DAILY PRAYER 2017

Sunday Year A • Weekday Year I

A book of prayer for each day of the liturgical year.

Mary C. Dumm
Randall R. Phillips

Nihil Obstat
Very Reverend Daniel A. Smilanic, JCD
Vicar for Canonical Services
Archdiocese of Chicago
February 22, 2016

Imprimatur
Very Reverend Ronald A. Hicks
Vicar General
Archdiocese of Chicago
February 22, 2016

The *Nihil Obstat* and *Imprimatur* are declarations that the material is free from doctrinal or moral error, and thus is granted permission to publish in accordance with c. 827. No legal responsibility is assumed by the grant of this permission. No implication is contained herein that those who have granted the *Nihil Obstat* and *Imprimatur* agree with the content, opinions, or statements expressed.

As a publisher, LTP works toward responsible stewardship of the environment. Visit www.LTP.org/environment to learn more about how this book was manufactured.

Daily Prayer is based in part on the pattern established in *Children's Daily Prayer*, by Elizabeth McMahon Jeep. This book was edited by Mary Fox. Christopher Magnus was the production editor. Kari Nicholls was the designer and production artist.

Printed in the United States of America.

ISBN: 978-1-61671-266-2

DP17

Table of Contents

Introduction

Rejoice always.
Pray without ceasing.
In all circumstances give thanks,
for this is the will of God for
you in Christ Jesus.

1 Thessalonians 5:16–18

Welcome to *Daily Prayer 2017,* Sunday Year A and Weekday Year I! This edition of the well-loved prayer book provides a familiar order of prayer for each day of the liturgical year, from the First Sunday of Advent, November 27, 2016, through December 31, 2017. Readings from the daily Mass are provided, and the prayer texts and reflections are connected to the liturgical time, solemnities, feasts of the Lord, and the memorials of the saints. The prayers on these pages will inspire and bring you to a deeper appreciation for the Word that is proclaimed and for Eucharist that is shared in the liturgical life of the Church.

The Order of Prayer

Daily Prayer 2017 follows a simple order of prayer: it begins with an opening verse with the Sign of the Cross, followed by a psalm, a reading from the daily Mass, a brief reflection, the Prayer of the Faithful, the Lord's Prayer, a closing prayer, and a closing verse with the Sign of the Cross. This order remains consistent for each day of the liturgical year, allowing its repetition to become part of your daily rhythm and routine.

Daily Prayer 2017 is organized by liturgical time, and the Psalter is located in the back of the book (pages 401–423). Everything you need is conveniently contained in this resource. Refer to the table of contents for easy reference.

DAILY HEADING

Daily Prayer 2017 is easy to use. A heading is provided for each day of prayer so you will always know where you are and what you should pray. The heading includes the date and the name of the liturgical observance. Typically, optional memorials are not celebrated in this edition of *Daily Prayer 2017*; however, if celebrated, the optional memorial will be noted in the heading. The liturgical observances are those according to the norms prescribed by the Secretariat of Divine Worship.

OPENING AND CLOSING VERSICLE WITH SIGN OF THE CROSS

The order of prayer begins each day with the Sign of the Cross and a versicle, or opening verse. The versicles are taken from the refrains proper to the Responsorial Psalms from the Mass; antiphons from *The Liturgy of the Hours* and *The Roman Missal*; verses from the Acclamation before the Gospel (*Lectionary for Mass*); and lines from Scripture, especially the psalms.

PSALMODY

The psalms are an important part of Catholic prayer. As poetic readings from Sacred Scripture, the psalms reflect upon God's saving work in various ways —praise, thanksgiving, and lamentation. The psalms in *Daily Prayer 2017* have been selected for their liturgical significance. Psalms for Advent implore God's return; psalms for Christmas

Time shout for joy; psalms for Lent evoke the need for God's mercy and forgiveness; psalms for Easter Time give praise for his glory and salvation; and psalms for Ordinary Time give thanks for all that is good. For many of the Marian solemnities and feasts, the psalm has been replaced by the Canticle of Mary. This canticle is included on page 422.

READING

Each day of prayer includes a reading from the daily Mass. This enables further reflection upon the Word of God proclaimed during the Eucharistic celebration (Mass)—the source and summit of our faith. On some days, excerpts, not the full text, from the Scripture passage have been selected. The Gospel is used for each Sunday, solemnity, and feast of the Lord.

REFLECTION

The authors for this year have provided insights for meditation and reflection. These reflections guide the reader to a deeper relationship with God, neighbor, and self.

UNIVERSAL PRAYER

Universal Prayer, sometimes referred to as the Prayer of the Faithful, is a prayer of the baptized who, through Christ, voice their concerns to God regarding the Church, the world, the oppressed, local needs, and other concerns. Thus, the prayers in this book connect the individual and small faith groups to the universal Church and those in most need of God's love and mercy. Although specific prayers are provided in this resource, others may be added.

THE LORD'S PRAYER

Jesus taught us how to pray. It is fitting to follow the Universal Prayer with the Lord's Prayer, for it encapsulates the humility and reverence we give to our God—and neighbor—while asking for his mercy and forgiveness.

CLOSING PRAYER

The closing prayer follows the form of the traditional Collect. This prayer "is usually addressed to God the Father, through Christ, in the Holy Spirit" (*General Instruction of the Roman Missal*, 54). Essentially, this prayer "collects" our daily prayer, the prayers found in this book, and those of our hearts and minds, those as individuals or groups, into one Trinitarian prayer, concluding with our assent of faith in the response "Amen."

Using the Book

This resource may be used by individuals, families, or prayer groups; on retreats; to begin meetings or catechetical sessions, formational and youth ministry events; or as prayer with the aged, sick, and homebound. The prayers may be used at any time during the day, and, given this book's convenient size, it is easily transported to meet various prayer needs and situations.

The order of prayer may be prayed silently or, especially for group prayer, prayed aloud. If used for prayer gatherings, it might be helpful to designate someone to open the prayer, lead the Prayer of the Faithful, begin the Lord's Prayer, and to conclude the prayer. Select an additional volunteer to proclaim the reading. Allow the faithful to read the psalm together either as an entire group, or divide the stanzas among the faithful with alternating recitation.

Feel free to adapt these prayers for specific needs—intercessions (or petitions) may be added, music may begin and conclude the service, and the psalm response to the Universal Prayer and the Lord's Prayer may be chanted or sung.

Other Uses for Daily Prayer

Daily Prayer 2017 also may be used in other situations or for various needs.

- Use the Prayer of the Faithful during the Mass. The prayers have been written in accordance with paragraphs 69 and 70 of the *General Instruction of the Roman Missal.* Since this book contains prayers for each day of the liturgical year, you may use the intercessions for every day of the year for Mass.
- Use the included reflections as homily sparkers and catechetical tools.

Customer Feedback

Daily Prayer 2017 is the sixteenth edition of an annual publication; *Daily Prayer 2018* is already being prepared. Because it is an annual, it can be changed from year to year to become a better tool for your daily prayer. As you use this book and adapt it for yourself, you may have ideas about how it can be made more useful for your prayer. Feel free to e-mail us at DailyPrayer@LTP.org.

About the Authors

Mary C. Dumm, DMIN, has ministered in the Archdiocese of Detroit for more than thirty years. She is presently the pastoral associate at St. Blase Church, Sterling Heights, Michigan, and is an adjunct professor at Siena Heights University.

Rev. Randall Phillips, STD, has been a priest of the Archdiocese of Detroit for more than thirty years. He is the pastor of St. Blase Parish, Sterling Heights, Michigan. He holds a doctorate in sacred theology from the Pontifical Gregorian University.

Sunday, November 27, 2016

First Sunday of Advent

✝ Maranatha! Come, Emmanuel!

Psalm 85

page 411

Reading

Matthew 24:37–44

Jesus said to his disciples: "As it was in the days of Noah, so will it be at the coming of the Son of Man. In those days before the flood, they were eating and drinking, marrying and giving in marriage, up to the day that Noah entered the ark. They did not know until the flood came and carried them all away. So will it be also at the coming of the Son of Man. Two men will be out in the field; one will be taken, and one will be left. Two women will be grinding at the mill; one will be taken, and one will be left. Therefore, stay awake! For you do not know on which day the Lord will come. Be sure of this: if the master of the house had known the hour of night when the thief was coming, he would have stayed awake and not let his house be broken into. So too, you also must be prepared, for at an hour you do not expect, the Son of Man will come."

Reflection

"Stay awake!" How often do we ignore our surroundings? Many times we arrive at our destination without realizing the twists and turns of our travel. Our mind is elsewhere. Advent commands us to pay attention. The difference between the men in the field or the women grinding is not the work they do but the attention they pay. God is in our midst. Let us be mindful this Advent, and see God with us.

Prayers

others may be added

To Emmanuel, we pray:

◆ Draw near, Lord.

May your Church be a beacon of justice and hope for the distraught, we pray: ◆ May our world leaders seek to bring peace, we pray: ◆ May patience and understanding overpower hatred and bigotry, we pray: ◆ May all who live in the shadow of death, rest in peace, we pray: ◆

Our Father . . .

Emmanuel,
you offer your presence to us.
Open our eyes that we may see you
in our brothers and sisters
and be ever attentive to their needs.
We ask this through our Lord Jesus
Christ, your Son,
who lives and reigns with you in the unity
of the Holy Spirit,
one God, for ever and ever.
Amen.

✝ Maranatha! Come, Emmanuel!

Monday, November 28, 2016
Advent Weekday

✝ Maranatha! Come, Emmanuel!

Psalm 85

page 411

Reading

Isaiah 4:2–6

On that day, / The branch of the LORD will be luster and glory, / and the fruit of the earth will be honor and splendor / for the survivors of Israel. / He who remains in Zion / and he who is left in Jerusalem / Will be called holy: / every one marked down for life in Jerusalem. / When the LORD washes away / the filth of the daughters of Zion, / And purges Jerusalem's blood from her midst / with a blast of searing judgment, / Then will the LORD create, / over the whole site of Mount Zion / and over her place of assembly, / A smoking cloud by day / and a light of flaming fire by night. / For over all, the LORD's glory will be shelter and protection: / shade from the partial heat of day, / refuge and cover from storm and rain.

Reflection

Often we pray for Emmanuel to come; that the day of the Lord may be present in all its fullness. But what will that mean? There are two sides to the coin. Isaiah commands us to be aware of the filth in our midst. What are those events and actions in our lives that are not of God? Where are our sins? Not everything is just, good, and holy. Now is the time to see sins clearly and excise them from our lives. Then, the presence of God will overshadow and protect us.

Prayers

others may be added

To Emmanuel, we pray:

◆ Draw near, Lord.

As Church, may we purify ourselves, removing all that keeps us from living the Gospel, we pray: ◆ May leaders of nations turn to actions of light and truth, we pray: ◆ May the poor, victims of violence, and the homeless be shrouded in security and healing, we pray: ◆ May we see our sinful attitudes and actions and in courage, repent, we pray: ◆

Our Father . . .

Merciful Lord,
you provide justice for all.
Help us to place our trust in you
and seek to do your will
that we might be called holy.
We ask this through Christ our Lord.
Amen.

✝ Maranatha! Come, Emmanuel!

Tuesday, November 29, 2016
Advent Weekday

✝ Maranatha! Come, Emmanuel!

Psalm 85

page 411

Reading

Isaiah 11:1–3, 6–9

On that day, / A shoot shall sprout from the stump of Jesse, / and from his roots a bud shall blossom. / The Spirit of the LORD shall rest upon him: / a Spirit of wisdom and of understanding, / A Spirit of counsel and of strength, / a spirit of knowledge and fear of the LORD, / and his delight shall be the fear of the LORD. / Not by appearance shall he judge, / nor by hearsay shall he decide. /

Then the wolf shall be a guest of the lamb, / and the leopard shall lie down with the kid; / The calf and the young lion shall browse together, / with a little child to guide them. / The cow and the bear shall be neighbors, / together their young shall rest; / the lion shall eat hay like the ox. / The baby shall play by the cobra's den, / and the child lay his hand on the adder's lair. / There shall be no harm or ruin on all my holy mountain; / for the earth shall be filled with knowledge of the LORD, / as water covers the sea.

Reflection

The peaceable kingdom. When God's Spirit pervades the world, even enemies will live in peace. During this Advent, we may want to consider what we are doing to bring about the Kingdom. Isaiah shows animals giving up the urge to kill those who would naturally be their prey. What do you need to give up for the Reign of God to be fulfilled?

Prayers

others may be added

To Emmanuel, we pray:

◆ Draw near, Lord.

May your Spirit, Lord, enliven our Church, we pray: ◆ May opposing nations value each other and learn to live in community, we pray: ◆ May the forsaken, excluded, and abandoned find a welcome home, we pray: ◆ May we see your truth in the world, rejecting values contrary to the Gospel, we pray: ◆

Our Father . . .

Dear Lord,
your peace demands a change of hearts and minds.
Renew your Spirit within us
so that we are open to the beauty of others
and willing to abandon
all that causes them hardship or pain.
We ask this through Christ our Lord.
Amen.

✝ Maranatha! Come, Emmanuel!

Wednesday, November 30, 2016

Feast of St. Andrew, Apostle

☩ Maranatha! Come, Emmanuel!

Psalm 85

page 411

Reading

Romans 10:9–10

Brothers and sisters: If you confess with your mouth that Jesus is Lord and believe in your heart that God raised him from the dead, you will be saved. For one believes with the heart and so is justified, and one confesses with the mouth and so is saved.

Reflection

Andrew and his brother Simon Peter were among the first called to follow the Lord. As a disciple, Andrew listened to Jesus and then followed his example. Paul reminds us that disciples train their hearts in the ways of the Master, and in their actions, they image the one they follow. We need to seek an internal, complete transformation to the Lord. Our actions replicate what we believe: that Jesus is Lord. This Advent, may all we do be a sign to others of what we believe, that the Kingdom of God is in our midst.

Prayers

others may be added

To Emmanuel, we pray:

◆ Draw near, O Lord.

May our Church reach out in mission to all who have not yet been transformed by the Gospel, we pray: ◆ May leaders of nations and communities guide in ways that heed the needs of the least, lost, and broken, we pray: ◆ May those who suffer from depression, mental illness, or a listless spirit, find healing and hope, we pray: ◆ May our communities proclaim in word and action the way of the Lord, we pray: ◆

Our Father . . .

God of Light,
you called Andrew to follow you
and so transformed his life.
Help us to yield to your call
so that we may be just and true disciples
of your Word.
We ask this through Christ our Lord.
Amen.

☩ Maranatha! Come, Emmanuel!

Thursday, December 1, 2016
Advent Weekday

✝ Maranatha! Come, Emmanuel!

Psalm 85 *page 411*

Reading *Isaiah 26:1–6*

On that day they will sing this song in the land of Judah: / "A strong city have we; / he sets up walls and ramparts to protect us. / Open up the gates / to let in a nation that is just, / one that keeps faith. / A nation of firm purpose you keep in peace; / in peace, for its trust in you."

Trust in the LORD forever! / For the LORD is an eternal Rock. / He humbles those in high places, / and the lofty city he brings down; / He tumbles it to the ground, / levels it with the dust. / It is trampled underfoot by the needy, / by the footsteps of the poor.

Reflection

Today we see God making a choice. Who gets to be safe and secure in the city of God and who is brought down and humbled? The just may live in peace. Those who are just and trust in God find themselves in a strong city, but those who build up walls and methods of protection are not safe. This truth is in conflict with our world's values. In vulnerability, we find shelter. In faith, we find peace.

Prayers *others may be added*

To Emmanuel, we pray:

◆ Draw near, O Lord.

May our Church remain vulnerable, trusting in the Lord always, we pray: ◆ May our world abandon ways of exclusion and domination, we pray: ◆ May those in nursing homes and hospitals, feel protected and loved, we pray: ◆ May our days be guided by humility, peace, and faith, we pray: ◆

Our Father . . .

Gentle Father,
you provide for your children
and gather them in your holy city.
Keep us firm in faith and justice.
We ask this through Christ our Lord.
Amen.

✝ Maranatha! Come, Emmanuel!

Friday, December 2, 2016
Advent Weekday

☩ Maranatha! Come, Emmanuel!

Psalm 85
page 411

Reading
Isaiah 29:18–21

Thus says the Lord GOD: / On that day the deaf shall hear / the words of a book; / And out of gloom and darkness, / the eyes of the blind shall see. / The lowly will ever find joy in the LORD / and the poor rejoice in the Holy One of Israel. / For the tyrant will be no more / and the arrogant will have gone; / All who are alert to do evil will be cut off, / those whose mere word condemns a man, / Who ensnare his defender at the gate, / and leave the just man with an empty claim.

Reflection
To condemn implies power over another and a viciousness that belies understanding and compassion. Yet, we often condemn others by our words and attitudes. The next time you consider condemning another, even if only in your mind, consider empathy. Is there a way to reach out to the individual with kindness and concern?

Prayers
others may be added

To Emmanuel, we pray:

◆ Draw near, Lord.

May our Church be a place of compassion, we pray: ◆ May our lawmakers put an end to the death penalty, we pray: ◆ May all bound up by harsh judgment be released, we pray: ◆ May we form communities of care and forgiveness, we pray: ◆

Our Father . . .

Forgiving One,
you alone know the pains of our hearts
and the cause our actions.
Have mercy on us
and teach us to be merciful to others.
We ask this through Christ our Lord.
Amen.

☩ Maranatha! Come, Emmanuel!

Saturday, December 3, 2016
Memorial of St. Francis Xavier, Priest

☩ Maranatha! Come, Emmanuel!

Psalm 85
page 411

Reading
1 Corinthians 9:16–19, 22–23

Brothers and sisters: If I preach the Gospel, there is no reason for me to boast, for an obligation has been imposed on me, and woe to me if I do not preach it! If I do so willingly, I have a recompense, but if unwillingly, then I have been entrusted with a stewardship. What then is my recompense? That, when I preach, I offer the Gospel free of charge so as not to make full use of my right in the Gospel. Although I am free in regard to all, I have made myself a slave to all so as to win over as many as possible. To the weak I became weak, to win over the weak. I have become all things to all, to save at least some. All this I do for the sake of the Gospel, so that I too may have a share in it.

Reflection

St. Francis Xavier was a missionary who tirelessly proclaimed the Gospel in lands as far as India and Japan. We are all missionaries and should proclaim the Gospel daily. But how do we do it? Paul tells us that we need to listen to those we wish to evangelize and meet them where they are. It's necessary to adapt our proclamation to our hearers. Pope Francis has used the image of a field hospital. We must go to people, empathize, listen, and preach the Gospel, using words only as necessary.

Prayers
others may be added

To Emmanuel, we pray:

◆ Draw near, Lord.

May the work of missionaries bear much fruit, we pray: ◆ May the Gospel transform the lives of all who hear it, we pray: ◆ May our nation's leaders not be lost in the ways of world, but hear the cry of the Lord who beckons all to himself, we pray: ◆ May our evangelizing be filled with compassion, we pray: ◆

Our Father . . .

Heavenly Father,
you gave Francis Xavier the zeal of
  a missionary
so that your words reached many who
  had not heard the Good News.
May we too be willing to reach out
  to others,
respecting their culture and proclaiming
  your truth.
We ask this through Christ our Lord.
Amen.

☩ Maranatha! Come, Emmanuel!

Sunday, December 4, 2016

Second Sunday of Advent

† Behold, our Savior will come; you need no longer fear.

Psalm 72

page 410

Reading

Matthew 3:1–6

John the Baptist appeared, preaching in the desert of Judea and saying, "Repent, for the kingdom of heaven is at hand!" It was of him that the prophet Isaiah had spoken when he said: / *A voice of one crying out in the desert, / Prepare the way of the Lord, / make straight his paths.* / John wore clothing made of camel's hair and had a leather belt around his waist. His food was locusts and wild honey. At the time Jerusalem, all Judea, and the whole region around the Jordan were going out to him and were being baptized by him in the Jordan River as they acknowledged their sins.

Reflection

John the Baptist is quite a character. He is strong, forthright, and rather unpresentable with his wild clothing and odd food. Perhaps he is just what we need to shake us from our complacency. While he preaches a message of repentance, he wants more than empty words and he's not afraid to tell us so. How are you seeking conversion this Advent?

Prayers

others may be added

To the Sun of Justice, we pray:

◆ Graciously hear us, Lord.

Inspire your Church, that we may be a sign of your light in a world driven by darkness, we pray: ◆ With your mighty arm, guide leaders of nations to build bridges of peace and communities of justice, we pray: ◆ Melt hardened hearts, soften minds filled with vengeance, and enliven spirits slowed by atrophy, we pray: ◆ Draw near to all who have died, may they now live forever in your light, we pray: ◆

Our Father . . .

Lord of all,
you provided John the Baptist
the courage to live in your truth.
Purify us
that all we do may be pleasing to you.
We ask this through our Lord Jesus
Christ, your Son,
who lives and reigns with you in the unity
of the Holy Spirit,
one God, for ever and ever.
Amen.

† Behold, our Savior will come; you need no longer fear.

Monday, December 5, 2016
Advent Weekday

✝ Behold, our Savior will come; you need no longer fear.

Psalm 72 *page 410*

Reading *Isaiah 35:6b–8a, 10*

Streams will burst forth in the desert, / and rivers in the steppe. / The burning sands will become pools, / and the thirsty ground, springs of water; / The abode where jackals lurk / will be a marsh for the reed and papyrus. / A highway will be there, / called the holy way. / Those whom the LORD has ransomed will return / and enter Zion singing, / crowned with everlasting joy; / They will meet with joy and gladness, / sorrow and mourning will flee.

Reflection

We pray so often for God to transform our pain, sadness, and loss. Sometimes this happens quickly, but often it is a slow journey. What is our response to God's goodness? How often do we acknowledge the gifts, insights, and gentle joys with which God has graced us? Isaiah's image is of unabashed joy with singing and gladness. Take time to consider the sense of joyfulness in your life. Even if you are going through some unhappiness, you can feel the joy of the Gospel, the joy that comes from knowing that God is with us.

Prayers *others may be added*

To the Sun of Justice, we pray:

◆ Hear us, Lord.

For a message of gladness emanating from our Church, we pray: ◆ For a world filled with laughter, fraternity, and optimism, we pray: ◆ For our community leaders, that they are beacons of hope for those in distress, we pray: ◆ For the ability to share the gifts we have been given and the peace in which we abide, we pray: ◆

Our Father . . .

God of grace,
you provide blessings for us each day.
May our discouragement at pain and loss
never overwhelm the confidence of faith.
We ask this through Christ our Lord.
Amen.

✝ Behold, our Savior will come; you need no longer fear.

Tuesday, December 6, 2016
Advent Weekday

✝ Behold, our Savior will come; you need no longer fear.

Psalm 72 *page 410*

Reading *Isaiah 40:1–2, 10–11*

Comfort, give comfort to my people, / says your God. / Speak tenderly to Jerusalem, and proclaim to her / that her service is at an end, / her guilt is expiated; / Indeed, she has received from the hand of the LORD / double for all her sins.

Here comes with power / the Lord God / who rules by his strong arm; / Here is his reward with him, / his recompense before him, / Like a shepherd he feeds his flock; / in his arms he gathers the lambs, / Carrying them in his bosom, / and leading the ewes with care.

Reflection

Today's First Reading provides an image of the gentleness of God. We can get worn out this time of year so easily. We are overburdened by shopping and cooking, or frayed by trying so hard to make everything perfect. God simply speaks of comfort and tenderness. Lay it all down today. Accept the embrace of the Shepherd who carefully, gently, carries and feeds us, and trust in the Lord's restfulness.

Prayers *others may be added*

To the Sun of Justice, we pray:

◆ Hear us, Lord.

For pastors with voices of compassion, we pray: ◆ For world leaders, that they exercise consideration for the least among us, we pray: ◆ For an end to human trafficking, sweatshops, and unfair labor practices, we pray: ◆ For an ability to rest in the arms of our loving Savior, we pray: ◆

Our Father . . .

Shepherd of souls,
you offer healing to all in your care.
Forgive our sins, comfort our souls,
and bring peace to our spirits.
We ask this through Christ our Lord.
Amen.

✝ Behold, our Savior will come; you need no longer fear.

Wednesday, December 7, 2016

Memorial of St. Ambrose, Bishop and Doctor of the Church

☩ **Behold, our Savior will come; you need no longer fear.**

Psalm 72

page 410

Reading

Isaiah 40:25–31

To whom can you liken me as an equal? / says the Holy One. / Lift up your eyes on high / and see who has created these things: / He leads out their army and numbers them, / calling them all by name. / By his great might and the strength of his power / not one of them is missing! / Why, O Jacob, do you say / and declare, O Israel, / "My way is hidden from the LORD, / and my right is disregarded by my God"?

Do you not know / or have you not heard? / The LORD is the eternal God, / creator of the ends of the earth. / He does not faint nor grow weary, / and his knowledge is beyond scrutiny. / He gives strength to the fainting; / for the weak he makes vigor abound. / Though young men faint and grow weary, / and youths stagger and fall, / They that hope in the LORD will renew their strength, / they will soar as with eagles' wings; / They will run and not grow weary, / walk and not grow faint.

Reflection

The folk song "God is God," by Steve Earle, reminds us of the simple fact that "God ain't me . . . God ain't us." Yet how often we want to claim equality with God and tell God what to do. When we act and think in such ways, we have lost our appropriate place. It's important that we keep in mind the difference it makes to live with such humility. As this reading notes, those who hope in the Lord, will "run and not grow weary."

Prayers

others may be added

To the Sun of Justice, we pray:

◆ **Hear us, Lord.**

For your Church pregnant with signs of your life among us, we pray: ◆ For a softening of hardened hearts, we pray: ◆ For parents, teachers, and all who guide others, for wisdom inspired by God, we pray: ◆ For humility, that we may remember that God is God, we pray: ◆

Our Father . . .

God of all,
yours is power and majesty.
Help us to seek humility
so that we may acknowledge your work
among all of creation.
We ask this through Christ our Lord.
Amen.

☩ **Behold, our Savior will come; you need no longer fear.**

Thursday, December 8, 2016

Solemnity of the Immaculate Conception of the Blessed Virgin Mary

✝ Hail Mary full of grace! The Lord is with you.

Canticle of Mary

page 422

Reading

Luke 1:26–30a, 35b–38a

The angel Gabriel was sent from God to a town of Galilee called Nazareth, to a virgin betrothed to a man named Joseph, of the house of David, and the virgin's name was Mary. And coming to her, he said, "Hail, full of grace! The Lord is with you." But she was greatly troubled at what was said and pondered what sort of greeting this might be. Then the angel said to her, "Do not be afraid, Mary, . . . the Holy Spirit will come upon you, and the power of the Most High will overshadow you. Therefore the child to be born will be called holy, the Son of God. And behold, Elizabeth, your relative, has also conceived a son in her old age, and this is the sixth month for her who was called barren; for nothing will be impossible for God." Mary said, "Behold, I am the handmaid of the Lord. May it be done to me according to your word."

Reflection

Was Mary's "yes" both easy and difficult? What the angel told her was both amazing and seemingly impossible. Still, she said, "Yes." Mary's heart is filled with love for God, and with that love, trust. When confronted with difficulty, what level of trust do we have in God?

Prayers

others may be added

To the Sun of Justice, we pray:

◆ Send us peace with justice, Lord.

May our Church be open to the incomprehensible movement of the Spirit, we pray: ◆ May we trust in the grace of God alive in our world, we pray: ◆ May world leaders work for peace, we pray: ◆ May love overwhelm hatred, trust quench fear, and faith dispel distress, we pray: ◆

Our Father . . .

Eternal Father,
you filled the Blessed Virgin Mary
with the grace to say "yes"
to her role in your plan for salvation.
Teach us to trust as she did
that we too may help build up your reign
in our world.
We ask this through our Lord Jesus
Christ, your Son,
who lives and reigns with you in the unity
of the Holy Spirit,
one God, for ever and ever.
Amen.

✝ Hail Mary full of grace! The Lord is with you.

Friday, December 9, 2016
Advent Weekday

✝ Behold, our Savior will come; you need no longer fear.

Psalm 72 *page 410*

Reading *Isaiah 48:17–19*

Thus says the LORD, your redeemer, / the Holy One of Israel: / I , the LORD, your God, / teach you what is for your good, / and lead you on the way you should go. / If you would hearken to my commandments, / your prosperity would be like a river, / and your vindication like the waves of the sea; / Your descendants would be like the sand, / and those born of your stock like its grains, / their name never cut off / or blotted out from my presence.

Reflection

The words in the Book of Isaiah bring us to the essentials. In today's reading, we hear that God teaches and leads us. If we follow the Lord, we will prosper and stay in his presence. You may want to sit in the stillness of Advent to meditate on these verses. In the quiet, consider why you listen to and follow other voices when you prefer Christ's.

Prayers *others may be added*

To the Sun of Justice, we pray:

◆ Send us peace with justice, Lord.

Open our mouths that your Church may proclaim comfort to the oppressed, challenge to the self-righteous, and blessed assurance to all who walk in your way, we pray: ◆ Raise up true leaders to guide others in your ways of justice and peace, we pray: ◆ Open the coffers of the greedy that they too may discover the joy of sharing with others, we pray: ◆ Excise fear and sin from our lives, so that we may conduct ourselves in holiness and devotion seeking first the Reign of God, we pray: ◆

Our Father . . .

O Lord,
you have made your way clear to us.
Wash us anew and renew us during this holy season
so that your teaching takes root deeply within us.
We ask this through Christ our Lord.
Amen.

✝ Behold, our Savior will come; you need no longer fear.

Saturday, December 10, 2016
Advent Weekday

✝ Behold, our Savior will come; you need no longer fear.

Psalm 72 *page 410*

Reading *Sirach 48:1–4, 9–11*

In those days, like a fire there appeared the prophet Elijah / whose words were as a flaming furnace. / Their staff of bread he shattered, / in his zeal he reduced them to straits; / By the Lord's word he shut up the heavens / and three times brought down fire. / How awesome are you, Elijah, in your wondrous deeds! / Whose glory is equal to yours? / You were taken aloft in a whirlwind of fire, / in a chariot with fiery horses. / You were destined, it is written, in time to come / to put an end to wrath before the day of the LORD, / to turn back the hearts of fathers toward their sons, / and to reestablish the tribes of Jacob. / Blessed is he who shall have seen you / and who falls asleep in your friendship.

Reflection

Elijah was a strong and powerful prophet. His deeds are remembered even more than his words. From a contest of fire on Mount Carmel to raising a dead son, Elijah was filled with power. But to remember Elijah is to remember also his exhaustion and his visit from God in a still, gentle whisper. We recall our sinfulness during Advent; let us also remember the power God provides to us. In God is our power to do amazing things. With God we can change people's hearts and lives.

Prayers *others may be added*

To the Sun of Justice, we pray:

◆ Lord, hear our prayer.

Guide your Church to eagerly await your advent in our world, we pray: ◆ Rain down a spirit of your peace upon our president and all world leaders, we pray: ◆ Speak tenderly to our catechumens and candidates, and soften hearts hardened by bitterness and anger, we pray: ◆ Support us as we reach out to those who are lonely and depressed, we pray: ◆

Our Father . . .

All powerful God,
you bid us to use our abilities
and influence
for your Reign.
Grant us insight into our gifts
and courage to use them in your service.
We ask this through Christ our Lord.
Amen.

✝ Behold, our Savior will come; you need no longer fear.

Sunday, December 11, 2016

Third Sunday of Advent

✝ Rejoice the Lord is near!

Psalm 146

page 420

Reading

Matthew 11:7–11

As they were going off, Jesus began to speak to the crowds about John, "What did you go out to the desert to see? A reed swayed by the wind? Then what did you go out to see? Someone dressed in fine clothing." Those who wear fine clothing are in royal palaces. Then why did you go out? To see a prophet? Yes, I tell you, and more than a prophet. This is the one about whom it is written: / *Behold, I am sending my messenger ahead of you; / he will prepare your way before you.* / Amen, I say to you, among those born of women there has been none greater than John the Baptist; yet the least in the kingdom of heaven is greater than he."

Reflection

Rejoice! The Lord is near. Can you see him? Where is God to be found? In fine clothing? In royal palaces? We are so often intrigued by the lives of the rich and famous. Spectators seem willing to do just about anything to get their face on the "big screen" at a sporting event. However, the place of the prophet is in the desert. The Lord is not found with "the most" but with "the least." How are you preparing for Christmas? With two weeks left, how are you spending your time and energy?

Prayers

others may be added

Turning to the Lord, with joy and patience, we pray:

◆ Lord, hear our prayer.

May your Church be roused to strengthen the weak and bring hope to all trapped in adversity, we pray: ◆ For our hearts to be open to those who need food and shelter, we pray: ◆ May patience be restored that we may listen before judging, and trust in your way above all else, we pray: ◆ For our beloved dead, may they be at peace in your Kingdom, we pray: ◆

Our Father . . .

Lord of the prophets,
you sent John the Baptist to prepare
the way.
Heal us and cleanse us
that all we do may be accomplished
in sincerity of mind and heart.
We ask this through our Lord Jesus
Christ, your Son,
who lives and reigns with you in the unity
of the Holy Spirit,
one God, for ever and ever.
Amen.

✝ Rejoice the Lord is near!

Monday, December 12, 2016

Feast of Our Lady of Guadalupe

☩ Rejoice the Lord is near!

Psalm 146 *page 420*

Reading *Zechariah 2:14–17*

Sing and rejoice, O daughter Zion! See I am coming to dwell among you, says the LORD. Many nations shall join themselves to the LORD on that day, and they shall be his people, and he will dwell among you, and you shall know that the LORD of hosts has sent me to you. The LORD will possess Judah as his portion in the holy land, and he will again choose Jerusalem. Silence, all mankind, in the presence of the LORD! For he stirs forth from his holy dwelling.

Reflection

When St. Juan Diego met Our Lady, he saw a young woman with features resembling his. Mary is in solidarity with the poor and oppressed; she dwells among them. The prophet Zechariah reiterates the covenant of God, once made with the people of Israel on Mount Sinai, but now meant for everyone. All nations are God's people and God dwells among them. Do we consider God as dwelling among those whose ways are foreign to us, who speak another language, who may be undocumented? Are we willing to act in solidarity with others as Mary did with Juan Diego?

Prayers *others may be added*

Turning to the Lord, with joy and patience, we pray:

◆ Lord, hear our prayer.

As the Church reaches to the ends of the earth, so may we embrace all that is good in each culture and each people, we pray: ◆ May nations seek ways of peace together, we pray: ◆ For refugees, immigrants, and strangers in a new land, we pray: ◆ For our nation's leaders, that they may enact fair immigration laws, we pray: ◆

Our Father . . .

Lord of all,
you sent Our Lady of Guadalupe
as a sign of your love for the people
 of Mexico
and of your solidarity with them in the
 face of tyranny.
Again hear the cry of all who are
 oppressed
and cry for freedom with justice.
Protect all who call upon your name
and aid us as we reach out to all of our
 sisters and brothers.
We ask this through Christ our Lord.
Amen.

☩ Rejoice the Lord is near!

Tuesday, December 13, 2016
Memorial of St. Lucy, Virgin and Martyr

✝ Rejoice the Lord is near!

Psalm 146 *page 420*

Reading *Zephaniah 3:1–2, 9–13*

Thus says the LORD: / Woe to the city, rebellious and polluted, / to the tyrannical city! / She hears no voice, / accepts no correction; / In the LORD she has not trusted, / to her God she has not drawn near.

For then I will change and purify / the lips of the peoples, / That they all may call upon the name of the LORD, / to serve him with one accord; / From beyond the rivers of Ethiopia / and as far as the recesses of the North, / they shall bring me offerings.

But I will leave as a remnant in your midst / a people humble and lowly, / Who shall take refuge in the name of the LORD: / the remnant of Israel. / They shall do no wrong / and speak no lies; / Nor shall there be found in their mouths / a deceitful tongue; / They shall pasture and couch their flocks / with none to disturb them.

Reflection

Life is a mixed bag of people. Our routine errands bring us into contact with many individuals with different values. Zephaniah reminds us that, on the mountain of the Lord, there were both the humble and the braggarts. In the days to come the rebellious will be removed, but a remnant of the lowly will remain. Do we let ourselves be influenced by the attitudes of others or can we remain true to the Lord?

Prayers *others may be added*

Turning to the Lord, with joy and patience, we pray:

◆ **Lord, hear our prayer.**

Lord Jesus, sustain the power of the Spirit in your Church that we may render constant thanks, we pray: ◆ Instruct the mighty and powerful in ways of humility and self-sacrifice, we pray: ◆ Heal those who are broken, free those who are bound, and liberate all held captive, we pray: ◆ Teach us to heed the voices of the prophets, we pray: ◆

Our Father . . .

Light of the world,
by your daughter Lucy's actions,
the Gospel was preached
even to those whose eyes were closed to
your Word.
May we too have such confidence in
our faith
so that others may see your goodness and
your Gospel.
We ask this through Christ our Lord.
Amen.

✝ Rejoice the Lord is near!

Wednesday, December 14, 2016

Memorial of St. John of the Cross, Priest and Doctor of the Church

✝ Rejoice the Lord is near!

Psalm 146

page 420

Reading

Isaiah 45:6c–8

I am the LORD and there is no other; / I form the light, and create the darkness, / I make well-being and create woe; / I, the LORD, do all these things. / Let justice descend O heavens, like dew from above, / like gentle rain let the skies drop it down. / Let the earth open and salvation bud forth; / let justice also spring up! / I, the LORD have created this.

Reflection

The picture that Isaiah paints portrays justice as part of creation. We hear in these verses that God not only created the light and darkness but that justice springs from the Lord. If we live as God intends, then all will flourish. During this Advent, you may want to examine how you work for God and creation. If you have not done so, you might want to begin reading Pope Francis' encyclical *Laudato Si'*.

Prayers

others may be added

Turning to the Lord, with joy and patience, we pray:

◆ Lord, come and save us

For our Holy Father, bishops, priests, deacons, and lay ministers, may they be voices of truth in the midst of the cacophony of discord, we pray: ◆ For our nation's leaders, that they may seek to protect the environment, we pray: ◆ For reformers and prophets, may they hear your Word and proclaim it fearlessly, as did John of the Cross, we pray: ◆ For all in nursing homes, hospitals, and hospice units, we pray: ◆

Our Father . . .

Gracious God,
you sent John of the Cross,
who drew ever closer to you in solitude
and prayer.
In his holy season,
may we embrace the darkness and silence
to hear your gentle voice calling our name.
We ask this through Christ our Lord.
Amen.

✝ Rejoice the Lord is near!

Thursday, December 15, 2016
Advent Weekday

☩ Rejoice the Lord is near!

Psalm 146

page 420

Reading

Isaiah 54:4–8

Fear not, you shall not be put to shame; / you need not blush, for you shall not be disgraced. / The shame of your youth you shall forget, / the reproach of your widowhood no longer remember / For he who has become your husband is your Maker; / his name is the LORD of hosts; / Your redeemer is the Holy One of Israel, / called God of all the earth. / The LORD calls you back, / like a wife forsaken and grieved in spirit, / A wife married in youth and then cast off, / says your God. / For a brief moment I abandoned you, / but with great tenderness I will take you back. / In an outburst of wrath, for a moment / I hid my face from you; / but with enduring love I take pity on you, / says the LORD your redeemer.

Reflection

How often do you feel isolated and alone? Do you ever feel abandoned even by God? But God is near. Isaiah reminds us that God will be with us at all times. Though we have sinned, God calls us with tenderness and mercy. With Christmas ten days away, prepare for the Lord with a repentant heart.

Prayers

others may be added

Turning to the Lord, with joy and patience, we pray:

◆ Lord, come and save us.

That in the Church's ministry of reconciliation more people will feel the balm of mercy, we pray: ◆ That world leaders will choose forgiveness over vengeance, we pray: ◆ That prisoners will seek atonement, we pray: ◆ That we may generously forgive all who have trespassed against us, as we too have been forgiven, we pray: ◆

Our Father . . .

Merciful One,
you are always with us,
healing, protecting, and forgiving.
Make us ever aware of our sins,
and with contrite hearts,
let us be transformed by your love.
We ask this through Christ our Lord.
Amen.

☩ Rejoice the Lord is near!

Friday, December 16, 2016
Advent Weekday

✝ Rejoice the Lord is near!

Psalm 146
page 420

Reading
Isaiah 56:6–8

The foreigners who join themselves to the LORD, / ministering to him, / Loving the name of the LORD, / and becoming his servants— / All who keep the sabbath free from profanation / and hold to my covenant. / Them I will bring to my holy mountain / and make joyful in my house of prayer; / Their burnt offerings and sacrifices / will be acceptable on my altar, / For my house shall be called / a house of prayer for all peoples. / Thus says the Lord GOD, / who gathers the dispersed of Israel: / Others will I gather to him / besides those already gathered.

Reflection
The people of Israel saw themselves as the Chosen People, in a unique relationship with God. While this may have been true in the past, the prophet says that all this has changed. Loving God is not an exclusive right of a few; rather, all people are gathered to the Lord. Are we as open as the Lord? How do we receive new Catholics, new parishioners, or guests? Now is the time to open wide the doors of hospitality. If God welcomes all, how can we not do the same?

Prayers
others may be added

Turning to the Lord, with joy and patience, we pray:

◆ Lord, come and save us.

For a spirit of openness to all people who seek the Lord, we pray: ◆ For a world that embraces diversity, we pray: ◆ For the isolated and rejected, we pray: ◆ For all who feel excluded, we pray: ◆

Our Father . . .

God of all,
you wrap all the world in your
loving embrace.
Remove our rigidity and blindness.
Allow us the freedom
to embrace all our sisters and brothers
as coheirs to your promise.
We ask this through Christ our Lord.
Amen.

✝ Rejoice the Lord is near!

Saturday, December 17, 2016
Advent Weekday

✝ Come, O Wisdom.

Psalm 146

page 420

Reading

Genesis 49:2, 8, 10

Jacob called his sons and said to them: / "Assemble and listen, sons of Jacob, / listen to Israel, your father. /

"You, Judah, shall your brothers praise / —your hand on the neck of your enemies; / the sons of your father shall bow down to you. . . . / The scepter shall never depart from Judah, / or the mace from between his legs, / While tribute is brought to him, / and he receives the people's homage."

Reflection

As we turn to the last days of Advent we recall the work that God has done. Through Jacob, King David was of the tribe of Judah and, of course, Jesus is often referred to as "son of David." Lineage in the Scriptures is more than a bloodline; however, it does not provide the right to wield power as terror or demand tribute that deprives another of sustenance. Both Jesus and David teach us that true leadership is about service. Those with power are held to a higher standard and have responsibilities to others.

Prayers

others may be added

Turning to the Lord, with joy and patience, we pray:

◆ **Lord, come and save us.**

For leaders in our Church, may they possess a spirit of wisdom, we pray: ◆ For leaders in the world, may they prefer service to honors, compassion to hard-heartedness, we pray: ◆ For those in need of wisdom, we pray: ◆ For an end to selfish pride, we pray: ◆

Our Father . . .

O Wisdom,
enlighten our minds and hearts.
Help us to see the world as you do.
May we act in love
and respond with kindness to all we meet.
We ask this through Christ our Lord.
Amen.

✝ Come, O Wisdom.

Sunday, December 18, 2016
Fourth Sunday of Advent

✝ Come, O Lord of Power and Might.

Canticle of Mary *page 422*

page 422

Reading *Matthew 1:18–21*

This is how the birth of Jesus Christ came about. When his mother Mary was betrothed to Joseph, but before they lived together, she was found with child through the Holy Spirit. Joseph her husband, since he was a righteous man, yet unwilling to expose her to shame, decided to divorce her quietly. Such was his intention when, behold, the angel of the Lord appeared to him in a dream and said, "Joseph, son of David, do not be afraid to take Mary your wife into your home. For it is through the Holy Spirit that this child has been conceived in her. She will bear a son and you are to name him Jesus, because he will save his people from their sins."

Reflection

Earlier in Advent we heard Mary's "yes" when the angel appeared to her. Today we hear the story of another messenger from God asking Joseph to care for Mary and Jesus. Joseph's "yes" is often lost in the busyness of these last days before Christmas. Joseph was willing to look beyond the rules and conventions of his time. He was willing to risk and trust the voice of the Spirit over the letter of the law. Do we put such trust in the Spirit? God's will can be messy and inconvenient. It disrupted Joseph's life. Do you let it disrupt yours?

Prayers *others may be added*

Looking to the Lord, with hopeful expectation, we pray:

◆ Graciously hear us, Lord.

Motivate your Church that we may bravely proclaim your Gospel to all we meet, we pray: ◆ Draw near to those who suffer from catastrophe and disaster, may they receive food, clothing, and financial support, we pray: ◆ Protect our vulnerable ones, from conception to natural death, we pray: ◆ Gather all the dead into your eternal home, we pray: ◆

Our Father . . .

Almighty Lord,
with great power you forged a covenant
with your servant Israel,
promising them to always be their God,
as they shall be your beloved people.
Renew in us this harmony with you.
May we hear your Spirit alive within us
and follow all that you ask.
We ask this through our Lord Jesus
Christ, your Son,
who lives and reigns with you in the unity
of the Holy Spirit,
one God, for ever and ever.
Amen.

✝ Come, O Lord of Power and Might.

Monday, December 19, 2016
Advent Weekday

✝ Come, O Root of Jesse.

Psalm 24 *page 403*

Reading *Judges 13:2–7, 24–25a*

There was a certain man from Zorah, of the clan of the Danites, whose name was Manoah. His wife was barren and had borne no children. An angel of the LORD appeared to the woman and said to her, "Though you are barren and have had no children, yet you will conceive and bear a son. Now, then, be careful to take no wine or strong drink and to eat nothing unclean. As for the son you will conceive and bear, no razor shall touch his head, for this boy is to be consecrated to God from the womb. It is he who will begin the deliverance of Israel from the power of the Philistines."

The woman went and told her husband, "A man of God came to me; he had the appearance of an angel of God, terrible indeed. I did not ask him where he came from, nor did he tell me his name. But he said to me, 'You will be with child and will bear a son. So take neither wine nor strong drink, and eat nothing unclean. For the boy shall be consecrated to God from the womb, until the day of his death.'"

The woman bore a son and named him Samson. The boy grew up and the LORD blessed him; the Spirit of the LORD stirred him.

Reflection

A preponderance of barren women are in the Old Testament. Today we meet the wife of Manoah, who will bear Samson. Like her sisters in faith, this mother is told to dedicate her son to the Lord from the moment of his conception. Samson will stray a bit from the faith; however, his roots are strong and he will return home, willing to offer his life for the sake of the community. How have you passed on your faith to friends and family?

Prayers *others may be added*

Looking to the Lord, with hopeful expectation, we pray:

◆ May your Spirit change us Lord.

Guide parents, catechists, and all teachers in our Church as they pass on the truths of faith, we pray: ◆ May our nation's leaders show the way to sharing our resources, we pray: ◆ May all people share with each other, work with integrity, and live righteously, we pray: ◆ May your light of love shine on those who struggle with depression, we pray: ◆

Our Father . . .

Bountiful One,
you raise up among your people
teachers and prophets
to help guide us in ways of truth.
May they speak courageously
to the lost, the powerful, and the forgotten
of our world.
We ask this through Christ our Lord.
Amen.

✝ Come, O Root of Jesse.

Tuesday, December 20, 2016
Advent Weekday

☩ Come, O Key of David.

Psalm 24
page 403

Reading
Isaiah 7:10–14

The LORD spoke to Ahaz: Ask for a sign from the LORD, your God; let it be deep as the nether world, or high as the sky! But Ahaz answered, "I will not ask! I will not tempt the LORD!" Then Isaiah said: Listen, O house of David! Is it not enough for you to weary men, must you also weary my God? Therefore the Lord himself will give you this sign: the virgin shall conceive and bear a son, and shall name him Emmanuel.

Reflection
Despite the instruction from the prophet, King Ahaz will not do as the Lord asks. He is playing at false pride, refusing to ask for a sign. This is what wearies God. Do we too weary God? Do we hide our agenda behind passive-aggressive behavior and fabricated piety? All our showy holiness is not the same as a converted heart and true charity.

Prayers
others may be added

Looking to the Lord, with hopeful expectation, we pray:

◆ Hear us, Lord.

May your Church model your love to the world, we pray: ◆ May world leaders bring peace where there is conflict, we pray: ◆ May the homeless find homes and the jobless secure employment, we pray: ◆ May the suffering that breeds bitterness end, we pray: ◆

Our Father . . .

O Key of David,
you are the way to the Father.
Unlock our hearts when they are closed to truth.
May our actions be honest,
our thoughts be yours,
and our lives speak of the integrity of the Gospel.
We ask this through Christ our Lord.
Amen.

☩ Come, O Key of David.

Wednesday, December 21, 2016
Advent Weekday

✝ Come, O Radiant Dawn.

Psalm 24 *page 403*

Reading *Song of Songs 2:8, 11–13*

Hark! my lover—here he comes / springing across the mountains, / leaping across the hills. / "For see, the winter is past, / the rains are over and gone. / The flowers appear on the earth, / the time of pruning the vines has come, / and the song of the dove is heard in our land. / The fig tree puts forth its figs, / and the vines, in bloom, give forth fragrance. / Arise, my beloved, my beautiful one, / and come!"

Reflection

What a beautiful book is the Song of Songs. It is the story of lovers—lost and found—questing, seeking, loving. So too is our relationship with God. God seeks us and desires a deep, intimate relationship. Are we excited or afraid by this? Intimacy means that all is revealed.

To be loved is one of our deepest fears and most profound needs. Can we accept the all-encompassing love of God? In love, the winter of our lives can give way to flowers and the song of the dove. Beauty will abound. Let the dawn of love shine in this late Advent.

Prayers *others may be added*

Looking to the Lord, with hopeful expectation, we pray:

◆ Hear us, Lord.

That your Church may glow as a herald of love in the world, we pray: ◆ That all peoples live freely in love, we pray: ◆ That married couples are a witness of love, commitment, and sincere faith, we pray: ◆ That we may find everlasting joy, we pray: ◆

Our Father . . .

O Everlasting Light,
illumine the gloom of these dark days.
May your love for us serve
as both solace and beacon,
guiding us into the arms of your consolation.
Help us to be open to you
and grow in your radiance.
We ask this through Christ our Lord.
Amen.

✝ Come, O Radiant Dawn.

Thursday, December 22, 2016
Advent Weekday

✝ Come, O King of Nations.

Psalm 24
page 403

Reading
I Samuel 1:24–28

In those days, Hannah brought Samuel with her, along with a three-year-old bull, an ephah of flour, and a skin of wine, and presented him at the temple of the LORD in Shiloh. After the boy's father had sacrificed the young bull, Hannah, his mother, approached Eli and said: "Pardon, my lord! As you live, my lord, I am the woman who stood near you here, praying to the LORD. I prayed for this child, and the LORD granted my request. Now I, in turn, give him to the LORD; as long as he lives, he shall be dedicated to the LORD." She left Samuel there.

Reflection
Hannah is one of the barren women of the Old Testament, and she was ridiculed for being so. She desperately wanted a son, and in time God gave her Samuel. In return, she dedicated him back to the Lord.

The gifts God has given us are for the common good and are meant to be offered to others. As we use these gifts, they bring joy to ourselves and others. Perhaps during this Christmas, you will want to consider how your gifts can enrich others. You will then, like Hannah, give your gift back to the Lord.

Prayers
others may be added

Looking to the Lord, with hopeful expectation, we pray:

◆ Hear us, Lord.

That we use our talents for the building up of your Church, we pray: ◆ That world leaders respect the diversity of the many cultures and peoples, we pray: ◆ For artists, musicians, and all who bring beauty to the world, we pray: ◆ That we rededicate ourselves to doing your will, we pray: ◆

Our Father . . .

O King of Nations,
the entire world is yours.
May we embrace the great mosaic you
have created,
loving all people
and rejoicing in their gifts and talents.
We ask this through Christ our Lord.
Amen.

✝ Come, O King of Nations.

Friday, December 23, 2016
Advent Weekday

✝ Come, O Emmanuel.

Psalm 24
page 403

Reading
Malachi 3:1–4, 23–24

Thus says the Lord GOD: / Lo, I am sending my messenger / to prepare the way before me; / And suddenly there will come to the temple / the LORD whom you seek, / And the messenger of the covenant whom you desire. / Yes, he is coming, says the LORD of hosts. / But who will endure the day of his coming? / And who can stand when he appears? / For he is like the refiner's fire, / or like the fuller's lye. / He will sit refining and purifying silver, / and he will purify the sons of Levi, / Refining them like gold or like silver / that they may offer due sacrifice to the LORD. / Then the sacrifice of Judah and Jerusalem / will please the LORD, / as in the days of old, as in years gone by.

Lo, I will send you / Elijah, the prophet, / Before the day of the LORD comes, / the great and terrible day, / To turn the hearts of the fathers to their children, / and the hearts of the children to their fathers, / Lest I come and strike / the land with doom.

Reflection

The day of the Lord is coming. Will it be today? Even as we count down to the celebration of our Lord's Incarnation, we look forward to his coming at the end of time. Malachi speaks of the refiner's fire and purification. This is our story of formation. Every day of our journey we open ourselves to God to purify us ever more. Sometimes it's easy, but often it hurts. It demands we let go of impurities. We need to release all that the binds us to sin. What do you need to release today? What is holding you back from celebrating Christmas in all of its fullness?

Prayers
others may be added

Looking to the Lord, with hope, we pray:

◆ Hear us, Lord.

Purify your Church, we pray: ◆ Cleanse our lawmakers so that they may see the truth, we pray: ◆ Heal those attached to money or power, we pray: ◆ Refine us that we too may shine with your radiant light, we pray: ◆

Our Father . . .

O Emmanuel,
you are able to see our inmost thoughts.
Purify our desires
so that our actions and attitudes
may be those of the Gospel.
Let us recognize you in all we meet,
for you are God with us.
We ask this through Christ our Lord.
Amen.

✝ Come, O Emmanuel.

Saturday, December 24, 2016
Advent Weekday

✝ Maranatha! Come, Emmanuel!

Psalm 24 *page 403*

Reading *2 Samuel 7:1–5, 8b–12, 14a, 16*

When King David was settled in his palace, and the LORD had given him rest from his enemies on every side, he said to Nathan the prophet, "Here I am living in a house of cedar, while the ark of God dwells in a tent!" Nathan answered the king, "Go, do whatever you have in mind, for the LORD is with you." But that night the LORD spoke to Nathan and said: "Go, tell my servant David, 'Thus says the LORD: Should you build me a house to dwell in?'

"It was I who took you from the pasture and from the care of the flock to be commander of my people Israel. I have been with you wherever you went, and I have destroyed all your enemies before you. And I will make you famous like the great ones of the earth. I will fix a place for my people Israel; I will plant them so that they may dwell in their place without further disturbance. Neither shall the wicked continue to afflict them as they did of old, since the time I first appointed judges over my people Israel. I will give you rest from all your enemies. The LORD also reveals to you that he will establish a house for you. And when your time comes and you rest with your ancestors, I will raise up your heir. . . . I will be a father to him, and he shall be a son to me. Your house and your Kingdom shall endure forever before me; your throne shall stand firm forever.'"

Reflection

David thinks he is doing something good by building God a temple; however, this is not what God wants. In obedience, David changes his plan and, in the end, his son Solomon will construct a temple for the Lord.

This evening we begin the celebration of the Incarnation. The marvel of God's generous gift is a reminder to us. Let us live in the freedom of the children of God, trusting in God's abundant and bountiful love.

Prayers *others may be added*

Looking to God, with hopeful expectation, we pray:

◆ Hear us, Lord.

That the Church follows your will for her and the world, we pray: ◆ That hearts will be transformed and all nations may respect the least among us, we pray: ◆ That we embrace harmony with the poor, hungry, and vulnerable in our midst, we pray: ◆ That even as we cling to earthly blessings, our heart will belong to you, we pray: ◆

Our Father . . .

Emmanuel,
you seek to reign in our hearts.
May your reign come in its fullness
as we seek to convert our hearts to follow
your will and way.
You live and reign with the Father in the
unity of the Holy Spirit,
one God, for ever and ever.
Amen.

✝ Maranatha! Come, Emmanuel!

Sunday, December 25, 2016

Solemnity of the Nativity of the Lord (Christmas)

☩ All the ends of the earth have seen the saving power of God.

Psalm 98

page 414

Reading

John 1:1–5, 14

In the beginning was the Word, / and the Word was with God, / and the Word was God. / He was in the beginning with God. / All things came to be through him, / and without him nothing came to be. / What came to be through him was life, / and this life was the light of the human race; / the light shines in the darkness, / and the darkness has not overcome it.

And the Word became flesh / and made his dwelling among us, / and we saw his glory, / the glory as of the Father's only Son, / full of grace and truth. /

Reflection

Christmas is described as the beginning of our salvation. Perhaps it is also the end, or the goal of our salvation. We transform the cross into the tree of blessing and abundance: charity toward the poor; forgiveness of others and our self; the spirit of generosity and good will, these all speak to the presence of the Reign of God in our midst. Even as Advent begins by drawing us to the Second Coming, so we honor the Incarnation by anticipating Christ's return in glory through the holy and celebratory character that makes today unique. Glory to God in the highest, and on earth peace to people of good will!

Prayers

others may be added

The Word became flesh and so we pray:

◆ Son of God and son of Mary, hear us.

Emmanuel, God with us, come live in the hearts of all the faithful, we pray: ◆ Prince of Peace, guide us in the ways of peace and nonviolence, we pray: ◆ Wonder Counselor, be with those who are alone, we pray: ◆ Father Forever, warm our hearts to embrace the immigrant, aid the refugee, and welcome the stranger, we pray: ◆ God-Hero, be with those who are homeless, we pray: ◆

Our Father . . .

Lord our God,
in the fullness of time,
you sent us your Son:
Light from Light, true God from true God,
consubstantial with you, our Father.
Hear our prayer this Christmas
and kindle within us
the joy, charity, forgiveness, and peace
which is your reign,
through our Lord Jesus Christ, your Son,
who lives and reigns with you in the unity
of the Holy Spirit,
one God, for ever and ever.
Amen.

☩ All the ends of the earth have seen the saving power of God.

Monday, December 26, 2016

Feast of St. Stephen, the First Martyr

✝ All the ends of the earth have seen the saving power of God.

Psalm 98

page 414

Reading

Acts 6:8–10; 7:54–59

Stephen, filled with grace and power, was working great wonders and signs among the people. Certain members of the so-called Synagogue of Freedmen, Cyrenians, and Alexandrians, and people from Cilicia and Asia, came forward and debated with Stephen, but they could not withstand the wisdom and the spirit with which he spoke.

When they heard this, they were infuriated, and they ground their teeth at him. But he, filled with the Holy Spirit, looked up intently to heaven and saw the glory of God and Jesus standing at the right hand of God, and he said, "Behold, I see the heavens opened and the Son of Man standing at the right hand of God." But they cried out in a loud voice, covered their ears, and rushed upon him together. They threw him out of the city, and began to stone him. . . . As they were stoning Stephen, he called out "Lord Jesus, receive my spirit."

Reflection

The painful reality of martyrdom is not to be glossed over as we keep today's feast. What amazing faith, what conviction and depth of devotion to Christ Jesus are afforded by the blood of martyrs. Stephen's death mirrors that of Christ's and is another way in which Christmas and the Paschal Triduum are united.

Prayers

others may be added

To the Word made flesh, we pray:

◆ Prince of Peace, enlighten us.

For the Church persecuted, we pray: ◆ May the witness of the martyrs inspire us, we pray: ◆ For lawmakers, that they will seek peace, we pray: ◆ For those we persecute in our minds and hearts, we pray: ◆ That the kindness and goodwill of this Christmastide will endure, we pray: ◆

Our Father . . .

Lord God,
you gave us the servant Stephen
as a model of fidelity.
True to you until death, he is the first
of so many who have given their lives
in witness to your Son and his Reign.
May the witness of the martyrs
deepen our faith and strengthen
our resolve
to be people who embody the
undying love
of our Lord Jesus Christ, your Son,
who lives and reigns with you in the unity
of the Holy Spirit,
one God, for ever and ever.
Amen

✝ All the ends of the earth have seen the saving power of God.

Tuesday, December 27, 2016

Feast of St. John, Apostle and Evangelist

☩ All the ends of the earth have seen the saving power of God.

Psalm 98

page 414

Reading

I John 1:1–4

Beloved:
What was from the beginning, / what we have heard, / what we have seen with our eyes, / what we looked upon / and touched with our hands / concerns the Word of life— / for the life was made visible; / we have seen it and testify to it / and proclaim to you the eternal life / that was with the Father and was made visible to us— / what we have seen and heard / we proclaim now to you, / so that you too may have fellowship with us; / for our fellowship is with the Father / and with his Son, Jesus Christ. / We are writing this so that our joy may be complete.

Reflection

In our Catholic tradition a feast day occurs on the date of the individual's death, the time of their birth into eternal life. The disciple John is indicated to be among Jesus' most intimate followers. There is no way of knowing the date of John's death. It is, however, appropriate that his feast be kept within the Octave of Christmas. The Gospel that bears his name explicitly informs us of the mystery of the Incarnation. Today, you may want to slowly and prayerfully read the Prologue of the Gospel according to John, perhaps in conjunction with the first chapter of Genesis.

Prayers

others may be added

To the Word made flesh, we pray:

◆ Light of the World, hear us.

For the Church, may we proclaim the Incarnation in word and deed, we pray: ◆ For N., our (arch) bishop, and for our local church, we pray: ◆ May we see the seed of the new creation in the beauty of nature, we pray: ◆ For novelists, lyricists, screenwriters, and all who inspire us through words, we pray: ◆ May we appreciate the sacredness of our words and respect the words of others, we pray: ◆

Our Father . . .

Lord God,
you sent your Word, Jesus Christ,
to speak spirit and life to us.
May our words speak the truth of
our lives,
even when we are fearful or
self-conscious.
May the Holy Spirit give us the courage
to speak truth to power
and to faithfully abide
in you even as your Son abides in us.
We ask this through our Lord Jesus
Christ, your Son,
who lives and reigns with you in the unity
of the Holy Spirit,
one God, for ever and ever.
Amen.

☩ All the ends of the earth have seen the saving power of God.

Wednesday, December 28, 2016

Feast of the Holy Innocents, Martyrs

✝ All the ends of the earth have seen the saving power of God.

Psalm 98 *page 414*

Reading *Matthew 2:16–18*

When Herod realized that he had been deceived by the magi, he became furious. He ordered the massacre of all the boys in Bethlehem and its vicinity two years old and under, in accordance with the time he had ascertained from the magi. Then was fulfilled what had been said through Jeremiah the prophet: *A voice was heard in Ramah, / sobbing and loud lamentation; / Rachel weeping for her children, / and she would not be consoled, / since they were no more.*

Reflection

Today we observe the Slaughter of the Innocents. The story leads us to recall Pharaoh's edict against the Hebrew newborns (Exodus 1) and the Exodus. Moses guided the Hebrew people from slavery to freedom. The newborn king will be even greater than Moses, leading humanity from death to eternal life. In Matthew's Gospel, this account is a literary device, not a historical event. Even so, in the wake of abortion, human trafficking, child abuse, neglect, starvation, and bullying, to name a few, the slaughter of the innocents is all too real.

Prayers *others may be added*

To the Word made flesh, we pray:

◆ Son of God and son of Mary, hear us.

For the Church, that she may continue to seek to protect the unborn, we pray: ◆ For children bought and sold, we pray: ◆ For victims of clergy sexual abuse, we pray: ◆ For our nation's leaders, that they may work with the interest of orphans, those in foster care, and homeless children, we pray: ◆ For those who feel unloved or unlovable, we pray: ◆

Our Father . . .

Lord Jesus,
you entered fully into our humanity,
including the experience of childhood.
Help your Church and all who serve in
public office
to be mindful of the world of children.
May those young people
who dwell in darkness and the shadow
of death
come to know of your presence,
protection, and love,
for you live and reign with God the Father
in the unity of the Holy Spirit,
one God, for ever and ever.
Amen.

✝ All the ends of the earth have seen the saving power of God.

Thursday, December 29, 2016

Optional Memorial of St. Thomas Becket, Bishop and Martyr

✝ All the ends of the earth have seen the saving power of God.

Psalm 98

page 414

Reading

1 John 2:3–11

Beloved: The way we may be sure that we know Jesus is to keep his commandments. Whoever says, "I know him," but does not keep his commandments is a liar, and the truth is not in him. But whoever keeps his word, the love of God is perfected in him. This is the way we are to know we are in union with him: whoever claims to abide in him ought to walk just as he walked.

Beloved, I am writing no new commandment to you but an old commandment that you had from the beginning. The old commandment is the word that you have heard. . . . Whoever says he is in the light, yet hates his brother, is still in the darkness. Whoever loves his brother remains in the light, and there is nothing in him to cause a fall. Whoever hates his brother is in darkness; he walks in darkness and does not know where he is going because the darkness has blinded his eyes.

Reflection

Today's optional memorial recalls the role of conscience during a conflict between church and state. Thomas Becket, the archbishop of Canterbury, England, was murdered under the orders of King Henry II. Becket had resisted the king's attempts to impinge on the freedom of the Church and weaken the connections of clergy to Rome. When news spread of his assassination, English Catholics acclaimed Becket as a saint. Just two years later, the Church canonized him. Becket's name remains synonymous with obeying one's conscience.

Prayers

others may be added

To the Word made flesh, we pray:

◆ Prince of Peace, hear us.

That the Church may continue to be a bold advocate for the freedom of religion, we pray: ◆ For those newly elected to public office, we pray: ◆ That governments respect free speech, free press, and the right to peaceful dissent, we pray: ◆ For the grace and courage to follow one's conscience, we pray: ◆ That the witness of peaceful individuals who die by violence may inspire us to nonviolence, we pray: ◆

Our Father . . .

Lord of all creation,
in every generation
you raise up men and women outstanding
in holiness.
May Thomas Beckett's witness of fidelity
to you,
loyalty to his faith,
and obedience to his conscience
continue to challenge and inspire us
to confidently proclaim and live
the faith we profess,
through our Lord Jesus Christ, your Son,
who lives and reigns with you in the unity
of the Holy Spirit,
one God, for ever and ever.
Amen.

✝ All the ends of the earth have seen the saving power of God.

Friday, December 30, 2016

Feast of the Holy Family of Jesus, Mary, and Joseph

† All the ends of the earth have seen the saving power of God.

Psalm 98

page 414

Reading

Matthew 2:13–15

When the magi had departed, behold, the angel of the Lord appeared to Joseph in a dream and said, "Rise, take the child and his mother, flee to Egypt, and stay there until I tell you. Herod is going to search for the child to destroy him." Joseph rose and took the child and his mother by night and departed for Egypt. He stayed there until the death of Herod, that what the Lord had said through the prophet might be fulfilled, / *Out of Egypt I called my son.*

Reflection

Being family often is not easy. For Joseph, it meant taking on the role of a protector, fleeing from home in the middle of the night. When we think of the issues, tensions, and chaos in our family, we can look to the Holy Family, knowing that they dealt with problems too. It can be comforting to know that Jesus, Mary, and Joseph needed to deal with turmoil. After the Holy Family was forced to flee into Egypt, Joseph remained fearful of returning to Judea. Just as Joseph trusted in the Lord, today's families need to turn to God to guide them during distress.

Prayers

others may be added

To the Word made flesh, we pray:

◆ Son of God and son of Mary, hear us.

May the ministry of ecumenism bring unity to the Christian family, we pray: ◆ May families strive to model the bond of love and communion of the Father, Son, and Holy Spirit, we pray: ◆ For families in which members are alienated from one another, we pray: ◆ For our family and loved ones, we pray: ◆ For the family of faith that has gone before us yet remains forever part of us, we pray: ◆

Our Father . . .

Lord Jesus,
you are the Word made flesh.
Help us to make your words flesh to those we love.
May we share ourselves openly, honestly, and safely with one another.
May we receive those we love and those who share our common humanity
with tenderness and respect.
Bless our family, your family of the Church, and the entire family of humanity.
You live and reign with God the Father in the unity of the Holy Spirit,
one God, for ever and ever.
Amen.

† All the ends of the earth have seen the saving power of God.

Saturday, December 31, 2016

Seventh Day within the Octave of the Nativity of the Lord

✝ All the ends of the earth have seen the saving power of God.

Psalm 98 *page 414*

Reading *John 1:10–13, 15*

He was in the world, / and the world came to be through him, / but the world did not know him. / He came to what was his own, / but his own people did not accept him.

But to those who did accept him he gave power to become children of God, to those who believe in his name, who were born not by natural generation nor by human choice nor by a man's decision but of God.

John testified to him and cried out, saying, "This was he of whom I said, 'The one who is coming after me ranks ahead of me because he existed before me.' "

Reflection

We do not live apart from the world but bring the life of the world into our faith. Still, at times, we feel apart from the world. Tonight is celebrated as New Year's Eve; our new liturgical year began weeks ago. This New Year is kept with revelry; the liturgical year begins with Advent, quietly and almost as imperceptibly as the Son of God entering into Mary's womb. Tonight people make resolutions. There is no need to critique the world tonight. Smile, enjoy, and claim the presence of Christ that is unknown and unacknowledged but there nonetheless.

Prayers *others may be added*

To the Word made flesh, we pray:

◆ **Lord Jesus, the Alpha and the Omega, hear us.**

For world peace, we pray: ◆ For safety and sobriety this night, we pray: ◆ May our elderly dream dreams and our young see visions, we pray: ◆ That we may forgive even as we have been forgiven, we pray: ◆ For all who have died this past year, may they rest in your loving embrace, we pray: ◆

Our Father . . .

O God of endless ages,
to whom a thousand years are as a day,
look upon us whose lives are shrouded in just one age
and for whom the years pass so quickly.
We thank you for the blessings, joys, and triumphs of the passing year
and yes, also for the sorrows shared and the burdens borne.
We remember with love those who have departed
and welcome in thanksgiving
those who have entered our lives.
We ask your help in remaining faithful to you
and to the Kingdom of your Son,
who lives and reigns with you in the unity of the Holy Spirit,
one God, for ever and ever.
Amen.

✝ All the ends of the earth have seen the saving power of God.

Sunday, January 1, 2017

Solemnity of Mary, the Holy Mother of God

☩ From this day all generations will call me blessed.

Canticle of Mary

page 422

Reading

Luke 2:16–20

The shepherds went in haste to Bethlehem and found Mary and Joseph, and the infant lying in the manger. When they saw this, they made known the message that had been told them about this child. All who heard it were amazed by what had been told them by the shepherds. And Mary kept all these things, reflecting on them in her heart. Then the shepherds returned, glorifying and praising God for all they had heard and seen, just as it had been told to them.

Reflection

"What good is it to me if Mary gave birth to the Son of God fourteen hundred years ago and I do not also give birth to the Son of God in my time and in my culture?" Meister Eckhart asked.

The title Mother of God flows from the Church's belief in Jesus as "consubstantial with the Father." While this title originated as a defense of Jesus' identity, as the words from Meister Eckhart indicate, today's solemnity gives us pause to ponder our Baptism into the priesthood of all believers. How will I render Christ present today?

Prayers

others may be added

The Word became flesh and so we pray:

◆ Son of God and son of Mary, hear us.

May the Church be the symbol of Christ to the world, we pray: ◆ For N. the bishop of Rome and for bishops throughout the world, we pray: ◆ That peace may reign in our hearts, our family, and our world, we pray: ◆ For all who share in the vocation of motherhood, we pray: ◆ For the safety of travelers, especially college students returning to school, we pray: ◆

Our Father . . .

Lord God,
you have given us Mary as a beacon of holiness.
We began anew in Advent,
and we do so again today.
May we keep in mind the Mother of God this year
as we greet the new beginnings that come to us
and seek her guidance to greater conversion
and a conscious living out of our Baptism.
We ask this through our Lord Jesus Christ, your Son,
who lives and reigns with you in the unity of the Holy Spirit,
one God, for ever and ever.
Amen.

☩ From this day all generations will call me blessed.

Monday, January 2, 2017

Sts. Basil the Great and Gregory Nazianzen,
Bishops and Doctors of the Church

☩ **Let the heavens be glad and the earth rejoice!**

Psalm 96 *page 413*

Reading *I John 2:22–28*

Beloved: Who is the liar? Whoever denies that Jesus is the Christ. Whoever denies the Father and the Son, this is the antichrist. Anyone who denies the Son does not have the Father, but whoever confesses the Son has the Father as well.

Let what you heard from the beginning remain in you. If what you heard from the beginning remains in you, then you will remain in the Son and in the Father. And this is the promise that he made us: eternal life. I write you these things about those who would deceive you. As for you, the anointing that you received from him remains in you, so that you do not need anyone to teach you. But his anointing teaches you about everything and is true and not false; just as it taught you, remain in him.

And now, children, remain in him, so that when he appears we may have confidence and not be put to shame by him at his coming.

Reflection

"Remain in the Son and in the Father" are words to reflect upon as we ponder the Incarnation. God desires that we remain in him so much that he came as one of us. St. Athanasius said, "The Son of God became man so that we might become God." Through Word and sacrament, especially the Eucharist, Christ dwells in us. To remain in Christ and the Father is to be mindful of who we are, of the Baptism we have received, and of the sacred Body and Blood that unites us to Christ and our sisters and brothers.

Prayers *others may be added*

To Christ, who humbled himself to share in our humanity, we pray:

◆ **Light from Light, enlighten us.**

For a greater appreciation of the holy Eucharist, we pray: ◆ For Eastern Rite Catholics, we pray: ◆ For the new evangelization, that it may draw us closer to Christ, we pray: ◆ For wise and learned theologians, we pray: ◆ For vocations to the priesthood, religious life, and lay ecclesial ministry, we pray: ◆

Our Father . . .

Lord God,
you joined your Son, Jesus Christ, to our humanity
with a bond that can never be broken.
May we, your Church,
unite ourselves to Christ,
who comes to us in the poor, the addicted, the frightened, and the lost.
Help us to remain in solidarity with these
and all whom the world deems
to be inconvenient and insignificant.
Guide us to ways that uphold the dignity
and the holiness of every person.
Through Christ our Lord.
Amen.

☩ **Let the heavens be glad and the earth rejoice!**

Tuesday, January 3, 2017

Christmas Weekday

✝ **Let the heavens be glad and the earth rejoice!**

Psalm 96

page 413

Reading

John 1:29–34

John the Baptist saw Jesus coming toward him and said, "Behold, the Lamb of God, who takes away the sin of the world. He is the one of whom I said, 'A man is coming after me who ranks ahead of me because he existed before me.' I did not know him, but the reason why I came baptizing with water was that he might be made known to Israel." John testified further, saying, "I saw the Spirit come down like a dove from heaven and remain upon him. I did not know him, but the one who sent me to baptize with water told me, 'On whomever you see the Spirit come down and remain, he is the one who will baptize with the Holy Spirit.' Now I have seen and testified that he is the Son of God."

Reflection

In referring to Christ, John declares that "he existed before me." Passages such as this help us to appreciate the mystery of Christmas because they speak of the preexistence of the Son. He is with God from the beginning. He is the Word, and he is the figure of Wisdom, whom the Old Testament portrays as being with God from "the beginning." When we reflect on this, we come to grasp why Christmas goes far beyond the miracle of birth; and why we keep Christmas beyond our cultural holiday season.

Prayers

others may be added

To Christ, who humbled himself to share in our humanity, we pray:

◆ **Light from Light, enlighten us.**

May Wisdom guide the Church, we pray: ◆ May world leaders seek the truth in their dealings with each other, we pray: ◆ For the forgiveness of our sins, we pray: ◆ For a deeper appreciation of the mystery of the Incarnation, we pray: ◆ For those to whom this day will be a burden rather than a joy, we pray: ◆

Our Father . . .

Lamb of God,
you were with God from all eternity;
you are the Wisdom of the Father.
In your compassion,
you take away the sins of the world.
May we trust in your mercy and love
and be confident that we stand before you
as sinners who have been forgiven.
You live and reign with God the Father in
the unity of the Holy Spirit,
one God, for ever and ever.
Amen.

✝ **Let the heavens be glad and the earth rejoice!**

Wednesday, January 4, 2017

Memorial of St. Elizabeth Ann Seton, Religious

✝ **Let the heavens be glad and the earth rejoice!**

Psalm 96 *page 413*

Reading *John 1:35–42*

John was standing with two of his disciples, and as he watched Jesus walk by, he said, "Behold, the Lamb of God." The two disciples heard what he said and followed Jesus. Jesus turned and saw them following him and said to them, "What are you looking for?" They said to him, "Rabbi" (which translated means Teacher), "where are you staying?" He said to them, "Come, and you will see." So they went and saw where he was staying, and they stayed with him that day. It was about four in the afternoon. Andrew, the brother of Simon Peter, was one of the two who heard John and followed Jesus. He first found his own brother Simon and told him, "We have found the Messiah," which is translated Christ. Then he brought him to Jesus. Jesus looked at him and said, "You are Simon the son of John; you will be called Cephas," which is translated Peter.

Reflection

Today we honor the first saint to be born in what would become the United States. Elizabeth Ann Seton was born two years prior to the Revolutionary War. She would eventually establish the first Catholic school in the United States and the nation's first congregation of religious women, the Sisters of Charity. Elizabeth Seton was not born into a Catholic family. Following the death of her husband, the kindness and support of Catholic neighbors and friends guided this future saint to Catholicism. Yes, our thoughtful words and compassionate actions can and do evangelize.

Prayers *others may be added*

To Christ, who humbled himself to share in our humanity, we pray:

◆ **Light from Light, enlighten us.**

That our words and actions may lead others to faith in Christ, we pray: ◆ For women religious, we pray: ◆ For leaders in Catholic schools, we pray: ◆ For widowed and widowers, we pray: ◆ For the grace to embrace new endeavors, we pray: ◆

Our Father . . .

Lord of Light,
you gave Elizabeth Ann Seton the wisdom and fortitude
to discern the crucial needs
of the Church in the eighteenth and early nineteenth centuries.
Enlighten us to read the signs of our times
and to respond to the needs of the Church in the twenty-first century.
Inspired by her conversion and ministry,
may we be aware of how our words and actions
might invite those we know to faith in you,
who live and reign with God the Father in the unity of the Holy Spirit,
one God, for ever and ever.
Amen.

✝ **Let the heavens be glad and the earth rejoice!**

Thursday, January 5, 2017
Memorial of St. John Neumann, Bishop

✝ Let the heavens be glad and the earth rejoice!

Psalm 96
page 413

Reading
1 John 3:14–21

Beloved: We know that we have passed from death to life because we love our brothers. Whoever does not love remains in death. Everyone who hates his brother is a murderer, and you know that no murderer has eternal life remaining in him. The way we came to know love was that he laid down his life for us; so we ought to lay down our lives for our brothers. If someone who has worldly means sees a brother in need and refuses him compassion, how can the love of God remain in him? Children, let us love not in word or speech but in deed and truth.

Now this is how we shall know that we belong to the truth and reassure our hearts before him in whatever our hearts condemn, for God is greater than our hearts and knows everything. Beloved, if our hearts do not condemn us, we have confidence in God.

Reflection

The First Letter of John was composed at a time when the author's community was under attack. That is why his writing is filled with dichotomy: love and hate, good and evil; life and murder. Today's passage is no different, except he provides reassurance and comfort when he writes, "God is greater than our hearts and knows everything."

Prayers
others may be added

To Christ, who humbled himself to share in our humanity, we pray:

◆ Light from Light, enlighten us.

For Christians living in the midst of war and repression, we pray: ◆ For the willingness to understand economic, gender, racial, and religious differences, we pray: ◆ For prisoners, especially those who await execution, we pray: ◆ For people living with obsessive-compulsive disorder, we pray: ◆ That legislators who disagree are respectful toward one another, we pray: ◆

Our Father . . .

God of life and creation,
you know our hearts better than we.
May the coming Epiphany of your Son
enlighten us.
Arouse us to be self-reflective
so that we better know ourselves
and inspire in us the desire to be more
understanding of others.
We ask this through our Lord Jesus
Christ, your Son,
who lives and reigns with you in the unity
of the Holy Spirit,
one God, for ever and ever.
Amen.

✝ Let the heavens be glad and the earth rejoice!

Friday, January 6, 2017
Christmas Weekday

✝ Light dawns for the just; and gladness, for the upright of heart.

Psalm 97 *page 414*

Reading *I John 5:5–9, 13*

Beloved: Who indeed is the victor over the world but the one who believes that Jesus is the Son of God?

This is the one who came through water and Blood, Jesus Christ, not by water alone, but by water and Blood. The Spirit is the one who testifies, and the Spirit is truth. So there are three that testify, the Spirit, the water, and the Blood, and the three are of one accord. If we accept human testimony, the testimony of God is surely greater. Now the testimony of God is this, that he has testified on behalf of his Son.

I write these things to you so that you may know that you have eternal life, you who believe in the name of the Son of God.

Reflection

There are devout Christians who could be poster children for what it means to be a faithful disciple. Still, they carry within themselves great anxiety as to whether they will be saved. The First Letter of John says that if you believe in the name of the Son of God, you have eternal life. It sounds too simple. Of course, faith in Christ will result in worshipping God and performing works of service. But in the end, eternal life is God's gift to us through Christ and the Holy Spirit. This is the gift of Christmas. Receive the gift with gladness.

Prayers *others may be added*

To Christ, who humbled himself to share in our humanity, we pray:

◆ Light from Light, hear us.

For the Church, may we be the symbol of God's salvific will, we pray: ◆ For the faith that leads to action on behalf of justice, we pray: ◆ For families experiencing marital distress, we pray: ◆ For community leaders, that they possess the humility to graciously accept the gifts of others, we pray: ◆ For those who have died, especially those whose faith is known only to God, we pray: ◆

Our Father . . .

Lord God,
you so loved the world
that in the fullness of time
you sent your only Son to be our Savior.
Such is your wondrous love, O God.
Help us to trust in your love always,
through our Lord Jesus Christ, your Son,
who lives and reigns with you in the unity
of the Holy Spirit,
one God, for ever and ever.
Amen.

✝ Light dawns for the just; and gladness, for the upright of heart.

Saturday, January 7, 2017
Christmas Weekday

✝ **Light dawns for the just; and gladness, for the upright of heart.**

Psalm 97 *page 414*

Reading *John 2:1–8, 10*

There was a wedding in Cana in Galilee, and the mother of Jesus was there. Jesus and his disciples were also invited to the wedding. When the wine ran short, the mother of Jesus said to him, "They have no wine." And Jesus said to her, "Woman, how does your concern affect me? My hour has not yet come." His mother said to the servers, "Do whatever he tells you." Now there were six stone water jars there for Jewish ceremonial washings, each holding twenty to thirty gallons. Jesus told them, "Fill the jars with water." So they filled them to the brim. Then he told them, "Draw some out now and take it to the headwaiter." So they took it. . . . The headwaiter called the bridegroom and said to him, "Everyone serves good wine first, and then when people have drunk freely, an inferior one; but you have kept the good wine until now."

Reflection

The prophet Joel saw an abundance of wine as a sign of the day of the Lord. That Jesus' ministry begins with the transformation of 120 to 180 gallons of water into wine is appropriate. Just as in the day of the Lord, the Spirit of God was about to be unleashed on God's people, so with the beginning of Jesus' preaching and healing. Today's Gospel is a fitting preparation for tomorrow's solemnity in that it signals the beginning of our movement out of Christmas and toward Jesus' ministry and our own. With what gifts have I been anointed this Christmas? What will I do with them? Who am I being called to serve?

Prayers *others may be added*

To Christ, who humbled himself to share in our humanity, we pray:

◆ **Light from Light, enlighten us.**

For the Church, may we be open to the gifts of the Holy Spirit, we pray: ◆ For world leaders, may they seek the common good of all, we pray: ◆ For those who are missing from Sunday worship, we pray: ◆ For the unemployed and the underemployed, we pray: ◆ May the spirit of Christmas continue to reign in our hearts throughout the year, we pray: ◆

Our Father . . .

Lord,
you have sent out your Spirit.
Ignite within us the sure resolve to renew the face of the earth.
May we work to end hunger, violence, abuse, prejudice,
and all that is contrary to your Reign,
for you live and reign with God the Father in the unity of the Holy Spirit,
one God, for ever and ever.
Amen.

✝ **Light dawns for the just; and gladness, for the upright of heart.**

Sunday, January 8, 2017
Solemnity of the Epiphany of the Lord

✝ Light dawns for the just; and gladness, for the upright of heart.

Psalm 97 *page 414*

Reading *Matthew 2:1–2, 9–12*

When Jesus was born in Bethlehem of Judea, in the days of King Herod, behold, magi from the east arrived in Jerusalem, saying, "Where is the newborn king of the Jews? We saw his star at its rising and have come to do him homage." . . . After their audience with the king they set out. And behold, the star that they had seen at its rising preceded them, until it came and stopped over the place where the child was. They were overjoyed at seeing the star, and on entering the house they saw the child with Mary his mother. They prostrated themselves and did him homage. Then they opened their treasures and offered him gifts of gold, frankincense, and myrrh. And having been warned in a dream not to return to Herod, they departed for their country by another way.

Reflection

The word *epiphany* means "manifestation," "enlightenment," and "revelation." Something or someone is revealed, and we are enlightened. The journey of the Magi is our journey too. What are the ways in which you have been enlightened as you have come to know Christ? How has Christ been made known to you? Commemorate the journey of the Magi today by prayerfully reflecting on your journey toward Christ, and the ways that your route has been changed.

Prayers *others may be added*

To Christ, who humbled himself to share in our humanity, we pray:

◆ Light from Light, enlighten us.

May the Church truly be a light to the nations, we pray: ◆ That all the descendants of Abraham: Jews, Christians, and Muslims, may find the way to dwell in harmony, we pray: ◆ For catechumens and candidates, we pray: ◆ For seekers, scholars, researchers, scientists, and all who seek enlightenment, we pray: ◆ That our leaders welcome immigrants and refugees, we pray: ◆

Our Father . . .

Lord Jesus Christ,
today you are revealed as the Light of the world
and the Savior of all humankind.
May your light, passed on to us on the day of our Baptism,
continue to shine brightly so that,
seeing the good we do in your name,
people will give praise to the Father,
for you live and reign with God the Father in the unity of the Holy Spirit,
one God, for ever and ever.
Amen.

✝ Light dawns for the just; and gladness, for the upright of heart.

Monday, January 9, 2017

Feast of the Baptism of the Lord

✝ Light dawns for the just; and gladness, for the upright of heart.

Psalm 97

page 414

Reading

Matthew 3:13–17

Jesus came from Galilee to John at the Jordan to be baptized by him. John tried to prevent him, saying, "I need to be baptized by you, and yet you are coming to me?" Jesus said to him in reply, "Allow it now, for thus it is fitting for us to fulfill all righteousness." Then he allowed him. After Jesus was baptized, he came up from the water and behold, the heavens were opened for him, and he saw the Spirit of God descending like a dove and coming upon him. And a voice came from the heavens, saying, "This is my beloved Son, with whom I am well pleased."

Reflection

Today is the last day of Christmas Time. Jesus is baptized by John in the Jordan River. I was baptized into Christ Jesus by (name of presider) at (name of church). The baptism of Jesus might lead us to think about our Baptism and our children's Baptism. Do we still have ours or our child's baptismal garment? Or baptismal candle? If so, display them today. What do you know about your Baptism? Tell that story today. Do your children know about the day of their Baptism? Tell or retell the story of that day. Discuss what does it mean to be baptized into Christ Jesus?

Prayers

others may be added

To Christ, who humbled himself to share in our humanity, we pray:

◆ Light from Light, hear us.

That our baptismal identity may mean more to us than our economic status or other way we identify ourselves, we pray: ◆ For a greater understanding that ministry flows from Baptism, we pray: ◆ For our parents and godparents, living and deceased, we pray: ◆ For our children, grandchildren, and godchildren, we pray: ◆ That all who have died with Christ in Baptism come to share in the glory of his Resurrection, we pray: ◆

Our Father . . .

Dear Lord,
to you, we are beloved.
Help me to see myself as you see me,
so that I may become the person you have called me to be.
We ask this through our Lord Jesus Christ, your Son,
who lives and reigns with you in the unity of the Holy Spirit,
one God, for ever and ever.
Amen.

✝ Light dawns for the just; and gladness, for the upright of heart.

Tuesday, January 10, 2017
Weekday

✝ O Lord, our Lord, how awesome is your name over all the earth!

Psalm 8

page 401

Reading

Hebrews 2:5–9

It was not to the angels that God subjected the world to come, of which we are speaking.

Instead, someone has testified somewhere: / *What is man that you are mindful of him, / or the son of man that you care for him? / You made him for a little while lower than the angels; / you crowned him with glory and honor, / subjecting all things under his feet.* / In "subjecting" all things [to him], he left nothing not "subject to him." Yet at present we do not see "all things subject to him," but we do see Jesus "crowned with glory and honor" because he suffered death, he who "for a little while" was made "lower than the angels," that by the grace of God he might taste death for everyone.

Reflection

The Letter to the Hebrews quotes Psalm 8, though the reference appears to be general, "Someone has testified somewhere . . . " Don't many of us know the Bible in a similar way? We can tell the plot and the detail of some of our favorite stories, such as the account of the prodigal son or the Good Samaritan by heart. These stories have been embedded in our hearts. What stories guide your heart today? Are there psalms that are meaningful to you? Do you turn to them for comfort?

Prayers

others may be added

Turning to God with confidence, we pray:

◆ Teach our hearts, O Lord.

May your Church preach words of faith to a troubled world, we pray: ◆ May our hearts embrace words of peace, we pray: ◆ May engineers and scientists revel in the beauty of God's creation, we pray: ◆ May the sick find peace and healing, we pray: ◆

Our Father . . .

Creator God,
your Scriptures teach us your will.
Their truths ring in our hearts
and the stories are on our lips.
May we take the time
to delve further into your holy Word
that your revelation may be the source of our actions.
We ask this through Christ our Lord.
Amen.

✝ O Lord, our Lord, how awesome is your name over all the earth!

Wednesday, January 11, 2017
Weekday

✝ O Lord, our Lord, how awesome is your name over all the earth!

Psalm 8

page 401

Reading

Hebrews 2:14–18

Since the children share in blood and Flesh, Jesus likewise shared in them, that through death he might destroy the one who has the power of death, that is, the Devil, and free those who through fear of death had been subject to slavery all their life. Surely he did not help angels but rather the descendants of Abraham; therefore, he had to become like his brothers and sisters in every way, that he might be a merciful and faithful high priest before God to expiate the sins of the people. Because he himself was tested through what he suffered, he is able to help those who are being tested.

Reflection

What does it mean to say that Jesus "had to become like us"? Hebrews says that this is so that he might be a merciful and a faithful high priest. Consider how you relate to others. Do you feel the pain of the mother who has lost her son in war, even if her son fought with the enemy? Do we see pictures of the poor lining up to get food and realize that could be us if our circumstances were slightly different? Do we experience the heat of a summer sun on their backs, the ice of winter under their feet? If Jesus became human like us, can we ignore the human suffering of our sisters and brothers?

Prayers

others may be added

Turning to the Lord with confidence, we pray:

◆ Teach our hearts, O Lord.

For worldwide vision in the Church, we pray: ◆ For world leaders to work to end war, we pray: ◆ For justice for the poor, we pray: ◆ For hearts open to the pain and sorrow of others, we pray: ◆ For compassion for our enemies, we pray: ◆

Our Father . . .

Father of the poor,
Jesus became our brother,
one like us in all things but sin.
May we truly become sister and brother
to all people of the world, feeling their
joys and sorrows, pain and pleasure.
We ask this through Christ our Lord.
Amen.

✝ O Lord, our Lord, how awesome is your name over all the earth!

Thursday, January 12, 2017
Weekday

☩ O Lord, our Lord, how awesome is your name over all the earth!

Psalm 8
page 401

Reading
Hebrews 3:7–14

The Holy Spirit says: / *Oh, that today you would hear his voice, / "Harden not your hearts as at the rebellion / in the day of testing in the desert, / where your ancestors tested and tried me / and saw my works for forty years. / Because of this I was provoked with generations / and I said, 'They have always been of erring heart, / and they do not know my ways.' / As I swore in my wrath, / 'They shall not enter into my rest.'"* / Take care, brothers and sisters, that none of you may have an evil and unfaithful heart, so as to forsake the living God. Encourage yourselves daily while it is still "today," so that none of you may grow hardened by the deceit of sin. We have become partners of Christ if only we hold the beginning of the reality firm until the end.

Reflection
Today's reading references the end of Psalm 95, which recalls the Israelites' hardened hearts. Though they had seen God's mighty works in Egypt, they still would not trust during their forty years in the desert. Does this sound like us? The excitement of Christmas is past, and the cold of January can harden us. Have we begun to complain and forgotten our blessings? Try to spend a few moments realizing the gifts God has given you.

Prayers
others may be added

Turning to the Lord with confidence, we pray:

◆ Teach our hearts, O Lord.

For a Church that speaks of blessings and God's graciousness, we pray: ◆ For softening of our nation's leaders' hearts, hardened by politics, we pray: ◆ For teenagers and all who seek God's voice, we pray: ◆ For an end to our bitterness and selfishness, we pray: ◆ For gratitude, we pray: ◆

Our Father . . .

Generous God, you bless us with abundance.
Renew in us a spirit of humility.
Help us to be more open to your will
and less concerned with the success of our hands.
We ask this through Christ our Lord.
Amen.

☩ O Lord, our Lord, how awesome is your name over all the earth!

Friday, January 13, 2017
Weekday

✝ O Lord, our Lord, how awesome is your name over all the earth!

Psalm 8 *page 401*

Reading *Hebrews 4:1–5, 11*

Let us be on our guard while the promise of entering into his rest remains, that none of you seem to have failed. For in fact we have received the Good News just as our ancestors did. But the word that they heard did not profit them, for they were not united in faith with those who listened. For we who believed enter into that rest, just as he has said: / *As I swore in my wrath, / "They shall not enter into my rest,"* / and yet his works were accomplished at the foundation of the world. For he has spoken somewhere about the seventh day in this manner, / *And God rested on the seventh day from all his works;* / and again, in the previously mentioned place, / *They shall not enter into my rest.* /

Therefore, let us strive to enter into that rest, so that no one may fall after the same example of disobedience.

Reflection

Sabbath rest has become a lost concept. The sacred author speaks in a solemn manner about what may seem a simple concept. We often feel that so much needs to be done. Yet as time with family decreases, heart attacks increase. What is so important that we cannot stop for one day? To stop working requires trust in God. Reexamine your practices on Sunday to strive to enter into rest with God.

Prayers *others may be added*

Turning to God with confidence,
we pray:

◆ Teach our hearts, O Lord.

May disciples trust deeply in God's providential care, we pray: ◆ May community leaders advocate for just wages and fair expectations, we pray: ◆ May the unemployed and underemployed find jobs, we pray: ◆ May those who work in social-service organizations, job placement, and in respite care be blessed in their work, we pray: ◆ In confidence, may we rest in the Lord, we pray: ◆

Our Father . . .

Almighty God,
you command us to rest,
to lay down our burdens weekly.
Increase our trust in you
that we may find rest
for our bodies and our souls.
We ask this through Christ out Lord.
Amen.

✝ O Lord, our Lord, how awesome is your name over all the earth!

Saturday, January 14, 2017
Weekday

✝ O Lord, our Lord, how awesome is your name over all the earth!

Psalm 8 *page 401*

Reading *Hebrews 4:12–13*

The word of God is living and effective, sharper than any two-edged sword, penetrating even between soul and spirit, joints and marrow, and able to discern reflections and thoughts of the heart. No creature is concealed from him, but everything is naked and exposed to the eyes of him, to whom we must render an account.

Reflection

The Word of God penetrates and discerns. Surgeons must work carefully to distinguish between healthy and unhealthy tissue. It's a slow, careful task. God's Word is like that. It is not a quick fix, but rather sees what we try to hide. Do we try to hide even from ourselves? Do we take the time to carefully assess our thoughts and actions, or do we move quickly, acting before thinking? Take it easy today. Move a bit slower and discern why you do the things that you do.

Prayers *others may be added*

Turning to God with confidence,
we pray:

◆ Teach our hearts, O Lord.

For confessors and spiritual directors, may they help us discern our intents and actions, we pray: ◆ For open dialogue among nations, we pray: ◆ For an end to lies, deception, and false business practices, we pray: ◆ For compassion for all who have hurt us, we pray: ◆ For a willingness to think before we act, we pray: ◆

Our Father . . .

Word of God,
you discern the motives of our heart
and actions.
Help us to see our lives more clearly
and acknowledge our sins.
In humility, may we grow in faith
and love.
We ask this through Christ our Lord.
Amen.

✝ O Lord, our Lord, how awesome is your name over all the earth!

Sunday, January 15, 2017

Second Sunday in Ordinary Time

✝ Here am I, Lord; I come to do your will.

Psalm 40

page 405

Reading

John 1:29–34

John the Baptist saw Jesus coming toward him and said, "Behold, the Lamb of God, who takes away the sin of the world. He is the one of whom I said, 'A man is coming after me who ranks ahead of me because he existed before me.' I did not know him, but the reason why I came baptizing with water was that he might be made known to Israel." John testified further, saying, "I saw the Spirit come down like a dove from heaven and remain upon him. I did not know him, but the one who sent me to baptize with water told me, 'On whomever you see the Spirit come down and remain, he is the one who will baptize with the Holy Spirit.' Now I have seen and testified that he is the Son of God."

Reflection

"I did not know him, but . . ." John baptized in the wilderness because God called him to do so. He did this without any idea of his role in history. Would you find it difficult to place that much trust in God? Do you find yourself desiring to know the end result during a difficult time or even during the routines of your life? Often we are tempted to think that our lives cannot be part of a cosmic plan. How wrong we can be. All we must do is serve the Lord as God wills it. Then step back and let God do the work of building his Kingdom.

Prayers

others may be added

To the Lord, who opens our ears to hear his will, we pray:

◆ Lord, hear our prayer.

For grace and unity, that they be upon the entire Church, consecrated and called to be a holy people, we pray: ◆ For wisdom and prudence for government officials, we pray: ◆ For relief for those who suffer from hunger, oppression, or war, we pray: ◆ For a spirit of generosity and compassion upon our catechumens and candidates, we pray: ◆ For life and glory upon all who have crossed the threshold of death, we pray: ◆

Our Father . . .

God of wisdom and power,
you called John the Baptist to
preach repentance.
You call each of us to a different part
of your mission.
Help us to discern your will
and trust even when the way is not clear.
We ask this through our Lord Jesus
Christ, your Son,
who lives and reigns with you in the unity
of the Holy Spirit,
one God, for ever and ever.
Amen.

✝ Here am I, Lord; I come to do your will.

Monday, January 16, 2017
Weekday

✝ Here am I, Lord; I come to do your will.

Psalm 40

page 405

Reading

Hebrews 5:1–6

Brothers and sisters: Every high priest is taken from among men and made their representative before God, to offer gifts and sacrifices for sins. He is able to deal patiently with the ignorant and the erring, for he himself is beset by weakness and so, for this reason, must make sin offerings for himself as well as for the people. No one takes this honor upon himself but only when called by God, just as Aaron was. In the same way, it was not Christ who glorified himself in becoming high priest, but rather the one who said to him: / *You are my Son: / this day I have begotten you;* / just as he says in another place, / *You are a priest forever according to the order of Melchizedek.* /

Reflection

A key image in Hebrews is that of Jesus as high priest. The priest offers prayer for others and their sins, because he too is a sinner. A priest is patient, because he too is weak. While it may be easy to pass all these qualities off to our pastors, in Baptism we are anointed as priest. These are our responsibilities too. Recognizing that, we should pray for others, especially for the sins of our world. We should feel solidarity with all, knowing that we too are weak and sinful.

Prayers

others may be added

To our Lord, whose will we seek, we pray:

◆ Lord, hear our prayer.

For humility in our Church, we pray: ◆ For leaders of nations, that they will seek solidarity with the weakest among us, we pray: ◆ For life and love for the not yet born, we pray: ◆ For food for the hungry, we pray: ◆ For an increase of faith, we pray: ◆

Our Father . . .

Gentle Lord,
you humbled yourself,
becoming like us.
Teach us to see the world
through the eyes of the weak, powerless, and struggling.
May we live in solidarity with all your holy people.
You live and reign with God the Father in the unity of the Holy Spirit,
one God, for ever and ever.
Amen.

✝ Here am I, Lord; I come to do your will.

Tuesday, January 17, 2017
Memorial of St. Anthony, Abbot

✝ Here am I, Lord; I come to do your will.

Psalm 40
page 405

Reading
Hebrews 6:10–12

Brothers and sisters: God is not unjust so as to overlook your work and the love you have demonstrated for his name by having served and continuing to serve the holy ones. We earnestly desire each of you to demonstrate the same eagerness for the fulfillment of hope until the end, so that you may not become sluggish, but imitators of those who, through faith and patience, are inheriting the promises.

Reflection
What does the author of Hebrews mean when he encourages the community to keep the faith? The passage calls for an eagerness in living the values of the Gospel. That means that we show our love in caring for others. Do we do as well with living out the teachings of the catechism as we do with memorizing its precepts? Do we allow the loving words of God to take root in our hearts? As St. Francis is believed to have said, "Preach the Gospel at all times. Use words if necessary."

Prayers
others may be added

To the Lord, who opens our ears, we pray:

◆ That we may know your will.

May your Church preach the Gospel, in actions as well as words, we pray: ◆ May monks and all in religious life, find joy in their vocation, we pray: ◆ May the poor be cared for and the hungry fed, we pray: ◆ May the values of the Gospel pervade our thoughts, we pray: ◆ May all that is contrary to love have no place in our hearts, we pray: ◆

Our Father . . .

Lord,
your actions of love fill the world.
As your disciples,
we seek to model your way
and so lead others to you.
May your teachings take deep root in our hearts
that in all we do your love may be evident.
We ask this through Christ our Lord.
Amen.

✝ Here am I, Lord; I come to do your will.

Wednesday, January 18, 2017
Weekday

☩ Here am I, Lord; I come to do your will.

Psalm 40

page 405

Reading

Hebrews 7:1–3

Melchizedek, king of Salem and priest of God Most High, met Abraham as he returned from his defeat of the kings and blessed him. And Abraham apportioned to him *a tenth of everything.* His name first means "righteous king," and he was also "king of Salem," that is, king of peace. Without father, mother, or ancestry, without beginning of days or end of life, thus made to resemble the Son of God, he remains a priest forever.

Reflection

Not much is known about Melchizedek other than that he offered Abraham bread and wine after a victorious battle (see Genesis 14). This action occurred before the covenant was made, before Isaac was born. In many ways, Abraham is no one special. Whom do we take time to take care of? How do you show care to the numerous individuals you meet each day: the clerk at the drive-through window, the cashier at the store, for example?

Prayers

others may be added

To the Lord, who opens our ears, we pray:

◆ **Lord, hear our prayer.**

May the Church continue to boldly proclaim a preferential option for the poor, we pray: ◆ For those who suffer in unknown wars and conflicts, we pray: ◆ For a media less attuned to the lives of the famous, we pray: ◆ For an ability to take time with each person we meet today, we pray: ◆ For lawmakers, that in their legislation they see the value of each person, we pray: ◆

Our Father . . .

Lord of all,
you enter into our lives daily.
Enlighten us, O Lord.
May we see what you see,
and view each person with your eyes.
We ask this through Christ our Lord.
Amen.

☩ Here am I, Lord; I come to do your will.

Thursday, January 19, 2017
Weekday

✝ Here am I, Lord; I come to do your will.

Psalm 40

page 405

Reading

Hebrews 8:1–2

The main point of what has been said is this: we have such a high priest, who has taken his seat at the right hand of the throne of the Majesty in heaven, a minister of the sanctuary and of the true tabernacle that the Lord, not man, set up.

Reflection

We often speak of Jesus in his humility, but today we reflect on his majesty. He is God. He has taken his rightful seat in heaven. What does this mean to us? Majesty is a powerful term. Does this image give us hope? It should not make us fearful, for he is accessible to us and loves us. The image of dominion has been misused by human kings and made into domination and control. This is not our Lord. Rather, his power is for justice and defense of the weak. Can we take comfort in the Lord's power today?

Prayers

others may be added

To the Lord, who opens our ears, we pray:

◆ Graciously hear us, Lord.

For the rightful authority of the Church, may it be used in clemency and mercy, we pray: ◆ For kings, presidents, and other leaders, may they use their power for the powerless, we pray: ◆ For the voiceless, we pray: ◆ For refugees, we pray: ◆ For discernment to use power wisely, we pray: ◆

Our Father . . .

All powerful God,
you are supreme in authority and majesty.
Hear your people as they cry out to you.
Vindicate the battered.
Bind up the injured.
Comfort the neglected.
May we become more like you
and be a shield for all who are ill-treated.
We ask this through Christ our Lord.
Amen.

✝ Here am I, Lord; I come to do your will.

Friday, January 20, 2017
Weekday

✝ Here am I, Lord; I come to do your will.

Psalm 40 *page 405*

Reading *Hebrews 8:6–10*

Brothers and sisters: Now our high priest has obtained so much more excellent a ministry as he is mediator of a better covenant, enacted on better promises.

For if that first covenant had been faultless, no place would have been sought for a second one. But he finds fault with them and says: / *Behold, the days are coming, says the Lord, / when I will conclude a new covenant with the house of Israel and the house of Judah. / It will not be like the covenant I made with their fathers / the day I took them by the hand to lead them forth from the land of Egypt; / for they did not stand by my covenant / and I ignored them, says the Lord. / But this is the covenant I will establish with the house of Israel / after those days, says the Lord: I will put my laws in their minds / and I will write them upon their hearts. / I will be their God, / and they shall be my people. /*

Reflection

Unlike a contract, a covenant forms a deep relationship. The "new covenant" is written on fleshy hearts, not stone tablets. That makes it a bit messy. It demands we internally process our actions. Take time today to evaluate your relationship with God and how you regard being in a covenant with God.

Prayers *others may be added*

To the Lord, who opens our ears, we pray:

◆ Lord, hear our prayer.

May the Church guide us to a deeper relationship with the Lord, we pray: ◆ For perseverance and joy for peacemakers, we pray: ◆ For all who work for justice, we pray: ◆ For deliverance and relief for all who suffer from hunger, oppression, or war, we pray: ◆ For strength and courage upon all who face hatred and misunderstanding, we pray: ◆

Our Father . . .

Loving One,
you call us into a deeper relationship with you.
You write your law of love on our hearts and bid us to love in return.
Help us to travel this covenant journey with you.
We ask this through Christ our Lord.
Amen.

✝ Here am I, Lord; I come to do your will.

Saturday, January 21, 2017

Memorial of St. Agnes, Virgin and Martyr

✝ Here am I, Lord; I come to do your will.

Psalm 40

page 405

Reading

I Corinthians 1:26–29

Consider your calling, brothers and sisters. Not many of you were wise by human standards, not many were powerful, not many were of noble birth. Rather, God chose the foolish of the world to shame the wise, and God chose the lowly and despised of the world, those who count for nothing, to reduce to nothing those who are something, so that no human being might boast before God.

Reflection

Who is nothing and who is something? Who matters and who doesn't? We confront these questions again and again. How can the weak shame the strong or the foolish dishonor the wise? It demands a different set of values than those of the popular culture. St. Agnes was martyred while a teenager. She refused to marry, instead choosing the Lord and therefore her own death. A simple girl, Agnes' name and commitment have lasted through the centuries, though those of the rich and powerful who killed have been forgotten. Can we leave these questions of importance behind and instead focus only on the Lord?

Prayers

others may be added

To the Lord, who opens our ears,
we pray:

◆ Graciously hear us, Lord.

That prudence and peace be upon the Church consecrated and called to be a holy people, we pray: ◆ For unity and communion among Christian Churches, we pray: ◆ For courage and wisdom for the world's leaders, we pray: ◆ That protection and safety be upon travelers, we pray: ◆ That healing and comfort be upon the sick, we pray: ◆

Our Father . . .

God of the martyrs,
you gave St. Agnes the courage to offer
her life rather than sacrifice
her dignity.
May her love for you and the Gospel
be our example that even
worldly pressures
seek to ensnare our hearts.
We ask this through Christ our Lord.
Amen.

✝ Here am I, Lord; I come to do your will.

Sunday, January 22, 2017

Third Sunday in Ordinary Time

† The Lord is my light and my salvation.

Psalm 27

page 404

Reading

Matthew 4:12–17

When Jesus heard that John had been arrested, he withdrew to Galilee. He left Nazareth and went to live in Capernaum by the sea, in the region of Zebulun and Naphtali, that what had been said through Isaiah the prophet might be fulfilled:

Land of Zebulun and land of Naphtali, / the way to the sea, beyond the Jordan, / Galilee of the Gentiles, / the people who sit in darkness / have seen a great light, / on those dwelling in a land overshadowed by death light has arisen.

From that time on, Jesus began to preach and say, "Repent, for the kingdom of heaven is at hand."

Reflection

Change. The world for Jesus shifts. John the Baptist is arrested. Jesus withdraws to Galilee and moves to Capernaum. Now he begins to preach. Our lifetime journey is full of change. Like Jesus, circumstances may motivate us to press forward. It's as if all is in alignment. Now it is our turn to begin a new phase in life. When was the last time you made a profound shift in your life? When we feel the movement of the Spirit, God is beckoning us to take our rightful and necessary place in mission.

Prayers

others may be added

To the Lord, who helps us discern his will, we pray:

◆ Graciously hear us, Lord.

May the Church seek unity, proclaiming the Gospel in every land, we pray: ◆ May world leaders seek an end to genocide, we pray: ◆ May discrimination and hatred cease, we pray: ◆ May we have the courage to abandon our comfortable lives to follow Jesus, we pray: ◆ May those who have entered the shadow of death, live now in the light of Christ, we pray: ◆

Our Father . . .

Gentle Lord,
you stay with us along our daily journey as the road winds,
and changes challenge us.
May all of our steps draw our hearts ever closer to you.
We ask this through our Lord, Jesus Christ, your Son,
who lives and reigns with you in the unity of the Holy Spirit,
one God, for ever and ever.
Amen.

† The Lord is my light and my salvation.

Monday, January 23, 2017
Day of Prayer for the Legal Protection of Unborn Children

☩ The Lord is my light and my salvation.

Psalm 27 *page 404*

Reading *Hebrews 9:15, 28*

Christ is mediator of a new covenant: since a death has taken place for deliverance from transgressions under the first covenant, those who are called may receive the promised eternal inheritance.

Just as it is appointed that human beings die once, and after this the judgment, so also Christ, offered once to take away the sins of many, will appear a second time, not to take away sin but to bring salvation to those who eagerly await him.

Reflection

Christians who await the Second Coming of Christ do so with eagerness. While we wait, we are charged with Christ's mission: to build up his Reign. Fundamental to God's Reign is a respect for life from conception to natural death. Yet, abortion is still a legal option in our country. Even more fundamental is the lack of concern for this vulnerable life and the life of the mother. The spiritual bond between a mother and her unborn child is rarely spoken of, yet clearly is there. In many ways it is a metaphor for God's love for us. Let us pray today for a respect for all life, for solutions to the problems that lead some women to abortion, for a love for mother and child, and for Christians to embrace these women in their pain.

Prayers *others may be added*

To the Lord, who helps us discern, we pray:

◆ Graciously hear us, Lord.

May our Church work to end abortion, we pray: ◆ May legislators seek policies that respect all life, from conception to natural death, we pray: ◆ May women who have had abortions find healing and reconciliation, we pray: ◆ May children be assured of food, safe homes, and education, we pray: ◆ May all people of good will work for justice, we pray: ◆

Our Father . . .

Lord,
you have given us the precious gift of life.
Show us ways to end abortion
and change attitudes about the lives of
the vulnerable.
May women and children
find safety, shelter, and love.
We ask this through Christ our Lord.
Amen.

☩ The Lord is my light and my salvation.

Tuesday, January 24, 2017
Memorial of St. Francis de Sales,
Bishop and Doctor of the Church

✝ The Lord is my light and my salvation.

Psalm 27 *page 404*

Reading *Hebrews 10:1, 3–10*

Brothers and sisters: Since the law has only a shadow of the good things to come, and not the very image of them, it can never make perfect those who come to worship by the same sacrifices that they offer continually each year. In those sacrifices there is only a yearly remembrance of sins, for it is impossible that the blood of bulls and goats take away sins. For this reason, when he came into the world, he said:

Sacrifice and offering you did not desire, / but a body you prepared for me; / in burnt offerings and sin offerings you took no delight. / Then I said, As is written of me in the scroll, / Behold, I come to do your will, O God.

First he says, / *Sacrifices and offerings, / burnt offerings and sin offerings, / you neither desired nor delighted in.* These are offered according to the law. Then he says, *Behold, I come to do your will.* He takes away the first to establish the second. By this "will," we have been consecrated through the offering of the Body of Jesus Christ once for all.

Reflection

Laws and rules. Sacrifices and sin offerings. We may rail against laws, like adolescents do, but secretly we love them. Laws can make life easy. Just follow all the rules and no thought required. However, the Scriptures are opposed to this attitude. The law is supportive but not directive. Sacrifice must emerge from our faith. God cannot be fooled by sin offerings without conversion. What rules do we follow that may need to be changed? What laws keep us from being better disciples of Jesus?

Prayers *others may be added*

To the Lord, who helps us discern his will, we pray:

◆ Guide our steps along your path.

May the laws of the Church serve our discipleship, we pray: ◆ May leaders free prisoners of conscience, we pray: ◆ May human trafficking end, we pray: ◆ May journalists and preachers be guided by the Holy Spirit, we pray: ◆ May unjust laws be discerned and changed, we pray: ◆

Our Father . . .

Lord,
you gave the world your servant Francis de Sales, who reached out to others in compassion.
May we too avoid using the law to hurt and instead bring mercy and love to all we meet.
We ask this through Christ our Lord.
Amen.

✝ The Lord is my light and my salvation.

Wednesday, January 25, 2017
Feast of the Conversion of St. Paul the Apostle

✝ The Lord is my light and my salvation.

Psalm 27

page 404

Reading

Acts 22:6–11

Paul addressed the people in these words: "On that journey as I drew near to Damascus, about noon a great light from the sky suddenly shone around me. I fell to the ground and heard a voice saying to me, 'Saul, Saul, why are you persecuting me?' I replied, 'Who are you, sir?' And he said to me, 'I am Jesus the Nazorean whom you are persecuting.' My companions saw the light but did not hear the voice of the one who spoke to me. I asked, 'What shall I do, sir?' The Lord answered me, 'Get up and go into Damascus, and there you will be told about everything appointed for you to do.' Since I could see nothing because of the brightness of that light, I was led by hand by my companions and entered Damascus."

Reflection

We revel in the story of great sinners leaving behind their way of life and turning to Christ. But to be honest, the Church was as skeptical of Paul's conversion as we may be today. Yet, Ananias took a risk and embraced Paul, helping him move into the Christian community. Are we as open? How do we greet new parishioners or strangers worshipping with us? Do we welcome the catechumens? This Sunday look for someone at church that you can welcome.

Prayers

others may be added

To the Lord, who helps us discern, we pray:

◆ Guide our steps along your path.

May the Church continue to boldly give witness to Jesus Christ to the ends of the earth, we pray: ◆ May nations strive for freedom, not power; food, not dominance, we pray: ◆ May our catechumens and candidates find in our assembly love and acceptance, we pray: ◆ May we embrace all who seek to know the Lord, we pray: ◆ May strangers and outcasts find acceptance, we pray: ◆

Our Father . . .

Lord God,
you gave your servant Paul the courage to change his life.
He is our model of embracing conversion and evangelization.
May we too reach out to others and proclaim your Gospel of love,
welcoming all into our community.
We ask this through Christ our Lord.
Amen.

✝ The Lord is my light and my salvation.

Thursday, January 26, 2017

Memorial of Sts. Timothy and Titus, Bishops

✝ The Lord is my light and my salvation.

Psalm 27

page 404

Reading

2 Timothy 1:1–6

Paul, an Apostle of Christ Jesus by the will of God for the promise of life in Christ Jesus, to Timothy, my dear child: grace, mercy, and peace from God the Father and Christ Jesus our Lord.

I am grateful to God, whom I worship with a clear conscience as my ancestors did, as I remember you constantly in my prayers, night and day. I yearn to see you again, recalling your tears, so that I may be filled with joy, as I recall your sincere faith that first lived in your grandmother Lois and in your mother Eunice and that I am confident lives also in you.

For this reason, I remind you to stir into flame the gift of God that you have through the imposition of my hands.

Reflection

Timothy and Titus were both companions of St. Paul. But what was the origin of their faith? For Timothy, it was his grandmother and mother. They who had faith, nurtured it in their grandson and son. That's the case for many of us. While we must make the faith ours, the seeds were planted and watered by our families. The Church calls the family the "domestic church." The family is our first crucible of faith, where we learn to pray, to keep the Sabbath, the meaning and practice of our faith. How are we doing in handing on the faith?

Prayers

others may be added

To the Lord, who helps us discern his will, we pray:

◆ Graciously hear us, Lord.

May the Church continue to work to support families, we pray: ◆ May world leaders work to reunite families that are separated by war or famine, we pray: ◆ For an end to domestic violence, we pray: ◆ For forgiveness and acceptance in our families, we pray: ◆ For parents, grandparents, and all who seek to pass on the faith, we pray: ◆ For families with special needs, we pray: ◆

Our Father . . .

Dear Father,
you offer us people of faith
in our families and communities.
Help us to look to their example as we seek to live out your Word.
We ask this through Christ our Lord.
Amen.

✝ The Lord is my light and my salvation.

Friday, January 27, 2017
Weekday

✝ The Lord is my light and my salvation.

Psalm 27 *page 404*

Reading *Hebrews 10:32–36*

Remember the days past when, after you had been enlightened, you endured a great contest of suffering. At times you were publicly exposed to abuse and affliction; at other times you associated yourselves with those so treated. You even joined in the sufferings of those in prison and joyfully accepted the confiscation of your property, knowing that you had a better and lasting possession. Therefore, do not throw away your confidence; it will have great recompense. You need endurance to do the will of God and receive what he has promised.

Reflection

The theology that bad things only occur to those who have sinned occurs nowhere in the New Testament. The author of Hebrews asks the community to recall their suffering. The pains they endured for the sake of the Gospel are prized as evidence of their faith. Do we suffer for the Gospel? Are there friendships we've lost because we care about human trafficking or don't support an evil of our time? Are there those who do not understand that we prioritize worship on Sunday? Do coworkers think we are strange for not eating meat during Lent? The point is not to purposely antagonize others by actions but to witness to our faith.

Prayers *others may be added*

To the Lord, who helps us discern,
we pray:

◆ Guide our steps along your path.

For faith communities with the audacity to believe in the Gospel, despite hardship, we pray: ◆ For an end to religious persecution, we pray: ◆ For hope, we pray: ◆ For freedom of faith in our workplaces, we pray: ◆ For a spirit of courage in our sufferings, we pray: ◆

Our Father . . .

Lord,
you know our suffering.
You hear the cry of the oppressed.
When we face affliction for the sake
of the Gospel,
may your resolution be sure
and our conviction always rest in you.
We ask this through Christ our Lord.
Amen.

✝ The Lord is my light and my salvation.

Saturday, January 28, 2017

Memorial of St. Thomas Aquinas,
Priest and Doctor of the Church

✝ The Lord is my light and my salvation.

Psalm 27

page 404

Reading

Hebrews 11:1–2, 8–12

Brothers and sisters: Faith is the realization of what is hoped for and evidence of things not seen. Because of it the ancients were well attested.

By faith Abraham obeyed when he was called out to a place that he was to receive as an inheritance; he went out, not knowing where he was to go. By faith he sojourned in the promised land as in a foreign country, dwelling in tents with Isaac and Jacob, heirs of the same promise; for he was looking forward to the city with foundations, whose architect and maker is God. By faith he received power to generate, even though he was past the normal age—Sarah herself was sterile—for he thought that the one who had made the promise was trustworthy. So it was that there came forth from one man, himself as good as dead, descendants as numerous as the stars in the sky and as countless as the sands on the seashore.

Reflection

What is faith? Too often we align it with creedal confession or use it as a contract formulation for membership. That is not what Hebrews has in mind. Faith is spirit and it is concrete. Christians do things that may seem foolish to others, but for people of faith they are as sure as the sun rising. Dr. Martin Luther King Jr. believed in his Beloved Community, and so all the fire hoses, jails or beatings did not deter him. Archbishop Desmond Tutu saw a world without apartheid and eventually laws changed. What dreams does your faith foster in you?

Prayers

others may be added

To the Lord, who helps us discern his will, we pray:

◆ Graciously hear us, Lord.

May faith undergird the Church's cry for justice, we pray: ◆ May famine and war end, we pray: ◆ May missionaries and all who preach the Gospel proclaim freedom of heart and faith in Jesus, we pray: ◆ May we prefer the foolishness of the Gospel to the wisdom of this world, we pray: ◆ May our profession of faith lead us to actions for justice, we pray: ◆

Our Father . . .

Dear Lord,
you are our refuge and strength.
Guide us so that our every action has its source in our faith.
May the dreams of your Reign be a reality;
and may justice and peace be found,
even in some small way, today.
We ask this through Christ our Lord.
Amen

✝ The Lord is my light and my salvation.

Sunday, January 29, 2017
Fourth Sunday in Ordinary Time

☩ Blessed are the poor, the reign of God is theirs.

Psalm 146 *page 420*

Reading *Matthew 5:3–12a*

"Blessed are the poor in spirit, / for theirs is the kingdom of heaven. / Blessed are they who mourn, / for they will be comforted. / Blessed are the meek, / for they will inherit the land. / Blessed are they who hunger and thirst for righteousness, / for they will be satisfied. / Blessed are the merciful, / for they will be shown mercy. / Blessed are the clean of heart, / for they will see God. / Blessed are the peacemakers, / for they will be called children of God. / Blessed are they who are persecuted for the sake of righteousness, / for theirs is the kingdom of heaven. / Blessed are you when they insult you and persecute you / and utter every kind of evil against you falsely because of me. / Rejoice and be glad, / for your reward will be great in heaven."

Reflection

It's easy to get lost in the images of the Beatitudes and lose sight of the challenges. Mourning is painful, but it only happens if we love. Meekness and cleanliness of heart are not values we see on the average television show. What models do we have to cultivate the Beatitudes? Mercy isn't part of our world either; vengeance is much more common. Finally, we will be persecuted. Which of the Beatitudes do you find most challenging today?

Prayers *others may be added*

To the Lord, who blesses us, we pray:

◆ Graciously hear us, Lord.

For the Church of Jesus Christ, may we loudly boast in the Lord, we pray: ◆ For people ravaged by war and poverty, may they acquire comfort and assistance, we pray: ◆ For our catechumens and candidates, may they live always in the light of Christ, we pray: ◆ For peacemakers and all who work for justice, may their labors yield a fruitful harvest, we pray: ◆ For the dead, may they rejoice in the presence of God, we pray: ◆

Our Father . . .

Blessed are you Lord, our God.
Yours is a reign of truth, peace, and justice.
May we, your disciples,
embody your values in this world
and welcome all people to a community of love.
We ask this through our Lord Jesus Christ, your Son,
who lives and reigns with you in the unity of the Holy Spirit,
one God, for ever and ever.
Amen.

☩ Blessed are the poor, the reign of God is theirs.

Monday, January 30, 2017
Weekday

✝ Blessed are the poor, the reign of God is theirs.

Psalm 146 *page 420*

Reading *Hebrews 11:32–38*

Brothers and sisters: What more shall I say? I have not time to tell of Gideon, Barak, Samson, of David, Samuel, and the prophets, who by faith conquered kingdoms, did what was righteous, obtained the promises; they closed the mouths of lions, put out raging fires, escaped the devouring sword; out of weakness, they were made powerful, became strong in battle, and turned back foreign invaders. Women received back their dead through resurrection. Some were tortured and would not accept deliverance, in order to obtain a better resurrection. Others endured mockery, scourging, even chains and imprisonment. They were stoned, sawed in two, put to death at sword's point; they went about in skins of sheep or goats, needy, afflicted, tormented. The world was not worthy of them. They wandered about in deserts and on mountains, in caves and in crevices in the earth.

Reflection

The author of Hebrews paints a great picture of Old Testament heroes. By faith they did wonderful things, yet they also were tortured and wandered in the deserts. It's all about ups and downs. If you ever think that life isn't fair, you're right. Some days are great, others are not. When you wake up, you can never be sure what will happen. What are we to do? As the saying goes, "Keep on keeping on." It's not about what happens, but our choice in how we act, what we believe, how we reflect on the challenges and blessings. As today moves forward, take time to stop a bit and meet each moment in faith.

Prayers *others may be added*

To the Lord, who blesses us, we pray:

◆ Graciously hear us, Lord.

For the holy People of God, by our actions may we witness the Lord's love to all we meet, we pray: ◆ For all whose lives are saturated with hatred and violence, may they experience conversion, we pray: ◆ For those who console the mourning, may serenity be theirs, we pray: ◆ For all who visit the sick and care for the infirmed, may patience fill their souls, we pray: ◆ For the sick and suffering, may they feel God's deep healing, we pray: ◆

Our Father . . .

Gracious God,
you bless our days with opportunities
to herald your goodness.
Help us to greet each challenge
as a source of insight and each blessing
as a delight.
We ask this through Christ our Lord.
Amen.

✝ Blessed are the poor, the reign of God is theirs.

Tuesday, January 31, 2017

Memorial of St. John Bosco, Priest

✝ Blessed are the poor, the Reign of God is theirs.

Psalm 146

page 420

Reading

Hebrews 12:1–4

Brothers and sisters: Since we are surrounded by so great a cloud of witnesses, let us rid ourselves of every burden and sin that clings to us and persevere in running the race that lies before us while keeping our eyes fixed on Jesus, the leader and perfecter of faith. For the sake of the joy that lay before him, Jesus endured the cross, despising its shame, and has taken his seat at the right of the throne of God. Consider how he endured such opposition from sinners, in order that you may not grow weary and lose heart. In your struggle against sin you have not yet resisted to the point of shedding blood.

Reflection

What a solidarity we have with our ancestors. They who have gone before us, who know our pains, struggles, and joys, are cheering us on. The veil between this world and the next is sheer, says Hebrews. We are surrounded by these witnesses who understand us and will us to persevere. Who are your mentors who have gone before you? How can they help you thrive in the faith? Can you see in their lives the determination to live the Gospel?

Prayers

others may be added

To the Lord, who blesses us, we pray:

◆ Graciously hear us, Lord.

As Church may we continually root ourselves in the authority of Jesus and the Gospel, we pray: ◆ When evil threatens and falsehood arises, with courage and integrity, may we speak the truth of the Reign of God, we pray: ◆ In the midst of conflict, war, and discord, may justice and love prevail, we pray: ◆ For those parishes that recognize St. John Bosco as their patron, we pray: ◆ May the communion of saints welcome the dead into their eternal home, we pray: ◆

Our Father . . .

O God,
you gave your servant John Bosco the
  fortitude to dedicate himself
to teaching and service of the young.
May we too protect the vulnerable
and raise them up to love and serve you.
We ask this through Christ our Lord.
Amen.

✝ Blessed are the poor, the Reign of God is theirs.

Wednesday, February 1, 2017
Weekday

✝ Blessed are the poor, the Reign of God is theirs.

Psalm 146 *page 420*

Reading *Mark 6:1–6*

Jesus departed from there and came to his native place, accompanied by his disciples. When the sabbath came he began to teach in the synagogue, and many who heard him were astonished. They said, "Where did this man get all this? What kind of wisdom has been given him? What mighty deeds are wrought by his hands! Is he not the carpenter, the son of Mary, and the brother of James and Joseph and Judas and Simon? And are not his sisters here with us?" And they took offense at him. Jesus said to them, "A prophet is not without honor except in his native place and among his own kin and in his own house." So he was not able to perform any mighty deed there, apart from curing a few sick people by laying his hands on them. He was amazed at their lack of faith.

Reflection

When my nephew was very young, he came home from school and informed his mother that "God is in everyone." Later, when he returned from play, crying and angry with his friend, Jimmy, his mother chided, "I thought you told me God was in everyone." My nephew, befuddled, paused for a moment and then said, "God is in everyone, except Jimmy." When individuals challenge, disturb, or taunt us, we can fail to see Christ in their person and their lives. We might want to examine whether we sometimes fail to see the presence of Christ in another.

Prayers *others may be added*

To the Lord, who blesses us, we pray:

◆ **Graciously hear us, Lord.**

As disciples of the Lord, may we recognize his presence among us, we pray: ◆ May we heed the prophets in our midst, we pray: ◆ For families in which members are estranged from one another, we pray: ◆ For the chronically ill, we pray: ◆ For those who lack faith, we pray: ◆

Our Father . . .

God of the universe,
you offer us your presence in so many ways and in all we encounter.
May we honor your divine image in one another
and practice being aware of your perpetual presence.
We ask this through Christ our Lord.
Amen.

✝ Blessed are the poor, the Reign of God is theirs.

Thursday, February 2, 2017
Feast of the Presentation of the Lord

✝ The Lord keeps faith forever.

Psalm 146 *page 420*

Reading *Luke 2:25–32*

Now there was a man in Jerusalem whose name was Simeon. This man was righteous and devout, awaiting the consolation of Israel, and the Holy Spirit was upon him. It had been revealed to him by the Holy Spirit that he should not see death before he had seen the Christ of the Lord. He came in the Spirit into the temple; and when the parents brought in the child Jesus to perform the custom of the law in regard to him, he took him into his arms and blessed God, saying: / "Now, Master, you may let your servant go / in peace, according to your word, / for my eyes have seen your salvation, / which you prepared in sight of all the peoples, / a light for revelation to the Gentiles, / and glory for your people Israel."

Reflection

It has been forty days since Christmas. We move from manger to the Temple, for in Luke's Gospel, Jesus is the Temple. We move from the fear and wonder of the shepherds to the righteous and devout Simeon who speaks of "a light of revelation to the Gentiles, and the glory of your people, Israel." The light of the world fills the earth. This day had been called "Candlemas," as candles were blessed at Mass and brought home, to bring the message that "the light shines in the darkness and the darkness has not overcome it" (John 1:5).

Prayers *others may be added*

To Jesus, who decreed, blessed are they who hunger and thirst for righteousness, we pray:

◆ Light from Light, hear our prayer.

May the Church's witness to Christ and the Reign of God shine before all, we pray: ◆ That Christ, the light of the world, will guide us to peace, we pray: ◆ May the flame of faith that we received at our Baptism burn brightly, we pray: ◆ For beekeepers, candle makers and all who create our liturgical appointments, we pray: ◆ For community leaders, that they will reflect God's light, we pray: ◆

Our Father . . .

Lord of Life,
today we honor the gift of your Son
and commemorate his being presented
to you:
God from God, Light from Light, true
God from true God.
May his light shine within us
that we may be beacons of faith
and charity.
Through our Lord Jesus Christ, your Son,
who lives and reigns with you in the unity
of the Holy Spirit,
one God, for ever and ever.
Amen.

✝ The Lord keeps faith forever.

Friday, February 3, 2017
Optional Memorial of St. Blaise, Bishop and Martyr

☩ Blessed are the poor, the reign of God is theirs.

Psalm 146
page 420

Reading
Mark 6:17–20

Herod was the one who had John the Baptist arrested and bound in prison on account of Herodias, the wife of his brother Philip, whom he had married. John had said to Herod, "It is not lawful for you to have your brother's wife." Herodias harbored a grudge against him and wanted to kill him but was unable to do so. Herod feared John, knowing him to be a righteous and holy man, and kept him in custody. When he heard him speak he was very much perplexed, yet he liked to listen to him.

Reflection
King Herod had no intention of beheading John the Baptist, but he erred in making an open-ended promise to Herodias' daughter. In a sense, the martyrdom of Blaise (316), bishop of Sebastea in Armenia (modern-day Turkey), also came about through poor communication. The Edict of Milan, which had been issued three years prior (313), granted Christians the freedom of worship. In the fourth century, however, news traveled slowly. St. Blaise was executed for being a Christian, which was no longer a criminal act, let alone a capital offense. Having saved a child from choking, Blaise is honored by the blessing of throats today.

Prayers
others may be added

To the Lord, who blesses us, we pray:

◆ Graciously hear us, Lord.

May the witness of the martyrs fill the Church with fortitude, we pray: ◆ For our bishops, we pray: ◆ That leaders will seek the release of those wrongly imprisoned, we pray: ◆ For those who suffer with maladies of the throat, we pray: ◆ For the repose of the souls of innocent people who have been executed, we pray: ◆

Our Father . . .

Through the intercession of St. Blaise,
bishop and martyr,
may God protect you from diseases of
the throat
and from every other illness;
and may those unjustly condemned find
light, happiness, and peace,
through our Lord Jesus Christ, your Son,
who lives and reigns with you in the unity
of the Holy Spirit,
one God, for ever and ever.
Amen.

☩ Blessed are the poor, the reign of God is theirs.

Saturday, February 4, 2017
Weekday

† Blessed are the poor, the reign of God is theirs.

Psalm 146 *page 420*

Reading *Mark 6:30–34*

The Apostles gathered together with Jesus and reported all they had done and taught. He said to them, "Come away by yourselves to a deserted place and rest a while." People were coming and going in great numbers, and they had no opportunity even to eat. So they went off in the boat by themselves to a deserted place. People saw them leaving and many came to know about it. They hastened there on foot from all the towns and arrived at the place before them.

When Jesus disembarked and saw the vast crowd, his heart was moved with pity for them, for they were like sheep without a shepherd; and he began to teach them many things.

Reflection

Who of us has not needed some respite from the world but have been alerted to a need? We have come through a time of stress, busyness, or crisis and when we think we can catch our breath, a text message, a phone call, or someone is at our door requesting our help. Moved with compassion, we rise. Of course, there are times we need to say, "No." There are times we need to reverence our own needs. But more often than not, we do what Jesus did, for we are his disciples, and have been baptized to be "Christ-bearers."

Prayers *others may be added*

To the Lord, who blesses us, we pray:

◆ Graciously hear us, Lord.

May the Church be a balm of healing for a hurting planet, we pray: ◆ May world leaders be attentive to the cry of the poor, we pray: ◆ For those who have been there in our times of need, we pray: ◆ May we never tire of doing what is right, we pray: ◆ That we may see Christ in those who ask for our help, we pray: ◆

Our Father . . .

God of grace and mercy,
you have shown us the importance of prayer and service.
Help us to discern wisely when to put others first and when to rest in you.
We ask this through Christ our Lord.
Amen.

† Blessed are the poor, the reign of God is theirs.

Sunday, February 5, 2017
Fifth Sunday in Ordinary Time

☩ O bless the Lord, my soul.

Psalm 104 *page 416*

Reading *Matthew 5:13–16*

Jesus said to his disciples: "You are the salt of the earth. But if salt loses its taste, with what can it be seasoned? It is no longer good for anything but to be thrown out and trampled underfoot. You are the light of the world. A city set on a mountain cannot be hidden. Nor do they light a lamp and then put it under a bushel basket; it is set on a lampstand, where it gives light to all in the house. Just so, your light must shine before others, that they may see your good deeds, and glorify your heavenly Father."

Reflection

Being the "light of the world," a phrase usually mentioned in relation to Christ, and "the salt of the earth," can seem overwhelming. "I find it lonely being luminous," laments Father Edward Hays (*Psalms for Zero Gravity* [Ave Maria Press, 1998]). Do we do what we do to get credit from God or prove ourselves to another? The last line in today's Gospel provides the answer. We are called to be "light and salt" neither for ourselves nor for others, but "to glorify your heavenly Father." It is always about God, not about us.

Prayers *others may be added*

To our Lord, who calls us to be light and salt, we pray:

◆ Lord, hear our prayer.

That the Church continues to place herself in service to the Reign of God, we pray: ◆ May our parishes be communities of light and salt for the world, we pray: ◆ For vocations to the priesthood, religious life, and lay ecclesial ministry, we pray: ◆ For teachers who enlighten us, we pray: ◆ For those who labor underground as miners, we pray: ◆

Our Father . . .

Lover of humankind,
you enlighten our mind and heart with your Word.
Fortify our character and will with your Spirit,
that we may do all for the glory of your name.
Through our Lord Jesus Christ, your Son,
who lives and reigns with you in the unity of the Holy Spirit,
one God, for ever and ever.
Amen.

☩ O bless the Lord, my soul.

Monday, February 6, 2017

Memorial of St. Paul Miki and Companions, Martyrs

✝ O bless the Lord, my soul.

Psalm 104

page 416

Reading

Mark 6:53–56

After making the crossing to the other side of the sea, Jesus and his disciples came to land at Gennesaret and tied up there. As they were leaving the boat, people immediately recognized him. They scurried about the surrounding country and began to bring in the sick on mats to wherever they heard he was. Whatever villages or towns or countryside he entered, they laid the sick in the marketplaces and begged him that they might touch only the tassel on his cloak; and as many as touched it were healed.

Reflection

When we hear of Nagasaki, Japan, we first think of one of two cities destroyed by the dropping of the atomic bomb. Both prior to that act and today, Nagasaki enjoys the largest population of Catholics in Japan. This is due, in part, to the ministry and eventual martyrdom of Paul Miki. Miki was a native of Japan and a Jesuit who preached the Gospel in his homeland during the sixteenth century. Twenty-four others—priests, brothers, and laity—were martyred with him. Prior to his death, Miki spoke words of forgiveness toward the emperor and all who desired his death.

Prayers

others may be added

To our Lord, who calls us to be light and salt, we pray:

◆ Lord, hear our prayer.

May the blood of the martyrs inspire zeal for the Gospel throughout the Church, we pray: ◆ For the Church in Japan, we pray: ◆ That governments will respect the right to freedom of religion, we pray: ◆ For those living with cancer, we pray: ◆ For all who seek reconciliation, we pray: ◆

Our Father . . .

God of all the earth,
look on us with kindness and mercy.
May we live as witnesses to the Gospel
of your Son
and persevere in fidelity through the end
of our days.
Through our Lord Jesus Christ, your Son,
who lives and reigns with you in the
unity of the Holy Spirit,
one God, for ever and ever.
Amen.

✝ O bless the Lord, my soul.

Tuesday, February 7, 2017
Weekday

✝ O bless the Lord, my soul.

Psalm 104 *page 416*

page 416

Reading *Mark 7:5–13*

The Pharisees and the scribes questioned [Jesus], "Why do your disciples not follow the tradition of the elders but instead eat a meal with unclean hands?" He responded, "Well did Isaiah prophesy about you hypocrites, as it is written: / *This people honors me with their lips, / but their hearts are far from me; / In vain do they worship me, / teaching as doctrines human precepts.* / You disregard God's commandment but cling to human tradition." He went on to say, "How well you have set aside the commandment of God in order to uphold your tradition! For Moses said, *Honor your father and your mother,* and *Whoever curses father or mother shall die.* Yet you say, 'If a person says to father or mother, "Any support you might have had from me is *qorban*"' (meaning, dedicated to God), you allow him to do nothing more for his father or mother. You nullify the word of God in favor of your tradition that you have handed on. And you do many such things."

Reflection

Neither God's Commandments nor human traditions are unimportant. These are passed on as helpers and guides to living our faith and knowing God. But we have a habit of making our customs and traditions the goal in and of themselves rather than a means and instrument serving a greater end, as is their true purpose. When we do this, we cling to our traditions but fail to see and hear the person or situation. The ministry of Pope Francis, like that of Jesus, constantly reminds us that the person is the priority.

Prayers *others may be added*

To the Lord, who calls to be light and salt, we pray:

◆ **Lord, hear our prayer.**

May the Church be open to continuous conversion, we pray: ◆ May the faithful be devoted to spiritual growth, we pray: ◆ For those who hide behind human rules and traditions, we pray ◆: For the courage to name our hypocrisy, we pray: ◆ For parents, living and deceased, we pray: ◆

Our Father . . .

Lord God,
you have shown us what is important.
May we imitate the ministry of your Son,
and of holy ones who have followed him,
in observing your Word over and above
our human customs and traditions.
We ask this through Christ our Lord.
Amen.

✝ O bless the Lord, my soul.

Wednesday, February 8, 2017
Weekday

✝ O bless the Lord, my soul.

Psalm 104 *page 416*

Reading *Mark 7:14–15, 21–23*

Jesus summoned the crowd again and said to them, "Hear me, all of you, and understand. Nothing that enters one from outside can defile that person; but the things that come out from within are what defile.

"From within the man, from his heart, come evil thoughts, unchastity, theft, murder, adultery, greed, malice, deceit, licentiousness, envy, blasphemy, arrogance, folly. All these evils come from within and they defile."

Reflection

The expression "You are what you eat" is intended to encourage a healthy diet. While taking care of our bodies is a form of stewardship, we might hear Jesus quietly clearing his throat at the above expression. Jesus routinely violated laws of purity by touching lepers and the dead, and by dining with sinners. From these singular examples, he forms a general concept: impurity does not come from the outside but from the inside. Contrast the amount of time and effort you put into your appearance and the externals of life with the time and effort with which you ponder your motives, attitudes, and internal dispositions.

Prayers *others may be added*

To the Lord, who calls us to be light and salt, we pray:

◆ Lord, hear our prayer.

That the Church encourage her members to confession, contrition, and reconciliation, we pray: ◆ May we be cleansed of our prejudices, we pray: ◆ For victims of violence, we pray: ◆ For those who perceive themselves to be unloved and unlovable, we pray: ◆ For those who have loved us enough to speak hard truths to us, we pray: ◆

Our Father . . .

Lord God,
you show us the way to goodness.
May we hear the wisdom of your Son
and seek to cleanse our minds and hearts.
Help us to make our attitude that of
your Son,
who lives and reigns with you in the unity
of the Holy Spirit,
one God, for ever and ever.
Amen.

✝ O bless the Lord, my soul.

Thursday, February 9, 2017
Weekday

✝ O bless the Lord, my soul.

Psalm 104 *page 416*

Reading *Mark 7:24–30*

Jesus went to the district of Tyre. He entered a house and wanted no one to know about it, but he could not escape notice. Soon a woman whose daughter had an unclean spirit heard about him. She came and fell at his feet. The woman was a Greek, a Syrophoenician by birth, and she begged him to drive the demon out of her daughter. He said to her, "Let the children be fed first. For it is not right to take the food of the children and throw it to the dogs." She replied and said to him, "Lord, even the dogs under the table eat the children's scraps." Then he said to her, "For saying this, you may go. The demon has gone out of your daughter." When the woman went home, she found the child lying in bed and the demon gone.

Reflection

Martin Luther offered an insight on this passage. Luther states that the woman is willing to be a labeled a dog, if that's what it takes to gain a cure for her daughter. In doing so, she has Jesus cornered. He has no more moves to make, save to concede her amazing faith and do as she requested. Sometimes God seems distant and silent. Luther said in times such as these we need to have faith like the Syrophoenician woman, a faith that refuses to accept that God could be anything but gracious (William C. Placher, Mark [Louisville: Westminster John Knox Press, 2010]).

Prayers *others may be added*

To the Lord, who calls us to be light and salt, we pray:

◆ Lord, hear our prayer.

For interreligious dialogue, we pray: ◆ May the community of believers be a place of welcome, we pray: ◆ For those who are alienated from the Church, we pray: ◆ For perseverance, we pray: ◆ That we act as signs of God's love and mercy, we pray: ◆

Our Father . . .

Lord God,
you granted goodness in each of us.
When we are beset, hurt, or angry
due to the shortcomings of others,
may we not lose sight of another's
inherent dignity
but continue to afford them respect.
We ask this through Christ our Lord.
Amen.

✝ O bless the Lord, my soul.

Friday, February 10, 2017
Memorial of St. Scholastica, Virgin

† O Lord, open my lips and my mouth shall declare your praise.

Psalm 51

page 406

Reading

Mark 7:31–37

Jesus left the district of Tyre and went by way of Sidon to the Sea of Galilee, into the district of the Decapolis. And people brought to him a deaf man who had a speech impediment and begged him to lay his hand on him. He took him off by himself away from the crowd. He put his finger into the man's ears and, spitting, touched his tongue; then he looked up to heaven and groaned, and said to him, "*Ephphatha*!" (that is, "Be opened!") And immediately the man's ears were opened, his speech impediment was removed, and he spoke plainly. He ordered them not to tell anyone. But the more he ordered them not to, the more they proclaimed it. They were exceedingly astonished and they said, "He has done all things well. He makes the deaf hear and the mute speak."

Reflection

The liturgical flavor of the healing of the deaf man might provide a glimpse into the ritual life of Mark's community. The man is brought to Jesus by people (perhaps his sponsors). Jesus takes him away from the crowd (a period of instruction). The ritual that follows includes both word and action. Also suggested is that the man cannot hear or speak because of the crowd. It is hard for us to hear the voice of God when our lives are filled with noise. We need to get away from the crowd and the noise to hear and be healed by the Lord.

Prayers

others may be added

To the Lord, who calls us to be light and salt, we pray:

◆ Lord, hear our prayer.

For those who serve the Church in monastic life, we pray: ◆ For Benedictine priests, brothers, and sisters, we pray: ◆ For a greater awareness of the interplay between liturgy and daily life, we pray: ◆ For those who have speech or hearing impairments, we pray: ◆ For all who sleep in Christ, we pray: ◆

Our Father . . .

God of many voices,
you seek our listening ear.
May we discern your presence
in the hustle and bustle of our lives.
May we hear you speak in silence
and the stillness of our hearts.
We ask this through Christ our Lord.
Amen.

† O Lord, open my lips and my mouth shall declare your praise.

Saturday, February 11, 2017
Weekday

✝ O bless the Lord, my soul.

Psalm 104 *page 416*

Reading *Mark 8:2–9*

[Jesus said], "My heart is moved with pity for the crowd, because they have been with me now for three days and have nothing to eat. If I send them away hungry to their homes, they will collapse on the way, and some of them have come a great distance." His disciples answered him, "Where can anyone get enough bread to satisfy them here in this deserted place?" Still he asked them, "How many loaves do you have?" "Seven," they replied. He ordered the crowd to sit down on the ground. Then, taking the seven loaves he gave thanks, broke them, and gave them to his disciples to distribute, and they distributed them to the crowd. They also had a few fish. He said the blessing over them and ordered them distributed also. They ate and were satisfied. They picked up the fragments left over—seven baskets. There were about four thousand people.

Reflection

The multiplication of loaves occurs twice in Mark: once in Jewish territory and once in Gentile territory. It is the latter we read today. These events look forward to the Eucharist and most readily see that. There is one detail easy to overlook. We are told that the crowd has been with Jesus for three days and has had nothing to eat. That is quite impressive. I am hard pressed to think of a guest speaker for whom the people of my community would go without food for three days just to hear. Perhaps, though, the three days that the people fast are suggestive of the paschal fast.

Prayers *others may be added*

To the Lord, who calls us to be light and salt, we pray:

◆ **Lord, hear our prayer.**

May the Eucharist truly be the source and summit of the Church's life, we pray: ◆ May we hunger for the bread of life and thirst for the cup of salvation, we pray: ◆ That more individuals will make the time to go on a retreat and spend time with Christ, we pray: ◆ For those who hunger for acceptance, recognition, or approval, we pray: ◆ For those who will go without food this day, we pray: ◆

Our Father . . .

Lord Jesus,
you are manna in our desert
and water in our wilderness.
May we approach your table
in awe and wonder,
with joy and thanksgiving.
You live and reign with God the Father in
the unity of the Holy Spirit,
one God, for ever and ever.
Amen.

✝ O bless the Lord, my soul.

Sunday, February 12, 2017
Sixth Sunday in Ordinary Time

✝ Blessed are they who follow the law of the Lord.

Psalm 119 *page 417*

Reading *Matthew 5:17–20*

Jesus said to his disciples: "Do not think that I have come to abolish the law or the prophets. I have come not to abolish but to fulfill. Amen, I say to you, until heaven and earth pass away, not the smallest letter or the smallest part of a letter will pass from the law, until all things have taken place. Therefore, whoever breaks one of the least of these commandments and teaches others to do so will be called least in the kingdom of heaven. But whoever obeys and teaches these commandments will be called greatest in the kingdom of heaven."

Reflection

Jesus fulfills the Law by challenging us to go beyond it. It is not enough not to kill, we must also guard our anger. We need to examine whether we deal with our anger appropriately or respond furiously after letting it build inside. Or perhaps, we pout and never talk things out. Jesus calls us to see others, not as objects that might fill our desires but as subjects made in God's image. In all of what Jesus says, he gives priority to the dignity God has bestowed upon humankind.

Prayers *others may be added*

Turning to Christ, who seeks that we reconcile with one another, we pray:

◆ Lord, have mercy.

That the Church and her ministers act as agents of reconciliation to a divided world, we pray: ◆ That we express our anger in appropriate ways, we pray: ◆ That we may honor our body and the bodies of others, we pray: ◆ For those who are separated or divorced, we pray: ◆ That world leaders seek peaceful ways of responding to aggressive acts, we pray: ◆

Our Father . . .

Lord,
you have given us laws
that your Kingdom might come to pass.
May you strengthen us to teach your ways
to others
and guide them to a life of fullness
in you.
Through our Lord Jesus Christ, your Son,
who lives and reigns with you in the unity
of the Holy Spirit,
one God, for ever and ever.
Amen.

✝ Blessed are they who follow the law of the Lord.

Monday, February 13, 2017
Weekday

✝ Blessed are they who follow the law of the Lord.

Psalm 119 *page 417*

Reading *Mark 8:11–13*

The Pharisees came forward and began to argue with Jesus, seeking from him a sign from heaven to test him. He sighed from the depth of his spirit and said, "Why does this generation seek a sign? Amen, I say to you, no sign will be given to this generation." Then he left them, got into the boat again, and went off to the other shore.

Reflection

The Pharisees seek a sign but Jesus refuses to give one. In Mark's Gospel, Jesus performs mighty or powerful deeds directed toward the welfare of another. These deeds are never about Jesus himself nor do they point to him. Whenever we, in our humanity, seek a sign, most often we are thinking of ourselves. We are seeking clarity over a decision or reassurance in grief or anxiety. Like the Pharisees, we get caught up in our need for certitude and miss opportunities to extend God's mercy to those we encounter.

Prayers *others may be added*

Turning to Christ, who seeks that we reconcile with one another, we pray:

◆ Lord, have mercy.

That the Church be the sign of Christ's love and work mighty deeds in his name, we pray: ◆ For N., the bishop of Rome, and N., our bishop, we pray: ◆ For peace in the world, we pray: ◆ For the poor, the homeless, and the unemployed, we pray: ◆ That we may seek to be reconciled with those with whom we are estranged, we pray: ◆

Our Father . . .

Lord Jesus,
in humility,
you have shown us the way to God.
Help us to honor the signs that you send to us through those we meet and the events in our lives.
You are the only sign we need.
To you be the glory and praise, laud and honor,
for you live and reign with God the Father in the unity of the Holy Spirit,
one God, for ever and ever.
Amen.

✝ Blessed are they who follow the law of the Lord.

Tuesday, February 14, 2017

Memorial of Sts. Cyril, Monk, and Methodius, Bishop

✝ Blessed are they who follow the law of the Lord.

Psalm 119

page 417

Reading

Mark 8:14–21

The disciples had forgotten to bring bread, and they had only one loaf with them in the boat. Jesus enjoined them, "Watch out, guard against the leaven of the Pharisees and the leaven of Herod." They concluded among themselves that it was because they had no bread. When he became aware of this he said to them, "Why do you conclude that it is because you have no bread? Do you not yet understand or comprehend? Are your hearts hardened? Do you have eyes and not see, ears and not hear? And do you not remember, when I broke the five loaves for the five thousand, how many wicker baskets full of fragments you picked up?" They answered him, "Twelve." "When I broke the seven loaves for the four thousand, how many full baskets of fragments did you pick up?" They answered him, "Seven." He said to them, "Do you still not understand?"

Reflection

Despite healing the deaf and the blind and even raising the dead, Jesus cannot break through to his disciples. They are concerned because they have only one loaf of bread with them. The "one loaf," Jesus himself, is all they, or we, need. Sts. Cyril and Methodius are co-patrons of Europe and known as "the apostles to the Slavs" for bringing the Gospel to the Slavic people.

Prayers

others may be added

Turning to Christ, who seeks that we reconcile with one another, we pray:

◆ Lord, have mercy.

For those who serve God's people as missionaries, we pray: ◆ For the Slavic peoples, we pray: ◆ That we may be attentive to the voice of God, we pray: ◆ For those joined in marriage, we pray: ◆ For those who are lonely, we pray: ◆

Our Father . . .

Lord,
you are the glory of the saints.
Open our minds and hearts
with a desire to better comprehend
the Sacred Scriptures and our faith,
which comes to us from the Apostles.
We ask this through Christ our Lord.
Amen.

✝ Blessed are they who follow the law of the Lord.

Wednesday, February 15, 2017
Weekday

✝ Blessed are they who follow the law of the Lord.

Psalm 119 *page 417*

page 417

Reading *Mark 8:22–26*

When Jesus and his disciples arrived at Bethsaida, people brought to him a blind man and begged him to touch him. He took the blind man by the hand and led him outside the village. Putting spittle on his eyes he laid his hands on him and asked, "Do you see anything?" Looking up he replied, "I see people looking like trees and walking." Then he laid hands on his eyes a second time and he saw clearly; his sight was restored and he could see everything distinctly. Then he sent him home and said, "Do not even go into the village."

Reflection

Once again Jesus leads someone away from the crowd, outside of the village, before he cures him. Mark greatly underlines that we need one-on-one time with the Lord if we seek healing.

We might see humor and relief in this story. Seemingly, it takes Jesus two attempts to get it right—how very human and we can readily relate. From the blind man's perspective, coming to sight, or coming to faith, occurs gradually. So often we want healing, or deeper faith, or peace of mind "right now." Here we are reminded that most growth and insight occurs slowly.

Prayers *others may be added*

Turning to Christ, who seeks that we reconcile with one another, we pray:

◆ Lord, have mercy.

For the new evangelization, we pray: ◆ For godparents and sponsors, we pray: ◆ For retreat directors and those who staff retreat houses, we pray: ◆ For people who are blind or have diseases of the eye, we pray: ◆ For those who are emotionally or spiritually blind, we pray: ◆

Our Father . . .

Lord God,
you answer our prayers for healing.
Assist us in seeking your will in all things
and, aided by the Holy Spirit,
have the resolve to act in accord with your will.
We ask this through our Lord Jesus Christ, your Son,
who lives and reigns with you in the unity of the Holy Spirit,
one God, for ever and ever
Amen.

✝ Blessed are they who follow the law of the Lord.

Thursday, February 16, 2017
Weekday

✝ Blessed are they who follow the law of the Lord.

Psalm 119 *page 417*

Reading *Mark 8:27–33*

Jesus and his disciples set out for the villages of Caesarea Philippi. Along the way he asked his disciples, "Who do people say that I am?" They said in reply, "John the Baptist, others Elijah, still others one of the prophets." And he asked them, "But who do you say that I am?" Peter said to him in reply, "You are the Christ." Then he warned them not to tell anyone about him.

He began to teach them that the Son of Man must suffer greatly and be rejected by the elders, the chief priests, and the scribes, and be killed, and rise after three days. He spoke this openly. Then Peter took him aside and began to rebuke him. At this he turned around and, looking at his disciples, rebuked Peter and said, "Get behind me, Satan. You are thinking not as God does, but as human beings do."

Reflection

In this passage we are drawn to Peter's confession of faith. He is the first to declare Jesus, "the Christ" (Messiah). The location of this event is crucial to this story. Jesus and his disciples are on the way to Caesarea Philippi. This city was named both for the emperor, the Caesar, and for Philip, the son of Herod the Great. Peter is confessing his faith, and he is committing high treason: acknowledging that Jesus is the true "Christ," the true king, over and against the emperor and the Herod family. Jesus and his reign are lord of our political life as well as our spiritual life.

Prayers *others may be added*

Turning to Christ, who seeks that we reconcile with one another, we pray:

◆ **Lord, have mercy.**

May the Church boldly proclaim Christ and his reign to the world, we pray: ◆ May the baptized embrace the preferential option for the poor, we pray: ◆ That politicians and world leaders devote themselves to the common good, we pray: ◆ May we work to replace our culture of death with the Gospel of life, we pray: ◆ That leaders of nations that are estranged from another nation seek dialogue and nonviolent resolution we pray: ◆

Our Father . . .

Lord Jesus,
you are our King.
May we believe in the Gospel
enough to bring it to bear on our political and social views,
for you live and reign with God the Father in the unity of the Holy Spirit,
one God, for ever and ever.
Amen.

✝ Blessed are they who follow the law of the Lord.

Friday, February 17, 2017
Weekday

✝ A heart contrite and humbled,
O God, you will not spurn.

Psalm 51 *page 406*

Reading *Mark 8:34—9:1*

Jesus summoned the crowd with his disciples and said to them, "Whoever wishes to come after me must deny himself, take up his cross, and follow me. For whoever wishes to save his life will lose it, but whoever loses his life for my sake and that of the Gospel will save it. What profit is there for one to gain the whole world and forfeit his life? What could one give in exchange for his life? Whoever is ashamed of me and of my words in this faithless and sinful generation, the Son of Man will be ashamed of when he comes in his Father's glory with the holy angels."

He also said to them, "Amen, I say to you, there are some standing here who will not taste death until they see that the Kingdom of God has come in power."

Reflection

Some standing with Jesus would not taste death until they see that the Kingdom of God has come. Yet, those standing with him all died, and we continue to pray, "thy kingdom come." This is no contradiction. The Kingdom or Reign of God is not only a future reality; it is a present reality. To that end, Jesus proclaims that the Kingdom is at hand (Mark 1:15). We experience the Reign of God in moments of transcendence—at worship, a sunrise, the hug of a close friend, a world event, etc. The disciples saw the Kingdom in Jesus' Passion, Death, and Resurrection and, upon later reflection, in his person and ministry.

Prayers *others may be added*

Turning to Christ, who seeks that we reconcile with one another, we pray:

◆ Lord, have mercy.

May the Church, especially in worship, be an experience of God's Reign, we pray: ◆ May we, in our vocations and ministries, be a sign of God's Reign, we pray: ◆ For those who have helped us to encounter the Reign of God, we pray: ◆ May we seek the Reign of God before all else, we pray: ◆ May those who are dying feast at the banquet in the Kingdom of Heaven, we pray: ◆

Our Father . . .

King of all creation,
you offer us the chance to dwell with you
in your Kingdom.
Help us to live in such a way
that we witness to salvation in the here
and now.
We ask this through Christ our Lord.
Amen.

✝ A heart contrite and humbled,
O God, you will not spurn.

Saturday, February 18, 2017
Weekday

✝ Blessed are they who follow the law of the Lord.

Psalm 119 *page 417*

Reading *Mark 9:2–9*

Jesus took Peter, James, and John and led them up a high mountain apart by themselves. And he was transfigured before them, and his clothes became dazzling white, such as no fuller on earth could bleach them. Then Elijah appeared to them along with Moses, and they were conversing with Jesus. Then Peter said to Jesus in reply, "Rabbi, it is good that we are here! Let us make three tents: one for you, one for Moses, and one for Elijah." . . . Then a cloud came, casting a shadow over them; from the cloud came a voice, "This is my beloved Son. Listen to him." Suddenly, looking around, they no longer saw anyone but Jesus alone with them.

As they were coming down from the mountain, he charged them not to relate what they had seen to anyone, except when the Son of Man had risen from the dead.

Reflection

This is the third time we have read of Jesus taking individuals away to be alone with him. We need to have time alone with the Lord. Given the busyness of life, and that may mean scheduling it, just as we would make a date with a friend. Lent is fast approaching. Consider going up the mountain too (a retreat) or plan for some other time away with the Lord.

Prayers *others may be added*

Turning to Christ, who seeks that we reconcile with one another, we pray:

◆ Lord, have mercy.

That the Church encourage members to spend time in quiet with God, we pray: ◆ For those leading parish missions and for spiritual directors, we pray: ◆ For all who minister in the liturgy, we pray: ◆ That we might be a people of prayer, we pray: ◆ For leaders of nations, that they see value in setting aside time for prayer, we pray: ◆

Our Father . . .

Eternal God,
you are beyond time but have given us
the gift of time.
May our days not be so full
so as to have no time to set aside
intentionally for you.
We ask this through Christ our Lord.
Amen.

✝ Blessed are they who follow the law of the Lord.

Sunday, February 19, 2017
Seventh Sunday in Ordinary Time

✝ The Lord is kind and merciful.

Psalm 103 *page 415*

Reading *Matthew 5:38, 43–48*

Jesus said to his disciples: "You have heard that it was said, / *You shall love your neighbor and hate your enemy.* / But I say to you, love your enemies and pray for those who persecute you, that you may be children of your heavenly Father, for he makes his sun rise on the bad and the good, and causes rain to fall on the just and the unjust. For if you love those who love you, what recompense will you have? Do not the tax collectors do the same? And if you greet your brothers only, what is unusual about that? Do not the pagans do the same? So be perfect, just as your heavenly Father is perfect."

Reflection

Terrorist threats, mass shootings, Internet breeches, home invasions—all of it can make us wary of others. Jesus' command to "love your enemies and pray for those who persecute you" sometimes seems out of place in a world in which so much goes wrong. During difficult times, we are most in need of heeding Jesus' challenging words. We need to pray both for the victims of crime and for those who have caused harm to others.

Prayers *others may be added*

Directing our prayer to Christ, who calls us to love our enemies, we pray:

◆ Lord, hold us in your mercy.

For those who hold the Church in disdain, we pray: ◆ For those who commit acts of terrorism, we pray: ◆ For those who take innocent life, we pray: ◆ For those who exploit the poor, we pray: ◆ For those who abuse children and teens, we pray: ◆

Our Father . . .

Gracious God,
you have set before us
the way to be holy.
Sustain in us a desire
to be perfect as the heavenly Father is perfect and to love those who have caused harm.
Through our Lord Jesus Christ, your Son,
who lives and reigns with you in the unity of the Holy Spirit,
one God, for ever and ever.
Amen.

✝ The Lord is kind and merciful.

Monday, February 20, 2017
Weekday

✝ The Lord is kind and merciful

Psalm 103
page 415

Reading
Sirach 1:1–9

All wisdom comes from the LORD / and with him it remains forever, / and is before all time / The sand of the seashore, the drops of rain, / the days of eternity: who can number these? / Heaven's height, earth's breadth, / the depths of the abyss: who can explore these? / Before all things else wisdom was created; / and prudent understanding, from eternity. / The word of God on high is the fountain of wisdom / and her ways are everlasting. / To whom has wisdom's root been revealed? / Who knows her subtleties? / To whom has the discipline of wisdom been revealed? / And who has understood the multiplicity of her ways? / There is but one, wise and truly awe-inspiring seated upon his throne. / There is but one, Most High / all-powerful creator-king and truly awe-inspiring one, seated upon his throne and he is the God of dominion.

Reflection

The Book of Sirach, which was written during the second century before Christ, contains a number of maxims or proverbs on how to how to live a good life. Today's passage tells of God's transcendence. Speaking of divine wisdom, the author implies, rightly, that, rather than question God, we stand in awe, and are grateful that God has poured wisdom on all his works and has lavished wisdom upon his friends.

Prayers
others may be added

Directing our prayer to Christ, who calls us to love our enemies, we pray:

◆ Lord, hold us in your mercy.

For those who persecute Christians, we pray: ◆ For those who turn away refugees and immigrants, we pray: ◆ For those who profit from pornography, we pray: ◆ For those who use power and position for personal gain, we pray: ◆ For those who turn their heads, pretending not to see, we pray: ◆

Our Father . . .

Dear Lord,
in you is contained all of wisdom.
When we cannot understand,
when we question you,
when we doubt you,
in our darkness may we recall your words to us.
We ask this through Christ our Lord.
Amen.

✝ The Lord is kind and merciful.

Tuesday, February 21, 2017
Weekday

✝ The Lord is kind and merciful.

Psalm 103 *page 415*

page 415

Reading *Sirach 2:1–9*

My son, when you come to serve the LORD, / stand in justice and fear, / prepare yourself for trials. / Be sincere of heart and steadfast, / incline your ear and receive the word of understanding, / undisturbed in time of adversity. / Wait on God, with patience, cling to him, forsake him not; / thus will you be wise in all your ways. / Accept whatever befalls you, / when sorrowful, be steadfast, / and in crushing misfortune be patient; / For in fire gold and silver are tested, / and worthy people in the crucible of humiliation. / Trust God and God will help you; / trust in him, and he will direct your way; / keep his fear and grow old therein. /

You who fear the LORD, wait for his mercy, / turn not away lest you fall. You who fear the LORD, trust him, / and your reward will not be lost. / You who fear the LORD, hope for good things, / for lasting joy and mercy. / You who fear the LORD, love him, / and your hearts will be enlightened.

Reflection

We hear in these verses that those who serve the Lord should prepare themselves for trials. These are not words we want to hear, yet experience tells us it is so. The greater question is how to we deal with adversity when it comes. The reading tells us that we need to be sincere, undisturbed, and steadfast; waiting with patience and trusting the Lord. Being undisturbed in times of adversity is difficult to embody. But if we are patient and trust in God, we can do so. When you are beset with adversity, monitor your reaction.

Prayers *others may be added*

Directing our prayer to Christ, who calls us to love our enemies, we pray:

◆ Lord, hold us in your mercy.

For the Church, that we trust in the wisdom of the Lord, we pray: ◆ For those who suffer misfortune, that they will rely on the Lord, we pray: ◆ For leaders in our community, that when tested with adversity they remain steadfast, we pray: ◆ For those who prevent another from pursuing their calling, we pray: ◆

Our Father . . .

Lord Jesus, Wisdom of the Father,
you offer us enlightenment.
Amid the bumps and bruises, the surgeries and scars,
may we always trust in you,
who live and reign with God the Father in the unity of the Holy Spirit,
one God, for ever and ever.
Amen.

✝ The Lord is kind and merciful.

Wednesday, February 22, 2017

Feast of the Chair of St. Peter the Apostle

✝ The Lord is kind and merciful.

Psalm 103

page 415

Reading

Matthew 16:13–19

When Jesus went into the region of Caesarea Philippi he asked his disciples, "Who do people say that the Son of Man is?" They replied, "Some say John the Baptist, others Elijah, still others Jeremiah or one of the prophets." He said to them, "But who do you say that I am?" Simon Peter said in reply, "You are the Christ, the Son of the living God." Jesus said to him in reply, "Blessed are you, Simon son of Jonah. For flesh and blood has not revealed this to you, but my heavenly Father. And so I say to you, you are Peter, and upon this rock I will build my Church, and the gates of the netherworld shall not prevail against it. I will give you the keys to the Kingdom of heaven. Whatever you bind on earth shall be bound in heaven; and whatever you loose on earth shall be loosed in heaven."

Reflection

Colleges and universities have what is called "the chair" in departments. The "chair" is a position of leadership and teaching authority. In ancient times the traditional posture for teaching (and preaching) was to be seated. The word *cathedral* is derived from the Latin word *cathedra*, for this is the seat or chair of the bishop. In celebrating the Chair of St. Peter, we honor the leadership of Peter and, by extension, the teaching office of the Bishop of Rome.

Prayers

others may be added

Turning to Christ, who founded the Church, we pray:

◆ Lord, save your people.

For the entire Church of Christ, we pray: ◆ For our pope and all bishops in union with him, we pray: ◆ That the work of ecumenism will lead to true and lasting unity, we pray: ◆ That hearts and minds will be open to the teachings of the Church, we pray: ◆ For those who have doubted or denied Christ, we pray: ◆

Our Father . . .

All-powerful Father,
you have built your Church
on the rock of St. Peter's confession
of faith.
May nothing divide or weaken our unity
in faith and love.
Grant this through our Lord Jesus Christ,
your Son,
who lives and reigns with you in the unity
of the Holy Spirit,
one God, for ever and ever.
Amen. (*Liturgy of the Hours*)

✝ The Lord is kind and merciful.

Thursday, February 23, 2017

Memorial of St. Polycarp, Bishop and Martyr

✝ The Lord is kind and merciful.

Psalm 103

page 415

Reading

Sirach 5:1–4, 6–8

Rely not on your wealth; / say not: "I have the power." / Rely not on your strength / in following the desires of your heart. / Say not: "Who can prevail against me?" / or, "Who will subdue me for my deeds?" / for God will surely exact the punishment. / Say not: "I have sinned, yet what has befallen me? / for the Most High bides his time. / Delay not your conversion to the LORD, / put it not off from day to day. / For suddenly his wrath flames forth; / at the time of vengeance you will be destroyed. / Rely not upon deceitful wrath, / for it will be no help on the day of wrath.

Reflection

Sirach counsels against relying on one's wealth or power—the very things so many rely on today for their sense of security and status! Neither of these is a guarantor of character or godliness nor do they indicate a person of love and conscientiousness. Nor, Sirach states, are we to be overconfident of forgiveness. We can be confident in God's mercy yet we must be aware of our sin, acknowledge the harm it does to others, ourselves, and our relationship with God.

St. Polycarp is an important Church Father. He was formed in the faith by Jesus' disciple John, thus creating a link between the apostolic age and that of the Fathers of the Church.

Prayers

others may be added

Addressing God, who is our strength,
we pray:

◆ **Lord, save your people.**

That the Church, founded on the Apostles, bear witness to God's mercy, we pray: ◆ For peace in Jerusalem and peace in the world, we pray: ◆ For victims of war, rape, abduction, or torture, we pray: ◆ That we not cling to wealth or status for our security, we pray: ◆ For the willingness to name and confess our sins, we pray: ◆

Our Father . . .

Compassionate and merciful God,
you provide for our needs.
May we know that to place our security
in anyone or anything that is not you
is idolatry.
May we place all our hope in you.
We ask this through Christ our Lord.
Amen.

✝ The Lord is kind and merciful.

Friday, February 24, 2017
Weekday

† The Lord is kind and merciful.

Psalm 103 *page 415*

Reading *Sirach 6:5–8, 14–17*

A kind mouth multiplies friends and appeases enemies, / and gracious lips prompt friendly greetings. / Let your acquaintances be many, / but one in a thousand your confidant. / When you gain a friend, first test him, / and be not too ready to trust him. / For one sort is a friend when it suits him, / but he will not be with you in time of distress. / A faithful friend is a sturdy shelter; / he who finds one finds a treasure. / A faithful friend is beyond price, / no sum can balance his worth. / A faithful friend is a life-saving remedy, / such as he who fears God finds; / For he who fears God behaves accordingly, / and his friend will be like himself.

Reflection

Friendship, the sacred author understands, is key in our lives. The pain of broken promises and trust is highly destructive. What type of friends do you have? Are there people in your life who are more than acquaintances and people of worth who hold your life as sacred? Which friendships are most precious to you? Do people trust you enough to share what is confidential? How do you nurture your friendships? Take some time to evaluate your friendships today and your role in these relationships.

Prayers *others may be added*

Surrounded by a great cloud of witnesses, we pray:

◆ Lord, save your people.

For our Church, may we be a place of solace, we pray: ◆ For our brothers and sisters who today live with war, we pray: ◆ For our lawmakers, that they will act with honor, we pray: ◆ For all who suffer from cold and storm, we pray: ◆ For the wisdom to reach out in friendship to the stranger, we pray: ◆

Our Father . . .

You bless us with friendship, Holy One.
Our friends help us bear our burdens and share our joys.
Help us to value our friends and be true to them.
We ask this through Christ our Lord.
Amen.

† The Lord is kind and merciful.

Saturday, February 25, 2017
Weekday

✝ The Lord is kind and merciful.

Psalm 103 *page 415*

Reading *Sirach 17:1–8*

God from the earth created man, / and in his own image he made him. / He makes man return to earth again, / and endows him with a strength of his own. / Limited days of life he gives him, / with power over all things else on earth. / He puts the fear of him in all flesh, / and gives him rule over beasts and birds. / He created for them counsel, and a tongue and eyes and ears, / and an inventive heart, / and filled them with the discipline of understanding. / He created in them knowledge of the spirit; / With wisdom he fills their heart; / good and evil he shows them. / He put the fear of himself upon their hearts, / and showed them his mighty works, / That they might glory in the wonder of his deeds / and praise his holy name.

Reflection

This creation story paints a picture of right relationship with God. It speaks of humanity's inventive heart, capability for wisdom, and responsibility for the earth. Is our life as balanced as this portrait? Do we take time to nourish our minds, bodies, and spiritual selves? Too often at least one of these is neglected. Lent is just around the corner. Now is a good time to make a self-assessment and plan for the season. Perhaps you will find that you need to place more priority on your spiritual self.

Prayers *others may be added*

Surrounded by a great cloud of witnesses, we pray:

◆ Lord, save your people.

May the Church continue to speak out against every kind of evil and injustice, we pray: ◆ May world leaders abandon acts of revenge and violence, we pray: ◆ For artists and musicians, we pray: ◆ May those who are ill be refreshed by God, we pray ◆ May we embrace the spirit that lives within us and calls us to fullness of life, we pray: ◆

Our Father . . .

Creator God,
you made us in your image and likeness,
setting us over the whole world in all its wonder.
You breathed into us your spirit and charged us
to avoid evil and build a relationship with you.
In wisdom, sustain us.
In joy, be with us.
Help us to live as you intend, loving you, ourselves, and others.
We ask this through Christ our Lord.
Amen.

✝ The Lord is kind and merciful.

Sunday, February 26, 2017
Eighth Sunday in Ordinary Time

✝ Only in God is my soul at rest.

Psalm 62 *page 407*

Reading *Matthew 6:24–27*

Jesus said to his disciples: "No one can serve two masters. He will either hate one and love the other, or be devoted to one and despise the other. You cannot serve God and mammon.

"Therefore I tell you, do not worry about your life, what you will eat or drink, or about your body, what you will wear. Is not life more than food and the body more than clothing? Look at the birds in the sky: they do not sow or reap. they gather nothing into barns, your heavenly Father feeds them. Are not you more important than they? Can any one of you by worrying add a single moment to your life-span?"

Reflection

Can you count how many commercials point us to worry? We should be worried about our retirement, the lines in our face, the clothes we wear. This is exactly opposite of the Gospel. Our lives are in God's hands. The lesson here is not irresponsibility, but priorities and trust. Can we let go of our worries that feed our obsessions? Overwork doesn't allow us time with friends. Overeating is done out of stress. Overscheduling turns simple joys into tasks to be accomplished. Seek to let go today and take a Sabbath's rest.

Prayers *others may be added*

To our gentle God, who opens our hearts, we pray:

◆ Lord, hear our prayer.

For a Church faithful to the love of the Lord, we pray: ◆ For a world free from hunger and war, we pray: ◆ For all who are trapped by drugs, prostitution, violence, or abuse, that they may find a way out, we pray: ◆ For grace to rest in the Lord, we pray: ◆ For all who have died and now rest from their labors, we pray: ◆

Our Father . . .

All powerful God,
you provide us with the essentials.
Help us to trust in your promise and
your grace
to be the foundation of each day.
We ask this through our Lord Jesus
Christ, your Son,
who lives and reigns with you in the unity
of the Holy Spirit,
one God, for ever and ever.
Amen.

✝ Only in God is my soul at rest.

Monday, February 27, 2017
Weekday

✝ Only in God is my soul at rest.

Psalm 62 *page 407*

Reading *Sirach 17:20–21*

To the penitent God provides a way back, / he encourages those who are losing hope / and has chosen for them the lot of truth. / Return to him and give up sin, / pray to the LORD and make your offenses few. / Turn again to the Most High and away from your sin, / hate intensely what he loathes, / and know the justice and judgments of God, / Stand firm in the way set before you, / in prayer to the Most High God.

Reflection

With Ash Wednesday only two days away, we may feel a certain trepidation about the beginning of Lent. The author Sirach puts our mind at ease. Penitence is about hope and truth. God is always there, not as a harsh judge waiting to trip us up, but rather as our champion, helping and encouraging us. Lent demands prayer, time spent with God. As we anticipate its beginning, let us pray now for open hearts. Let God reveal to us our sins and errors. Then our forty-day journey will be rooted in the Lord's care.

Prayers *others may be added*

To our gentle God, who opens our hearts, we pray:

◆ Lord, hear our prayer.

For preachers and prophets in the Church, we pray: ◆ For ears to hear the truth of the Gospel, we pray: ◆ For courage to trust in God, even when times are difficult and the road is long, we pray: ◆ For people who live in the midst poverty, we pray: ◆ For community leaders, that they will bring hope to those they serve, we pray: ◆

Our Father . . .

Merciful One,
you long for the repentant sinner.
You reach out to the lost
in the tangle of the world's vices.
We seek to live in your love,
yet sin has blocked our path.
Help us to remove whatever keeps us
from you
and sustain us as we prepare for our
Lenten journey.
We ask this through Christ our Lord.
Amen.

✝ Only in God is my soul at rest.

Tuesday, February 28, 2017

Weekday

✝ Only in God is my soul at rest.

Psalm 62

page 407

Reading

Sirach 35:1–9

To keep the law is a great oblation, / and he who observes the commandments sacrifices a peace offering. / In works of charity one offers fine flour, / and when he gives alms he presents his sacrifice of praise. / To refrain from evil pleases the LORD, / and to avoid injustice is an atonement. / Appear not before the LORD empty-handed, / for all that you offer is in fulfillment of the precepts. / The just one's offering enriches the altar / and rises as a sweet odor before the Most High. / The just one's sacrifice is most pleasing, / nor will it ever be forgotten. / In a generous spirit pay homage to the LORD, / be not sparing of freewill gifts. / With each contribution show a cheerful countenance, / and pay your tithes in a spirit of joy. / Give to the Most High as he has given to you, / generously, according to your means.

Reflection

As we contemplate what we will do for Lent, Sirach provides valuable guidance. Charity and almsgiving are meant to be sacrifices that come from the heart. If the joy of the Gospel is within our hearts, our sacrifice will be joyful. As you consider your Lenten fast, reflect on your spirit of giving. How can you sacrifice with a cheerful countenance?

Prayers

others may be added

To our gentle God, who opens our hearts, we pray:

◆ Lord, hear our prayer.

May the Church offer us a spirit of joy for our sacrifice, we pray: ◆ May world leaders work for an end to war, we pray: ◆ May we offer the Lord obedience, we pray: ◆ May our hearts be full of mercy and compassion, we pray: ◆ May our piety be supported by love, our charity by justice, our prayer by action, we pray: ◆

Our Father . . .

Lord of all,
you will for us to live in solidarity with each other.
Teach us to truly love others
and embrace the stranger as a friend.
We ask this through Christ our Lord.
Amen.

✝ Only in God is my soul at rest.

Wednesday, March 1, 2017
Ash Wednesday

✝ Have mercy on me, O God, in your goodness.

Psalm 51

page 406

Reading

Joel 2:12–18

Even now, says the LORD, / return to me with your whole heart, / with fasting, and weeping, and mourning; / Rend your hearts, not your garments, / and return to the LORD, your God. / For gracious and merciful is he, / slow to anger, rich in kindness, / and relenting in punishment. / Perhaps he will again relent / and leave behind him a blessing, / Offerings and libations / for the LORD, your God.

Blow the trumpet in Zion! / Proclaim a fast, / call an assembly; / Gather the people, / notify the congregation; / Assemble the elders, / gather the children / and the infants at the breast / . . . Between the porch and the altar / let the priests, the ministers of the LORD, weep, / And say, "Spare, O LORD, your people / and make not your heritage a reproach, / with the nations ruling over them! / Why should they say among the peoples, / 'Where is their God?' "

Then the LORD was stirred to concern for his land and took pity on his people.

Reflection

The word *Lent* translates as spring. We often think of the end of springtime with buds on the trees bursting forth and tulips peeking out from the cold earth. But what about early spring? As the snow and ice melt in warmer air, we have fog. The rains come, bringing slush and mud. Temperatures fluctuate. We are never quite sure even how to dress for the weather. This is the spring of Lent: a slow, gradual, messy movement of change. How will you change toward the Lord this Lent? Remember, it will likely be messy and fraught with good days and struggles.

Prayers

others may be added

Turning to God, who is merciful,
we pray:

◆ Change us, O Lord.

That the Church proclaim God's love and mercy to the world, we pray: ◆ That our world is transformed wherever hatred exists, we pray: ◆ May people know less terror and more justice, we pray: ◆ That the lost, seeking, and discouraged find direction, hope, and healing, we pray: ◆ That our Lenten disciplines renew us to be better disciples of Christ, we pray: ◆

Our Father . . .

Merciful One,
you see our need for forgiveness.
Open our minds and our eyes to our sinfulness,
so that on our Lenten journey,
we will clearly see the changes we need to make in our lives.
We ask this through Christ our Lord.
Amen.

✝ Have mercy on me, O God, in your goodness.

Thursday, March 2, 2017

Thursday after Ash Wednesday

✝ Have mercy on me, O God, in your goodness.

Psalm 51 *page 406*

Reading *Deuteronomy 30:15–20*

Moses said to the people: "Today I have set before you life and prosperity, death and doom. If you obey the commandments of the LORD, your God, which I enjoin on you today, loving him, and walking in his ways, and keeping his commandments, statutes and decrees, you will live and grow numerous, and the LORD, your God, will bless you in the land you are entering to occupy. If, however, you turn away your hearts and will not listen, but are led astray and adore and serve other gods, I tell you now that you will certainly perish; you will not have a long life on the land that you are crossing the Jordan to enter and occupy. I call heaven and earth today to witness against you: I have set before you life and death, the blessing and the curse. Choose life, then, that you and your descendants may live, by loving the LORD, your God, heeding his voice, and holding fast to him. For that will mean for you a long life for you to live on the land that the LORD swore he would give to your fathers Abraham, Isaac and Jacob."

Reflection

"Choose life." The choice for life includes our daily decisions to live in God. Do we love the Lord with our whole heart? How does that affect our choices in food, investments, shopping, and housing? Nothing is outside of our love for God.

Prayers *others may be added*

Turning to the Lord, who is merciful, we pray:

◆ **Lord, hear our prayer.**

May our Church be a place of life, love, and reconciliation, we pray: ◆ May our world respect life from conception to natural death, we pray: ◆ May all who serve our gods of power, control, or money, know conversion, we pray: ◆ May all of our decisions be rooted in our love of the Lord, we pray: ◆

Our Father . . .

Lord of Life,
you show us the way to prosperity
but allow us to choose you or other gods.
We choose to love you above all else.
Give us insight to know your way
and courage to live it in our
daily decisions.
We ask this through Christ our Lord.
Amen.

✝ Have mercy on me, O God, in your goodness.

Friday, March 3, 2017
Friday after Ash Wednesday

✝ Have mercy on me, O God, in your goodness.

Psalm 51 *page 406*

Reading *Isaiah 58:6–9a*

Thus says the Lord God: / This, rather, is the fasting that I wish: / releasing those bound unjustly, / untying the thongs of the yoke; / Setting free the oppressed, / breaking every yoke; / Sharing your bread with the hungry, / sheltering the oppressed and the homeless; / Clothing the naked when you see them, / and not turning your back on your own. / Then your light shall break forth like the dawn, / and your wound shall quickly be healed; / Your vindication shall go before you, / and the glory of the Lord shall be your rear guard. / Then you shall call, and the Lord will answer, / you shall cry for help, and he will say: Here I am!

Reflection

Isaiah cuts to the heart of penitence; it is not the externals that matter, but an inward conversion and actions of justice; it is not a bowed head but sheltering the homeless and caring for the oppressed. It is not a fast of going without food, but sharing bread with the hungry. What does our Lent look like? Is it self-serving private penance or actions for immigrants, prisoners, the hungry, and homeless? Can we move beyond the externals, giving up our ambivalence to the poor?

Prayers *others may be added*

With trust in God's mercy, we pray:

◆ Lord, hear our prayer.

May our Church proclaim justice, we pray: ◆ May nations enact policies that embrace immigrants, the hungry, and all the vulnerable, we pray: ◆ May all who struggle in this world find food for their bellies, safety for their bodies, and sustenance for their souls, we pray: ◆ May we live in courage as people of justice, we pray: ◆ May this Lent be marked by inner conversion, we pray: ◆

Our Father . . .

Lord of the poor,
you hear the cry of the hungry
and demand that we too open our ears.
In this sacred time, may their pleas
for justice
become ours.
May we share our bounty
with our sisters and brothers in need.
We ask this through Christ our Lord.
Amen.

✝ Have mercy on me, O God, in your goodness.

Saturday, March 4, 2017

Saturday after Ash Wednesday

✝ Have mercy on me, O God, in your goodness.

Psalm 51

page 406

Reading

Isaiah 58:13–14

Thus says the LORD: If you hold back your foot on the sabbath / from following your own pursuits on my holy day; / If you call the sabbath a delight, / and the LORD's holy day honorable; / If you honor it by not following your ways, / seeking your own interests, or speaking with malice— / Then you shall delight in the LORD, / and I will make you ride on the heights of the earth; / I will nourish you with the heritage of Jacob, your father, / for the mouth of the LORD has spoken.

Reflection

The prophet Isaiah continues to address his people's false piety with an attack on their Sabbath practices. The Sabbath was a day set aside for rest in the Lord. So integral is the Sabbath that it is safeguarded by both commandment and laws. The intent is clear: rest in God. No work, no malicious speech, no personal interests. Lay it all down for a day. Renew, regroup, and relish the love and blessedness of God. What do our Sundays look like? Do we rest? Not to work seems anathema in our society. Perhaps a good Lenten discipline would be to return Sunday to its rightful place. Remember that we don't run the world, God does. We need a weekly reminder of that.

Prayers

others may be added

Turning to our merciful Lord, we pray:

◆ Hear us, O Lord.

May the Church be a constant symbol of God's abiding power in our world, we pray: ◆ May all in authority recognize that ultimate power resides in the Lord, we pray: ◆ May those who struggle with workaholism embrace the joy of rest, we pray: ◆ May we relish our blessings from God, we pray: ◆ May the Sabbath be a time of rest and trust in God's abundant blessings, we pray: ◆

Our Father . . .

Lord of the Sabbath,
you provide a day to honor you.
Help us to abandon an unhealthy love of work
and make our Sundays times of goodness, family, and healing.
We ask this through Christ our Lord.
Amen.

✝ Have mercy on me, O God, in your goodness.

Sunday, March 5, 2017
First Sunday of Lent

✝ Lord, do not condemn us according to our sins.

Psalm 79

page 410

Reading

Matthew 4:1–4

At the time Jesus was led by the Spirit into the desert to be tempted by the devil. He fasted for forty days and forty nights, and afterwards he was hungry. The tempter approached and said to him, "If you are the Son of God, command that these stones become loaves of bread." He said in reply, "It is written: / *One does not live by bread alone, / but by every word that comes forth / from the mouth of God.*"

Reflection

The evangelists place the story of Jesus' temptation immediately following his baptism and before his public ministry. As we enter Lent, it is comforting to know that even the Lord is tempted. Ash Wednesday may have begun in great enthusiasm, but just a few days later, are we rethinking the idea of penance? Are we making excuses for our failures? The Gospel portrays Jesus as tired and alone when temptation strikes. His firm foundation and commitment allow him to reject the easy solutions offered. Is our foundation in the Lord firm? In our inevitable exhaustion, can we remain true to this Lent?

Prayers

others may be added

With confidence in God's power,
we pray:

◆ Hear us, O God.

That temptation to wield power be removed from those in the Church, we pray: ◆ That community leaders work for an end to poverty, we pray: ◆ That the voices of hatred and bigotry are silenced, we pray: ◆ That our elect and candidates draw near to you this Lent as they prepare for the Easter sacraments, we pray: ◆ That those in the shadow of death rest in the gentle arms of your peace, we pray: ◆

Our Father . . .

Christ our Lord,
you resisted temptation
throughout forty days in the desert.
Be near us as we journey
in the desert seeking your way and truth.
May our Lenten disciplines mold us into truer disciples
and in temptation may we find strength in your love.
We ask this through our Lord Jesus Christ, your Son,
who lives and reigns with you in the unity of the Holy Spirit,
one God, for ever and ever.
Amen.

✝ Lord, do not condemn us according to our sins.

Monday, March 6, 2017
Lenten Weekday

✝ Lord, do not condemn us according to our sins.

Psalm 79

page 410

Reading

Leviticus 19:1–2, 17–18

The LORD said to Moses, "Speak to the whole assembly of the children of Israel and tell them: Be holy, for I, the LORD, am holy.

"You shall not bear hatred for your brother in your heart. Though you may have to reprove him, do not incur sin because of him. Take no revenge and cherish no grudge against your fellow countrymen. You shall love your neighbor as yourself. I am the LORD."

Reflection

Be holy because God is holy. What a huge endeavor. As disciples we say we will follow God, but being like God is an even bigger step. We have our ideas of what this should look like, but in Leviticus, God defines holiness. It is very practical: Love our neighbor as ourselves. Treat them with justice. No slander, no partiality, no unfair business practices. We can see holiness as beyond us, but it is right in front of us. Can we accept this?

Prayers

others may be added

With confidence in God's power, we pray:

◆ Hear us, gracious God.

That all in our Church will seek to be holy, we pray: ◆ That our world's leaders will seek harmony, we pray: ◆ That we will seek to appreciate the goodness of all and defend the rights of others, we pray: ◆ That we will try to remove from our hearts actions of revenge, grudges, and slander, we pray: ◆

Our Father . . .

Lord,
you show us the way
to be holy as you are holy.
Help us to remove the stains of bitterness
that sour relationships.
Aid us as we seek to be compassionate
to the pain of others.
We ask this through Christ our Lord.
Amen.

✝ Lord, do not condemn us according to our sins.

Tuesday, March 7, 2017
Optional Memorial of Sts. Perpetua and Felicity, Martyrs

✝ Lord, do not condemn us according to our sins.

Psalm 79

page 410

Reading

Romans 8:35–39

What will separate us from the love of Christ? Will anguish, or distress, or persecution, or famine, or nakedness, or peril, or the sword? As it is written: / *For your sake we are being slain all the day; / we are looked upon as sheep to be slaughtered.* / No, in all these things we conquer overwhelmingly through him who loved us. For I am convinced that neither death, nor life, nor angels, nor principalities, nor present things, nor future things, nor powers, nor height, nor depth, nor any other creatures will be able to separate us from the love of God in Christ Jesus our Lord.

Reflection

Perpetua and Felicity were martyrs of the early third century. One was a noblewoman, the other a slave. Both were young mothers, Felicity having given birth while imprisoned. They went to their deaths confessing their faith. Faith in our culture often serves convenience. We look for a Mass time that fits into our schedule. We shop where we want, despite a retailer's documented unfair business practices. We support unjust political policies that are not mindful of the vulnerable. Perpetua and Felicity put faith first, even in the face of torture and death, even when it meant losing their children. We must ask ourselves where we place faith in our lives.

Prayers

others may be added

With confidence in God's power,
we pray:

◆ Hear us, O God.

For those who offer their lives for the sake of the Gospel, we pray: ◆ For the poor, that they may be empowered, we pray: ◆ For refuge for the homeless, we pray: ◆ For a voice to proclaim liberty for the voiceless, we pray: ◆ For legislators, that they will have courage to listen to God's will, we pray: ◆

Our Father . . .

Father of all,
you provided Sts. Perpetua and Felicity
with the courage to stand up for their faith.
They stand as models of young women
willing to commit their lives to you,
no matter the cost.
May their lives challenge our actions.
Inspire us to look to them and
face opposition
with courage and love.
We ask this through Christ our Lord.
Amen.

✝ Lord, do not condemn us according to our sins.

Wednesday, March 8, 2017
Lenten Weekday

☩ Lord, do not condemn us according to our sins.

Psalm 79 *page 410*

Reading *Jonah 3:1–5*

The word of the LORD came to Jonah a second time: "Set out for the great city of Nineveh, and announce to it the message that I will tell you." So Jonah made ready and went to Nineveh, according to the LORD's bidding. Now Nineveh was an enormously large city; it took three days to go through it. Jonah began his journey through the city, and had gone but a single day's walk announcing, "Forty days more and Nineveh shall be destroyed," when the people of Nineveh believed God; they proclaimed a fast and all of them, great and small, put on sackcloth.

Reflection

Jonah is a model of Lenten springtime: He runs from God. He listens to God. He does God's will. He needs another reprimand. Today's reading is Jonah on a good day. His preaching of God's word of conversion has an effect. The people of Nineveh repent. Note that it is not Jonah's perfection that is important but that he keeps trying and allows God to do the rest. As we move through our Lenten disciplines it's important to persist. Even in our failure, God is there. And when we succeed, it is still God to whom the success belongs.

Prayers *others may be added*

Turning to God, who is all powerful, we pray:

◆ Sustain us, O God.

May the Church preach a word of conversion and repentance, we pray: ◆ May prisoners find justice and freedom, we pray: ◆ May our world be free from acts of terror and thoughts of hatred, we pray: ◆ May we persist in our Lenten disciplines, we pray: ◆ May we hear the voices of prophets in our midst, we pray: ◆

Our Father . . .

Merciful One,
you sent your prophet Jonah
to proclaim repentance
to a people who had grown away
from you.
May our voices also preach your message
of renewal
and may all return to the arms of
your love.
We ask this through Christ our Lord.
Amen.

☩ Lord, do not condemn us according to our sins.

Thursday, March 9, 2017
Lenten Weekday

✝ **Lord, do not condemn us according to our sins.**

Psalm 79 *page 410*

Reading *Esther C 12, 14–16, 23–25*

Queen Esther, seized with mortal anguish, had recourse to the LORD. She lay prostrate upon the ground, together with her handmaids, from morning until evening, and said: "God of Abraham, God of Isaac, and God of Jacob, blessed are you. Help me, who am alone and have no help but you, for I am taking my life in my hand. As a child I used to hear from the books of my forefathers that you, O LORD, always free those who are pleasing to you. Now help me, who am alone and have no one but you, O LORD, my God.

"And now, come to help me, an orphan. Put in my mouth persuasive words in the presence of the lion and turn his heart to hatred for our enemy, so that he and those who are in league with him may perish. Save us from the hand of our enemies; turn our mourning into gladness and our sorrows into wholeness."

Reflection

Queen Esther could hide her identity and faith and protect herself, but instead she prays for courage, takes a risk, and saves her people. How courageous are we? How willing are we to take risks to help others? Do our politics reflect the Gospel? In changing our hearts this Lent, are we willing to speak out for the cause of justice?

Prayers *others may be added*

With confidence in God's power,
we pray:

◆ Sustain us, O God.

That the Church will preach love when the world cries out in hatred, we pray: ◆ That neighbors and friends will join with widows, the orphans, and the lonely when they need help, we pray: ◆ That world leaders will listen to prophets who speak against war, we pray: ◆

Our Father . . .

Compassionate God,
you created the world in love,
and are always ready to comfort the persecuted.
Give us the courage of Esther to sacrifice for truth
and live in commitment to goodness.
We ask this through Christ our Lord.
Amen.

✝ **Lord, do not condemn us according to our sins.**

Friday, March 10, 2017
Lenten Weekday

✝ Lord, do not condemn us according to our sins.

Psalm 51
page 406

Reading
Ezekiel 18:21–22

Thus says the Lord God: If the wicked man turns away from all the sins he committed, if he keeps all my statutes and does what is right and just, he shall surely live, he shall not die. None of the crimes he committed shall be remembered against him; he shall live because of the virtue he has practiced.

Reflection
This reading may leave us with a question of whether we are good or bad people. But perhaps it should leave us examining how we define those terms and if we label others as "wicked" or "good." Most of us would claim to be good people. Ezekiel reminds us that to be good or wicked is a daily choice. Some of us may have a reputation for being "good," still the good may perform wicked actions and the wicked may embrace conversion. Reputation is nothing in the face of choice. As we move through Lent, let us honestly evaluate ourselves. Are our actions that of the Gospel? Let us also be open to the conversion of others.

Prayers
others may be added

Turning to God, who is all powerful, we pray:

◆ Hear us, O God.

May the Church be challenged to greater goodness, we pray: ◆ May victims of war and genocide find a home and security, we pray: ◆ May those who struggle with addictions find healing, we pray: ◆ May peace be our constant prayer, we pray: ◆ May we willingly evaluate our lives in the light of the Gospel, we pray: ◆

Our Father . . .

Merciful God,
you created us from your goodness
to be holy as you are holy.
Make clear our sins
that we may turn from them
and become ever closer to you.
We ask this through Christ our Lord.
Amen.

✝ Lord, do not condemn us according to our sins.

Saturday, March 11, 2017
Lenten Weekday

✝ Lord, do not condemn us according to our sins.

Psalm 79
page 410

Reading
Deuteronomy 26:16–19

Moses spoke to the people, saying: "This day the LORD, your God, commands you to observe these statutes and decrees. Be careful, then, to observe them with all your heart and with all your soul. Today you are making this agreement with the LORD: he is to be your God and you are to walk in his ways and observe his statutes, commandments and decrees, and to hearken to his voice. And today the LORD is making this agreement with you: you are to be a people peculiarly his own, as he promised you; and provided you keep all his commandments, he will then raise you high in praise and renown and glory above all other nations he has made, and you will be a people sacred to the LORD, your God, as he promised."

Reflection
God has called the people to a covenant relationship. Relationships, however, demand a commitment. We can't just say we belong to God without acting like it. It's more than just how we feel on any given day. Our culture sees laws as intrusive, a hindrance to freedom. In the light of a relationship, they provide guidance and help. They are parameters that form us. Which laws will help your Lenten journey? Can you see the grace of discipline in your life?

Prayers
others may be added

Turning to God, who is all powerful, we pray:

◆ Hear us, O God.

May your Church be sustained in your mercy, we pray: ◆ May the laws of nations guide their people toward an option for the poor, we pray: ◆ May police officers, firefighters, judges, and all who enforce our laws, work in justice with mercy, we pray: ◆ May married people be true to their covenant commitment, we pray: ◆ May we accept the disciplines of this Lenten season that we may grow in our relationship with Jesus, we pray: ◆

Our Father . . .

Great Lawgiver,
you call us into relationship
and teach us your ways.
May we understand your laws
as discipline that leads to freedom.
Help us embrace this holy season
as a time to draw nearer to you.
We ask this through Christ our Lord.
Amen.

✝ Lord, do not condemn us according to our sins.

Sunday, March 12, 2017

Second Sunday of Lent

✝ May your kindness be on us, O Lord,
as we place our trust in you.

Psalm 33

page 405

Reading

Matthew 17:1–5

Jesus took Peter, James, and John his brother, and led them up a high mountain by themselves. And he was transfigured before them; his face shone like the sun and his clothes became white as light. And behold, Moses and Elijah appeared to them, conversing with him. Then Peter said to Jesus in reply, "Lord, it is good that we are here. If you wish, I will make three tents here, one for you, one for Moses, and one for Elijah." While he was still speaking, behold, a bright cloud cast a shadow over them, then from the cloud came a voice that said, "This is my beloved Son, with whom I am well pleased; listen to him."

Reflection

The glimpse of glory the disciples received at the Transfiguration provided a moment of clarity. At times, we also see some of God's majesty. These times might be while witnessing a birth, when feeling at peace, or while immersed in music. Such glimpses may be rare gifts but can give us the respite to go on. Are we open to these moments or do we rationalize them away? Can we accept the movement of the Spirit blowing in our world?

Prayers

others may be added

Looking to the Lord, who transforms us, we pray:

◆ Hear us, gracious Lord.

That the Church will speak out courageously against war, we pray: ◆ That our sisters and brothers living in poverty will be provided hope, we pray: ◆ That our elect and candidates will be drawn to your love, we pray: ◆ That our community leaders will seek solidarity with those they serve, we pray: ◆ That those who are dying today feel embraced by your loving mercy, we pray: ◆

Our Father . . .

All powerful Lord,
you showed the disciples your majesty
at the Transfiguration.
Open our eyes this Lent
to see what you dream for us
so that we may become closer to an
image of you.
We ask this through our Lord Jesus
Christ, your Son,
who lives and reigns with you in the unity
of the Holy Spirit,
one God, for ever and ever.
Amen.

✝ May your kindness be on us, O Lord,
as we place our trust in you.

Monday, March 13, 2017
Lenten Weekday

✝ May your kindness be on us, O Lord,
as we place our trust in you.

Psalm 33 *page 405*

Reading *Daniel 9:4b–10*

"Lord, great and awesome God, you who keep your merciful covenant toward those who love you and observe your commandments! We have sinned, been wicked and done evil; we have rebelled and departed from your commandments and your laws. We have not obeyed your servants the prophets, who spoke in your name to our kings, our princes, our fathers, and all the people of the land. Justice, O Lord, is on your side; we are shamefaced even to this day: we, the men of Judah, the residents of Jerusalem, and all Israel, near and far, in all the countries to which you have scattered them because of their treachery toward you. O LORD, we are shamefaced, like our kings, our princes, and our fathers, for having sinned against you. But yours, O Lord, our God, are compassion and forgiveness! Yet we rebelled against you and paid no heed to your command, O LORD, our God, to live by the law you gave us through your servants the prophets."

Reflection

Daniel is brutally honest in his prayer. He acknowledges that the people are in exile because they broke the covenant and did not listen to the prophets calling them to repentance. Where do we stand before God? Do we try to justify our behavior or can we admit our sin? Prophets preach challenge. They command us to change in significant ways. This can be difficult to hear and may even hurt our feelings. In today's reading, do you hear a message for your life?

Prayers *others may be added*

Turning to our merciful God, we pray:

◆ Graciously hear us, Lord

That in the wake of disaster we are strong as a Church, we pray: ◆ That our nation's leaders seek to protect the poor, we pray: ◆ That provisions are made to protect the earth, we pray: ◆ That the world pays attention to prophets who speak words of challenge, we pray: ◆

Our Father . . .

Lord God,
you sent your prophets to guide
your people to live justly.
Send your Holy Spirit into our lives
to give us strength to continue to repent
as we seek conversion during our
Lenten journey.
We ask this through Christ our Lord.
Amen.

✝ May your kindness be on us, O Lord,
as we place our trust in you.

Tuesday, March 14, 2017
Lenten Weekday

✝ May your kindness be on us, O Lord,
as we place our trust in you.

Psalm 33 *page 405*

Reading *Isaiah 1:10, 16–20*

Hear the word of the LORD, / princes of Sodom! / Listen to the instruction of our God / people of Gomorrah!

Wash yourselves clean! / Put away your misdeeds from before my eyes; / cease doing evil; learn to do good. / Make justice your aim: redress the wronged, / hear the orphan's plea, defend the widow.

Come now, let us set things right, says the LORD: / Though your sins be like scarlet / they may become white as snow; / Though they be crimson red, / they may become white as wool. / If you are willing, and obey, / you shall eat the good things of the land; / But if you refuse and resist, / the sword shall consume you: / for the mouth of the LORD has spoken!

Reflection

Hear the plea of the widow and the orphan. In our day of social services, it is difficult to imagine the vulnerability of those without male protection in the time of Isaiah. Yet in our society many people are left susceptible and defenseless. In every locale, people suffer from poverty or abuse. We need to keep our eyes open that we may help those who have little or no resources.

Prayers *others may be added*

To our Lord, who has given us the power of the Gospel, we pray:

◆ Hear us, gracious Lord.

That the Church seeks to protect the defenseless, we pray: ◆ That the nation's leaders work to provide resources for those left orphaned and widowed because of war, we pray: ◆ That we will try to keep the abused safe from harm, we pray: ◆ That hatred and bigotry cease, we pray: ◆ That we not allow disaster to weaken our faith, we pray: ◆

Our Father . . .

Loving Father,
you hear the pleas of all your people.
Draw into your embrace
the weak and helpless of our sisters
and brothers.
Hold them tenderly
and show us the way to ease their burdens.
We ask this through Christ our Lord.
Amen.

✝ May your kindness be on us, O Lord,
as we place our trust in you.

Wednesday, March 15, 2017
Lenten Weekday

☩ May your kindness be on us, O Lord,
as we place our trust in you.

Psalm 33

page 405

Reading

Jeremiah 18:18–20

The people of Judah and the citizens of Jerusalem said, "Come, let us contrive a plot against Jeremiah. It will not mean the loss of instruction from the priests, nor of counsel from the wise, nor of messages from the prophets. And so, let us destroy him by his own tongue; let us carefully note his every word."

Heed me, O LORD, / and listen to what my adversaries say. / Must good be repaid with evil / that they should dig a pit to take my life? / Remember that I stood before you / to speak in their behalf, / to turn away your wrath from them.

Reflection

The prophet Jeremiah spent his life proclaiming the unpopular message of the destruction of Judah. The people's reaction was to plot against him and do him harm rather than listen to the Word of the Lord. Do you ever suddenly realize that your conversation or actions are not God's will? When that occurs, does it take you awhile to fully admit this to yourself? Do you ever consult someone to see how you might change? Would it be helpful to bring this to the Sacrament of Penance?

Prayers

others may be added

To the Lord, who protects his people, we pray:

◆ Graciously hear us, Lord.

That the Church will not shirk from challenging her members' actions, we pray: ◆ That those in authority will serve with humility, we pray: ◆ That leaders of nations will gather at tables to seek peace, we pray: ◆ That our community will work for unity among our diversity, we pray: ◆ That the Word of the Lord falls on open ears, we pray: ◆

Our Father . . .

God of the prophets,
throughout the ages you choose men and women
to courageously proclaim your Word.
Help us to be open to legitimate critique and faithful honesty.
May we honor the prophets among us
and protect the message they give in your name.
We ask this through Christ our Lord.
Amen.

☩ May your kindness be on us, O Lord,
as we place our trust in you.

Thursday, March 16, 2017
Lenten Weekday

✝ May your kindness be on us, O Lord,
as we place our trust in you.

Psalm 33 *page 405*

Reading *Jeremiah 17:5–10*

Thus says the LORD: / Cursed is the man who trusts in human beings, / who seeks his strength in flesh, / whose heart turns away from the LORD. He is like a barren bush in the desert / that enjoys no change of season, / But stands in a lava waste, / a salt and empty earth. / Blessed is the man who trusts in the LORD, / whose hope is the LORD. / He is like a tree planted beside the waters / that stretches out its roots to the stream: / It fears not the heat when it comes, / its leaves stay green; / In the year of drought it shows no distress, / but still bears fruit. / More torturous than all else is the human heart, / beyond remedy; who can understand it? / I, the LORD, alone probe the mind and test the heart, / To reward everyone according to his ways, / according to the merit of his deeds.

Reflection

We hear from Jeremiah that those who put their trust in others and turn from the Lord are cursed. Heeding the prophet's caution will bring a fruitful life. However, it is so easy to place our trust in what is visible. We must keep our eyes on what is truly of God. And to do that, it is essential that we spend time with God. Today, sit quietly with God and lay bare your heart, remembering God is merciful.

Prayers *others may be added*

Turning to God, who gives us his Word, we pray:

◆ Graciously hear us, Lord.

For the Church, that she will help her members be accountable to each other, we pray: ◆ For farmers enduring a drought, that they will receive help, we pray: ◆ For leaders of nations, that they will protect ethnic minorities, we pray: ◆ For those at the end of life who have trusted in the Lord, that they may die peacefully, we pray: ◆

Our Father . . .

O Omniscient One,
you probe the deepest center of our being.
You know us better than we know ourselves.
Root out our sinfulness and purify us.
Grow within us a heart in union with you.
We ask this through Christ our Lord.
Amen.

✝ May your kindness be on us, O Lord,
as we place our trust in you.

Friday, March 17, 2017

Optional Memorial of St. Patrick, Bishop

☩ Have mercy on me, O God, in your goodness.

Psalm 51

page 406

Reading

1 Peter 4:7b–11

Beloved: Be serious and sober-minded so that you will be able to pray. Above all, let your love for one another be intense, because love covers a multitude of sins. Be hospitable to one another without complaining. As each one has received a gift, use it to serve one another as good stewards of God's varied grace. Whoever preaches, let it be with the words of God; whoever serves, let it be with the strength that God supplies, so that in all things God may be glorified through Jesus Christ, to whom belong glory and dominion forever and ever. Amen.

Reflection

The legends of Patrick abound as we dye both our rivers and beer green, and don the attire of mythical wee folks. Patrick was real, however, and how he lived is a model for us. Captured as a slave from Britain, he escaped, but returned to bring the Gospel to the Celts. His love for his captors was great, for he saw beyond their actions and grudges to a need to know the love of the Lord. Bishop Patrick cannot sit idly on a shelf; his story is easily found. This year, imagine what it was like for him. What difficulties he faced: the cold, exclusion, ridicule, the struggle to forgive. His love was intense. May we seek to model our faith and love on his.

Prayers

others may be added

Turning to God, who gives us his Word, we pray:

◆ Graciously hear us, Lord.

For Pope N., our Bishop N., and the College of Bishops, may they serve with intense love for their people, we pray: ◆ For an end to slavery and human trafficking, we pray: ◆ For peace among nations, we pray: ◆ For a willingness to forgive, we pray: ◆ For the spirit and courage to evangelize, we pray: ◆

Our Father . . .

Heavenly Father,
you gave your bishop, Patrick,
a courageous spirit
to fearlessly proclaim the Gospel
and change the hearts of many.
May we too have the courage of
our conviction
and an intense love for your people,
especially our enemies.
We ask this through Christ our Lord.
Amen.

☩ Have mercy on me, O God, in your goodness.

Saturday, March 18, 2017
Lenten Weekday

† May your kindness be on us, O Lord,
as we place our trust in you.

Psalm 33 *page 405*

Reading *Micah 7:14–15, 18–20*

Shepherd your people with your staff, / the flock of your inheritance, / That dwells apart in a woodland, / in the midst of Carmel. / Let them feed in Bashan and Gilead; / as in the days of old; / As in the days when you came from the land of Egypt, / show us wonderful signs.

Who is there like you, the God who removes guilt / and pardons sin for the remnant of his inheritance; / Who does not persist in anger forever, but delights rather in clemency, / And will again have compassion on us, treading underfoot our guilt? / You will cast into the depths of the sea all our sins; / You will show faithfulness to Jacob, / and grace to Abraham, / As you have sworn to our fathers / from the days of old.

Reflection

The Lord delights in clemency. This seems to be the opposite of much of our culture. Our popular "reality" shows portray people hurting and belittling others. The method of communication is screaming. If TV cameras were turned on our lives, what would they show? Do we prefer leniency and clemency as God does, or are we hard on others? Do we speak gently with each other, or are we filled with accusation?

Prayers *others may be added*

To our God of compassion, we pray:

◆ Graciously hear us, Lord.

For your Church, that she acts with mercy and forgivenesss, we pray: ◆ For world leaders, that they seek peace not vengeance, we pray: ◆ For all who need a compassionate ear, that they may find a person to listen, we pray: ◆ For anyone who suffers from bitterness, may their wounds be healed, we pray: ◆ For those who face the death penalty, may they see the face of God, we pray: ◆

Our Father . . .

God of mercy,
you joyfully forgive and offer clemency
to all.
Remember no more our sins
and teach us to forgive
all who trespass against us.
May we treat others with concern
and empathy.
We ask this through Christ our Lord.
Amen.

† May your kindness be on us, O Lord,
as we place our trust in you.

Sunday, March 19, 2017

Third Sunday of Lent

✝ If today you hear God's voice,
harden not your hearts.

Psalm 95

page 413

Reading

John 4:6–10

Jesus, tired from his journey, sat down there at the well. It was about noon.

A woman of Samaria came to draw water. Jesus said to her, "Give me a drink." His disciples had gone into the town to buy food. The Samaritan woman said to him, "How can you, a Jew, ask me, a Samaritan woman, for a drink?" . . . Jesus answered and said to her, "If you knew the gift of God and who is saying to you, 'Give me a drink,' you would have asked him and he would have given you living water."

Reflection

The number of rules and conventions Jesus destroys in this Gospel text are almost too numerable to count. Throwing caution to the wind he sits with a Samaritan woman. Students of the Old Testament know what happens between women and men at wells. Now, of course, Jesus isn't going to marry her, but a bond of truthfulness is formed. She grows to know him for who he is. Her self-hatred, doubts, and rigid rules are washed away in the flowing water of love. Do we allow the same thing to happen within us?

Today is the first Scrutiny for those preparing to receive the initiation sacraments at the Easter Vigil. The elect are called to discern in their life what needs to be washed away.

Prayers

others may be added

Remembering our Baptism, turning to the Lord, we pray:

◆ Lord, hear our prayer.

That your Church will boast in the beneficence of your grace, we pray: ◆ That all who wander in the wilderness of greed, despair, hurt, or anger are guided back to your loving arms, we pray: ◆ That diversity is embraced, we pray: ◆ That the hearts of our elect will be purified by the water of eternal life, we pray: ◆ That the dying will be embraced in the gentleness of love, we pray: ◆

Our Father . . .

Loving Father,
you cleansed our sins in water
and made us new creations in you.
Renew us again this Lent,
making our lives fertile and fruitful,
and providing us spirits ready to do
your will.
We ask this through our Lord Jesus
Christ, your Son,
who lives and reigns with you in the unity
of the Holy Spirit,
one God, for ever and ever.
Amen.

✝ If today you hear God's voice,
harden not your hearts.

Monday, March 20, 2017
Solemnity of St. Joseph, Spouse of the Blessed Virgin Mary

☩ If today you hear God's voice,
harden not your hearts.

Psalm 95 *page 413*

Reading *2 Samuel 7:4–5a, 12–14a, 16*

The LORD spoke to Nathan and said: "Go, tell my servant David, 'When your time comes and you rest with your ancestors, I will raise up your heir after you, sprung from your loins, and I will make his kingdom firm. It is he who shall build a house for my name. And I will make his royal throne firm forever. I will be a father to him, and he shall be a son to me. Your house and your kingdom shall endure forever before me; your throne shall stand firm forever.'"

Reflection

This is the story of the solemn covenant made with King David. Despite David's failures, God reaches out and makes a promise to him. We look to this story as we remember Joseph. The genealogy of the Gospel of Matthew says that Joseph is a descendent of David, but the contrast is striking. There is much written on David, little about Joseph. David's sins are legendary; Joseph is peaceful. The faith of both men, though, is rooted in their relationship with God. When Joseph finds out Mary is pregnant, he feels compassion and does not expose her to the law. He trusts in dreams. Where is our faith rooted? When temptations arise, where do we turn? Do we find solace in our heart or in laws and convention?

Prayers *others may be added*

Remembering our Baptism, turning to the Lord, we pray:

◆ Lord, hear our prayer.

May pastors in the Church place their trust in compassion and mercy, we pray: ◆ May pregnant women find compassion and support, we pray: ◆ May refugees have shelter and safe passage, we pray: ◆ May fathers gently guide their children, we pray: ◆ May faith support and guide our actions, we pray: ◆

Our Father . . .

Maker of the covenant,
you instilled a faithful and merciful heart
in St. Joseph.
Keep our hearts faithful
and root our actions in love.
We ask this through Christ our Lord.
Amen.

☩ If today you hear God's voice,
harden not your hearts.

Tuesday, March 21, 2017
Lenten Weekday

✝ If today you hear God's voice,
harden not your hearts.

Psalm 95 *page 413*

Reading *Daniel 3:25, 37–43*

Azariah stood up in the fire and prayed aloud: [. . .] "For we are reduced, O Lord, beyond any other nation, brought low everywhere in the world this day because of our sins. We have in our day no prince, prophet, or leader, no burnt offering, sacrifice, oblation, or incense, no place to offer first fruits, to find favor with you. But with contrite heart and humble spirit let us be received; as though it were burnt offerings of rams and bullocks, or thousands of fat lambs, so let our sacrifice be in your presence today as we follow you unreservedly; for those who trust in you cannot be put to shame. And now we follow you with our whole heart, we fear you and we pray to you. Do not let us be put to shame, but deal with us in your kindness and great mercy. Deliver us by your wonders, and bring glory to your name, O Lord."

Reflection

The Book of Daniel is set in the time of the Babylonian captivity. The people are removed from all that they know. In many ways they have been brought low and destroyed. But the covenant with God is not null and void. No matter what had happened, the author of this prayer knows that God is there. God is always there. Do we know this? Has this Lent revealed to us sins, deep and dark? Has our life become a shell of what it was? God is there. Are there pains and sorrows so hurtful we keep them locked away? God is there. Let us open ourselves to the Lord and allow God to sit with us in our pain.

Prayers *others may be added*

Turning to the Lord, we pray:

◆ **Lord, hear our prayer.**

May the sins of the Church be washed away, we pray: ◆ May ancient wounds between peoples give way to understanding, we pray: ◆ May bitterness in families end, we pray: ◆ May parishes experiencing closings, clustering, and merging find a path of healing, we pray: ◆ May we have the courage to rest in the Lord even with pain and sorrow, we pray: ◆

Our Father . . .

O Lord,
you are always open to forgive us.
Help us as we strive to release
feelings of resentment and animosity
during this Lent as we seek
to draw ever closer to you.
We ask this through Christ our Lord.
Amen.

✝ If today you hear God's voice,
harden not your hearts.

Wednesday, March 22, 2017
Lenten Weekday

☩ If today you hear God's voice,
harden not your hearts.

Psalm 95 *page 413*

Reading *Deuteronomy 4:1, 5–8*

Moses spoke to the people and said: "Now, Israel, hear the statutes and decrees which I am teaching you to observe, that you may live, and may enter in and take possession of the land which the LORD, the God of your fathers, is giving you. Therefore, I teach you the statutes and decrees as the LORD, my God, has commanded me, that you may observe them in the land you are entering to occupy. Observe them carefully, for thus will you give evidence of your wisdom and intelligence to the nations, who will hear of all these statutes and say, 'This great nation is truly a wise and intelligent people.' For what great nation is there that has gods so close to it as the LORD, our God, is to us whenever we call upon him? Or what great nation has statutes and decrees that are as just as this whole law which I am setting before you today?"

Reflection

Memories. The Scriptures are based on them. Family dinners are filled with them. Memories tell us who we are. Moses, after telling the people to keep laws, urges them with even more vigor to remember. These memories are what shall be taught from generation unto generation. It's more than history; it's identity. What are your faith memories? How do they define you? Sunday morning Mass with a dinner afterwards? Your mother praying the Rosary when grandma was sick? Funerals filled with deepest mourning, yet still the Paschal candle stands by the coffin? First Communion and the party afterward? What were you taught and why do you remember?

Prayers *others may be added*

As we remember our Baptism, turning to the Lord, we pray:

◆ Lord, hear our prayer.

Let the memories of the saints guide our Church in truth, we pray: ◆ Let memories of liberty inspire freedom fighters, we pray: ◆ Let memories of wholeness encourage all who struggle with depression, we pray: ◆ Let our memories of faith sustain us in times of emptiness, we pray: ◆ Let the memories of the saints give us courage, we pray: ◆

Our Father . . .

God of our ancestors,
you have led your people through centuries
of doubt and joy, pain and jubilation.
May we continue to tell the stories
of the faith of our ancestors as we recount
your steadfast love and mercy
to our children and our children's children.
We ask this through Christ our Lord.
Amen.

☩ If today you hear God's voice,
harden not your hearts.

Thursday, March 23, 2017
Lenten Weekday

✝ If today you hear God's voice,
harden not your hearts.

Psalm 95

page 413

Reading

Jeremiah 7:23–28

Thus says the LORD: This is what I commanded my people: Listen to my voice; then I will be your God and you shall be my people. Walk in all the ways that I command you, so that you may prosper.

But they obeyed not, nor did they pay heed. They walked in the hardness of their evil hearts and turned their backs, not their faces, to me. From the day that your fathers left the land of Egypt even to this day, I have sent you untiringly all my servants the prophets. Yet they have not obeyed me nor paid heed; they have stiffened their necks and done worse than their fathers. When you speak all these words to them, they will not listen to you either; when you call to them, they will not answer you. Say to them: This is the nation that does not listen to the voice of the LORD, its God, or take correction. Faithfulness has disappeared; the word itself is banished from their speech.

Reflection

Jeremiah hears the crux of the Sinai Covenant: "I will be your God and you shall be my people. However, the fundamental problem is that the people do not listen. In the midst of their everyday lives they have lost sight of the basics. They cannot be faithful if they miss this essential point. Throughout Lent we fast and abstain from meat on Fridays. Perhaps our parish participates in the annual Catholic Relief Service's Rice Bowl program. Consider today why you participate in fasting and sacrifice.

Prayers

others may be added

As we remember our Baptism, turning to the Lord, we pray:

◆ Lord, hear our prayer.

May the Church be renewed in the
mystery of our symbols and actions,
we pray: ◆ May victims of natural
disasters return home to safety,
we pray: ◆ May teachers create a firm
foundation for success for their students,
we pray: ◆ May we return to the
foundation of our faith, which is love
for you, we pray: ◆ May this Lenten
journey help us experience conversion,
we pray: ◆

Our Father . . .

Dear Lord,
you have molded and shaped us
with your love.
As we seek this Lent
to renew our commitment
to discipleship,
we seek your help.
We ask this through Christ our Lord.
Amen.

✝ If today you hear God's voice,
harden not your hearts.

Friday, March 24, 2017
Lenten Weekday

✝ Have mercy on me, O God, in your goodness.

Psalm 51 *page 406*

Reading *Hosea 14:2–5*

Thus says the LORD: / Return, O Israel, to the LORD, your God; / you have collapsed through your guilt. / Take with you words, / and return to the LORD; / Say to him, "Forgive all iniquity, / and receive what is good, that we may render / as offerings the bullocks from our stalls. / Assyria will not save us, / nor shall we have horses to mount; / We shall say no more, 'Our god,' / to the work of our hands; / for in you the orphan finds compassion." /

I will heal their defection, says the LORD, / I will love them freely; / for my wrath is turned away from them.

Reflection

Worshipping a piece of stone seems silly to us. But don't we do the same thing? We look admiringly at the rich and famous and long for luxurious homes and goods. There is no end to our desire for consumption. When a new phone, computer, tablet, or other technology is marketed, we often think we need it. Our wants are so often called needs and though technology was meant to free up our lives, we often find it hard to spend time with the Lord. Where is our heart? Who is our God? What are we realizing about ourselves this Lent?

Prayers *others may be added*

As we remember our Baptism,
we pray:

◆ Lord, hear our prayer.

Make your Church a beacon of your love, we pray: ◆ Hear the cry of the lost, O Lord, and guide all who wander in the wilderness, we pray: ◆ Transform your world, we pray: ◆ May we share our food, resources and power, we pray: ◆ May we worship only you, Lord, spending time in your loving presence, we pray: ◆

Our Father . . . :

Lord,
you are our God, living and true,
yet our days are spent with the work of our hands.
Redirect us. Change us. Challenge us.
Let us see our folly
and focus our lives on you and your will.
We ask this through Christ our Lord.
Amen.

✝ Have mercy on me, O God, in your goodness.

Saturday, March 25, 2017
Solemnity of the Annunciation of the Lord

✝ Hail Mary full of grace! The Lord is with you.

Canticle of Mary *page 422*

Reading *Luke 1:26–29, 38*

The angel Gabriel was sent from God to a town of Galilee called Nazareth, to a virgin betrothed to a man named Joseph, of the house of David, and the virgin's name was Mary. And coming to her, he said, "Hail, full of grace! The Lord is with you." But she was greatly troubled at what was said and pondered what sort of greeting this might be. Mary said, "Behold, I am the handmaid of the Lord. May it be done to me according to your word."

Reflection

The liturgical year provides a vision of Jesus' conception. Within a week we celebrate the Solemnity of St. Joseph and hear of his role in accepting Mary's pregnancy and the Annunciation and Mary's "yes" to God. Both stories call for human collaboration. God's will in the here and now demands our "yes." Let us model ourselves after Mary. How is God asking for our involvement in the building up of the Lord's Reign? Is it through working for care for the environment or a nonviolent world?

Prayers *others may be added*

Remembering our Baptism, as we turn to the Lord, we pray:

◆ Lord, hear our prayer.

That your Church acts as an agent of change and herald of your Reign, we pray: ◆ That our nation's leaders transform policy so our laws reflect true justice, we pray: ◆ That the poor and marginalized feel your love, we pray: ◆ That our world will be healed from the scars of deforestation and other forms of waste, we pray: ◆ That we will comply with your command of love, we pray: ◆.

Our Father . . .

Your Reign, O Lord,
is one of justice and peace.
You have asked us
to live in collaboration with you
in accomplishing your Reign.
May all our actions be directed toward it
and may our children's children know
its love.
We ask this through Christ our Lord.
Amen.

✝ Hail Mary full of grace! The Lord is with you.

Sunday, March 26, 2017
Fourth Sunday of Lent

✝ **The law of the Lord is perfect, refreshing the soul.**

Psalm 19 *page 402*

Reading *John 9:1–3, 5–7*

As Jesus passed by he saw a man blind from birth. His disciples asked him, "Rabbi, who sinned, this man or his parents, that he was born blind?" Jesus answered, "Neither he nor his parents sinned; it is so that the works of God might be made visible through him." When he had said this, he spat on the ground and made clay with the saliva, and smeared the clay on his eyes, and said to him, "Go wash in the Pool of Siloam"—which means Sent—. So he went and washed, and came back able to see.

Reflection

Most of us cannot imagine blindness. We've always been able to see. Spiritual blindness, however, is more common. For example, we look back in history and can't imagine how people could own slaves and still consider themselves good Christians. Blindness still exists and we need to hear this reading often. The Pharisees' blindness is called out by Jesus. What about our own? Do we judge others and not see our sinfulness? What about our prejudices? Do we hide behind language such as "hate the sin but love the sinner"? We need to be careful of our attitudes. Let's start today with our blindness. Where do we not see our evil? Do we have the courage to ask another to help us see?

Prayers *others may be added*

To our Lord, who brings sight to the blind, we pray:

◆ **Lord, hear our prayer.**

May the Church clearly and with confidence live your Gospel, we pray: ◆ May the blindness of hatred, the darkness of war, and the gloom of greed, be transformed by the Light of Christ, we pray: ◆ May truth prevail, we pray: ◆ May our elect and candidates, prefer the folly of the cross to the wisdom of this world, we pray: ◆ May those who walk in the valley of the shadow of death live forever in the Reign of God, we pray: ◆

Our Father . . .

Lord,
you opened the eyes of the blind man and can open our eyes too.
Help us to see your truth.
and embrace the power of light over darkness so that we will be transformed.
We ask this through our Lord Jesus Christ, your Son,
who lives and reigns with you in the unity of the Holy Spirit,
one God, for ever and ever.
Amen.

✝ **The law of the Lord is perfect, refreshing the soul.**

Monday, March 27, 2017
Lenten Weekday

☩ The law of the Lord is perfect,
refreshing the soul.

Psalm 19 *page 402*

Reading *Isaiah 65:17–21*

Thus says the LORD: / Lo, I am about to create new heavens / and a new earth; / The things of the past shall not be remembered / or come to mind. / Instead, there shall always be rejoicing and happiness / in what I create; / For I create Jerusalem to be a joy / and its people to be a delight; / I will rejoice in Jerusalem / and exult in my people. / No longer shall the sound of weeping be heard there, / or the sound of crying; / no longer shall there be in it / an infant who lives but a few days, / or an old man who does not round out his full lifetime; / He dies a mere youth who reaches but a hundred years, / and he who fails of a hundred shall be thought accursed. / They shall live in the houses they build, / and eat the fruit of the vineyards they plant.

Reflection

Halfway through Lent, our spirits may be lagging. All is not lost. Our reading from the end of the Book of Isaiah is a breath of fresh air. There is an end in sight. God will not even remember the past, the sins, failings, and false starts. There is the reality of a new heaven and new earth. In this spring, as rain begins to water the earth, there is a renewed hope. Can you feel it? Rejoicing is almost within our grasp. What can you see over the horizon?

Prayers *others may be added*

To our Lord, who brings sight to the blind, we pray:

◆ Lord, hear our prayer.

May the People of God see a new earth dawning, we pray: ◆ May all those who seek to rebuild their homes after war and conflict find help, support, and healing, we pray: ◆ May all who struggle with cancer find healing, we pray: ◆ May victims of sexual abuse find solace and grow in wholeness, we pray: ◆ May we trust in the joy of the Lord, we pray: ◆

Our Father . . .

God of the new day,
you have showered us with gifts
that bring us joy.
As the sun rises this day,
we give you praise.
May the light of your power
sustain us on our Lenten journey.
We ask this through Christ our Lord.
Amen.

☩ The law of the Lord is perfect,
refreshing the soul.

Tuesday, March 28, 2017

Lenten Weekday

✝ The law of the Lord is perfect,
refreshing the soul.

Psalm 19 *page 402*

Reading *Ezekiel 47:1, 6–9, 12*

The angel brought me, Ezekiel, back to the entrance of the temple of the LORD, and I saw water flowing out from beneath the threshold of the temple toward the east, for the façade of the temple was toward the east; the water flowed down from the right side of the temple, south of the altar. He asked me, "Have you seen this, son of man?" Then he brought me to the bank of the river, where he had me sit. Along the bank of the river I saw very many trees on both sides. He said to me, "This water flows into the eastern district down upon the Arabah, and empties into the sea, the salt waters, which it makes fresh. Wherever the river flows, every sort of living creature that can multiply shall live, and there shall be abundant fish, for wherever this water comes the sea shall be made fresh. Along both banks of the river, fruit trees of every kind shall grow; their leaves shall not fade, nor their fruit fail. Every month they shall bear fresh fruit, for they shall be watered by the flow from the sanctuary. Their fruit shall serve for food, and their leaves for medicine."

Reflection

Today's reading from Ezekiel is similar in theme to yesterday's reading from Isaiah. Here we have an image of water flowing from the temple. The water turns into a river; fish fill the river while trees line its banks. Certainly the creation stories from Genesis come to mind. There is abundance here. Can we open wide the doors and live instead in God's bounty?

Prayers *others may be added*

To the Lord, who gives sight to the blind, we pray:

◆ Help us to see, Lord.

May the children of God embrace mercy and compassion, we pray: ◆ May the hungry be fed and the homeless find shelter, we pray: ◆ May the forgotten and alone know companionship, we pray: ◆ May the bounty of the earth be freely shared among all, we pray: ◆ May we unburden ourselves of needless possessions and trust in the Lord's goodness, we pray: ◆

Our Father . . .

God of the harvest,
your grace and blessings are boundless.
Teach us to trust and to share
so that through these simple disciplines,
we may find the freedom to live.
We ask this through Christ our Lord.
Amen.

✝ The law of the Lord is perfect,
refreshing the soul.

Wednesday, March 29, 2017
Lenten Weekday

✝ The law of the Lord is perfect,
refreshing the soul

Psalm 19 *page 402*

Reading *Isaiah 49:8–9, 12*

Thus says the LORD: / In a time of favor I answer you, / on the day of salvation I help you; / and I have kept you and given you as a covenant to the people, / To restore the land / and allot the desolate heritages, / Saying to the prisoners: Come out! / To those in darkness: Show yourselves! / Along the ways they shall find pasture, / on every bare height shall their pastures be. /

But Zion said, "The LORD has forsaken me; / my Lord has forgotten me." / Can a mother forget her infant, / be without tenderness for the child of her womb? / Even should she forget, / I will never forget you.

Reflection

In the reading we are given the image of God as a mother carrying her child. In her body the woman nourishes an infant. Pregnancy is not an easy gift. The baby moves, kicks, flips, and causes discomfort. Yet mothers, in the midst of it all, love the child. So it is with God and us. We squirm, fight, and push ourselves around. God continues to feed us. God keeps us safe. Like the infant in the womb, God is our lifeline. Let us remember God's motherhood with us. Can we see how intricately bound we are to God?

Prayers *others may be added*

To the Lord, who gives sight to the blind, we pray:

◆ Help us to see, Lord.

May the Church be a compassionate mother, loving the world with the concern of God, we pray: ◆ May pregnant women with few resources receive health care, we pray: ◆ For an end to abortion, we pray: ◆ For children, and all who live without tenderness, we pray: ◆ For a childlike trust in God, we pray: ◆

Our Father . . .

Dear God,
you are the source of life.
In you is found food for our bodies
and souls.
May we too mirror your tenderness for
the world
and in gentleness, reach out to all in need
of care.
We ask this through Christ our Lord.
Amen.

✝ The law of the Lord is perfect,
refreshing the soul.

Thursday, March 30, 2017
Lenten Weekday

✝ The law of the Lord is perfect,
refreshing the soul.

Psalm 19 *page 402*

Reading *Exodus 32:7–13*

The LORD said to Moses, "Go down at once to your people whom you brought out of the land of Egypt, for they have become depraved. They have soon turned aside from the way I pointed out to them, making for themselves a molten calf and worshiping it, sacrificing to it and crying out, 'This is your God, O Israel, who brought you out of the land of Egypt!' The LORD said to Moses, "I see how stiff-necked this people is. Let me alone, then, that my wrath may blaze up against them to consume them. Then I will make of you a great nation."

But Moses implored the LORD, his God, saying, "Why, O LORD, should your wrath blaze up against your own people, whom you brought out of the land of Egypt with such great power and with so strong a hand? Why should the Egyptians say, 'With evil intent he brought them out, that he might kill them in the mountains and exterminate them from the face of the earth'? Let your blazing wrath die down; relent in punishing your people. Remember your servants Abraham, Isaac and Israel, and how you swore to them by your own self, saying, 'I will make your descendants as numerous as the stars in the sky; and all this land that I promised, I will give your descendants as their perpetual heritage.'"

Reflection

Despite God's love, in the face of God's power against the Egyptians, the Israelites create and worship a molten calf. It is likely that the people have tried to capture an image of God by making the calf. What are our images of God? Are they visions of aspects of God? How certain are we? Do we trap God into our way of thinking? Are there other ways of seeing God?

Prayers *others may be added*

To our Lord, who gives sight to the blind, we pray:

◆ Lord, hear our prayer.

May we as Church embrace worldwide diversity and the beauty of all cultures, we pray: ◆ May our world welcome a sharing of new ideas, thoughts, and opportunities, we pray: ◆ May we seek to image God's holiness, we pray: ◆ For an end to bullying and intimidation, we pray: ◆ May unity strengthen our faith, we pray: ◆

Our Father . . .

Lord,
you alone are God.
Stretch our feeble images and language.
Allow our minds to wander and find rest
among the myriad ways
you are present to us.
We ask this through Christ our Lord.
Amen.

✝ The law of the Lord is perfect,
refreshing the soul.

Friday, March 31, 2017
Lenten Weekday

✝ Have mercy on me, O God, in your goodness.

Psalm 51 *page 406*

Reading *Wisdom 2:1a, 12–16*

The wicked said among themselves, / thinking not aright: / "Let us beset the just one, because he is obnoxious to us; / he sets himself against our doings, / Reproaches us for transgressions of the law / and charges us with violations of our training. / He professes to have knowledge of God / and styles himself a child of the LORD. / To us he is the censure of our thoughts; / merely to see him is a hardship for us, / Because his life is not like that of others, / and different are his ways. / He judges us debased; / he holds aloof from our paths as from things impure. / He calls blest the destiny of the just / and boasts that God is his Father."

Reflection

Conflict. It is a harsh reality. For all our talk of unity we cannot escape the fact that there are enemies. The Book of Wisdom speaks of truth, the truth that throughout time the just are hated, maligned, and even killed. Do we still want to be just? Even today goodness is seen as foolish, truth succumbs to lies, and generosity is overpowered by greed. We tell teens to be strong and do the right thing in the face of peer pressure, but how are we doing as adults? Do we give in often? Consider this honestly in the light of your most difficult decisions.

Prayers *others may be added*

To our Lord, who gives sight to the blind, we pray:

◆ Help us to see, Lord.

May we be willing to preach the Gospel, despite persecution, we pray: ◆ For missionaries and all in danger for Christ, we pray: ◆ For anyone who has hurt us, we pray: ◆ For those who cannot face truth, we pray: ◆ For courage to be disciples, we pray: ◆

Our Father . . .

Lord God,
in your mercy, you sent your Son, Jesus Christ, to us,
though he would be tortured and die as he proclaimed justice and peace.
Your Kingdom is still a stumbling block for many.
May we who dare to wear the name of Christian
be ready for persecution and respond with faith.
We ask this through Christ our Lord.
Amen.

✝ Have mercy on me, O God, in your goodness.

Saturday, April 1, 2017
Lenten Weekday

✝ The law of the Lord is perfect,
refreshing the soul

Psalm 19

page 402

Reading

Jeremiah 11:18–20

I knew their plot because the LORD informed me; at that time you, O LORD, showed me their doings.

Yet I, like a trusting lamb led to slaughter, had not realized that they were hatching plots against me: "Let us destroy the tree in its vigor; let us cut him off from the land of the living, so that his name will be spoken no more."

But, you, O LORD of hosts, O just Judge, / searcher of mind and heart, / Let me witness the vengeance you take on them, / for to you I have entrusted my cause!

Reflection

Jeremiah is quite human in today's reading. He speaks of no lofty goals, no high ideals. He is afraid and angry. He knows there are plots against him. He cries out for vengeance on his enemies. Of note, however, is that Jeremiah trusts in God to take up the prophet's cause. He will not do anything himself (though he hopes to see God's wrath). Can we let God take care of our battles for us? Can we just accept what will happen, even when we experience pain, confusion, or anger? We can't deny our emotions, pretend they don't exist. We are human and feelings are an integral part of how God made us. Choices are what matter here. Are we ruled by our reactions or by our choice for Christ?

Prayers

others may be added

To our Lord, who gives sight to the blind, we pray:

◆ Lord, hear our prayer.

May our Church accept pain and yet preach love, we pray: ◆ May the powerful control their weapons by preferring peace to war and life to destruction, we pray: ◆ May those who struggle with the pain of victimization, hatred, and prejudice find solace and recovery, we pray: ◆ May the Holy Spirit guide the work of therapists, arbiters, and social workers, we pray: ◆ May the death penalty end, we pray: ◆

Our Father . . .

Almighty God,
you know our minds and hearts.
Heal us and help us always to trust in
your will,
no matter the outcome of our actions.
We ask this through Christ our Lord.
Amen.

✝ The law of the Lord is perfect,
refreshing the soul.

Sunday, April 2, 2017
Fifth Sunday of Lent

✝ With the Lord there is mercy, and fullness of redemption.

Psalm 130 *page 419*

Reading *John 11:17–23*

When Jesus arrived, he found that Lazarus had already been in the tomb for four days. Now Bethany was near Jerusalem, only about two miles away. And many of the Jews had come to Martha and Mary to comfort them about their brother. When Martha heard that Jesus was coming, she went to meet him; but Mary sat at home. Martha said to Jesus, "Lord, if you had been here, my brother would not have died. But even now I know that whatever you ask of God, God will give you." Jesus said to her, "Your brother will rise."

Reflection

When Martha saw Jesus after her brother Lazarus died, she said, "Lord, if you had been here, my brother would not have died."

We too are believers, and have witnessed death in many ways. Sometimes it is the death of a neighborhood, due to crime. Other times it is the death of an innocent and beloved individual. Discipleship never meant instant healing, wealth, or lives of prosperity. Discipleship is about a joy in being in relationship with the Lord. This brings a peace beyond human understanding, and with discipleship, comes life.

Prayers *others may be added*

To our Lord, who brings us life,
we pray:

◆ Give us new life in you.

Give your Church the courage to live in the freedom of the children of God, we pray: ◆ Open the graves of all those numbed by addictions and pain, made lifeless by overwork and exhaustion, we pray: ◆ Open our ears to those who cry out in poverty, we pray: ◆ From our elect and candidates, prune away all traces of sin. Unbind their hearts and let them go free, we pray: ◆ May all the dead share in the new life of resurrection, we pray: ◆

Our Father . . .

God of the living and the dead,
you offer us life in you.
Free us from expectations not worthy
of the Gospel that we will live freely
as your children.
We ask this through our Lord Jesus
Christ, your Son,
who lives and reigns with you in the unity
of the Holy Spirit,
one God, for ever and ever.
Amen.

✝ With the Lord there is mercy, and fullness of redemption.

Monday, April 3, 2017
Lenten Weekday

✝ With the Lord there is mercy, and fullness of redemption.

Psalm 130 *page 419*

Reading *Daniel 13:5–6, 15, 16, 19–26, 28, 36, 42, 45–49*

That year, two elders of the people were appointed judges. . . . These men, to whom all brought their cases, frequented the house of Joakim. When the people left at noon, Susanna used to enter her husband's garden for a walk.

One day, while they were waiting for the right moment, she entered the garden as usual, with two maids only. . . . Nobody else was there except the two elders, who had hidden themselves. . . .

As soon as the maids had left, the two old men got up and hurried to her. "Look," they said, "the garden doors are shut, and no one can see us; give in to our desire, and lie with us. "

"I am completely trapped," Susanna groaned. "If I yield, it will be my death; if I refuse, I cannot escape your power. Yet it is better for me to fall into your power without guilt than to sin before the Lord." Then Susanna shrieked, and the old men also shouted at her, as one of them ran to open the garden doors.

When the people came to her husband Joakim the next day, the two wicked elders also came, fully determined to put Susanna to death. Before all the people they ordered: "Send for Susanna . . . .

As she was being led to execution, God stirred up the holy spirit of a young boy named Daniel, and he cried aloud: "I will have no part in the death of this woman. . . . Return to court, for they have testified falsely against her."

Reflection

Susanna's trust in the Lord allowed her to choose to remain faithful to her husband and the law rather than to sin with the two elders. Their deception could have meant her downfall and death. Can we trust that all that matters is that our actions are known to God, despite what anyone says about us?

Prayers *others may be added*

To the Lord, who gives life, we pray:

◆ Give us new life in you.

That members of the Church stand firm in their convictions of faith, we pray: ◆
That our community leaders will be steadfast in what is right when others twist deeds and actions, we pray: ◆
That we continue charitable deeds when others call them foolish, we pray: ◆
That those who are persecuted for right will remain strong, we pray: ◆

Our Father . . .

God of truth,
you protect those who are virtuous.
Root us in honesty and integrity.
Though slander be spoken about us,
may we have courage to fearlessly live
the Gospel.
We ask this through Christ our Lord.
Amen.

✝ With the Lord there is mercy, and fullness of redemption.

Tuesday, April 4, 2017
Lenten Weekday

† With the Lord there is mercy, and fullness of redemption.

Psalm 130 *page 419*

Reading *Numbers 21:4–9*

From Mount Hor the children of Israel set out on the Red Sea road, to bypass the land of Edom. But with their patience worn out by the journey, the people complained against God and Moses, "Why have you brought us up from Egypt to die in this desert, where there is no food or water? We are disgusted with this wretched food!"

In punishment the LORD sent among the people saraph serpents, which bit the people so that many of them died. Then the people came to Moses and said, "We have sinned in complaining against the LORD, and you. Pray the LORD to take the serpents away from us." So Moses prayed for the people, and the LORD said to Moses, "Make a saraph and mount it on a pole, and whoever looks at it after being bitten will live." Moses accordingly made a bronze serpent and mounted it on a pole, and whenever anyone who had been bitten by a serpent looked at the bronze serpent, he lived.

Reflection

The consequence for complaining against the Lord's blessings is to be bitten by venomous snakes. The cure is to look upon the bronze serpent on the pole. When we sin, do we want to ignore or go around the situation? Do we pretend it didn't happen? The Israelites had to look at the snake to be healed. We too must acknowledge the sins we commit to address the problem and repent. In the Sacrament of Penance we confront the evil we have done and promise to try to sin no more.

Prayers *others may be added*

To our Lord, who gives us life,
we pray:

◆ Give us new life in you.

In this time of Lent, may the Church carefully examine herself and be freed from undue attachments, we pray: ◆ May those who struggle with addiction have the courage to find the assistance they need, we pray: ◆ May therapists and counselors know the wisdom of the Spirit, we pray: ◆ May legislators honestly evaluate our laws, seeking justice and not repudiation, we pray: ◆ May we avail ourselves of the grace of the Sacrament of Penance, seeking conversion and peace, we pray: ◆

Our Father . . .

O God,
you are merciful when we sin.
Help us commit ourselves to conversion
that we may seek you and and your will.
May your grace be enough for us.
We ask this through Christ our Lord.
Amen.

† With the Lord there is mercy, and fullness of redemption.

Wednesday, April 5, 2017
Lenten Weekday

✝ With the Lord there is mercy, and fullness of redemption.

Psalm 130 *page 419*

Reading *Daniel 3:14–20*

King Nebuchadnezzar said: "Is it true, Shadrach, Meshach, and Abednego, that you will not serve my god, or worship the golden statue that I set up? Be ready now to fall down and worship the statue I had made, whenever you hear the sound of the trumpet, flute, lyre, harp, psaltery, bagpipe, and all the other musical instruments; otherwise, you shall be instantly cast into the white-hot furnace; and who is the God who can deliver you out of my hands?" Shadrach, Meshach, and Abednego answered King Nebuchadnezzar, "There is no need for us to defend ourselves before you in this matter. If our God, whom we serve, can save us from the white-hot furnace and from your hands, O king, may he save us! But even if he will not, know, O king, that we will not serve your god or worship the golden statue that you set up."

King Nebuchadnezzar's face became livid with utter rage against Shadrach, Meshach, and Abednego. He ordered the furnace to be heated seven times more than usual and had some of the strongest men in his army bind Shadrach, Meshach, and Abednego and cast them into the white-hot furnace.

Reflection

When we stand for faith, we may be tested. Yes, there are times we will feel like we are in a fiery furnace. The fires of our lives can either kill us or forge faith. The difference is whether we trust in God or are destroyed by fear. Where are you in your faith journey? How are the flames of this Lent transforming you into a more faithful disciple?

Prayers *others may be added*

Turning to our Lord who gives us life, we pray:

◆ Give us new life in you.

Look with mercy on your Church, we pray: ◆ Burn away the decay of self-righteousness, we pray: ◆ Bind up wounds caused by vengeance, we pray: ◆ Free those bound by pain in mind, body, or spirit, we pray: ◆ Purge the power of inertia from our lives, we pray: ◆

Our Father . . .

Holy Spirit,
the flames of your love are hot
and boundless.
Remove from us impurities
of intent and insincerity of action.
Renew us in our baptismal convictions.
We ask this through Christ our Lord.
Amen.

✝ With the Lord there is mercy, and fullness of redemption.

Thursday, April 6, 2017
Lenten Weekday

✝ With the Lord there is mercy, and fullness of redemption.

Psalm 130 *page 419*

Reading *Genesis 17:3–8*

When Abram prostrated himself, God spoke to him: "My covenant with you is this: you are to become the father of a host of nations. No longer shall you be called Abram; your name shall be Abraham, for I am making you the father of a host of nations. I will render you exceedingly fertile; I will make nations of you; kings shall stem from you. I will maintain my covenant with you and your descendants after you throughout the ages as an everlasting pact, to be your God and the God of your descendants after you. I will give to you and to your descendants after you the land in which you are now staying, the whole land of Canaan, as a permanent possession; and I will be their God."

Reflection

Throughout the Scriptures, it is a significant event when God changes an individual's name. Names have great meaning. Brother Vince Reyes, a Capuchin friar who worked in a soup kitchen in Detroit, wrote the book *My Name Is . . .* (Detroit: Capuchin Soup Kitchen, 2007). In words and portrait pictures, the guests of the soup kitchen took back their names and told their stories. For Brother Vince it was a matter of basic dignity to know another person's name.

Prayers *others may be added*

Turning to our Lord, who gives us life, we pray:

◆ Give us new life in you.

May the Church be a place of safety and love for all people, we pray: ◆ May the rich and powerful know the homeless and poor, we pray: ◆ May the lonely find companions, we pray: ◆ May those in nursing homes and places of assisted living find ears to listen to their stories, we pray: ◆ May we treat everyone with equal dignity and respect, we pray: ◆

Our Father . . .

Lord,
you have created each of us in your image, in beauty and in love.
May we recognize our worth
and see in each person the dignity of a child of God.
We ask this through Christ our Lord.
Amen.

✝ With the Lord there is mercy, and fullness of redemption.

Friday, April 7, 2017
Lenten Weekday

✝ Have mercy on me, O God, in your goodness.

Psalm 51

page 406

Reading

Jeremiah 20:10–13

I hear the whisperings of many: / "Terror on every side! / Denounce! let us denounce him!" / All those who were my friends / are on the watch for any misstep of mine. / "Perhaps he will be trapped; then we can prevail, / and take our vengeance on him." / But the LORD is with me, like a mighty champion: / my persecutors will stumble, they will not triumph. / In their failure they will be put to utter shame, / to lasting, unforgettable confusion. / O LORD of hosts, you who test the just, / who probe mind and heart, / Let me witness the vengeance you take on them, / for to you I have entrusted my cause. / Sing to the LORD, / praise the LORD, / For he has rescued the life of the poor / from the power of the wicked!"

Reflection

In this passage, we see the tremendous amount of trust Jeremiah has in God. He knows that the Lord is with him "like a mighty champion," and that the Lord will rescue "the life of the poor." The prophet's words bring to mind the words of the *Magnificat*. There, Mary proclaims, "He has filled the hungry with good things, and the rich he has sent away empty." We come to our prayer trusting in the Lord. As disciples, we take that trust with us as we carry Christ's message to the world.

Prayers

others may be added

Turning to the Lord, who brings us life, we pray:

◆ Give us new life in you.

May the Church be one with the poor, we pray: ◆ May legislators hear the cry of the poor, we pray: ◆ May those who would be holy, be in solidarity with those in need, we pray: ◆ May workers find respect, employment, and fair wages, we pray: ◆ May this Lent transform us into advocates for justice for justice, we pray: ◆

Our Father . . .

Gracious God,
your heart is with the poor and broken.
Your anger is upon those who would do them harm
by action and inaction.
Help us as we seek to soften our hearts.
May we prefer places of the poor to the palaces of the rich.
We ask this through Christ our Lord.
Amen.

✝ Have mercy on me, O God, in your goodness.

Saturday, April 8, 2017
Lenten Weekday

✝ With the Lord there is mercy, and fullness of redemption.

Psalm 130 *page 419*

Reading *Ezekiel 37:21–22, 25–28*

Thus says the Lord God: I will take the children of Israel from among the nations to which they have come, and gather them from all sides to bring them back to their land. I will make them one nation upon the land, in the mountains of Israel, and there shall be one prince for them all. Never again shall they be two nations, and never again shall they be divided into two kingdoms.

They shall live on the land that I gave to my servant Jacob, the land where their fathers lived; they shall live on it forever, they, and their children, and their children's children, with my servant David their prince forever. I will make with them a covenant of peace; it shall be an everlasting covenant with them, and I will multiply them, and put my sanctuary among them forever. My dwelling shall be with them; I will be their God, and they shall be my people. Thus the nations shall know that it is I, the Lord, who make Israel holy, when my sanctuary shall be set up among them forever.

Reflection

God wants to dwell with us. The arrangement is simple: God is God and we are God's people, no matter what. How have you allowed God to dwell within you this Lent? Dwelling includes vulnerability. God understands.

Prayers *others may be added*

Turning to the Lord, who brings us life, we pray:

◆ Lord, hear our prayer.

May the Church be willing to be vulnerable to the will of God, we pray: ◆ May victims of flood and famine find security, we pray: ◆ May caregivers and nurses know respite and assistance, we pray: ◆ May families be places of trust and support, we pray: ◆ May we have the courage to dwell with God, allowing ourselves to share our days and nights with the Lord, we pray: ◆

Our Father . . .

Lord of the ages,
from the beginning,
you have sought to dwell with your people.
Strengthen our vulnerability that we may
open ourselves to you.
May we know the joy of living with you
all of our days.
We ask this through Christ our Lord.
Amen.

✝ With the Lord there is mercy, and fullness of redemption.

Sunday, April 9, 2017

Palm Sunday of the Passion of the Lord

✝ My God, my God, Why have you abandoned me?

Psalm 22 *page 402*

Reading *Matthew 21:1–11*

When Jesus and the disciples drew near Jerusalem and came to Bethphage on the Mount of Olives, Jesus sent two disciples, saying to them, "Go into the village opposite you, and immediately you will find an ass tethered, and a colt with her. Untie them and bring them here to me. And if anyone should say anything to you, reply, 'The master has need of them.' Then he will send them at once." This happened so that what had been spoken through the prophet might be fulfilled: / *Say to daughter Zion, / "Behold, your king comes to you, / meek and riding on an ass, / and on a colt, the foal of a beast of burden."* / The disciples went and did as Jesus had ordered them. They brought the ass and the colt and laid their cloaks over them, and he sat upon them. The very large crowd spread their cloaks on the road, while others cut branches from the trees and strewed them on the road. The crowds preceding him and those following kept crying out and saying: / "Hosanna to the Son of David; / blessed is he who comes in the name of the Lord; / hosanna in the highest." / And when he entered Jerusalem the whole city was shaken and asked, "Who is this?" And the crowds replied, "This is Jesus the prophet, from Nazareth in Galilee."

Reflection

In the midst of a city in a Passover fever, Jesus enters Jerusalem on a colt, not as a conquering king, but as a man of peace. In the middle of all this flurry, he remains committed to the Reign of God and is willing to see his mission to the end. As we walk these last days of Lent, where is our commitment? Where is our peace?

Prayers *others may be added*

To Christ, who is our triumphant King, we pray:

◆ Graciously hear us, Lord.

Son of David, purify your Church by your Passion, Death, and Resurrection, we pray: ◆ Lord of Lords, turn stubborn hearts to ways of justice and peace, we pray: ◆ Son of Man, guide your elect and candidates to the Easter sacraments, we pray: ◆ Victor over death, guide all the dead to eternal life, we pray: ◆

Our Father . . .

Ever-living God,
you sent your Son to us as a sacrifice.
As we begin our journey through this Holy Week,
purify our intent and actions
that our Easter celebration will be rooted in holiness.
Through Christ our Lord.
Amen.

✝ My God, my God, Why have you abandoned me?

Monday, April 10, 2017
Monday of Holy Week

✝ In you, O Lord, I take refuge

Psalm 71 *page 409*

Reading *Isaiah 42:1–7*

Here is my servant whom I uphold, / my chosen one with whom I am pleased, / Upon whom I have put my Spirit; / he shall bring forth justice to the nations, / Not crying out, not shouting, / not making his voice heard in the street. / A bruised reed he shall not break, / and a smoldering wick he shall not quench, / Until he establishes justice on the earth; / the coastlands will wait for his teaching.

Thus says God, the LORD, who created the heavens and stretched them out, / who spreads out the earth with its crops, / Who gives breath to its people / and spirit to those who walk on it: / I, the LORD, have called you for the victory of justice, / I have grasped you by the hand; / I formed you, and set you / as a covenant of the people, / a light for the nations, / To open the eyes of the blind, / to bring out prisoners from confinement, / and from the dungeon, those who live in darkness.

Reflection

This week we hear all four songs of the "Suffering Servant." The image in this first song is that of a steady, unobtrusive messenger. By gentle persistence, justice will be established. Not in one single action, but in daily commitment is God's will done. Is the slow burn of justice kindled within us? What simple actions do we perform to bring about the Kingdom of God?

Prayers *others may be added*

In humility, we pray:

◆ **Hear your people, Lord.**

For a consistent cry for justice in the Church, we pray: ◆ For peace in our neighborhoods, we pray: ◆ For an end to prejudice, we pray: ◆ For all who suffer pain in silence, we pray: ◆ For a flame of faith burning brightly in our lives, we pray: ◆

Our Father . . .

Sun of Justice,
you gave your servant a message
of justice for all people.
May the long journey of liberty
find many disciples on its road.
May we build up the broken, enliven
the downtrodden,
and bring peace to all who are heavily
burdened.
We ask this through Christ our Lord.
Amen.

✝ In you, O Lord, I take refuge.

Tuesday, April 11, 2017
Tuesday of Holy Week

✝ In you, O Lord, I take refuge.

Psalm 71 *page 409*

Reading *Isaiah 49:1–3*

Hear me, O islands, / listen, O distant peoples. / The LORD called me from birth, / from my mother's womb he gave me my name. / He made of me a sharp-edged sword / and concealed me in the shadow of his arm. / He made me a polished arrow, / in his quiver he hid me. / You are my servant, he said to me, / Israel, through whom I show my glory.

Reflection

In this passage the servant tells us that he was called from the womb. However, he was hidden for a while, like a sword in the shadow of God's arm, or an arrow in a quiver. Are we like this? We recognize that we have belonged to God from the beginning of our existence, but now it is time to do God's work in a very public way. Is now the time to speak up to family and friends about our discipleship? How will we prioritize our schedule that we may celebrate all of Triduum? What is God asking of us?

Prayers *others may be added*

Seeking the Lord who calls us,
we pray:

◆ Save your people, Lord.

For courage in the Church, we pray: ◆ For a world attuned to the will of God, we pray: ◆ For all who are in hospitals and treatment centers, we pray: ◆ For hearts focused on righteousness, we pray: ◆ For ears that will hear the Lord, we pray: ◆

Our Father . . .

Compassionate Lord,
you call your servants to your mission.
While we live in you always,
each day brings new challenges
and dreams.
In this Holy Week, renew in us our
baptismal call to prophecy.
Open our mouths at this time
to teach your truths to all we meet.
We ask this through Christ our Lord.
Amen.

✝ In you, O Lord, I take refuge.

Wednesday, April 12, 2017
Wednesday of Holy Week

✝ In you, O Lord, I take refuge.

Psalm 71 *page 409*

Reading *Isaiah 50:4–9a*

The Lord God has given me / a well-trained tongue, / That I might know how to speak to the weary / a word that will rouse them. / Morning after morning / he opens my ear that I may hear; / And I have not rebelled, / have not turned back. / I gave my back to those who beat me, / my cheeks to those who plucked my beard. / My face I did not shield / from buffets and spitting.

The Lord God is my help, / therefore I am not disgraced; / I have set my face like flint, / knowing that I shall not be put to shame. / He is near who upholds my right; / if anyone wishes to oppose me, / let us appear together. / Who disputes my right? / Let him confront me. / See, the Lord God is my help; / who will prove me wrong?

Reflection

"Speak to the weary a word that will rouse them." Easier said than done. Sometimes the demands of our work, ministry, and family leave us tired. Still, God is with us, and we rejoice in that. How might we encourage friends and family to join in prayer during the liturgies of the Sacred Triduum?

Prayers *others may be added*

Seeking the Lord who calls us,
we pray:

◆ Save your people, Lord.

For bishops, priests, deacons and all ministers of the Gospel, may weariness not dissuade them from preaching truth, we pray: ◆ For those who are exhausted by their work, we pray: ◆ For the jobless and underemployed, we pray: ◆ For the retired and all who rest from their labors, we pray: ◆ For hope in the face of depression, we pray: ◆

Our Father . . .

Lord God,
you are always near.
Awaken us from our slumber
and restore in us the joy of your Word.
As your holy days approach,
transform us ever more into
purer disciples.
We ask this through Christ our Lord.
Amen.

✝ In you, O Lord, I take refuge.

Thursday, April 13, 2017
Thursday of Holy Week (Holy Thursday)

☩ The cup of salvation I will take up, and I will call upon the name of the Lord.

Psalm 116 *page 416*

Reading *John 13:1–5, 12–15*

Before the feast of Passover, Jesus knew that his hour had come to pass from this world to the Father. He loved his own in the world and he loved them to the end. The devil had already induced Judas, son of Simon the Iscariot, to hand him over. So, during supper, fully aware that the Father had put everything into his power and that he had come from God and was returning to God, he rose from supper and took off his outer garments. He took a towel and tied it around his waist. Then he poured water into a basin and began to wash the disciples' feet and dry them with the towel around his waist.

So when he had washed their feet and put his garments back on and reclined at table again, he said to them, "Do you realize what I have done for you? You call me 'teacher' and 'master,' and rightly so, for indeed I am. If I, therefore, the master and teacher, have washed your feet, you ought to wash one another's feet. I have given you a model to follow, so that as I have done for you, you should also do."

Reflection

Tonight we wash feet as a symbolic gesture of Jesus' Commandment to love one another as he has loved us—laying down his life in love for us. There are many Catholics for whom tonight's liturgy is their favorite, as it profoundly blends noble simplicity with unfathomable mystery. May we watch and pray throughout these sacred three days.

Prayers *others may be added*

To Christ, who humbled himself to share in our humanity, we pray:

◆ Lord, sanctify your people.

For the whole Church throughout the world, we pray: ◆ That we may have greater appreciation and profound reverence for the Body and Blood of Christ, we pray: ◆ For those who share in the Sacrament of Holy Orders, we pray: ◆ For catechumens preparing for the Easter sacraments, we pray: ◆ For the poor, the hungry, the homeless, and the imprisoned, we pray: ◆

Our Father . . .

God of holiness,
your Son Jesus Christ is the great high priest
who gave his life once for all.
May your people, washed in his Blood through Baptism
and nourished by his Body and Blood,
embrace his command to love and to serve.
Through our Lord Jesus Christ, your Son,
who lives and reigns with you in the unity of the Holy Spirit,
one God, for ever and ever.
Amen.

☩ The cup of salvation I will take up, and I will call upon the name of the Lord.

Friday, April 14, 2017

Friday of the Passion of the Lord (Good Friday)

✝ My God, my God, why have you abandoned me?

Psalm 22 *page 402*

Readings *John 18:29–37*

So Pilate went back into the praetorium and summoned Jesus and said to him, "Are you the King of the Jews?" Jesus answered, "Do you say this on your own or have others told you about me?" Pilate answered, "I am not a Jew, am I? Your own nation and the chief priests handed you over to me. What have you done?" Jesus answered, "My kingdom does not belong to this world. If my kingdom did belong to this world, my attendants would be fighting to keep me from being handed over to the Jews. But as it is, my kingdom is not here." So Pilate said to him, "Then you are a king?" Jesus answered, "You say I am a king. For this I was born and for this I came into the world, to testify to the truth. Everyone who belongs to the truth listens to my voice."

Reflection

When Jesus says, "My kingdom does not belong to this world," we often assume a split between heaven and earth. Jesus' Kingdom is of heaven. Yet the pronoun "this" more likely refers to Pilate and Rome's world. This is a world where might makes right, where the poor are exploited, where you are a someone or nothing. It is a world in which religion itself is used (abused) to control and oppress rather than liberate and cultivate gifts. The Cross is God's judgment on such a world, the world of repression and futility that people continue to experience around the globe and within the walls of their homes.

Prayers *others may be added*

To Christ, who was obedient to death, we pray:

◆ Lord, have mercy on us.

For the Church living in the midst of suffering and oppression, we pray: ◆ For our ancestors in faith, the Jewish people, and for Muslims, who also share Abraham as our common ancestor, we pray: ◆ For those who do not believe in God, we pray: ◆ For all who are imprisoned, especially those condemned to death, we pray: ◆ For all the dead, especially those who have known torture, abuse, abandonment, or died in ignominy, we pray: ◆

Our Father . . .

God of loving kindness,
you have been described
as mercy within mercy within mercy.
The Cross of your Son is your judgment
on this world,
but it is also the sign of your prodigal love
for humanity,
of reconciliation and salvation.
Inspired by this act of love,
may we become people of forgiveness
and mercy.
Through Christ our Lord.
Amen.

✝ My God, my God, why have you abandoned me?

Saturday, April 15, 2017

Holy Saturday

✝ I will sing of your salvation.

Psalm 71

page 409

Reading

Matthew 28:8–10

[Mary Magdalene and the other Mary] went away quickly from the tomb, fearful yet overjoyed, and ran to announce the news to his disciples. And behold, Jesus met them on their way and greeted them. They approached, embraced his feet, and did him homage. Then Jesus said to them, "Do not be afraid. Go tell my brothers to go to Galilee, and there they will see me."

Reflection

Through the busyness and cacophony of making ready for this night of nights, there always seem to be a few faithful keeping vigil before the empty tabernacle. In the midst of the chaos, I often join them for awhile. Something about the empty tabernacle forces me to acknowledge my emptiness. And yet, it also mirrors the empty tomb. "He is not here. He has been raised." He is alive in you, me, the newly baptized, and the Church that readies to rejoice in this most sacred and festive night.

Prayers

others may be added

To Jesus Christ, over whom death has no dominion, we pray:

◆ Lord of Life, hear us.

That the holy Church will be renewed in the joy and fervor of this night, we pray: ◆ For all who die and rise in Baptism this night, we pray: ◆ That all humanity and all creation may come to share in the victory of this night, we pray: ◆ May the lonely, depressed, and abandoned know that no one is forgotten this night, we pray: ◆ That all liturgical ministers may serve with joy and gladness this night, we pray: ◆

Our Father . . .

Ever-living God,
may your people know the sanctifying power of this night
that dispels wickedness, washes faults away,
restores innocence to the fallen, and joy to mourners,
drives out hatred, fosters concord, and brings down the mighty.
Through our Lord Jesus Christ, your Son,
who lives and reigns with you in the unity of the Holy Spirit,
one God, for ever and ever.
Amen.

✝ I will sing of your salvation.

Sunday, April 16, 2017

Easter Sunday of the Resurrection of the Lord

✝ Alleluia, alleluia, alleluia.

Psalm 118 *page 417*

Reading *John 20:1–9*

On the first day of the week, Mary of Magdala came to the tomb early in the morning, while it was still dark, and saw the stone removed from the tomb. So she ran and went to Simon Peter and to the other disciple whom Jesus loved, and told them, "They have taken the Lord from the tomb, and we don't know where they put him." So Peter and the other disciple went out and came to the tomb. They both ran, but the other disciple ran faster than Peter and arrived at the tomb first; he bent down and saw the burial cloths there, and the cloth that had covered his head, not with the burial cloths but rolled up in a separate place. Then the other disciple also went in, the one who had arrived at the tomb first, and he saw and believed. For they did not yet understand the Scripture that he had to rise from the dead.

Reflection

The garden in which Jesus is buried in the Gospel of John recalls the first creation. With the Resurrection, John tells of a new creation. On Easter Sunday "everyone" comes to church. We see familiar faces, visitors, doubters . . . and if we look closely, we will notice our deceased loved ones, our favorite saint, maybe even a cherished pet or two. Resurrection is the re-creation not only of one species but of the entire cosmos. Alleluia!

Prayers *others may be added*

To Christ, who triumphed over the grave, we pray:

◆ Risen One, save us.

May the joy of the Gospel and the joy of Easter magnify the Church, we pray: ◆ For the neophytes, we pray: ◆ For the grace to proclaim the Good News, we pray: ◆ That the peace of Christ becomes the peace of the world, we pray: ◆ That those who struggle with the bondage of addiction may know the freedom of the children of God, we pray: ◆

Our Father . . .

Lord God of all life,
we rejoice and give thanks
for your Son's victory over death
and for our participation
in this mystery through Baptism.
May we share the joy of this holy day
with those we love, with the poor, and
those who are hurting and angry.
May our lives be faithful witnesses to the
triumph of life over all death.
Through our Lord Jesus Christ, your Son,
who lives and reigns with you in the unity
of the Holy Spirit,
one God, for ever and ever.
Amen.

✝ Alleluia, alleluia, alleluia.

Monday, April 17, 2017
Monday within the Octave of Easter

✝ Alleluia, alleluia, alleluia.

Psalm 118 *page 417*

Reading *Matthew 28:8–14*

Mary Magdalene and the other Mary went away quickly from the tomb, fearful yet overjoyed, and ran to announce the news to his disciples. And behold, Jesus met them on their way and greeted them. They approached, embraced his feet, and did him homage. Then Jesus said to them, "Do not be afraid. Go tell my brothers to go to Galilee, and there they will see me."

While they were going, some of the guard went into the city and told the chief priests all that had happened. The chief priests assembled with the elders and took counsel; then they gave a large sum of money to the soldiers, telling them, "You are to say to him, 'His disciples came by night and stole him while we were asleep. And if this gets to the ears of the governor, we will satisfy him and keep you out of trouble.' "

Reflection

As the women were going to announce the Good News to his disciples, the guards went into the city. The contrast in these two goings is striking. The guards go to proclaim the same tired story. Mary Magdalene and the other Mary go to proclaim the Resurrection—all is made new—the Kingdom of Heaven is begun in our midst. How will we be bearers of the news of Christ triumphant and victorious?

Prayers *others may be added*

To Christ, who triumphed over the grave, we pray:

◆ Risen One, save us.

May the Church always bear witness to the Gospel of life, we pray: ◆ For women who serve the Church in religious life, we pray: ◆ For those who struggle to find meaning in faith and worship, we pray: ◆ For those whose insecurity and fear guide them to make poor choices, we pray: ◆ For those who work in telecommunications, we pray: ◆

Our Father . . .

God of our journey,
you send many messengers
to announce the Good News.
Keep us faithful to the Baptism we
have received.
May we announce in word and deed
our belief in the Resurrection of your
Son, our Lord Jesus Christ,
who lives and reigns with you in the unity
of the Holy Spirit,
one God, for ever and ever.
Amen.

✝ Alleluia, alleluia, alleluia.

Tuesday, April 18, 2017
Tuesday within the Octave of Easter

✝ Alleluia, alleluia, alleluia.

Psalm 118 *page 417*

page 417

Reading *John 20:11–14*

Mary Magdalene stayed outside the tomb weeping. As she wept, she bent over the tomb and saw two angels in white sitting there, one at the head and one at the feet where the Body of Jesus had been. And they said to her, "Woman, why are you weeping?" She said to them, "They have taken my Lord, and I don't know where they laid him." When she had said this, she turned around and saw Jesus there, but did not know it was Jesus.

Reflection

Dying and rising are continuous in our lives. We die to childhood to enter adolescence, we die to our teenage self to enter young adulthood, and so it goes. Something similar occurs in our relationship with Christ. "They have taken away my Lord," a grief-stricken Mary Magdalene tells the guard. Our image of Christ, our understanding of Christ, must die and be "taken away," so that a clearer image, a closer relationship can come to fruition. And this must happen over and over again. Dying and rising are continuous in our lives.

Prayers *others may be added*

To Christ, who triumphed over the grave, we pray:

◆ Risen One, save us.

That the Church be continually renewed, we pray: ◆ For those experiencing a crisis of faith, we pray: ◆ For those navigating transitions in their lives, we pray: ◆ For those who find themselves overburdened, we pray: ◆ For ourselves, may we be open to the dying and rising of our lives, we pray: ◆

Our Father . . .

Lord Jesus,
you willingly emptied yourself
to share fully in our humanity,
to know our transitions, our dying
and risings.
May we trust in the Resurrection
and allow our faith to grow, deepen,
and mature,
for you live and reign for ever and ever.
Amen.

✝ Alleluia, alleluia, alleluia.

Wednesday April 19, 2017

Wednesday within the Octave of Easter

☩ Alleluia, alleluia, alleluia.

Psalm 118

page 417

Reading

Luke 24:28–32

As [the disciples] approached the village to which they were going, [Jesus] gave the impression that he was going on farther. But they urged him, "Stay with us, for it is nearly evening and the day is almost over." So he went in to stay with them. And it happened that, while he was with them at table, he took bread, said the blessing, broke it, and gave it to them. With that their eyes were opened and they recognized him, but he vanished from their sight. Then they said to each other, "Were not our hearts burning within us while he spoke to us on the way and opened the Scriptures to us?"

Reflection

Throughout the Octave of Easter we ponder various aspects of our Lord's Resurrection. Today we honor the Eucharistic presence of the Risen Christ. We, as did the disciples at Emmaus, recognize him in the breaking of bread. We recognize his body broken in the broken bodies of the sick, addicted, abused, and tortured, and all who share in his suffering. And we recognize his body broken in meals shared with family and friends, in joy and laughter. We affirm the grief and anguish, the joy and hope, and these lead us to the table of the Risen One who makes himself known again.

Prayers

others may be added

To Christ, who triumphed over the grave, we pray:

◆ Risen One, pray for us.

May the Church continue to know and recognize you in the breaking of bread, we pray: ◆ For catechists and teachers who open the Scriptures for us, we pray: ◆ For those preparing for their First Holy Communion, we pray: ◆ That eyes, ears, and hearts are opened among those who are estranged, we pray: ◆ For those who are dismayed and have lost heart, we pray: ◆

Our Father . . .

Risen Lord,
those who were dejected found their
hearts burning
as you spoke and revealed yourself
in the breaking of bread.
May we always honor your risen presence
in the most holy Sacrament of
the Eucharist
and be nourished with you,
the Bread of Life and Cup of Eternal
Salvation,
for you live and reign for ever and ever.
Amen.

☩ Alleluia, alleluia, alleluia.

Thursday, April 20, 2017
Thursday within the Octave of Easter

✝ Alleluia, alleluia, alleluia.

Psalm 118 *page 417*

Reading *Luke 24:35–43*

The disciples of Jesus recounted what had taken place along the way and how they had come to recognize him in the breaking of the bread.

While they were still speaking about this, he stood in their midst and said to them, "Peace be with you." But they were startled and terrified and thought that they were seeing a ghost. Then he said to them, "Why are you troubled? And why do questions arise in your hearts? Look at my hands and my feet, that it is I myself. Touch me and see, because a ghost does not have flesh and bones as you can see I have." And as he said this, he showed them his hands and his feet. While they were still incredulous for joy and were amazed, he asked them, "Have you anything here to eat?" They gave him a piece of baked fish; he took it and ate it in front of them.

Reflection

In the Creed, we proclaim belief in the resurrection of the body. We do not know exactly what a resurrected body is like. The Risen Jesus is not always recognized immediately, he appears and disappears and goes through doors as would a ghost. But he is no ghost. He is also able to be touched, to eat, to show, and invite others to examine his wounds. This physicality of the resurrection of the body, affirms the goodness and dignity of our body and the bodies of others. Today we honor our physicality, for Jesus has revealed that our bodies are designed for immortality.

Prayers *others may be added*

To Christ, who triumphed over the grave, we pray:

◆ Risen One, pray for us.

May the social teaching of the Church guide us to embrace the gift of our world, we pray: ◆ That our community leaders will seek to protect those who have been abused, we pray: ◆ For people who live with physical challenges, we pray: ◆ For those who have a negative image of their body, we pray: ◆ For those who mourn and who look forward to seeing their loved ones again, we pray: ◆

Our Father . . .

God of loving kindness,
in your Son you confirm the goodness of creation
and especially of our body.
Help us to treat ours and others' bodies
with dignity, honor, and respect
as Jesus has taught us
through his Incarnation, ministry, and Resurrection,
for he lives and reigns with you in the unity of the Holy Spirit,
one God, for ever and ever.
Amen.

✝ Alleluia, alleluia, alleluia.

Friday April 21, 2017

Friday within the Octave of Easter

✝ Alleluia, alleluia, alleluia.

Psalm 118

page 417

Reading

John 21:1–7a

Jesus revealed himself again to his disciples at the Sea of Tiberias. He revealed himself in this way. Together were Simon Peter, Thomas called Didymus, Nathanael from Cana in Galilee, Zebedee's sons, and two others of his disciples. Simon Peter said to them, "I am going fishing." They said to him, "We also will come with you." So they went out and got into the boat, but that night they caught nothing. When it was already dawn, Jesus was standing on the shore; but the disciples did not realize that it was Jesus. Jesus said to them, "Children, have you caught anything to eat?" They answered him, "No." So he said to them, "Cast the net over the right side of the boat and you will find something." So they cast it, and were not able to pull it in because of the number of fish. So the disciple whom Jesus loved said to Peter, "It is the Lord."

Reflection

When we come across stories of fishing in the New Testament, we are hearing stories of an evangelizing Church. At first, the idea of talking to others about our faith and its importance can be daunting. But once we feel the fear and do it anyway we discover that more people are open to that conversation than we expected. We can gently share our faith and invite others to come and see.

Prayers

others may be added

To Christ, who triumphed over the grave, we pray:

◆ Risen One, hear us

For the Bishop of Rome and the entire College of Bishops, may they teach in the spirit of Christ, we pray: ◆ For those who serve the Church as missionaries, we pray: ◆ That we, the People of God, will respond to our Lord's summons to evangelize, we pray: ◆ For children and teens, we pray: ◆ For those who have neglected or abandoned their faith, we pray: ◆

Our Father . . .

Lord God,
in the joy and power of the Resurrection
of your Son,
you inspire us to go forth and share the
Good News.
Help us to reveal our faith in word
and deed
so as to invite others to know the
Risen Christ,
who lives and reigns with you in the unity
of the Holy Spirit,
one God, for ever and ever.
Amen.

✝ Alleluia, alleluia, alleluia.

Saturday, April 22, 2017

Saturday within the Octave of Easter

✝ Alleluia, alleluia, alleluia.

Psalm 118

page 417

Reading

Mark 16:9–15

When Jesus had risen, early on the first day of the week, he appeared first to Mary Magdalene, out of whom he had driven seven demons. She went and told his companions who were mourning and weeping. When they heard that he was alive and had been seen by her, they did not believe.

After this he appeared in another form to two of them along on their way to the country. They returned and told the others; but they did not believe them either.

But later, as the Eleven were at table, he appeared to them and rebuked them for their unbelief and hardness of heart because they had not believed those who saw him after he had been raised. He said to them, "Go into the whole world and proclaim the Gospel to every creature."

Reflection

The Apostles do not believe the word of Mary Magdalene and later do not accept the story of the disciples to whom Jesus had appeared. At times it is difficult to believe in the Resurrection. The thought of eternal life and reunion with those we love sometimes seems like mere fantasy. Then we recall those moments when we too came to know Christ's presence. Then we know and believe. He lives.

Prayers

others may be added

To Christ, who triumphed over the grave, we pray:

◆ Risen One, hear us.

That the Church may be the risen Body and Blood of Christ to the world, we pray: ◆ For all neophytes, we pray: ◆ For those who are preparing for the Sacrament of Matrimony, we pray: ◆ That we may seek to understand more than to be understood, we pray: ◆ For those who cannot move forward in their mourning and grief, we pray: ◆

Our Father . . .

God of light and life,
you make yourself known to us
in many ways.
Help us to be mindful of your
saving presence,
and of the many times you have
guided us.
Confident in your love,
may we be your witnesses to the world.
We ask this through our Lord Jesus
Christ, your Son,
who lives and reigns with you in the unity
of the Holy Spirit,
one God, for ever and ever.
Amen.

✝ Alleluia, alleluia, alleluia.

Sunday, April 23, 2017

Second Sunday of Easter / Sunday of Divine Mercy

✝ I believe that I shall see the good things of the Lord in the land of the living.

Psalm 27 *page 404*

Reading *John 20:19–23*

On the evening of that first day of the week, when the doors were locked, where the disciples were, for fear of the Jews, Jesus came and stood in their midst and said to them, "Peace be with you." When he had said this, he showed them his hands and his side. The disciples rejoiced when they saw the Lord. Jesus said to them again, "Peace be with you. As the Father has sent me, so I send you." And when he had said this, he breathed on them and said to them, "Receive the Holy Spirit. Whose sins you forgive are forgiven them, and whose sins you retain are retained."

Reflection

The doors were locked. Today, they also may have had an alarm and been within a gated community. We live in an era of heightened security, passwords, and key codes. Maybe we are locked into ourselves too—both selfishly and emotionally. "Peace be with you," Jesus says. He brings peace, the Holy Spirit, forgiveness, and the power to forgive to set us free from the walls we have created, from our fear, and from ourselves. We need only to seek his peace.

Prayers *others may be added*

To Christ, the Alpha and the Omega, we pray:

◆ Revealer of God's mercy, hear our prayer.

For the holy Church throughout the world, we pray: ◆ For the grace to forgive even as we have been forgiven, we pray: ◆ For those who will receive the Holy Spirit in the Sacrament of Confirmation, we pray: ◆ For those who are unable to name their feelings or express their true self, we pray: ◆ For those who live in fear, be it real or perceived, we pray: ◆

Our Father . . .

God of tenderness and compassion,
you have given us your Son, our Lord Jesus Christ,
as our companion on this journey to you.
He has made known to us your boundless mercy.
May we extend that mercy,
understanding, and acceptance toward one another.
Through our Lord Jesus Christ, your Son,
who lives and reigns with you in the unity of the Holy Spirit,
one God, for ever and ever.
Amen.

✝ I believe that I shall see the good things of the Lord in the land of the living.

Monday, April 24, 2017
Easter Weekday

☩ I believe that I shall see the good things of the Lord in the land of the living.

Psalm 27

page 404

Reading

John 3:1–8

There was a Pharisee named Nicodemus, a ruler of the Jews. He came to Jesus at night and said to him, "Rabbi, we know that you are a teacher who has come from God, for no one can do these things that you are doing unless God is with him." Jesus answered and said to him, "Amen, amen, I say to you, unless one is born from above, he cannot see the Kingdom of God." Nicodemus said to him, "How can a man once grown old be born again? Surely he cannot reenter his mother's womb and be born again, can he?" Jesus answered, "Amen, amen, I say to you, unless one is born of water and Spirit he cannot enter the Kingdom of God. What is born of flesh is flesh and what is born of spirit is spirit. Do not be amazed that I told you, 'You must be born from above.' The wind blows where it wills, and you can hear the sound it makes, but you do not know where it comes from or where it goes; so it is with everyone who is born of the Spirit."

Reflection

It is next to impossible to hear these words from John's Gospel without thinking of our evangelical sisters and brothers calling us to accept Jesus Christ as our personal Lord and Savior. Of course he is and we do. Yet beyond a one-time conversion experience this passage invites us to reflect on our Baptism, when we were reborn in water and the Holy Spirit. Easter and Baptism are distinct but inseparable. Our journey from death to rising calls us to ongoing growth and conversion. Our Baptism is not only an event from our past but a reality to be lived daily.

Prayers

others may be added

To Christ, the Alpha and the Omega, we pray:

◆ Son of the living God, hear us.

For the People of God in their Catholic, Orthodox, and Protestant expressions, we pray: ◆ That we may grow in conscious awareness of our baptismal identity, we pray: ◆ For those who seek meaning and religious faith, we pray: ◆ For those who come to us at night, we pray: ◆

Our Father . . .

God of life,
with Baptism, you brought us a sharing in the Death and Resurrection of your Son.
Help us to claim that Baptism today.
May we know who we are, to whom we are joined, and to whom we belong.
Through our Lord Jesus Christ, your Son,
who lives and reigns with you in the unity of the Holy Spirit,
one God, for ever and ever.
Amen.

☩ I believe that I shall see the good things of the Lord in the land of the living.

Tuesday, April 25, 2017
Feast of St. Mark, Evangelist

† I believe that I shall see the good things of the Lord in the land of the living.

Psalm 27

page 404

Reading

I Peter 5:5b–11

Beloved: Clothe yourselves with humility in your dealings with one another, for: / *God opposes the proud / but bestows favor on the humble.* / So humble yourselves under the mighty hand of God, that he may exalt you in due time. Cast all your worries upon him because he cares for you.

Be sober and vigilant. Your opponent the Devil is prowling around like a roaring lion looking for someone to devour. Resist him, steadfast in faith, knowing that your brothers and sisters throughout the world undergo the same sufferings. The God of all grace who called you to his eternal glory through Christ Jesus will himself restore, confirm, strengthen, and establish you after you have suffered a little. To him be dominion forever. Amen.

Reflection

To be baptized is to become part of the Body of Christ, the Church. In today's Scripture we read of the early believers holding all things in common and renouncing any claim to private property. When a particular community was small this was possible, but as the Church grew in numbers this concept proved untenable. It would, however, become an inspiration for monastic communities and religious life. Nevertheless, this ideal establishes that being part of the Church makes a claim on each of us. What does it mean for you to belong to the Church?

Prayers

others may be added

To Christ, the Alpha and the Omega, we pray:

◆ Son of the living God, hear us.

That legislators may set the common good above all else, we pray: ◆ For those who proclaim the Gospel, we pray: ◆ That we may be open to the concerns and criticisms of those who are on the outside looking in, we pray: ◆ For a willingness to embrace the cross, we pray: ◆ For those communities that claim St. Mark as their patron, we pray: ◆

Our Father . . .

God of all compassion,
you give us the example of the early Church
whose concern was that there be no needy person among them.
May we as brothers and sisters
united by one Lord, faith, and Baptism,
be concerned for the good of all.
Through our Lord Jesus Christ, your Son,
who lives and reigns with you in the unity of the Holy Spirit,
one God, for ever and ever.
Amen.

† I believe that I shall see the good things of the Lord in the land of the living.

Wednesday, April 26, 2017
Easter Weekday

✝ I believe that I shall see the good things of the Lord in the land of the living.

Psalm 27

page 404

Reading

Acts 5:17–26

The high priest rose up and all his companions, that is, the party of the Sadducees, and, filled with jealousy, laid hands upon the Apostles and put them in the public jail. But during the night, the angel of the Lord opened the doors of the prison, led them out, and said, "Go and take your place in the temple area, and tell the people everything about this life." When they heard this, they went to the temple early in the morning and taught. When the high priest and his companions arrived, they convened the Sanhedrin, the full senate of the children of Israel, and sent to the jail to have them brought in. But the court officers who went did not find them in the prison, so they came back and reported, "We found the jail securely locked and the guards stationed outside the doors, but when we opened them, we found no one inside." When the captain of the temple guard and the chief priests heard this report, they were at a loss about them, as to what this would come to. Then someone came in and reported to them, "The men whom you put in prison are in the temple area and are teaching the people." Then the captain and the court officers went and brought them, but without force, because they were afraid of being stoned by the people.

Reflection

The greater point in this passage is that "the Word of God is not chained" (2 Timothy 2:9); it cannot be contained or imprisoned. Recall the martyrdom, persecution, and other hardships the faith has endured, not to mention the sin of its members. When we recall what others have gone through, we know that agonizing over faith, and because of our faith, is what disciples do.

Prayers

others may be added

To Christ, the Alpha and the Omega, we pray:

◆ Son of the Living God, hear us.

For the Church, as she continues to know persecution, we pray: ◆ That our nation's leaders will advocate for those whose human rights are denied, we pray: ◆ That we may be fearless in embracing the hardships the Gospel entails, we pray: ◆ For those who have been condemned to death, we pray: ◆ For people living in prisons of fear, we pray: ◆

Our Father . . .

God of the universe,
you have given us your Word.
May you give us the strength
to abide in your Word
so that it may achieve the end for which
you sent it.
Through Christ our Lord.
Amen.

✝ I believe that I shall see the good things of the Lord in the land of the living.

Thursday, April 27, 2017
Easter Weekday

✝ I believe that I shall see the good things of the Lord in the land of the living.

Psalm 27 *page 404*

Reading *Acts 5:27–33*

When the court officers had brought the Apostles in and made them stand before the Sanhedrin, the high priest questioned them, "We gave you strict orders did we not, to stop teaching in that name. Yet you have filled Jerusalem with your teaching and want to bring this man's blood upon us." But Peter and the Apostles said in reply, "We must obey God rather than men. The God of our ancestors raised Jesus, though you had him killed by hanging him on a tree. God exalted him at his right hand as leader and savior to grant Israel repentance and forgiveness of sins. We are witnesses of these things, as is the Holy Spirit whom God has given to those who obey him."

When they heard this, they became infuriated and wanted to put them to death.

Reflection

"We must obey God rather than men." What kind of resurrection would we come to know if we lived those words? Few people worship graven images, but in moments of conflict and stress, we often succumb to peer pressure and do what is popular. We need to trust in God to do what he desires.

Prayers *others may be added*

To Christ, the Alpha and the Omega, we pray:

◆ Son of the living God, hear us.

That the Church may continue to be the voice of God in the world, we pray: ◆ For the Holy Spirit's gift of fortitude, we pray: ◆ For those who face persecution or imprisonment for following the dictates of their conscience, we pray: ◆ For an end to racism, sexism, and ageism, we pray: ◆ For hearts that have been hardened by cynicism and skepticism, we pray: ◆

Our Father . . .

God of peace and freedom,
you are the source of all life,
the ground of our existence,
the Holy One who beckons us to yourself.
In a world filled with voices that run contrary to yours,
stir up our faith and, aided by the gifts of the Holy Spirit,
may we stand firm in obeying you and doing your will.
We ask this through Christ our Lord.
Amen.

✝ I believe that I shall see the good things of the Lord in the land of the living.

Friday, April 28, 2017
Easter Weekday

✝ I believe that I shall see the good things of the Lord in the land of the living.

Psalm 27

page 404

Reading

Acts 5:34–36, 38–39

A Pharisee in the Sanhedrin named Gamaliel, a teacher of the law, respected by all the people, stood up, ordered the Apostles to be put outside for a short time, and said to the Sanhedrin, "Fellow children of Israel, be careful what you are about to do to these men. Some time ago, Theudas appeared, claiming to be someone important, and about four hundred men joined him, but he was killed, and all those who were loyal to him were disbanded and came to nothing. So now I tell you, have nothing to do with these men, and let them go. For if this endeavor or this activity is of human origin, it will destroy itself. But if it comes from God, you will not be able to destroy them; you may even find yourselves fighting against God."

Reflection

We live in a culture of "the latest." We watch "breaking news" and follow what is trending and what (and who) is currently "hot." In contrast, the Church, for many people, appears to lag behind, to be slow to respond, to be out of touch. If something is of God, it will continue and bring forth good fruit, if not, it will be supplanted and replaced by the next trend. Patience is not easy. Yet, it has served Christians well for more than two thousand years.

Prayers

others may be added

To Christ, the Alpha and the Omega, we pray:

◆ Son of the living God, hear us.

That together with the Church, we might patiently wait and see, we pray: ◆ For peace in the world, we pray: ◆ For our ancestors in faith, the Jewish people, we pray: ◆ For the gifts of wisdom and discernment, we pray: ◆ For those who have gone before us in the hope of the resurrection, we pray: ◆

Our Father . . .

God of our ancestors,
you protect those who speak your Name.
Help us to accept our part in the history of salvation
and to remember that we are upheld
by a great cloud of witnesses,
as we work to advance the Reign of your Son,
who lives with you in the unity of the Holy Spirit,
one God, for ever and ever.
Amen.

✝ I believe that I shall see the good things of the Lord in the land of the living.

Saturday, April 29, 2017

Memorial of St. Catherine of Siena, Virgin and Doctor of the Church

✝ I believe that I shall see the good things of the Lord in the land of the living.

Psalm 27

page 404

Reading

John 6:16–20

When it was evening, the disciples of Jesus went down to the sea, embarked in a boat, and went across the sea to Capernaum. It had already grown dark, and Jesus had not yet come to them. The sea was stirred up because a strong wind was blowing. When they had rowed about three or four miles, they saw Jesus walking on the sea and coming near the boat, and they began to be afraid. But he said to them, "It is I. Do not be afraid."

Reflection

Catherine of Siena and Teresa of Avila were the first women to be declared "Doctors of the Church." Today's Gospel is fitting for Catherine, insofar as strong winds buffeted the Church in the fourteenth century. Catherine's profound dedication to the Eucharist inspired her to be an ambassador of peace and unity. A remarkable woman for any generation, she worked tirelessly to restore peace among the papal states and was instrumental in the seat of the papacy returning from France to Italy. In iconography, Catherine is sometimes depicted as carrying the "Bark of Peter," the Church, on her shoulders.

Prayers

others may be added

To Christ, the Alpha and the Omega, we pray:

◆ Son of the Living God, hear us.

For unity among Christians and within the Church, we pray: ◆ For lay women who devote themselves to Christ and the Church, we pray: ◆ For the Church in Italy, we pray: ◆ That our dedication to the Eucharist will guide us to be people of peace, we pray: ◆ For those undergoing trials, we pray: ◆

Our Father . . .

God of Providence,
in every generation
you provide refuge and strength
to your people.
As you once called St. Catherine of Siena,
so today open our hearts and minds
to work
for peace and unity in your Church and in
the world,
through your Son, Jesus Christ,
who lives and reigns with you in the unity
of the Holy Spirit,
one God, for ever and ever.
Amen.

✝ I believe that I shall see the good things of the Lord in the land of the living.

Sunday, April 30, 2017
Third Sunday of Easter

✝ Lord, you will show us the path of life.

Psalm 16
page 401

Reading
Luke 24:13–16

That very day, the first day of the week, two of Jesus' disciples were going to a village seven miles from Jerusalem called Emmaus, and they were conversing about all the things that had occurred. And it happened that while they were conversing and debating, Jesus himself drew near and walked with them, but their eyes were prevented from recognizing him.

Reflection

Understandably, we tend to zero in on the Eucharistic dimension of this Gospel. Yet, there are other aspects also to consider. Jesus comes as the stranger. He interprets and opens the Scriptures. We could wonder if the disciples would have recognized him otherwise. This passage is popular because it invites us to enter the world of metaphor. A visitor, a story, bread, wine, a lighted candle, all these and more tell us that the ordinary stuff of our lives is not so ordinary. Beyond function and practicality, the journey to Emmaus suggests the sacramentality of our lives.

Prayers
others may be added

To the Risen Lord, who walks beside us on our way, we pray:

◆ Word of the Father, stay with us.

That the Church may be hearers and servants of God's Word, we pray: ◆ For those celebrating their First Holy Communion, we pray: ◆ For our neophytes and the neophytes throughout the Church, we pray: ◆ That we may be open to Christ's presence in the stranger, we pray: ◆ For those who go hungry this day, we pray: ◆

Our Father . . .

Origin and Source of all that is good,
all that you have provided us can radiate your presence
if we but see with eyes of faith.
Help our eyes to be opened and our hearts to be burning
as we come to know you in Word and sacrament
in the stranger and in ourselves.
We ask this through our Lord Jesus Christ, your Son,
who lives and reigns with you in the unity of the Holy Spirit,
one God, for ever and ever.
Amen.

✝ Lord, you will show us the path of life.

Monday, May 1, 2017
Optional Memorial of St. Joseph the Worker

☩ Lord, you will show us the path of life.

Psalm 16 *page 401*

Reading *John 6:22–29*

[After Jesus had fed the five thousand men, his disciples saw him walking on the sea.] The next day, the crowd that remained across the sea saw that there had been only one boat there, and that Jesus had not gone along with his disciples in the boat, but only his disciples had left. Other boats came from Tiberias near the place where they had eaten the bread when the Lord gave thanks. When the crowd saw that neither Jesus nor his disciples were there, they themselves got into the boats and came to Capernaum looking for Jesus. And when they found him across the sea they said to him, "Rabbi, when did you get here?" Jesus answered them and said, "Amen, amen, I say to you, you are looking for me not because you saw signs but because you ate the loaves and were filled. Do not work for food that perishes but for the food that endures for eternal life, which the Son of Man will give you. For on him the Father, God, has set his seal." So they said to him, "What can we do to accomplish the works of God?" Jesus answered and said to them, "This is the work of God, that you believe in the one he sent."

Reflection

Joseph is described as an "upright man." Like his namesake from the Old Testament, God's messages are communicated to Joseph in his dreams. Joseph does as the angel of the Lord commands him. Joseph exemplifies the words of today's Gospel, "This is the work of God, that you believe in the one he sent." Looking at the example of Joseph, we too ask, "What can we do to accomplish the works of God?"

Prayers *others may be added*

To the Risen Christ, who walks beside us on our way, we pray:

◆ Word of the Father, stay with us.

That the Church may continue to uphold and defend the rights of workers, we pray: ◆ May all our labor be directed to your greater glory and honor, we pray: ◆ For the unemployed and underemployed, we pray: ◆ For those who labor and find life burdensome, we pray: ◆ For those forced to work in unsafe and inhumane conditions, we pray: ◆

Our Father . . .

God of creation,
you call us to be coworkers with you through our labor.
Help all find meaning and purpose in their work.
Help us to stand with those who are in dead-end jobs or cannot find work.
We ask this through Christ our Lord.
Amen.

☩ Lord, you will show us the path of life.

Tuesday, May 2, 2017

Memorial of St. Athanasius, Bishop and Doctor of the Church

† Lord, you will show us the path of life.

Psalm 16

page 401

Reading

John 6:30–35

The crowd said to Jesus: "What sign can you do, that we may see and believe in you? What can you do? Our ancestors ate manna in the desert, as it is written: / *He gave them bread from heaven to eat.*" / So Jesus said to them, "Amen, amen, I say to you, it was not Moses who gave the bread from heaven; my Father gives you the true bread from heaven. For the bread of God is that which comes down from heaven and gives life to the world."

So they said to Jesus, "Sir, give us this bread always." Jesus said to them, "I am the bread of life; whoever comes to me will never hunger, and whoever believes in me will never thirst."

Reflection

St. Gregory Nazianzen declared Athanasius to be "a pillar of the Church." When Bernini designed the Chair of St. Peter for St. Peter's Basilica, he apparently concurred as he made Athanasius one of the four Doctors of the Church upholding Peter's Chair. Athanasius was an assistant at the Council of Nicaea and, as bishop of Alexandria, was a staunch defender of the Creed. His insistence that both the Son and the Holy Spirit were consubstantial with the Father influenced subsequent Church councils.

Prayers

others may be added

To the Risen Lord, who walks beside us on our way, we pray:

◆ Word of the Father, stay with us.

For the Eastern Church, we pray: ◆
For bishops and theologians, we pray: ◆
For a greater appreciation of our spiritual heritage, we pray: ◆ For those who hunger and thirst for righteousness, we pray: ◆ For those living in exile, we pray: ◆

Our Father . . .

Almighty ever-living God,
who raised up St. Athanasius,
as an outstanding champion of your Son's divinity,
mercifully grant
that, rejoicing in his teaching and his protection,
we may never cease to grow in knowledge and love of you.
Through our Lord Jesus Christ, your Son,
who lives and reigns with you in the unity of the Holy Spirit,
one God, for ever and ever.
Amen. (*The Roman Missal*)

† Lord, you will show us the path of life.

Wednesday, May 3, 2017

Feast of Sts. Philip and James, Apostles

✝ Lord, you will show us the path of life.

Psalm 16 *page 401*

Reading *John 14:7–14*

Jesus said to his disciples: "If you know me, then you will also know my Father. From now on you do know him and have seen him." Philip said to him, "Master, show us the Father, and that will be enough for us." Jesus said to him, "Have I been with you for so long a time and you still do not know me, Philip? Whoever has seen me has seen the Father. How can you say, 'Show us the Father'? Do you not believe that I am the Father and the Father is in me? The words that I speak to you I do not speak on my own. The Father who dwells in me is doing his works. Believe me that I am in the Father and the Father is in me, or else, believe because of the works themselves. Amen, amen, I say to you, whoever believes in me will do the works that I do, and will be greater ones than these, because I am going to the Father. And whatever you ask in my name, I will do, so that the Father may be glorified in the Son. If you ask anything of me in my name, I will do it."

Reflection

Today we honor the Apostles Philip and James. This James is sometimes called James "the less." His father is Alphaeus. He is not the James who is the brother of John, nor should he be confused with the James that is related to Jesus; nor is he the author of the Letter of James. James was a very common name in the first century. Philip was from the same town as Peter and Andrew. He asks Jesus to "show us the Father." Earlier in this Gospel Philip invites Nathaniel to "come and see." Note how his words always revolve around seeing.

Prayers *others may be added*

To the Risen Lord, who walks beside us on our way, we pray:

◆ Word of the Father, stay with us.

For the successors to the Apostles, we pray: ◆ That we will invite others to come and see, we pray: ◆ May our words and actions reveal Christ to others, we pray: ◆ For those living in the midst of violence, we pray: ◆ For those parishes that celebrate their patronal feast day today, we pray: ◆

Our Father . . .

Lord our God,
your Son established the Church
on the ministry of the Apostles.
May we continue to faithfully build on that foundation
by proclaiming the Good News of your Reign,
celebrating the sacraments, ministering to the poor,
and laboring for justice and peace.
Through Christ our Lord.
Amen.

✝ Lord, you will show us the path of life.

Thursday, May 4, 2017
Easter Weekday

✝ Lord, you will show us the path of life.

Psalm 16 *page 401*

Reading *John 6:44–51*

[Jesus said to the crowds:] "No one can come to me unless the Father who sent me draw him, and I will raise him on the last day. It is written in the prophets: / *They shall all be taught by God.* / Everyone who listens to my Father and learns from him comes to me. Not that anyone has seen the Father except the one who is from God; he has seen the Father. Amen, amen, I say to you, whoever believes has eternal life. I am the bread of life. Your ancestors ate the manna in the desert but they died; this is the bread that comes from heaven so that one may eat it and not die. I am the living bread that came down from heaven; whoever eats this bread will live forever; and the bread that I will give is my Flesh for the life of the world."

Reflection

Jesus contrasts the bread he gives, his very self, with the manna of the Exodus account. Manna was literally the bread of survival for the tribes of Israel making their way to the Promised Land. Today, we take bread for granted. It doesn't occur to us that bread is the fundamental source of nourishment. When bread becomes an accessory, how can that not impact our appreciation of the Eucharist? Perhaps one needs to be hungry to grasp of Jesus' words.

Prayers *others may be added*

To the Risen Lord, who walks beside us on our way, we pray:

◆ Word of the Father, hear our prayer.

That the pilgrim Church may be nourished by the Bread of Life and Chalice of Blessing, we pray: ◆ For a greater understanding and respect for the Eucharist, we pray: ◆ For those living with celiac disease, we pray: ◆ For those who have no food to eat today, we pray: ◆ For the grace to live a simpler lifestyle, we pray: ◆

Our Father . . .

Lord Jesus,
you lovingly remind us not to fill our lives and ourselves
with that which fails to satisfy our deepest hungers.
You have already provided us with all we truly need,
the gift of yourself in the most holy sacrament of the altar,
for you live and reign with God the Father in the unity of the Holy Spirit,
one God, for ever and ever.
Amen.

✝ Lord, you will show us the path of life.

Friday, May 5, 2017
Easter Weekday

☩ Lord, you will show us the path of life.

Psalm 16 *page 401*

Reading *Acts 9:10–11, 13, 15–18*

There was a disciple in Damascus named Ananias, and the Lord said to him in a vision, "Ananias." He answered, "Here I am, Lord." The Lord said to him, "Get up and go . . . ask at the house of Judas for a man . . . named Saul. . . ." But Ananias replied, "Lord, I have heard from many sources about this man, what evil things he has done to your holy ones in Jerusalem. . . ." But the Lord said to him, "Go, for this man is a chosen instrument of mine to carry my name before Gentiles, kings, and children of Israel, and I will show him what he will have to suffer for my name." So Ananias went and entered the house; laying his hands on him, he said, "Saul, my brother, the Lord has sent me . . . that you may regain your sight and be filled with the Holy Spirit." Immediately things like scales fell from his eyes and he regained his sight.

Reflection

The story of Paul's conversion is fitting during this season. Paul journeyed from death to new life, from persecutor to apostle and evangelist. Perhaps there is another, somewhat disguised conversion in all this. We read of Saul "breathing murderous threats against the disciples of the Lord." We live in a time of renewed hostility rooted in religion. Yet the early Christians did not respond to Saul's threats with like threats or retaliation. They just tried to avoid him. Perhaps that is not a viable option in a global village. Then again, how easily can we dismiss the example and the witness of the early Church?

Prayers *others may be added*

To the Risen Lord, who walks beside us on our way, we pray:

◆ Word of the Father, hear our prayer.

That people of all faith traditions be able to worship freely and unhindered, we pray: ◆ For a lessening of violence in our world, our neighborhoods, and our hearts, we pray: ◆ For those who use religion to terrorize and oppress, that they may reform and receive a spirit of compassion, we pray: ◆ For the men and women serving in the Peace Corps, we pray: ◆ That perpetual light may shine on those who have died, we pray: ◆

Our Father . . .

Lord of Life,
you show us the way to you.
Help us to find a way beyond the fear
and violence
that so profoundly limits our love.
Through our Lord Jesus Christ, who lives
and reigns with you
in the unity of the Holy Spirit,
one God, for ever and ever.
Amen.

☩ Lord, you will show us the path of life.

Saturday, May 6, 2017
Easter Weekday

✝ Lord, you will show us the path of life

Psalm 16 *page 401*

Reading *Acts 9:32–33, 36–40*

As Peter was passing through every region, he went down to the holy ones living in Lydda. There he found a man named Aeneas, who had been confined to bed for eight years, for he was paralyzed. Peter said to him, "Aeneas, Jesus Christ heals you. Get up and make your bed." He got up at once.

Now in Joppa there was a disciple named Tabitha. . . . Now during those days she fell sick and died. . . . Since Lydda was near Joppa, the disciples, hearing that Peter was there, sent two men to him with the request, "Please come to us without delay." So Peter got up and went with them. When he arrived, they took him to the room upstairs where all the widows came to him weeping. . . . Peter sent them all out and knelt down and prayed. Then he turned to her body and said, "Tabitha, rise up."

Reflection

Earlier in the Acts of the Apostles, Peter healed a lame man (Acts 3) and today he cures a paralytic and then raises Tabitha from the dead. Luke, the author of the Acts of the Apostles, desires to show the continuity between Jesus and the Church, so he portrays the Church as continuing the healing ministry of Jesus. We do not have to limit our understanding of healing to the literal and physical. We can help the weak of faith to walk, we can release those frozen by fear, we can restore life to the downtrodden. How might you share in the ministry of healing?

Prayers *others may be added*

To the Risen Lord, who walks beside us on our way, we pray:

◆ Word of the Father, hear our prayer.

May the Church be a healing balm for the wounded, we pray: ◆ That our parishes will be communities that welcome the broken and hurting, we pray: ◆ For physicians, therapists, and all who work to heal others, we pray: ◆ For those experiencing conflict and pain in their marriage, we pray: ◆ For those living with depression, we pray: ◆

Our Father . . .

Lord Jesus,
you have conquered sin and death,
you are the healer of our every ill.
Let us know your presence in
our suffering
and allow you to touch us with healing,
even as we strive to be a balm to others
who live in pain and brokenness.
You live and reign with God the Father in
the unity of the Holy Spirit,
one God, for ever and ever.
Amen.

✝ Lord, you will show us the path of life.

Sunday, May 7, 2017
Fourth Sunday of Easter

✝ The Lord is my shepherd; there is nothing I shall want.

Psalm 23
page 403

Reading
John 10:1–6

Jesus said "Amen, amen, I say to you, whoever does not enter a sheepfold through the gate but climbs over elsewhere is a thief and a robber. But whoever enters through the gate is the shepherd of the sheep. The gatekeeper opens it for him, and the sheep hear his voice, as he calls his own sheep by name and leads them out. When he has driven out all his own, he walks ahead of them, and the sheep follow him, because they recognize his voice. But they will not follow a stranger; they will run away from him, because they do not recognize the voice of strangers." Although Jesus used this figure of speech, they did not realize what he was trying to tell them.

Reflection
The sheep follow their master because they recognize his voice. How do you listen for the voice of the Good Shepherd? To discern and hear our Lord requires practice. We practice being aware of living in God's presence, listening in prayer, immersing ourselves in the Scriptures and identifying our story in those stories, knowing him in the breaking of the bread and in the poor and needy.

Prayers
others may be added

To Christ, the Good Shepherd who guides us, we pray:

◆ Shepherd of Israel, hear us.

For all who shepherd the Church today, we pray: ◆ That all heads of state and leaders in government put service before self-interests, we pray: ◆ For the gift to discern and the faith to follow the voice of the Good Shepherd, we pray: ◆ For the sick and homebound, we pray: ◆ For an end to the abuse and torture of animals, we pray: ◆

Our Father . . .

God of all,
your care and providence extend to all that is.
By the sacrifice of the Good Shepherd laying down his life,
guide all creation to dwell peacefully in eternal pastures.
Through our Lord Jesus Christ, your Son,
who lives and reigns with you in the unity of the Holy Spirit,
one God, for ever and ever.
Amen.

✝ The Lord is my shepherd; there is nothing I shall want.

Monday, May 8, 2017
Easter Weekday

✝ The Lord is my shepherd; there is nothing I shall want.

Psalm 23 *page 403*

Reading *John 10:11–16*

Jesus said: "I am the good shepherd. A good shepherd lays down his life for the sheep. A hired man, who is not a shepherd and whose sheep are not his own, sees a wolf coming and leaves the sheep and runs away, and the wolf catches and scatters them. This is because he works for pay and has no concern for the sheep. I am the good shepherd, and I know mine and mine know me, just as the Father knows me and I know the Father; and I will lay down my life for the sheep. I have other sheep that do not belong to this fold. These also I must lead, and they will hear my voice, and there will be one flock, one shepherd."

Reflection

"I have other sheep that do not belong to this fold. These also I must lead." One of the remarkable teachings coming from the Second Vatican Council was that, "All are called to this catholic unity . . . and to it belong, or are related in different ways: the catholic faithful, others who believe in Christ, and finally all of humankind" (*Lumen Gentium*, 13). That which is true, holy, and beneficial to salvation in any faith is because Christ is present, albeit not fully. Today we honor those "that do not belong to this fold" but for whom even unknowingly Christ is present.

Prayers *others may be added*

To Christ, the Good Shepherd who guides us, we pray:

◆ Shepherd of Israel, hear us.

For all who profess faith in Christ Jesus, we pray: ◆ For neophytes, catechumens, and inquirers, we pray: ◆ For Jews and Muslims, who share with us Abraham, our ancestor in faith, we pray: ◆ For those who seek God in sincerity and obey the dictates of their conscience, we pray: ◆ For those who have not heard the Gospel, we pray: ◆

Our Father . . .

Almighty ever-living God,
you sent the Good Shepherd to guide us.
Grant to those who do not confess
Christ that,
by walking before you with a
sincere heart,
they may find the truth and that
we ourselves,
being constant in mutual love
and striving to understand more fully the
mystery of your life,
may be made more perfect witnesses
to your love in the world.
Through Christ our Lord.
Amen. (*The Roman Missal*)

✝ The Lord is my shepherd; there is nothing I shall want.

Tuesday, May 9, 2017
Easter Weekday

✝ The Lord is my shepherd; there is nothing I shall want.

Psalm 23

page 403

Reading

Acts 11:19–23

Those who had been scattered by the persecution that arose because of Stephen went as far as Phoenicia, Cyprus, and Antioch, preaching the word to no one but Jews. There were some Cypriots and Cyrenians among them, however, who came to Antioch and began to speak to the Greeks as well, proclaiming the Lord Jesus. The hand of the Lord was with them and a great number who believed turned to the Lord. The news about them reached the ears of the Church in Jerusalem, and they sent Barnabas to go to Antioch. When he arrived and saw the grace of God, he rejoiced and encouraged them all to remain faithful to the Lord in firmness of heart.

Reflection

We all want to belong. The nascent Church initially saw itself as part of Judaism. Then Gentiles began to convert in great numbers, as we read today. This resulted in tensions over the community's self-identity; who could belong and what practices to accept. For some communities of faith, these concerns remain today as we welcome Hispanic, Vietnamese, Arabic, Filipino, and others with varied and different customs to our parishes. Our focus, as we read today, must be "to remain faithful to the Lord in firmness of heart."

Prayers

others may be added

To the Good Shepherd, who guides us to abundant life, we pray:

◆ Shepherd of Israel, hear us.

That the Church will be a house of welcome and of prayer for all people, we pray: ◆ That disciples will remain faithful to Christ, we pray: ◆ That we will rejoice in the diversity of cultures and customs that comprise our Church, we pray: ◆ For parishes undergoing transitions, we pray: ◆ For those who do not believe in God, we pray: ◆

Our Father . . .

God of all,
you have embraced
peoples around the world.
May our fidelity to Christ,
the rich diversity of our Church,
and the witness of service to others,
invite more people to faith in your Son,
our Lord Jesus Christ,
who lives and reigns with you in the unity
of the Holy Spirit,
one God, for ever and ever
Amen.

✝ The Lord is my shepherd; there is nothing I shall want.

Wednesday, May 10, 2017

Optional Memorial of St. Damien de Veuster, Priest

✝ The Lord is my shepherd; there is nothing I shall want.

Psalm 23

page 403

Reading

Acts 12:24—13:5a

The word of God continued to spread and grow.

After Barnabas and Saul completed their relief mission, they returned to Jerusalem, taking with them John, who is called Mark.

Now there were in the Church at Antioch prophets and teachers: Barnabas, Symeon who was called Niger, Lucius of Cyrene, Manaen who was a close friend of Herod the tetrarch, and Saul. While they were worshiping the Lord and fasting, the holy Spirit said, "Set apart for me Barnabas and Saul for the work to which I have called them." Then, completing their fasting and prayer, they laid hands on them and sent them off.

So they, sent forth by the Holy Spirit, went down to Seleucia and from there sailed to Cyprus. When they arrived in Salamis, they proclaimed the word of God in the Jewish synagogues.

Reflection

If you are of a certain age, St. Damien is to you who St. Teresa of Calcutta would be to a subsequent generation. Like Barnabas and Saul, who were called for a particular work, Father Damien and St. Marianne Cope, OSF, went to the isolated Hawaiian island of Molokai to minister to lepers. At that time, those with leprosy were discarded and left to fend for themselves. Sts. Damien and Marianne brought the hope and healing of Christ, transforming chaos into community. Damien became fully one with those he served. He contracted leprosy and died in 1889.

Prayers

others may be added

To the Good Shepherd, who guides us to abundant life, we pray:

◆ Shepherd of Israel, hear us.

May the Church continue to be a symbol of hope and healing, we pray: ◆ That community leaders will seek to protect those whom others discard, we pray: ◆ That those who feel isolated may find companionship and community, we pray: ◆ For people afflicted with Hansen's disease (leprosy), we pray: ◆ For parishes under the patronage of St. Damien, celebrating their feast day today, we pray: ◆

Our Father . . .

Risen Christ,
vanquisher of death,
you did not deem equality with God
something to be grasped,
but humbled yourself to share in
our humanity.
May we humble ourselves to reach out
to those on the margins of our community
and so honor the humanity of all.
You live and reign with God the Father in
the unity of the Holy Spirit,
one God, for ever and ever.
Amen

✝ The Lord is my shepherd; there is nothing I shall want.

Thursday, May 11, 2017
Easter Weekday

✝ The Lord is my shepherd; there is nothing I shall want.

Psalm 23 *page 403*

Reading *Acts 13:16–18, 22–25*

So Paul got up, motioned with his hand, and said, "Fellow children of Israel . . . listen. The God of this people Israel chose our ancestors and exalted the people during their sojourn in the land of Egypt. With uplifted arm he led them out, and for about forty years he put up with them in the desert. [He] raised up David as their king; of him he testified, / *I have found David, son of Jesse, a man after my own heart; / he will carry out my every wish.* / From this man's descendants God, according to his promise, has brought to Israel a savior, Jesus. John heralded his coming by proclaiming a baptism of repentance to all the people of Israel; and as John was completing his course, he would say, 'What do you suppose that I am? I am not he. Behold, one is coming after me; I am not worthy to unfasten the sandals of his feet.'"

Reflection

New Testament scholars maintain that the Gospel of Luke and the Acts of the Apostles are written by the same author. One of the recurring themes in the writings of Luke/Acts is that of continuity from Israel to Christ to the Church. Here we have a portion of what must have been a lengthy exhortation delivered by Paul. Beginning with the Exodus, Paul recounts the story of salvation up through the ministry of John the Baptist. What do you know of your family's faith history? Perhaps you want to preserve that story so as to share it with future generations.

Prayers *others may be added*

To the Good Shepherd, who guides us to abundant life, we pray:

◆ Shepherd of Israel, hear us.

May Christians know and appreciate their rich spiritual history, we pray: ◆ That family members share their faith with one another, we pray: ◆ For orphans, refugees, and those removed from their family, we pray: ◆ For novelists, screenwriters, and playwrights who tell stories that move and inspire us, we pray: ◆ For the grace to hear the story of another, we pray: ◆

Our Father . . .

Loving God,
by the Holy Spirit you inspired the sacred authors
to share their faith and the experience of their faith communities
in which you revealed yourself.
In the fullness of time,
you sent us your Only Begotten Son,
the Word made flesh.
May we be so moved to share our sacred story with those we love.
We ask this through Christ our Lord.
Amen.

✝ The Lord is my shepherd; there is nothing I shall want.

Friday, May 12, 2017
Easter Weekday

✝ The Lord is my shepherd; there is nothing I shall want.

Psalm 23 *page 403*

Reading *John 14:1–6*

Jesus said to his disciples, "Do not let your hearts be troubled. You have faith in God; have faith also in me. In my Father's house there are many dwelling places. If there were not, would I have told you that I am going to prepare a place for you? And if I go and prepare a place for you, I will come back again and take you to myself, so that where I am you also may be. Where I am going you know the way." Thomas said to him, "Master, we do not know where you are going; how can we know the way?" Jesus said to him, "I am the way and the truth and the life. No one comes to the Father except through me."

Reflection

We have become accustomed to people sidestepping questions. So at first, when Thomas asks Jesus about the way and Jesus responds that he is the way, it might sound evasive. Jesus, in fact, is responding as directly as possible. Prior to the teachings in creeds and doctrines and in spiritual practices is faith in the person of Jesus Christ. In Jesus we do not merely learn about God, we meet God, we come to know and experience who God is. Jesus' invitation to "come and see" earlier in the Gospel is the invitation to intimately know Christ.

Prayers *others may be added*

To the Good Shepherd, who guides us to abundant life, we pray:

◆ Shepherd of Israel, hear us.

That the People of God may have a more intimate relationship with Christ, we pray: ◆ For an abiding hunger and thirst to know the Word of God, we pray: ◆ For those who struggle to find their way, we pray: ◆ For those who have prepared a place for us, we pray: ◆ For those whom our Risen Lord has taken to himself, we pray: ◆

Our Father . . .

Lord,
Son of the Father,
you have promised to prepare a place
for us
and to take us to yourself.
Hold us to yourself this day.
May we feel your loving and
understanding embrace today
and at the hour when you bring us to
your Father,
who lives and reigns with you in the unity
of the Holy Spirit,
one God, for ever and ever.
Amen.

✝ The Lord is my shepherd; there is nothing I shall want.

Saturday, May 13, 2017
Easter Weekday

☩ The Lord is my shepherd; there is nothing I shall want.

Psalm 23
page 403

Reading
Acts 13:44–47

On the following sabbath almost the whole city gathered to hear the word of the Lord. When the Jews saw the crowds, they were filled with jealousy and with violent abuse contradicted what Paul said. Both Paul and Barnabas spoke out boldly and said, "It was necessary that the word of God be spoken to you first, but since you reject it and condemn yourselves as unworthy of eternal life, we now turn to the Gentiles. For so the Lord has commanded us, *I have made you a light to the Gentiles, that you may be an instrument of salvation to the ends of the earth.*"

Reflection
In this selection from Acts, the message of Paul and Barnabas is soundly rejected by their own people. For many parents and grandparents, what occurs in this passage is way too close to home. Family elders, together with pastors and catechists, worry over, "What did I do wrong? How could I have done better? Is there something I'm missing or lacking?" We tend to be hard on ourselves in these matters. We must also humbly acknowledge our limitation. Many things play a part in an individual's not hearing the Good News. Sometimes we just need to be patient.

Prayers
others may be added

To the Good Shepherd, who guides us to abundant life, we pray:

◆ Shepherd of Israel, hear us.

That the Body of Christ never cease reaching out to nonpracticing members, we pray: ◆ For parents and grandparents who are hurting because of their family's lack of faith, we pray: ◆ For Catholics who have become estranged or alienated from the Church, we pray: ◆ For people who disrespect the faith of others, that they will come to know the Good News, we pray: ◆ That we do not become discouraged or lose heart, we pray: ◆

Our Father . . .

Abba, Father,
you have instilled faith within us.
Aid us as we seek to pass along our faith
in you to family and those we meet.
When some move away from the faith,
help us not to judge,
for that belongs to you alone.
We ask this through our Lord Jesus
Christ, your Son,
who lives and reigns with you in the unity
of the Holy Spirit,
one God, for ever and ever.
Amen.

☩ The Lord is my shepherd; there is nothing I shall want.

Sunday, May 14, 2017
Fifth Sunday of Easter

✝ May the peoples praise you, O God; may all the peoples praise you.

Psalm 67
page 408

Reading
John 14:1–6

Jesus said to his disciples, "Do not let your hearts be troubled. You have faith in God; have faith also in me. In my Father's house there are many dwelling places. If there were not, would I have told you that I am going to prepare a place for you? And if I go and prepare a place for you, I will come back again and take you to myself, so that where I am you also may be. Where I am going you know the way." Thomas said to him, "Master, we do not know where you are going; how can we know the way?" Jesus said to him, "I am the way and the truth and the life. No one comes to the Father except through me."

Reflection
Later in this Gospel, Jesus says, "Believe me that I am in the Father and the Father is in me, or else believe because of the works themselves." Though some struggle to confess faith in Christ, the works Christ performed can draw them toward faith. To that end, we must ensure that we and our parishes are doing what Christ did: healing, feeding, forgiving, and standing with the outcast and the sinner. This can be a powerful summons to Christ, especially to teens and young adults.

Prayers
others may be added

To Jesus Christ, who is our Way, our Truth, and our Life, we pray:

◆ Sun of Justice, hear our prayer.

May the Church reach out in hospitality to all, we pray: ◆ That the Holy Spirit inspire in us actions that are faithful to the example of Christ, we pray: ◆ For the neophytes throughout the Church, we pray: ◆ That the goodness of life, from conception to natural death, is recognized, we pray: ◆ For those who have lost their way, we pray: ◆

Our Father . . .

Risen Lord,
you are the way that leads us to
the Father,
the truth that reveals the Father,
the life that is one with the Father.
Through the gift of your Holy Spirit,
take us to yourself
so that we may always be in
your presence.
You live and reign with God the Father
in the unity of the Holy Spirit,
one God, for ever and ever.
Amen.

✝ May the peoples praise you, O God; may all the peoples praise you.

Monday, May 15, 2017

Easter Weekday

☩ May the peoples praise you, O God;
may all the peoples praise you.

Psalm 67

page 408

Reading

Acts 14:8–13

At Lystra there was a crippled man, lame from birth, who had never walked. He listened to Paul speaking, who looked intently at him, saw that he had the faith to be healed, and called out in a loud voice, "Stand up straight on your feet." He jumped up and began to walk about. When the crowds saw what Paul had done, they cried out in Lycaonian, "The gods have come down to us in human form." They called Barnabas "Zeus" and Paul "Hermes," because he was the chief speaker. And the priest of Zeus, whose temple was at the entrance to the city, brought oxen and garlands to the gates, for he together with the people intended to offer sacrifice.

Reflection

The crowds want to offer sacrifice to Paul and Barnabas, mistaking them to be gods in human form. It is funny, on one level; a twisted incarnation, on another; and yet, oddly contemporary as well. We live in a world of "the celebrity." The Church's ministers are not exempt from this. But when the messenger is the message we lose sight of Christ. While motives are never pure, there is a danger in performing ministry out of our need to be helpful or feel good about ourself. It is not about us. It is about Christ.

Prayers

others may be added

To Jesus Christ, who is our Way, our Truth, and our Life, we pray:

◆ Sun of Justice, hear our prayer.

That the Church will continue to be the sign of Christ and salvation, we pray: ◆ That those who serve others will be witnesses to the Reign of God, we pray: ◆ For those who worship the false gods of fame, wealth, and power, that they may see the Light, we pray: ◆ For the gift of humility, we pray: ◆ For those who are physically challenged, we pray: ◆

Our Father . . .

All-powerful God,
you have given us the task
of being Christ for others.
Instill in us humility that we may
honor those we meet in your Name.
May we find the presence of your Son in
those near and far,
for he lives and reigns with you in the
unity of the Holy Spirit,
one God, for ever and ever.
Amen.

☩ May the peoples praise you, O God;
may all the peoples praise you.

Tuesday, May 16, 2017
Easter Weekday

✝ May the peoples praise you, O God;
may all the peoples praise you.

Psalm 67

page 408

Reading

John 14:27–31a

Jesus said to his disciples: "Peace I leave with you; my peace I give to you. Not as the world gives do I give it to you. Do not let your hearts be troubled or afraid. You heard me tell you, 'I am going away and I will come back to you.' If you loved me, you would rejoice that I am going to the Father; for the Father is greater than I. And now I have told you this before it happens, so that when it happens you may believe. I will no longer speak much with you, for the ruler of the world is coming. He has no power over me, but the world must know that I love the Father and that I do just as the Father has commanded me."

Reflection

"Peace I leave with you; my peace I give to you." We pray these words before offering one another a sign of peace. We pray for the peace and unity of the Church, perhaps forgetting that the peace Jesus gives is not the peace the world gives. What the world considers peace is merely a façade of peace, a false peace that, more often than not, is merely the absence of conflict. And that lack of conflict is reserved for those who "count." Jesus offers a peace with justice, equality, mercy, and freedom; a peace that abides within and beyond our external condition.

Prayers

others may be added

To Jesus Christ, who is our Way,
our Truth, and our Life, we pray:

◆ Sun of Justice, hear our prayer.

That the Church, in the midst of conflict and division, has the courage to proclaim peace, we pray: ◆ That nations may seek the way of peace together, we pray: ◆ For those who serve as arbitrators and mediators, we pray: ◆ May the peace of Christ reign in our hearts, we pray: ◆ That we may be peacemakers, we pray: ◆

Our Father . . .

Good and gracious God,
peace is so elusive.
We often find it missing among nations,
neighbors, families, and within
our beings.
Yet Jesus gave us his gift of peace
so that our hearts would not be troubled
or afraid.
Help us to let go of all that prevents us
from this peace.
Through our Lord Jesus Christ, your Son,
who lives and reigns with you in the unity
of the Holy Spirit,
one God, for ever and ever
Amen.

✝ May the peoples praise you, O God;
may all the peoples praise you.

Wednesday, May 17, 2017
Easter Weekday

✝ May the peoples praise you, O God;
may all the peoples praise you.

Psalm 67 *page 408*

Reading *Acts 15:1–6*

Some who had come down from Judea were instructing the brothers, "Unless you are circumcised according to the Mosaic practice, you cannot be saved." Because there arose no little dissension and debate by Paul and Barnabas with them, it was decided that Paul, Barnabas, and some of the others should go up to Jerusalem to the Apostles and presbyters about this question. They were sent on their journey by the Church. . . . When they arrived in Jerusalem, they were welcomed by the Church, as well as by the Apostles and the presbyters, and they reported what God had done with them. But some from the party of the Pharisees who had become believers stood up and said, "It is necessary to circumcise them and direct them to observe the Mosaic law."

The Apostles and the presbyters met together to see about this matter.

Reflection

The young Church faces its first major internal hurdle: must Gentile converts observe the Law of Moses? Paul and Barnabas go to Jerusalem to consult with the Apostles and presbyters. This meeting in Jerusalem is sometimes considered the first council of the Church. The question will be answered in the negative. Still, it will take some time for that decision to be fully received. James, the leader of the Church in Jerusalem, is disappointed with the decision. This meeting establishes the practice of church councils. It also reminds us that the teaching of a council is never met with unanimous approval.

Prayers *others may be added*

To Jesus Christ, who is our Way, our Truth, and our Life, we pray:

◆ Sun of Justice, hear our prayer.

For our bishops, we pray: ◆ For unity among Christians, we pray: ◆ For our president, members of Congress, and Supreme Court justices, we pray: ◆ That we may be open to opinions that go against our own, we pray: ◆ For those who respectfully dissent, we pray: ◆

Our Father . . .

Lord God,
you are with us in our difficulties and conflicts.
Grant us perseverance and patience.
Teach us to respectfully listen to one another
and be open to dreams beyond our own.
Through our Lord Jesus Christ, your Son,
who lives and reigns with you in the unity of the Holy Spirit,
one God, for ever and ever.
Amen.

✝ May the peoples praise you, O God;
may all the peoples praise you.

Thursday, May 18, 2017
Easter Weekday

✝ **May the peoples praise you, O God; may all the peoples praise you.**

Psalm 67

page 408

Reading

Acts 15:7–12

Peter . . . said to the Apostles and the presbyters, "My brothers, you are well aware that . . . God made his choice among you that through my mouth the Gentiles would hear the word of the Gospel and believe. And God, who knows the heart, bore witness by granting them the Holy Spirit just as he did us. He made no distinction between us and them, for by faith he purified their hearts. Why, then, are you now putting God to the test by placing on the shoulders of the disciples a yoke that neither our ancestors nor we have been able to bear? On the contrary, we believe that we are saved through the grace of the Lord Jesus, in the same way as they." The whole assembly . . . listened while Paul and Barnabas described the signs and wonders God had worked among the Gentiles through them.

Reflection

"We believe that we are saved through the grace of the Lord Jesus, in the same way as they." Yes, but how hard is this to believe? Those of another religion are saved in the same way as ourselves. But shouldn't we be "more saved," don't we deserve a higher status, we are the followers of Jesus after all, does that not give us a prior claim, make us "special?" It is difficult, at times, for us to acknowledge the magnanimous love of God, especially when it comes to those we don't know or understand. We forget that God knows and understands them.

Prayers

others may be added

To Jesus Christ, who is our Way, our Truth, and our Life, we pray:

◆ **Sun of Justice, hear our prayer.**

That the Church have confidence and trust in the Holy Spirit, we pray: ◆ For our ancestors in faith, the Jewish people, we pray: ◆ For families in which members can be honest and feel safe, we pray: ◆ For those living with chronic illness, we pray: ◆ For those who struggle to believe or to remain faithful, we pray: ◆

Our Father . . .

Loving Father,
you love all of your children.
Teach us that our value and worth
come from being made
in your image and likeness
and redeemed by our Lord Jesus Christ,
your Son,
who lives and reigns with you in the unity
of the Holy Spirit,
one God, for ever and ever.
Amen.

✝ **May the peoples praise you, O God; may all the peoples praise you.**

Friday, May 19, 2017
Easter Weekday

† May the peoples praise you, O God;
may all the peoples praise you.

Psalm 67 *page 408*

Reading *John 15:12–16*

Jesus said to his disciples: "This is my commandment: love one another as I love you. No one has greater love than this, to lay down one's life for one's friends. You are my friends if you do what I command you. I no longer call you slaves, because a slave does not know what his master is doing. I have called you friends, because I have told you everything I have heard from my Father. It was not you who chose me, but I who chose you and appointed you to go and bear fruit that will remain, so that whatever you ask the Father in my name he may give you."

Reflection

Easter Time brings us face to face with our baptismal call to serve, to be priest, prophet, and king. "It was not you who chose me, but I who chose you." If we are baptized, then Christ has called us. Maybe we wish he hadn't. Perhaps like Jonah we want to run away, but to whom would we go? We have been chosen. God's choice does not make us privileged. We have been chosen to serve, to wash feet, to lay down our lives to love as the one who chose us loves.

Prayers *others may be added*

To Jesus Christ, who is our Way, our Truth, and our Life, we pray:

◆ Sun of Justice, hear our prayer.

May the Church be in the midst of the world as one who serves, we pray: ◆ That we may keep the day of our Baptism even as we keep the day of our birth, we pray: ◆ For community leaders, that they will nourish those in their care, we pray: ◆ For police, firefighters, emergency medical personnel, and other first responders, we pray: ◆ For family members and friends who have died, we pray: ◆

Our Father . . .

Lord Jesus,
you ask us to love as you love.
Help us to show your love even when we are weary.
You live and reign with God the Father in the unity of the Holy Spirit,
one God, for ever and ever.
Amen.

† May the peoples praise you, O God;
may all the peoples praise you.

Saturday, May 20, 2017
Easter Weekday

✝ May the peoples praise you, O God;
may all the peoples praise you.

Psalm 67 *page 408*

Reading *John 15:18–21*

Jesus said to his disciples: "If the world hates you, realize that it hated me first. If you belonged to the world, the world would love its own; but because you do not belong to the world, and I have chosen you out of the world, the world hates you. Remember the word I spoke to you, 'No slave is greater than his master.' If they persecuted me, they will also persecute you. If they kept my word, they will also keep yours. And they will do all these things to you on account of my name, because they do not know the One who sent me."

Reflection

We do not belong to this world. There is an ancient spiritual perspective that speaks of this life as being our exile. Our true home is with God in Christ. Sometimes we feel as if we don't belong. So we try hard to fit in and to be like everyone else. If we share this feeling, others will attempt to make us feel "at home." Perhaps, instead of running from feelings of not belonging, we may want to embrace them, as hard as that can be. How open am I to living "in exile"?

Prayers *others may be added*

To Jesus Christ, who is our Way, our Truth, and our Life, we pray:

◆ Sun of Justice, hear our prayer.

That our Church will reach out in welcome to all, we pray: ◆ That we may guard against materialism in our lives, we pray: ◆ That our nation's leaders will be concerned with seeking justice, we pray: ◆ For the poor, that they may feel God's comfort, we pray: ◆ For those who will die from starvation today, we pray: ◆

Our Father . . .

Creator of all,
you have provided us with a world of beauty and splendor,
teeming with life and abundance.
May we not become attached to wealth, fame, or material goods,
but as faithful stewards,
use your gifts for the welfare and care of others.
We ask this through Christ our Lord.
Amen.

✝ May the peoples praise you, O God;
may all the peoples praise you.

Sunday, May 21, 2017
Sixth Sunday of Easter

✝ All the ends of the earth have seen the saving power of God.

Psalm 98 *page 414*

Reading *John 14:15–17*

Jesus said to his disciples: "If you love me, you will keep my commandments. And I will ask the Father, and he will give you another Advocate to be with you always, the Spirit of truth, whom the world cannot accept, because it neither sees nor knows him. But you know him, because he remains with you, and will be in you."

Reflection

Julian of Norwich wrote of the experience of our union with God as "oneing." The language of today's Scripture is similar. Jesus promises that the Holy Spirit "will be in you." Of himself, Jesus says that, "I will come to you" and that "you are in me and I in you." Our relationship with Jesus is to be so close, so intimate, that we are as spouses or best friends—able to know and anticipate what the other would think, say, or do in a given situation. Jesus calls us to a "oneing" relationship with him.

Prayers *others may be added*

To the Conqueror of sin and death, we pray:

◆ Lord Jesus, abide with us.

That the Church be more fully the presence of Christ to the world, we pray: ◆ May all the baptized grow in their knowledge and experience of the Risen Lord, we pray: ◆ That we may truly honor the Sabbath, we pray: ◆ For those who share in the Sacrament of Matrimony, we pray: ◆ For those who are lonely, we pray: ◆

Our Father . . .

Lord God,
you declared us to be "very good"
and sent your Son to share in our humanity.
May we also seek you in prayer and worship,
in your Word and sacraments, in wisdom and service.
We ask this through our Lord Jesus Christ, your Son,
who lives and reigns with you in the unity of the Holy Spirit,
one God, for ever and ever.
Amen.

✝ All the ends of the earth have seen the saving power of God.

Monday, May 22, 2017
Easter Weekday

✝ All the ends of the earth have seen the saving power of God.

Psalm 98 *page 414*

Reading *Acts 16:11–15*

We set sail from Troas, making a straight run for Samothrace, and on the next day to Neapolis, and from there to Philippi, a leading city in that district of Macedonia and a Roman colony. We spent some time in that city. On the sabbath we went outside the city gate along the river where we thought there would be a place of prayer. We sat and spoke with the women who had gathered there. One of them, a woman named Lydia, a dealer in purple cloth, from the city of Thyatira, a worshiper of God, listened, and the Lord opened her heart to pay attention to what Paul was saying. After she and her household had been baptized, she offered us an invitation, "If you consider me a believer in the Lord, come and stay at my home," and she prevailed on us.

Reflection

Have you ever met someone whose expression of hospitality was not so much invitation as it was imperative, for example: "You will have dinner with us. You will stay at my home." That is the impression we get of Lydia. She was apparently an independent woman of business, a first-century rarity. No wonder that she "prevailed" on Paul, Silas, and Timothy. Lydia's example of hospitality prevails on us to be welcoming.

Prayers *others may be added*

To the Conqueror of sin and death, we pray:

◆ Lord, hear our prayer.

May the Church be a house of prayer for all people, we pray: ◆ For our brothers and sisters of the Orthodox Churches, we pray: ◆ That we may welcome visitors and guests as Christ, we pray: ◆ For the many faithful women who devotedly serve the Church in lay ministry, we pray: ◆ For servers, maids, cooks, and all who work in occupations of hospitality, we pray: ◆

Our Father . . .

Son of the Father,
after your Resurrection,
you first revealed yourself to the faithful
women who had followed you.
As your servant Lydia extended
hospitality to the Apostles,
so may we welcome the stranger at
our door,
for you live and reign with God the Father
in the unity of the Holy Spirit,
one God, for ever and ever.
Amen.

✝ All the ends of the earth have seen the saving power of God.

Tuesday, May 23, 2017
Easter Weekday

† All the ends of the earth have seen the saving power of God.

Psalm 98 *page 414*

Reading *Acts 16:25–31*

About midnight, while Paul and Silas were praying and singing hymns to God as the prisoners listened, there was suddenly such a severe earthquake that the foundations of the jail shook; all the doors flew open, and the chains of all were pulled loose. When the jailer woke up and saw the prison doors wide open, he drew his sword and was about to kill himself, thinking that the prisoners had escaped. But Paul shouted out in a loud voice, "Do no harm to yourself; we are all here." He asked for a light and rushed in and, trembling with fear, he fell down before Paul and Silas. Then he brought them out and said, "Sirs, what must I do to be saved?" And they said, "Believe in the Lord Jesus and you and your household will be saved."

Reflection

Paul and Silas refuse to take advantage of the earthquake and escape from jail. Such an action might have resulted in the jailer's death. Moved that the men did not flee, and by their subsequent preaching, the jailer seeks to be a follower. It would have been possible for Paul and Silas to view the earthquake as God's gift. They could have escaped. Instead, demonstrating concern for their jailer, they refused to take advantage of a serendipitous act of nature. How many of us would do the same?

Prayers *others may be added*

To the Conqueror of sin and death, we pray:

◆ Gracious Lord, hear us.

For Christians in conflict-ridden zones, and all the faithful who suffer persecution, we pray: ◆ For wardens and prison guards, and all who work in the criminal justice system, we pray: ◆ For those who are wrongly imprisoned, we pray: ◆ For those chained by fear, illiteracy, prejudice, or anger, we pray: ◆ For those who will show others God's grace this day, we pray: ◆

Our Father . . .

Lord Jesus,
you gained us freedom through the Cross.
Inspired by our Baptism,
may we live this day in the
glorious freedom
of the children of God.
You live and reign with God the Father in
the unity of the Holy Spirit,
one God, for ever and ever.
Amen.

† All the ends of the earth have seen the saving power of God.

Wednesday, May 24, 2017
Easter Weekday

† All the ends of the earth have seen the saving power of God.

Psalm 98 *page 414*

Reading *Acts 17:22–28, 32–34a*

Then Paul stood up at the Areopagus and said: "You Athenians, I see that in every respect you are very religious. For as I walked around looking carefully at your shrines, I even discovered an altar inscribed, 'To an Unknown God.' What therefore you unknowingly worship, I proclaim to you. The God who made the world and all that is in it, the Lord of heaven and earth, does not dwell in sanctuaries made by human hands, nor is he served by human hands because he needs anything. Rather it is he who gives to everyone life and breath and everything. He made from one the whole human race to dwell on the entire surface of the earth, and he fixed the ordered seasons and the boundaries of their regions, so that people might seek God, even perhaps grope for him and find him, though indeed he is not far from any one of us."

When they heard about resurrection of the dead, some began to scoff, but others said, "We should like to hear you on this some other time." And so Paul left them. But some did join him, and became believers.

Reflection

Paul endures a powerful rebuke in Athens. Despite his strong preaching, most walk away. The city of Athens at this time is greatly influenced by the thought of the philosopher Plato. Believers in this philosophy held firmly that a person's soul is trapped in their body and is only free after death. Therefore, to their ears, belief in the resurrection of the dead sounds like the soul being recaptured and imprisoned again. They want no part of that. Paul had little experience with failure. It is insightful and instructive how he handles it: he simply moves on.

Prayers *others may be added*

To the Conqueror of sin and death,
we pray:

◆ Lord, graciously hear us.

That the Church not become discouraged, we pray: ◆ For those who proclaim the Gospel, we pray: ◆ For those who cannot see beyond empiricism and rationalism, we pray: ◆ May we learn to let go of our faults and failures, we pray: ◆ For those who worship at the altar of their own ego, we pray: ◆

Our Father . . .

God of history,
you made the world and all that is in it.
May we remember that it is only in you
that we live and move and have our being.
We ask this through Christ our Lord.
Amen.

† All the ends of the earth have seen the saving power of God.

Thursday, May 25, 2017

Easter Weekday / Solemnity of the Ascension of the Lord

✝ God mounts his throne to shouts of joy.

Psalm 47

page 406

Reading

John 16:16–20

Jesus said to his disciples: "A little while and you will no longer see me, and again a little while later and you will see me." So some of his disciples said to one another, "What does this mean that he is saying to us, 'A little while and you will not see me, and again a little while and you will see me,' and 'Because I am going to the Father'?" So they said, "What is this 'little while' of which he speaks? We do not know what he means." Jesus knew that they wanted to ask him, so he said to them, "Are you discussing with one another what I said, 'A little while and you will not see me, and again a little while and you will see me'? Amen, amen, I say to you, you will weep and mourn, while the world rejoices; you will grieve, but your grief will become joy."

Reflection

In the Gospel according to John, everything takes place in the present. John has no coming judgment, for judgment occurs now. The one who believes in Jesus is already saved. In John, the Resurrection, Ascension, and sending of the Holy Spirit are virtually one event. And so we will see Jesus in a "little while." That is all it will take to recognize that, by his Resurrection and Ascension, he remains with us in new and glorious ways.

Prayers

others may be added

To the Risen Lord, we pray:

◆ King of glory, hear our prayer.

May the Church live out its preferential option for the poor and oppressed, we pray: ◆ That we may see Christ in one another, we pray: ◆ That we may be more contemplative and awed by mystery, we pray: ◆ For parents of children with special needs, we pray: ◆ For patience, we pray: ◆

Our Father . . .

God of grace and mercy,
draw us into greater mindfulness
and keep us in the present moment
so that we may discern the presence of
your Son, Jesus Christ,
who lives and reigns with you in the unity
of the Holy Spirit,
one God, for ever and ever.
Amen.

✝ God mounts his throne to shouts of joy.

Friday, May 26, 2017

Memorial of St. Philip Neri, Priest

✝ All the ends of the earth have seen the saving power of God

Psalm 98 *page 414*

Reading *Acts 18:9–15*

One night while Paul was in Corinth, the Lord said to him in a vision, "Do not be afraid. Go on speaking, and do not be silent, for I am with you. No one will attack and harm you, for I have many people in this city." He settled there for a year and a half and taught the word of God among them.

But when Gallio was proconsul of Achaia, the Jews rose up together against Paul and brought him to the tribunal, saying, "This man is inducing people to worship God contrary to the law." When Paul was about to reply, Gallio spoke to the Jews, . . . "[S]ince it is a question of arguments over doctrine and titles and your own law, see to it yourselves. I do not wish to be a judge of such matters."

Reflection

The admonition addressed to Paul, "Do not be afraid. Go on speaking," could easily have been addressed to Philip Neri. Born in Florence, Italy, Neri spent most of his life in Rome. His backdrop was the Protestant Reformation and the Council of Trent. To this anxious age Neri presented a playful disposition that refused to take himself or life too seriously. He served the sick and the poor, and founded a ministry providing care for poor pilgrims coming to the city. He was called "the apostle of Rome" because he would wander the streets engaging individuals in conversation that would deepen their faith and hope.

Prayers *others may be added*

To the Conqueror of sin and death,
we pray:

◆ Lord Jesus, hear our prayer.

May the Church bear witness to the joy of the Gospel, we pray: ◆ For our priests, we pray: ◆ For the safety of travelers, we pray: ◆ For humorists, comedians, and entertainers who bring laughter into our lives, we pray: ◆ For the sick and the dying, we pray: ◆

Our Father . . .

God of glory and majesty,
may we remember, especially when life isn't going our way,
the witness of Philip Neri
and find an inner confidence and a deeper joy
undefeated by passing circumstances.
We ask this through Christ our Lord.
Amen.

✝ All the ends of the earth have seen the saving power of God.

Saturday, May 27, 2017
Easter Weekday

✝ All the ends of the earth have seen the saving power of God.

Psalm 98 *page 414*

Reading *Acts 18:24–28*

A Jew named Apollos, a native of Alexandria, an eloquent speaker, arrived in Ephesus. He was an authority on the Scriptures. He had been instructed in the Way of the Lord and, with ardent spirit, spoke and taught accurately about Jesus, although he knew only the baptism of John. He began to speak boldly in the synagogue, but when Priscilla and Aquila heard him, they took him aside and explained to him the Way of God more accurately. And when he wanted to cross to Achaia, the brothers encouraged him and wrote to the disciples there to welcome him. After his arrival he gave great assistance to those who had come to believe through grace. He vigorously refuted the Jews in public, establishing from the Scriptures that the Christ is Jesus.

Reflection

We are introduced to a disciple named Apollos. He is described as "an eloquent speaker" and "an authority on the Scriptures." Though he speaks accurately about Jesus, his knowledge appears incomplete. He knows only the baptism of John the Baptist, and Priscilla and Aquila find it necessary to explain the faith more accurately. The figure of Apollos is a helpful reality check for all who serve. Is our understanding ever complete? Can our service ever be enough? But if we wait until we know enough we will never perform any ministry for Christ or the Church.

Prayers *others may be added*

To the Conqueror of sin and death, we pray:

◆ Lord Jesus, hear our prayer.

That those who serve the Church do so humbly and with hearts and minds that are open to insight, we pray: ◆ For theologians and biblical scholars, we pray: ◆ That our neophytes throughout the Church grow in wisdom, we pray: ◆ For business managers, bookkeepers, and maintenance and cleaning personnel who faithfully assist our parish, we pray: ◆ May we as people of faith make time for prayer in our daily lives, we pray: ◆

Our Father . . .

Lord God,
you have given us gifts to be used.
May we share these gifts in service
to your people, acknowledging
that all comes from you.
We ask this through Christ our Lord.
Amen.

✝ All the ends of the earth have seen the saving power of God.

Sunday, May 28, 2017

Solemnity of the Ascension of the Lord / Seventh Sunday of Easter

✝ God mounts his throne to shouts of joy.

Psalm 47 *page 406*

Reading *Matthew 28:16–20*

The eleven disciples went to Galilee, to the mountain to which Jesus had ordered them. When they saw him, they worshipped, but they doubted. Then Jesus approached and said to them, "All power in heaven and on earth has been given to me. Go, therefore, and make disciples of all nations, baptizing in the name of the Father, and of the Son, and of the Holy Spirit, teaching them to observe all that I have commanded you. And behold, I am with you always, until the end of the age."

Reflection

It is easy to get stuck in the literalism of the Ascension—Jesus "lifting off" from earth like a rocket! Today's solemnity purposely takes us away from the literal. We celebrate Jesus being glorified and going to the right hand of the Father. He commissions us and then bodily departs, so that, "Christ has no body but yours, no hands, no feet on earth but yours. . . . Yours are the hands, yours are the feet, yours are the eyes, you are his body. Christ has no body now but yours" (St. Teresa of Avila). "Go, therefore, and make disciples of all the nations."

Prayers *others may be added*

Turning to the Risen Lord, we pray:

◆ King of glory, hear our prayer.

For the gift of the Holy Spirit, we pray: ◆ May the entire People of God act as the Body and Blood of Christ, broken and poured out in loving service, we pray: ◆ For all bishops and all who hold and teach the Catholic faith that comes to us from the Apostles, we pray: ◆ That we may heed the call to evangelize, we pray: ◆ For peace, we pray: ◆

Our Father . . .

Lord Jesus Christ,
you have ascended in glory
and are at the right hand of the Father,
yet you remain here among us and
within us.
By the grace of the Holy Spirit,
empower us to be your faithful witnesses,
for you live and reign with God the Father
in the unity of the Holy Spirit,
one God, for ever and ever.
Amen.

✝ God mounts his throne to shouts of joy.

Monday, May 29, 2017
Easter Weekday

✝ Come Holy Spirit, come.

Psalm 47
page 406

Reading
Acts 19:1–7

While Apollos was in Corinth, Paul traveled through the interior of the country and down to Ephesus where he found some disciples. He said to them, "Did you receive the Holy Spirit when you became believers?" They answered him, "We have never even heard that there is a Holy Spirit." He said, "How were you baptized?" They replied, "With the baptism of John." Paul then said, "John baptized with a baptism of repentance, telling the people to believe in the one who was to come after him, that is, in Jesus." When they heard this, they were baptized in the name of the Lord Jesus. And when Paul laid his hands on them, the Holy Spirit came upon them, and they spoke in tongues and prophesied. Altogether there were about twelve men.

Reflection
"We have never even heard that there is a Holy Spirit." Odds are, you have at least heard of the Holy Spirit! But what part does the Spirit play in one's personal prayer or one's day-to-day faith? Dr. Stephen Covey said that the difference between someone who cannot read and someone who can read but doesn't, is negligible. Borrowing this, might we say that the difference between someone who doesn't know there is a Holy Spirit and someone who does but fails to consider the presence and action of the Holy Spirit, is negligible?

Prayers
others may be added

To our Risen and Ascended Lord,
we pray:

◆ Lord, send out your Spirit.

For the outpouring of the Holy Spirit on the People of God, we pray: ◆ For those who have been baptized, confirmed, or received their First Holy Communion in this Time of Easter, we pray: ◆ For those who hunger and thirst for righteousness, we pray: ◆ That caregivers receive support and encouragement, we pray: ◆ For those who have given their lives for the freedom of others, we pray: ◆

Our Father . . .

Lord God of hosts,
from the day of our Baptism,
your gift of the Holy Spirit has been sent
upon us.
May we reflect on the presence and action
of the Spirit in the life of the Church,
through our Lord Jesus Christ, your Son,
who lives and reigns with you in the unity
of the Holy Spirit,
one God, for ever and ever.
Amen.

✝ Come Holy Spirit, come.

Tuesday, May 30, 2017
Easter Weekday

✝ Come Holy Spirit, come.

Psalm 47

page 406

Reading

Acts 20:19–24

[Paul said:] "I served the Lord with all humility and with the tears and trials that came to me because of the plots of the Jews, and I did not at all shrink from telling you what was for your benefit, or from teaching you in public or in your homes. I earnestly bore witness for both Jews and Greeks to repentance before God and to faith in our Lord Jesus. But now, compelled by the Spirit, I am going to Jerusalem. What will happen to me there I do not know, except that in one city after another the Holy Spirit has been warning me that imprisonment and hardships await me. Yet I consider life of no importance to me, if only that I may finish my course and the ministry that I received from the Lord Jesus, to bear witness to the Gospel of God's grace."

Reflection

Paul strikes a foreboding tone in this passage. Certain that hardship and imprisonment await him in Jerusalem, he speaks as a terminally ill elder might when reflecting on life. His only wish is that he is able to finish his course, "to bear witness to the Gospel of God's grace." Not to warn of God's judgment, not to proclaim his self-righteousness, not to preach material success, but God's grace. How and in what ways do we make God's grace known? Do we embody the grace of God in our being?

Prayers

others may be added

Turning to our Risen and Ascended Lord, we pray:

◆ Font of Life, hear our prayer.

That the Church be both sign and instrument of God's grace, we pray: ◆ May we come to know salvation by grace through faith, we pray: ◆ May we demonstrate respect toward the elderly and hear their wisdom, we pray: ◆ That those who struggle with their faith find fortitude, we pray: ◆ For those who are about to give birth, we pray: ◆

Our Father . . .

Good and gracious God,
in you we live, move, and have our being.
All that we have, all that we are is
your gift.
In gratitude, may we bear witness to your
Gospel of grace.
We ask this through Christ our Lord.
Amen.

✝ Come Holy Spirit, come.

Wednesday, May 31, 2017
Feast of the Visitation of the Blessed Virgin Mary

☩ My soul proclaims the greatness of the Lord.

Canticle of Mary
page 422

Reading
Luke 1:39–47

Mary set out in those days and traveled to the hill country in haste to a town of Judah, where she entered the house of Zechariah and greeted Elizabeth. When Elizabeth heard Mary's greeting, the infant leaped in her womb, and Elizabeth, filled with the Holy Spirit, cried out in a loud voice and said, "Most blessed are you among women, and blessed is the fruit of your womb. And how does this happen to me, that the mother of my Lord should come to me? For at the moment the sound of your greeting reached my ears, the infant in my womb leaped for joy. Blessed are you who believed that what was spoken to you by the Lord would be fulfilled."

And Mary said: / "My soul proclaims the greatness of the Lord; / my spirit rejoices in God my savior."

Reflection
Mary, overshadowed by the Holy Spirit and with child, visits to her kinswoman, Elizabeth, pregnant with John the Baptist. This scene is of love and tenderness, joy and apprehension. Note that Elizabeth refers to Mary as "the mother of my Lord." It is only after Elizabeth has acknowledged the Lord that she turns her attention to Mary's faith in the Lord's promise.

Prayers
others may be added

Turning to our Risen and Ascended Lord, we pray:

◆ Son of God and son of Mary, hear us.

May the Church trust that God's promise will be fulfilled, we pray: ◆ May we live in the joy of the Holy Spirit, we pray: ◆ For expectant parents, we pray: ◆ That families may foster love, respect, understanding, and acceptance, we pray: ◆ For children longing to be adopted or to have a foster home, we pray: ◆

Our Father . . .

Eternal Father,
you inspired the Virgin Mary, mother of your Son,
to visit Elizabeth and assist her in her need.
Keep us open to the working of your Spirit,
and with Mary may we praise you forever.
We ask this through our Lord Jesus Christ, your Son,
who lives and reigns with you and the Holy Spirit, one God for ever and ever.
Amen. (*Liturgy of the Hours*)

☩ My soul proclaims the greatness of the Lord.

Thursday, June 1, 2017
Memorial of St. Justin, Martyr

✝ Come Holy Spirit, come.

Psalm 47 *page 406*

Reading *Acts 22:30; 23:6–7, 9*

Wishing to determine the truth about why Paul was being accused by the Jews, the commander freed him and ordered the chief priests and the whole Sanhedrin to convene. Then he brought Paul down and made him stand before them.

Paul was aware that some were Sadducees and some were Pharisees, so he called out before the Sanhedrin, "My brothers, I am a Pharisee, the son of Pharisees; I am on trial for hope in the resurrection of the dead." When he said this, a dispute broke out between the Pharisees and Sadducees, and the group became divided. . . . A great uproar occurred and some scribes belonging to the Pharisee party stood up and sharply argued, "We find nothing wrong with this man. Suppose a spirit or an angel has spoken to him."

Reflection

Despite instigating a near riot between the Sadducees and the Pharisees, Paul survives Jerusalem. Yet the ominous words are spoken to him, "You must also bear witness in Rome." Justin is also one who bore witness in Rome and like Peter and Paul, would be martyred there. Justin's writings are an invaluable link between the first- and third-century Church. In addition to a rigorous defense of Christian faith, Justin gives an account of how these early believers gathered on Sunday for the Eucharist.

Prayers *others may be added*

Turning to our Risen and Ascended Lord, we pray:

◆ Fire of Love, hear our prayer.

That believers today maintain a unity of consciousness with those who have gone before us, we pray: ◆ That the People of God experience harmony with one another through the Eucharist, we pray: ◆ For Christians experiencing persecution, we pray: ◆ That we may defend our faith through feeding the hungry and seeking justice for the oppressed, we pray: ◆ For parishes celebrating their patronal feast day today, we pray: ◆

Our Father . . .

Lord God,
you gave St. Justin the courage to be
steadfast in the faith.
Help us to follow the example of St.
Justin in our time.
May we reject the falsehoods of
consumerism,
materialism, and radical individualism
and by our example of loving service,
continue to proclaim Christ crucified,
for he lives and reigns with you in the
unity of the Holy Spirit,
one God, for ever and ever.
Amen.

✝ Come Holy Spirit, come.

Friday, June 2, 2017
Easter Weekday

✝ Come Holy Spirit, come.

Psalm 47
page 406

Reading
John 21:15–17

[Jesus] said to Simon Peter, "Simon, son of John, do you love me more than these?" He said to him, "Yes, Lord, you know that I love you." He said to him, "Feed my lambs." He then said to him a second time, "Simon, son of John, do you love me?" He said to him, "Yes, Lord, you know that I love you." He said to him, "Tend my sheep." He said to him the third time, "Simon, son of John, do you love me?" Peter was distressed that he had said to him a third time, "Do you love me?" and he said to him, "Lord, you know everything; you know that I love you." Jesus said to him, "Feed my sheep."

Reflection
The Gospel of John informs us that Jesus' words pertain to the kind of death Peter would undergo to glorify God. Yet there are many older adults in our communities that can readily relate to these words too. This is their experience: having others dress them and being taken where they do not want to go. In 1972 Bette Midler released "Hello in There" a song about the loneliness of the elderly. How do I and how does my community minister to and with older adults? Do we stop and say, "Hello in there"?

Prayers
others may be added

To our Risen and Ascended Lord,
we pray:

◆ Fire of Love, hear our prayer.

That the Church may gratefully cherish the legacy passed on from previous generations, we pray: ◆ May the gifts of our older adults be utilized and celebrated, we pray: ◆ For those afflicted with Alzheimer's disease and other forms of dementia, we pray: ◆ For those who are homebound, we pray: ◆ For children who are honoring their father or mother as their caregivers, we pray: ◆

Our Father . . .

God of the Covenant,
in calling a people to yourself,
you taught us to honor, respect, and learn
from our elders.
May we, your Church,
continue to be staunch advocates
and friends
of our senior members.
We ask this through Christ our Lord.
Amen.

✝ Come Holy Spirit, come.

Saturday, June 3, 2017

Memorial of St. Charles Lwanga and Companions, Martyrs

✝ Come Holy Spirit, come.

Psalm 47

page 406

Reading

Acts 28:16–17, 20, 30–31

When he entered Rome, Paul was allowed to live by himself, with the soldier who was guarding him.

Three days later he called together the leaders of the Jews. When they had gathered he said to them, "My brothers, although I had done nothing against our people or our ancestral customs, I was handed over to the Romans as a prisoner from Jerusalem. . . . It is on account of the hope of Israel that I wear these chains."

He remained for two full years in his lodgings. He received all who came to him, and with complete assurance and without hindrance he proclaimed the Kingdom of God and taught about the Lord Jesus Christ.

Reflection

Although Paul is the Apostle to the Gentiles, near the end of his life he tells the Jewish leaders that "it is on account of the hope of Israel that I wear these chains." Paul still longs for the conversion of his people. Charles Lwanga and his companions gave their lives so that Christianity might be preserved in their native Uganda. Today, Africa contains more than 16 percent of the world's Catholics and that number continues to grow. Most Catholics are in sub-Saharan Africa, while the northern part of Africa is mostly Muslim, thus the need for interreligious dialogue.

Prayers

others may be added

Turning to our Risen and Ascended Lord, we pray:

◆ Lord, hear our prayer.

For the Church in Africa, we pray: ◆
For interreligious dialogue between Christians and Muslims, we pray: ◆
For those who undergo torture, we pray: ◆ That peace and the desire for peace reign in our hearts, we pray: ◆
For parishes that invoke St. Charles Lwanga as their patron, we pray: ◆

Our Father . . .

God of all the earth,
you have bestowed the faith on many in Africa, and its gifts
to the Body of Christ are many.
May we claim the Church's heritage in Africa
and become more familiar with and connected
to the gifts and needs of Africa today.
We ask this through Christ our Lord.
Amen.

✝ Come Holy Spirit, come.

Sunday, June 4, 2017
Solemnity of Pentecost

✝ Lord, send out your Spirit and renew the face of the earth.

Psalm 104
page 416

Reading
John 20:19–23

On the evening of that first day of the week, when the doors were locked, where the disciples were, for fear of the Jews, Jesus came and stood in their midst and said to them, "Peace be with you." When he had said this, he showed them his hands and his side. The disciples rejoiced when they saw the Lord. Jesus said to them again, "Peace be with you. As the Father has sent me, so I send you." And when he had said this, he breathed on them and said to them, "Receive the Holy Spirit. Whose sins you forgive are forgiven them, and whose sins you retain are retained."

Reflection
In 1637, Anne Hutchinson was expelled from the Massachusetts Bay Colony for believing in an "unpredictable God and excessive grace." Her accuser, Thomas Hooker, declared, "I know there is wild love, and wild joy just as there are wild flowers, but we need a garden love and a garden joy of God's own planting." If we know anything about the Holy Spirit, it is the sharing of "unpredictable and excessive grace." How else can we account for the Incarnation, Resurrection, conversion of Paul, and so many of our life experiences? Unpredictable and excessive grace be praised.

Prayers
others may be added

To our Risen and Ascended Lord, we pray:

◆ Lord, send forth your Spirit.

May the gifts of the Holy Spirit fill the Church, we pray: ◆ That the gifts of wisdom, understanding, and knowledge guide us to truth, we pray: ◆ That the gifts of courage and right judgment make us witnesses to the Reign of God, we pray: ◆ That the gifts of piety and fear of the Lord awaken us to awe and wonder, we pray: ◆ May the Holy Spirit guide our feet in the way of peace, we pray: ◆

Our Father . . .

Come Holy Spirit, come.
Heal our wounds,
renew our strength,
bend the stubborn heart and will,
guide the steps that go astray.
On the faithful who adore and confess
you evermore,
give them virtue's sure reward;
give them your salvation, Lord;
give them joys that never end,
through Christ our Lord.
Amen. (Based on the Pentecost Sequence, Lectionary for Mass)

✝ Lord, send out your Spirit and renew the face of the earth.

Monday, June 5, 2017

Memorial of St. Boniface, Bishop and Martyr

✝ **Lord, send out your Spirit and renew the face of the earth.**

Psalm 104

page 416

Reading

Tobit 2:3–4

Tobiah went out to look for some poor kinsman of ours. When he returned he exclaimed, "Father!" I said to him, "What is it, son?" He answered, "Father, one of our people has been murdered! His body lies in the market place where he was just strangled!" I sprang to my feet, leaving the dinner untouched; and I carried the dead man from the street and put him in one of the rooms, so that I might bury him after sunset.

Reflection

The story of Tobit, his son Tobiah, and his wife Sarah is a wonderful tale of God working in individuals' lives. The picture painted in our reading could just as well be an image from today. A person lies dead on the streets and people just pass by. Why do the dead and suffering not bother us? What could be more important than someone's pain and loss? Funerals are even scheduled for convenience now. Children are left at home; we don't want them to know of death. Have we lost our ability to connect with others over death? Have we lost empathy? Tobiah hasn't.

Prayers

others may be added

Turning to our Risen and Ascended Lord, we pray:

◆ **Lord, hear our prayer.**

For the Church in England and Germany, we pray: ◆ For the condemned, tortured, and their families, we pray: ◆ For hospice workers and funeral directors, we pray: ◆ For legislators, that they work to put an end to the death penalty throughout our nation, we pray: ◆ For all the dead, we pray: ◆

Our Father . . .

God of the living and the dead,
your servant Boniface offered his life
for the Gospel and the people of Germany.
May we too be willing to live in
solidarity with others,
not counting the cost.
We ask this through Christ our Lord.
Amen.

✝ **Lord, send out your Spirit and renew the face of the earth.**

Tuesday, June 6, 2017
Weekday

✝ Lord, send out your Spirit and renew the face of the earth.

Psalm 104

page 416

Reading

Tobit 2:9–14

On the night of Pentecost, after I had buried the dead, I, Tobit, went into my courtyard to sleep next to the courtyard wall. My face was uncovered because of the heat. I did not know there were birds perched on the wall above me, till their warm droppings settled in my eyes, causing cataracts. I went to see some doctors for a cure but the more they anointed my eyes with various salves, the worse the cataracts became, until I could see no more. . . .

At that time, my wife Anna worked for hire at weaving cloth, the kind of work women do. When she sent back the goods to their owners, they would pay her. Late in winter on the seventh of Dystrus, she finished the cloth and sent it back to the owners. They paid her the full salary and also gave her a young goat for the table. On entering my house the goat began to bleat.

I called to my wife and said: "Where did this goat come from? Perhaps it was stolen! Give it back to its owners; we have no right to eat stolen food!" She said to me, "It was given to me as a bonus over and above my wages." Yet I would not believe her, and told her to give it back to its owners. I became very angry with her over this. So she retorted: "Where are your charitable deeds now? Where are your virtuous acts? See! Your true character is finally showing itself!"

Reflection

Tobit and his wife Anna have a fight. He has gone blind and she has to go to work to support them. After she has received a goat as a bonus, Tobit accuses her of stealing it! Marriage is both a difficult and blessed covenant. If we are truly intimate with each other, we share both good and bad moments. This is true with friends as well. We boldly allow another to see us as we are and find that we are loved. This love mirrors God's love for us.

Prayers

others may be added

Turning to our Risen and Ascended Lord, we pray:

◆ Lord, hear our prayer.

For an intimate relationship between God and the Church, we pray: ◆ For fair wages and safe working environments, we pray: ◆ For married people, we pray: ◆ For the openness to love as God loves us, we pray: ◆ For those who are divorced, we pray: ◆

Our Father . . .

Lord of love,
you give us friends and partners who share love with us.
Help us to accept their compassion and forgiveness.
May all our relationships reflect the great love you have for us.
We ask this through Christ our Lord.
Amen.

✝ Lord, send out your Spirit and renew the face of the earth.

Wednesday, June 7, 2017
Weekday

✝ Lord, send out your Spirit and renew the face of the earth.

Psalm 104

page 416

Reading

Tobit 3:1–3, 6a, 7–8a, 10

Grief-stricken in spirit, I, Tobit, groaned and wept aloud. Then with sobs I began to pray: / "You are righteous, O Lord, / and all your deeds are just; / All your ways are mercy and truth; / you are the judge of the world. / And now, O Lord, may you be mindful of me, / and look with favor upon me. / Punish me not for my sins, / nor for my inadvertent offenses, / nor for those of my ancestors. /

"So now, deal with me as you please, / and command my life breath to be taken from me, / that I may go from the face of the earth into dust. / It is better for me to die than to live, / because I have heard insulting calumnies, / and I am overwhelmed with grief." /

On the same day, at Ecbatana in Media, it so happened that Raguel's daughter Sarah also had to listen to abuse, from one of her father's maids. For she had been married to seven husbands, but the wicked demon Asmodeus killed them off before they could have intercourse with her, as it is prescribed for wives.

The girl was deeply saddened that day, and she went into an upper chamber of her house, where she planned to hang herself.

Reflection

Tobit and Sarah beg God for death. Tobit is in despair because of his blindness. Sarah has lost seven husbands and her maid is berating her. God will hear their pleas. Do you empathize with their pain? The torturous pain bullying inflicts can cause emotional turmoil that lasts for decades. How we treat each other is important to our wholeness and holiness. Today, let's pray for healing for all who have felt the sting of this torment and let us not forget to pray as well for those who inflict the anguish.

Prayers

others may be added

To the Risen Christ, we pray:

◆ Lord, send out your Spirit.

For a Church of healing and compassion, we pray: ◆ For nations who lead by intimidation and coercion, that they will know the way of the Lord, we pray: ◆ For victims of bullying, we pray: ◆ For those who consider suicide today, that they may have a spirit of courage and love, we pray: ◆

Our Father . . .

God of compassion,
you hear us in the depths of our pain.
You know the agony of the depressed
and the despair of the sorrowful.
Send your balm of healing
on all those injured by evil words and
slanderous tongues.
Renew in them a spirit of peace.
We ask this through Christ our Lord.
Amen.

✝ Lord, send out your Spirit and renew the face of the earth.

Thursday, June 8, 2017
Weekday

✝ Lord, send out your Spirit and renew the face of the earth.

Psalm 104 *page 416*

Reading *Tobit 7:13, 8:4–9a*

Raguel then called Sarah's mother and told her to bring a scroll, so that he might draw up a marriage contract stating that he gave Sarah to Tobiah as his wife according to the decree of the Mosaic law. Her mother brought the scroll, and Raguel drew up the contract, to which they affixed their seals.

When the girl's parents left the bedroom and closed the door behind them, Tobiah arose from bed and said to his wife, "My love, get up. Let us pray and beg our Lord to have mercy on us and to grant us deliverance." She got up, and they started to pray and beg that deliverance might be theirs.

And they began to say: / "Blessed are you, O God of our fathers, / praised be your name forever and ever. / Let the heavens and all your creation / praise you forever. / You made Adam and you gave him his wife Eve / to be his help and support; / and from these two the human race descended. / You said, 'It is not good for the man to be alone; / let us make him a partner like himself.' / Now, Lord, you know that I take this wife of mine / not because of lust, / but for a noble purpose. / Call down your mercy on me and on her, / and allow us to live together to a happy old age."

They said together, "Amen, amen," and went to bed for the night.

Reflection

The first thing that Tobiah and Sarah do as husband and wife is pray. There is a special closeness in praying with the one you love. Do you pray with those you love? Sometimes we treat prayer as if it should be totally private. While there is a dimension of this in our prayer life, there is also time to pray in community, even if it's a community of two. Consider the challenge to pray with someone you love.

Prayers *others may be added*

To the Risen Christ, we pray:

◆ Lord, send out your Spirit.

For Pope N., our bishop N., our pastor, N., may they be people of prayer, we pray: ◆ For religious freedom for people throughout the world, we pray: ◆ For an increase of prayer in family life, we pray: ◆ For our parish communities, for full, active, and conscious participation in our liturgies, we pray: ◆ For families lost, broken, and hurting, we pray:◆

Our Father . . .

We turn to you, O Lord,
and ask you to watch over us each day and night.
Hear our prayers too for our sisters and brothers in need.
May your Holy Spirit blanket us in your love.
We ask this through Christ our Lord.
Amen.

✝ Lord, send out your Spirit and renew the face of the earth.

Friday, June 9, 2017
Weekday

✝ Lord, send out your Spirit and renew the face of the earth.

Psalm 104 *page 416*

Reading *Tobit 11:5–7, 10–14*

Anna sat watching the road by which her son was to come. When she saw him coming, she exclaimed to his father, "Tobit, your son is coming, and the man who traveled with him!"

Raphael said to Tobiah before he reached his father: "I am certain that his eyes will be opened. Smear the fish gall on them. This medicine will make the cataracts shrink and peel off from his eyes; then your father will again be able to see the light of day."

Tobit got up and stumbled out through the courtyard gate. Tobiah went up to him with the fish gall in his hand, and holding him firmly, blew into his eyes. "Courage, father," he said. Next he smeared the medicine on his eyes, and it made them smart. Then, beginning at the corners of Tobit's eyes, Tobiah used both hands to peel off the cataracts.

When Tobit saw his son, he threw his arms around him and wept. He exclaimed, "I can see you, son, the light of my eyes!" Then he said: / "Blessed be God, / and praised be his great name, / and blessed be all his holy angels. / May his holy name be praised / throughout all the ages." /

Reflection

Sarah's pain has ended, now it is Tobit's turn. When Tobiah greets his father and applies a medicine on his eyes, Tobit's vision is restored. He then praises God and goes to meet his daughter-in-law. He accepts the good and bad from the hand of God. Though the son administers the medicine, it is God who gets the credit. Tobit understands that God is ultimately in charge of everything. We are often willing to blame God for the bad, we need to be sure to offer praise for the good that God provides.

Prayers *others may be added*

To the Risen Christ, we pray:

◆ Lord, hear our prayer.

May the Church offer a sacrifice of praise and thanksgiving to God, we pray: ◆
May medical care be available to all, we pray: ◆ For physicians, technicians, nurses, pharmacists, and all who practice the healing professions, we pray: ◆
For all who are blind, physically, emotionally, or spiritually, we pray: ◆
May we remember to pray, in good times and in bad, we pray: ◆

Our Father . . .

Praise be to you, Lord our God.
All things belong to you.
All life is found in you.
Every day may we bless your holy name.
Through our Lord Jesus Christ, your Son,
who lives and reigns with you in the unity of the Holy Spirit,
one God, for ever and ever.
Amen.

✝ Lord, send out your Spirit and renew the face of the earth.

Saturday, June 10, 2017
Weekday

✝ Lord, send out your Spirit and renew the face of the earth.

Psalm 104 *page 416*

Reading *Tobit 12:1, 5*

Tobit called his son Tobiah and said to him, "Son, see to it that you give what is due to the man who made the journey with you; give him a bonus too." So he called Raphael and said, "Take as your wages half of all that you have brought back, and go in peace."

Reflection

We thank God, but what about the others who share the journey with us? Do we thank them too? Tobit insists that Tobiah's companion not only be paid but receive a bonus as well. We need to be sure in business and relationships that we appreciate those who journey with us. Consider those who have shared difficult life experiences with you. Have you considered them to be angels, as Raphael is here?

Prayers *others may be added*

Turning to our Risen and Ascended Lord, we pray:

◆ Lord, hear our prayer.

May the Church continue to challenge business owners to practice Gospel values, we pray: ◆ May nations seek justice for laborers, we pray: ◆ For migrant workers and all who work our fields, we pray: ◆ For those in low-income jobs, that they may receive fair wages and benefits, we pray: ◆ For a heart bereft of greed and generous to our coworkers, we pray: ◆

Our Father . . .

Lord God,
you send your messengers to share
our journey with us.
May we appreciate their kindnesses
and be gracious for their friendship.
We ask this through Christ our Lord.
Amen.

✝ Lord, send out your Spirit and renew the face of the earth.

Sunday, June 11, 2017

Solemnity of the Most Holy Trinity

✝ Blessed are you, O Lord, the God of our ancestors!

Daniel 3 *page 421*

Reading *John 3:16–18*

God so loved the world that he gave his only Son, so that everyone who believes in him might not perish but might have eternal life. For God did not send his Son into the world to condemn the world, but that the world might be saved through him. Whoever believes in him will not be condemned, but whoever does not believe has already been condemned, because he has not believed in the name of the only Son of God.

Reflection

John 3:16. How many times have we seen the sign displaying this passage behind home plate or in the end zone of a football game? We need to give credit to these creative evangelizers. Proclaiming the Gospel is about these small, yet significant moments. It's just a sign, but people find it intriguing.

Each of us should consider how we evangelize. It's not just about going house to house. It can be as simple as a Nativity display on our lawn at Christmas, ashes on our head on Ash Wednesday, or the bumper stickers or magnets on our cars. But more importantly, it's how we live. Our coworkers will notice whether we handle death or illness with faith. Our lives are always witnesses to our love and belief in God.

Prayers *others may be added*

To the Most Holy Trinity, we pray:

◆ Hear us, Triune God.

Holy God, may the Church continue to ponder and teach the mysteries of your love and mercy, we pray: ◆ Ever-living God, empower those who are consumed with self-doubt, bitterness, and anger to live fully in the joy of your Spirit, we pray: ◆ Almighty God, end hatred, poverty, and war in this world you created, we pray: ◆ Spirit God, teach your children to act justly, we pray: ◆ Immortal God, lead all those who have died into everlasting life with you, we pray: ◆

Our Father . . .

O Most Holy Trinity,
one God, yet Three Persons,
you are the mystery in which we live.
Teach us to be faithful witnesses to you,
proclaiming Good News in many ways
throughout our day.
We ask this through our Lord Jesus
Christ, your Son,
who lives and reigns with you in the unity
of the Holy Spirit,
one God, for ever and ever.
Amen.

✝ Blessed are you, O Lord, the God of our ancestors!

Monday, June 12, 2017
Weekday

† Blessed are you, O Lord, the God of our ancestors!

Daniel 3 *page 421*

Reading *2 Corinthians 1:3–7*

Blessed be the God and Father of our Lord Jesus Christ, the Father of compassion and the God of all encouragement, who encourages us in our every affliction, so that we may be able to encourage those who are in any affliction with the encouragement with which we ourselves are encouraged by God. For as Christ's sufferings overflow to us, so through Christ does our encouragement also overflow. If we are afflicted, it is for your encouragement and salvation; if we are encouraged, it is for your encouragement, which enables you to endure the same sufferings that we suffer. Our hope for you is firm, for we know that as you share in the sufferings, you also share in the encouragement.

Reflection

Individuality or community? This ebb and flow, pull and push underlies most decisions. Do I choose for myself or the group? Scriptures show that we are inextricably bound to each other. Paul is clear on this. What he does is for the community and the community is also for each other. We share our lives. While we have an individual relationship with the Lord, it is in the community that we learn of Christ and live our Christianity. Do we see how our decisions affect others?

Prayers *others may be added*

To the Most Holy Trinity, we pray:

◆ Hear our prayer, Triune God.

Holy Trinity, bind your Church in unity, we pray: ◆ May nations live in solidarity and peace with each other, we pray: ◆ Open eyes to see the oneness of creation, we pray: ◆ Let diversity be rooted in harmony and difference, which is a sign of your grace, we pray: ◆ Teach us to accept the gifts of all, and may our parishes work for the common good, we pray: ◆

Our Father . . .

God of the nations,
you bring us together in community that
no one may live alone.
Teach us to share generosly our resources,
joys, and sorrows.
Help us to be open to all, forgiving,
loving, and witnessing together.
We ask this through Christ our Lord.
Amen.

† Blessed are you, O Lord, the God of our ancestors!

Tuesday, June 13, 2017

Memorial of St. Anthony of Padua, Priest and Doctor of the Church

✝ Blessed are you, O Lord, the God of our ancestors!

Daniel 3

page 421

Reading

2 Corinthians 1:18–22

Brothers and sisters: As God is faithful, our word to you is not "yes" and "no." For the Son of God, Jesus Christ, who was proclaimed to you by us, Silvanus and Timothy and me, was not "yes" and "no," but "yes" has been in him. For however many are the promises of God, their Yes is in him; therefore, the Amen from us also goes through him to God for glory. But the one who gives us security with you in Christ and who anointed us is God; he has also put his seal upon us and given the Spirit in our hearts as a first installment.

Reflection

St. Anthony of Padua was originally attached to the Augustinians, but the simplicity of the Franciscans and martyrdom of five friars changed him. Anthony joined the new order. He is known for simplicity and innocence and is the patron saint of lost articles.

Giving one's life for the faith sounds heroic. However, it was in viewing the awful reality of the martyred friars that Anthony experienced a conversion. He wanted to be like them. Offering one's life is not really about death, but about living. How do we offer our lives in such a meaningful way that others are attracted to the Gospel? Are our actions a compelling witness to the Lord?

Prayers

others may be added

To the Most Holy Trinity, we pray:

◆ Hear our prayer, Triune God.

For a spirit of witness alive in the Church, we pray: ◆ For all who are tortured this day and for all prisoners of conscience, we pray: ◆ For courage in the face of evil, we pray: ◆ For all who are lost, lonely, or forgotten, we pray: ◆ For the Franciscan community, we pray: ◆

Our Father . . .

Lord,
you sent St. Anthony to us as a bold
evangelizer of the Gospel.
Through Baptism, we too are called to be
your witnesses.
Help us shine with the light of Christ
that others may see your goodness and
hear your Good News.
We ask this through Christ our Lord.
Amen.

✝ Blessed are you, O Lord, the God of our ancestors!

Wednesday, June 14, 2017
Weekday

✝ Blessed are you, O Lord, the God of our ancestors!

Daniel 3 *page 421*

Reading *2 Corinthians 3:4–11*

Brothers and sisters: Such confidence we have through Christ toward God. Not that of ourselves we are qualified to take credit for anything as coming from us; rather, our qualification comes from God, who has indeed qualified us as ministers of a new covenant, not of letter but of spirit; for the letter brings death, but the Spirit gives life.

Now if the ministry of death, carved in letters on stone, was so glorious that the children of Israel could not look intently at the face of Moses because of its glory that was going to fade, how much more will the ministry of the Spirit be glorious? For if the ministry of condemnation was glorious, the ministry of righteousness will abound much more in glory. Indeed, what was endowed with glory has come to have no glory in this respect because of the glory that surpasses it. For if what was going to fade was glorious, how much more will what endures be glorious.

Reflection

St. Paul and his companions are clear. They deserve no credit, all is from God. Quite a statement of abandonment. Are we willing to be so transparent? We are proud of our achievements. But everything we have is gift; all is from God. Does that break our heart, or give us freedom? Can we be more generous with the money we possess, because it's God's not ours? What about our time? Where can we make changes today to show thanks for the Lord's graciousness?

Prayers *others may be added*

To the Most Holy Trinity, we pray:

◆ Hear our prayer, Triune God.

May the Church be open and transparent to the will of God, we pray: ◆ May generosity transform the miserly, we pray: ◆ May the poor receive freely all that they need, we pray: ◆ May workers know just wages and benefits, we pray: ◆ May our hearts receive and give freely the beneficence of God, we pray: ◆

Our Father . . .

Lord,
you are generous to all.
Need is a human creation born of greed and power.
Open our hearts and our coffers.
May we lively freely, sharing all that we have with others.
We ask this through Christ our Lord.
Amen.

✝ Blessed are you, O Lord, the God of our ancestors!

Thursday, June 15, 2017
Weekday

✝ Blessed are you, O Lord, the God of our ancestors!

Daniel 3 *page 421*

Reading *2 Corinthians 3:15—4:1, 3–6*

Brothers and sisters: To this day, whenever Moses is read, a veil lies over the hearts of the children of Israel, but whenever a person turns to the Lord the veil is removed. Now the Lord is the Spirit and where the Spirit of the Lord is, there is freedom. All of us, gazing with unveiled face on the glory of the Lord, are being transformed into the same image from glory to glory, as from the Lord who is the Spirit.

Therefore, since we have this ministry through the mercy shown us, we are not discouraged. And even though our Gospel is veiled, it is veiled for those who are perishing, in whose case the god of this age has blinded the minds of the unbelievers, so that they may not see the light of the Gospel of the glory of Christ, who is the image of God. For we do not preach ourselves but Jesus Christ as Lord, and ourselves as your slaves for the sake of Jesus. For God who said, *Let light shine out of darkness*, has shone in our hearts to bring to light the knowledge of the glory of God on the face of Jesus Christ.

Reflection

Freedom is a powerful concept. For people who are enslaved, it is the prize they long for. Do we recognize our shackles? How have we tied ourselves up? Are there ways of thinking or behaving we insist upon, never realizing they are not of the Spirit? Do we even pull passages from the Scriptures out of context just to bolster our preconceived ideas? Do we place burdens on others, insisting they live by our standards, not God's? Where the Spirit is, there is freedom. Freedom can be scary, but it is a hallmark of God's presence. Let us live in freedom. What is stopping you?

Prayers *others may be added*

To the Most Holy Trinity, we pray:

◆ Hear our prayer, Triune God.

Holy Spirit, guide your Church that we may live in the freedom of the children of God, we pray: ◆ Release those oppressed by poverty, we pray: ◆ Liberate all condemned by hatred or held captive in the chains of fear, we pray: ◆ Empower legislators to end the death penalty, abortion, and all sins against life, we pray: ◆

Our Father . . .

Liberating God,
send your power to emancipate all who live in darkness, pain, and poverty of spirit.
Help us to recognize your way
in the joy that freedom brings our sisters and brothers.
May your way of truth reign.
We ask this through Christ our Lord.
Amen.

✝ Blessed are you, O Lord, the God of our ancestors!

Friday, June 16, 2017
Weekday

✝ Blessed are you, O Lord, the God of our ancestors!

Daniel 3
page 421

Reading
2 Corinthians 4:7–11

Brothers and sisters: We hold this treasure in earthen vessels, that the surpassing power may be of God and not from us. We are afflicted in every way, but not constrained; perplexed, but not driven to despair; persecuted, but not abandoned; struck down but not destroyed; always carrying about in the Body the dying of Jesus, so that the life of Jesus may also be manifested in our body. For we who live are constantly being given up to death for the sake of Jesus, so that the life of Jesus may be manifested in our mortal flesh.

Reflection
Paul's reflection is simple and yet perhaps painful. It flies in the face of a sanitized Christianity. First, all power is God's not ours. But second, affliction is real and Christians should expect it. How different that is from some contemporary portrayals of the faith. Yet, though we know affliction and persecution, faith in God's ultimate power sustains us. When was the last time you felt betrayed, lost, or alone? Do you know the pain of abandonment? Yet, deeper than all this, is God's power. Let us remember our pains today and be in solidarity with those who suffer.

Prayers
others may be added

To the Most Holy Trinity, we pray:

◆ Hear our prayer, Triune God.

Almighty God, may your Church live in solidarity with the abused, lost, and abandoned, we pray: ◆ May the powerful defend the poor, the wealthy care for the lost, we pray: ◆ May victims of war, rape, and torture find peace and healing, we pray: ◆ May those in nursing homes find friendship, we pray: ◆ May we trust in the deep abiding power of God, we pray: ◆

Our Father . . .

All powerful Father,
you are our refuge.
Defend us in times of pain, weakness,
or assault.
Hear our cry when life becomes lonely
or difficult.
Train us to trust in your love.
We ask this through Christ our Lord.
Amen.

✝ Blessed are you, O Lord, the God of our ancestors!

Saturday, June 17, 2017
Weekday

✝ Blessed are you, O Lord, the God of our ancestors!

Daniel 3 *page 421*

Reading *2 Corinthians 5:14, 20–21*

Brothers and sisters: The love of Christ impels us, once we have come to the conviction that one died for all; therefore, all have died. He indeed died for all, so that those who live might no longer live for themselves but for him who for their sake died and was raised.

So we are ambassadors for Christ, as if God were appealing through us. We implore you on behalf of Christ, be reconciled to God. For our sake he made him to be sin who did not know sin, so that we might become the righteousness of God in him.

Reflection

We are ambassadors for Christ. We are not Christ, but official representatives. It is his will that we must proclaim, not ours. That can be difficult. Sometimes, we can want the Gospel to say what we desire it to say. Perhaps that would be easier. But that is not our decision. The Good News is about forgiveness, love of enemies, doing good to those who hate us. Jesus embraces all people in all places. What part of the Gospel do you find difficult to proclaim? Why? Reflect on how you can own this tough teaching.

Prayers *others may be added*

To the Most Holy Trinity, we pray:

◆ Hear our prayer, Triune God.

For the Church, may we respect diversity as we strive for unity, we pray: ◆ For patience when others regard God's will in our lives with suspicion, we pray: ◆ For graduates, may the Holy Spirit guide them on the new journeys of their lives, we pray: ◆ For the sick, though their bodies may be weak, may their spirits be strong, we pray: ◆ For enemies and friends, for those who accept the Gospel and those who reject it, we pray: ◆

Our Father . . .

Lord of all,
your truth is for all people,
your goodness reaches to the ends of
the earth.
Purify our hearts, minds, and speech
that in all ways we may proclaim your
Gospel in sincerity.
We ask this through Christ our Lord.
Amen.

✝ Blessed are you, O Lord, the God of our ancestors!

Sunday, June 18, 2017

Solemnity of the Most Holy Body and Blood of Christ (Corpus Christi)

✝ I will call on the name of the Lord.

Psalm 116 *page 416*

Reading *John 6:52–57*

The Jews quarreled among themselves, saying, "How can this man give us his flesh to eat?" Jesus said to them, "Amen, amen, I say to you, unless you eat the flesh of the Son of Man and drink his blood, you do not have life within you. Whoever eats my flesh and drinks my blood has eternal life, and I will raise him on the last day. For my flesh is true food, and my blood is true drink. Whoever eats my flesh and drinks my blood remains in me and I in him. Just as the living Father sent me and I have life because of the Father, so also the one who feeds on me will have life because of me."

Reflection

The gift of the Eucharist. As we approach the Eucharist Sunday after Sunday we are different each time. Sometimes we are attentive. Other times, distracted. We see the little one with hands barely large enough to hold a host. We see arthritic ones, stumbling toward the Lord. The world over we come to share in the feast. Saints and sinners, we come, beckoned by the Lord.

There are many images, theologies, thoughts, and reflection on the Body and Blood of the Lord. Which is your favorite? Which challenges you? As the bread and wine are transformed into the Real Presence of the Lord, may we too be changed this day.

Prayers *others may be added*

To the Lamb of God, who takes away the sin of the world, we pray:

◆ Have mercy on us.

Lamb of God, in your Blood the new covenant is sealed, bind your Church together forever in you, we pray: ◆ Lord Jesus, Bread of Life, may we who eat at this table, believe in your Real Presence guiding our lives, we pray: ◆ Lord Jesus, Fire of Love, brand into our hearts and our world, a deep respect for all people, of every race, language, and way of life, we pray: ◆ Jesus Christ, Cup of Salvation, heal hearts and bodies broken down by rape, abuse, war, and all acts of violence, we pray: ◆ Lord Jesus, hope for all, may those have died through your holy Body and Blood come to everlasting life, we pray: ◆

Our Father . . .

Loving Lord,
in the gift of the Eucharist,
you share your presence with us and bind us close to you.
May we who share in this feast mirror your presence to others
and build up your Reign in our world.
We ask this through our Lord Jesus Christ, your Son,
who lives and reigns with you in the unity of the Holy Spirit,
one God, for ever and ever.
Amen.

✝ I will call on the name of the Lord.

Monday, June 19, 2017
Weekday

✝ I will call on the name of the Lord.

Psalm 116 *page 416*

Reading *2 Corinthians 6:1–10*

Brothers and sisters: As your fellow workers, we appeal to you not to receive the grace of God in vain. For he says: / *In an acceptable time I heard you, / and on the day of salvation I helped you.* / Behold, now is a very acceptable time; behold, now is the day of salvation. We cause no one to stumble in anything, in order that no fault may be found with our ministry; on the contrary, in everything we commend ourselves as ministers of God, through much endurance, in afflictions, hardships, constraints, beatings, imprisonments, riots, labors, vigils, fasts; by purity, knowledge, patience, kindness, in the Holy Spirit, in unfeigned love, in truthful speech, in the power of God; with weapons of righteousness at the right and at the left; through glory and dishonor, insult and praise. We are treated as deceivers and yet are truthful; as unrecognized and yet acknowledged; as dying and behold we live; as chastised and yet not put to death; as sorrowful yet always rejoicing; as poor yet enriching many; as having nothing and yet possessing all things.

Reflection

Now is the moment. Now is the time. Now is the day of salvation. Too often we get it in our head that salvation is getting to heaven after we die. That's not enough. The Lord proclaimed that the Reign of God is at hand. It is now. If we are the ambassadors, then we are to build up the Kingdom here and now. Now, no one should suffer discrimination. Now, no one should be hungry, homeless, or live in violence. Now should love rule. How can you work to make the Kingdom visible?

Prayers *others may be added*

To the Lamb of God, who takes away the sin of the world, we pray:

◆ Have mercy on us.

May all the baptized labor for the Lord as ministers of the Church, we pray: ◆ May we live as a holy nation, we pray: ◆ May all children play safely, may the ill live in comfort, we pray: ◆ May we learn to give generously, without counting the cost, we pray: ◆ May our actions be faithful to the Gospel's vision of God's Reign, we pray: ◆

Our Father . . .

Holy One,
our Lord Jesus ushered in your Reign in this world.
Yet, poverty, hunger, and hatred remain.
Purify us and our actions.
May our neighbors see your goodness
and may we continue to build up your Gospel of justice.
We ask this through Christ our Lord.
Amen.

✝ I will call on the name of the Lord.

Tuesday, June 20, 2017
Weekday

✝ I will call on the name of the Lord.

Psalm 116
page 416

Reading
2 Corinthians 8:1–4, 7–8

We want you to know, brothers and sisters, of the grace of God that has been given to the churches of Macedonia, for in a severe test of affliction, the abundance of their joy and their profound poverty overflowed in a wealth of generosity on their part. For according to their means, I can testify, and beyond their means, spontaneously, they begged us insistently for the favor of taking part in the service to the holy ones. Now as you excel in every respect, in faith, discourse, knowledge, all earnestness, and in the love we have for you, may you excel in this gracious act also.

I say this not by way of command, but to test the genuineness of your love by your concern for others.

Reflection

How generous are we? How greedy? My parents taught me to share my toys with my brothers. In fact, my toys weren't really mine; they were gifts from my parents. I didn't earn them, buy them, or deserve them. They were freely given because mom and dad knew they would make me happy. So what was I sharing? It is the same with all of our possessions. Everything belongs to God, so why are we covetous? When we see all as God's gift, perhaps we will more freely share with others.

Prayers
others may be added

To the Lamb of God, who takes away the sin of the world, we pray:

◆ Have mercy on us.

For a Church, alive in the graciousness of God, we pray: ◆ For hearts, generous with the love of the Lord, we pray: ◆ For lavishness toward the poor, we pray: ◆ For thankfulness for God's gifts, we pray: ◆ For an end to stinginess, false security, and covetousness, we pray: ◆

Our Father . . .

O Lord,
your blessings are many.
Your grace fills the world.
Yet, we hold fast to our meager possessions,
and in doing so, deny others their daily bread.
Pry open our hands.
Unleash our stores of bounty,
that all may have their needs met today.
We ask this through Christ our Lord.
Amen.

✝ I will call on the name of the Lord.

Wednesday, June 21, 2017
Memorial of St. Aloysius Gonzaga, Religious

✝ I will call on the name of the Lord.

Psalm 116 *page 416*

Reading *2 Corinthians 9:6–8*

Brothers and sisters, consider this: Whoever sows sparingly will also reap sparingly, and whoever sows bountifully will also reap bountifully. Each must do as already determined, without sadness or compulsion, for God loves a cheerful giver. Moreover, God is able to make every grace abundant for you, so that in all things, always having all you need, you may have an abundance for every good work.

Reflection

Aloysius Gonzaga joined the Jesuits (also known as the Society of Jesus) at a young age, against the wishes of his family. But this was not his only challenge. He also had to redirect himself. His ideas on faith, penance, and sacrifice were to change. Penitential actions such as fasting are good, but they are not meant to be self-serving. All that we do should be for love of God and neighbor. Gonzaga found his peace and true penance in serving others in a hospital when a plague struck Rome. Do we separate holy actions from everyday actions? Can we unlock the wall between them and us and serve the Lord as we serve each other?

Prayers *others may be added*

To the Lamb of God, who takes away the sin of the world, we pray:

◆ Have mercy on us.

For a Church that serves, we pray: ◆ For a world where sacred and secular are united in care for one another, we pray: ◆ For physicians, nurses, and all health-care workers, we pray: ◆ For hospice chaplains and spiritual directors, we pray: ◆ For members of the Society of Jesus, we pray: ◆

Our Father . . .

Healer of our every ill,
nurture us and repair our souls.
May we learn the meaning of care and
comfort for others,
and in loving them, so also love you.
We ask this through Christ our Lord.
Amen.

✝ I will call on the name of the Lord.

Thursday, June 22, 2017
Weekday

✝ I will call on the name of the Lord.

Psalm 116 *page 416*

Reading *2 Corinthians 11:1–6*

Brothers and sisters: If only you would put up with a little foolishness from me! Please put up with me. For I am jealous of you with the jealousy of God, since I betrothed you to one husband to present you as a chaste virgin to Christ. But I am afraid that, as the serpent deceived Eve by his cunning, your thoughts may be corrupted from a sincere and pure commitment to Christ. For if someone comes and preaches another Jesus than the one we preached, or if you receive a different spirit from the one you received or a different gospel from the one you accepted, you put up with it well enough. For I think that I am not in any way inferior to these "superapostles." Even if I am untrained in speaking, I am not so in knowledge; in every way we have made this plain to you in all things.

Reflection

Why is Paul so agitated? It seems there are others who have also proclaimed the Gospel to this community, but in a slightly different form. There are people who claim to preach the Good News, but they are imposters. We have seen this too. Their message just doesn't sound like the truth. In some cases, it even changes the Gospel for self-serving purposes. How shall we know? Prayer. Reading the Bible. Reflection. We must trust our hearts, formed in the truth.

Prayers *others may be added*

To the Lamb of God, who takes away the sin of the world, we pray:

◆ Have mercy on us.

May the Church preach the Gospel, fully, carefully, and honestly, we pray: ◆ May refugees find homes, we pray: ◆ May false prophets be silenced, we pray: ◆ May farmers and all who work the land, yield an abundant crop, we pray: ◆ May the truth live in our hearts, we pray: ◆

Our Father . . .

Lord of Truth,
you proclaim eternal truth
and our ears are attuned to your voice.
Silence the cacophony of falsehood,
and in clarity may your message of justice
be announced in all lands.
We ask this through Christ our Lord.
Amen.

✝ I will call on the name of the Lord.

Friday, June 23, 2017
Solemnity of the Most Sacred Heart of Jesus

✝ I will call on the name of the Lord.

Psalm 116 *page 416*

Reading *Deuteronomy 7:6–11*

Moses said to the people: "You are a people sacred to the LORD, your God; he has chosen you from all the nations on the face of the earth to be a people peculiarly his own. It was not because you are the largest of all nations that the LORD set his heart on you and chose you, for you are really the smallest of all nations. It was because the LORD loved you and because of his fidelity to the oath he had sworn to your fathers, that he brought you out with his strong hand from the place of slavery, and ransomed you from the hand of Pharaoh, king of Egypt. Understand, then, that the LORD, your God, is God indeed, the faithful God who keeps his merciful covenant down to the thousandth generation toward those who love him and keep his commandments, but who repays with destruction a person who hates him; he does not dally with such a one, but makes them personally pay for it. You shall therefore carefully observe the commandments, the statutes and the decrees that I enjoin on you today."

Reflection

Too often the image of God in the Old Testament is caricatured as angry. Today's passage challenges this stereotype. The Lord chose Israel in love. The Chosen People did not earn the covenant. They weren't the mightiest nation. It is simply by God's gift of love that they have been chosen. Israel had a difficult time with this idea of a free gift. Can we accept this love? There is no deserving or meriting involved. We are loved simply because we exist. When we look in the mirror, do we see the person God loves? As we celebrate the Sacred Heart of Jesus, let us pray that our love for others mirrors the Lord's.

Prayers *others may be added*

To the Lamb of God, who takes away the sin of the world, we pray:

◆ Have mercy on us.

Heart of Jesus, inspire all leaders of the Church to joyfully do your will, we pray: ◆ Heart of Jesus, source of justice and love, unite nations and peoples throughout the world, we pray: ◆ Heart of Jesus, most worthy of all praise, fill our summer with safe, relaxing days, we pray: ◆ Heart of Jesus, our peace and reconciliation, forgive sins and bring wholeness to all in pain, we pray: ◆ Heart of Jesus, fountain of life and holiness, bless farmers and all who grow our food, we pray: ◆

Our Father . . .

Father of love,
you draw us to you, holding us gently.
Guide our hearts and our steps
that we may be more like you.
We ask this through Christ our Lord.
Amen.

✝ I will call on the name of the Lord.

Saturday, June 24, 2017

Solemnity of the Nativity of St. John the Baptist

☩ I will call on the name of the Lord.

Psalm 116

page 416

Reading

Luke 1:57–66

When the time arrived for Elizabeth to have her child she gave birth to a son. Her neighbors and relatives heard that the Lord had shown his great mercy toward her, and they rejoiced with her. When they came on the eighth day to circumcise the child, they were going to call him Zechariah after his father, but his mother said in reply, "No. He will be called John." But they answered her, "There is no one among your relatives who has this name." So they made signs, asking his father what he wished him to be called. He asked for a tablet and wrote, "John is his name," and all were amazed. Immediately his mouth was opened, his tongue freed, and he spoke blessing God. Then fear came upon all their neighbors, and all these matters were discussed throughout the hill country of Judea. All who heard these things took them to heart, saying, "What, then, will this child be?" For surely the hand of the Lord was with him.

Reflection

Today we honor John the Baptist, a scriptural hinge between the Old and New Testaments. John was called as a prophet in the tradition of his ancestors to proclaim repentance for sins. However, he also points to Jesus, and then John recedes into history. Various texts suggest John, while acknowledging Jesus, didn't fully understand who the Lord was. Is this not like us? Do we really understand Jesus? Even when we say "yes" to discipleship, do we know what it will entail? The birth of John reminds us that though we follow, we are not in charge. Our lives are part of God's plan, not our own.

Prayers

others may be added

To the Lamb of God, who takes away the sin of the world, we pray:

◆ Have mercy on us.

Empower your Church with leaders who passionately proclaim the Gospel, we pray: ◆ Call forth new prophets for our age. Like John the Baptist, may they courageously confront wickedness, and power that oppresses, we pray: ◆ Fill us with faith in your amazing promises. Like Elizabeth, may we place all our hope in your word, we pray: ◆ Give us a spirit of repentance and conversion. Like Zechariah, teach us to return to your way, we pray: ◆ Make of your Word a sharp-edged sword. Let truth cut down the power of evil, and integrity shear the fabric of lies, we pray: ◆

Our Father . . .

Lord of the prophets,
you called John to announce repentance
and to reveal the Lord Jesus to
a community.
Use us as well.
May our actions show the power
of the Risen Lord alive in our midst.
We ask this through Christ our Lord.
Amen.

☩ I will call on the name of the Lord.

Sunday, June 25, 2017
Twelfth Sunday in Ordinary Time

✝ Lord, in your great love, answer me.

Psalm 69 *page 408*

Reading *Matthew 10:28–33*

[Jesus said to the Twelve:] "Do not be afraid of those who kill the body but cannot kill the soul; rather, be afraid of the one who can destroy both soul and body in Gehenna. Are not two sparrows sold for a small coin? Yet not one of them falls to the ground without your Father's knowledge. Even all the hairs of your head are counted. So do not be afraid; you are worth more than many sparrows. Everyone who acknowledges me before others I will acknowledge before my heavenly Father. But whoever denies me before others, I will deny before my heavenly Father."

Reflection

Today Jesus is sending the disciples on mission with a rather ominous expectation. "Do not be afraid" implies there is a reason to be fearful. Jesus' vocation is not without peril. We speak of a new evangelization with high hopes. But what if the message is not received? What happens if friends and coworkers ignore the Gospel? Jesus says that will happen. If guaranteed success is our goal, then evangelization is not for us. So, what does a disciple do? Preach anyway. What roadblocks have you encountered in your quest to share the Good News? What did you do?

Prayers *others may be added*

To the Lord, whose kindness is bountiful, we pray:

◆ Gracious Lord, hear our prayer.

For love of the people, may the Church's leaders serve in holiness and integrity, we pray: ◆ For the love of justice, may rulers, presidents, and representatives seek the common good, we pray: ◆ For the love of life, may we continue to uphold the value of all humanity from the moment of conception to natural death, we pray: ◆ For the love of God, may we have the courage to proclaim the Gospel to all, we pray: ◆ For the promise of eternal life in heaven, we pray: ◆

Our Father . . .

Holy One,
your love conquers all things.
Pain, affliction, and darkness are
overwhelmed in your goodness.
Send a balm of peace upon the earth
that we may live in safety, joy, and dignity.
We ask this through our Lord Jesus
Christ, your Son,
who lives and reigns with you in the unity
of the Holy Spirit,
one God, for ever and ever.
Amen.

✝ Lord, in your great love, answer me.

Monday, June 26, 2017
Weekday

✝ Lord, in your great love, answer me.

Psalm 69

page 408

Reading

Genesis 12:1–4

The LORD said to Abram: "Go forth from the land of your kinsfolk and from your father's house to a land that I will show you.

"I will make of you a great nation, / and I will bless you; I will make your name great, / so that you will be a blessing. / I will bless those who bless you / and curse those who curse you. / All the communities of the earth / shall find blessing in you."

Abram went as the LORD directed him, and Lot went with him. Abram was seventy-five years old when he left Haran.

Reflection

You will be a blessing, says God to Abram. All the earth finds blessing in you. In Baptism we are filled with the Spirit and put on Christ. We share in his Body and Blood in the Eucharist. But we should periodically ask ourselves how we are perceived. Do people see Christ in us or a sour-faced person? We must take our faith seriously, but as Pope Francis states in *The Joy of the Gospel*, we should not look as though we have just come from a funeral. Evaluate your life today and determine to live as a baptized person who is a blessing to the world.

Prayers

others may be added

To the Lord, whose kindness is bountiful, we pray:

◆ Gracious Lord, hear our prayer.

May the Church be a blessing to the lost, lonely, and poor, we pray: ◆ May those who suffer from low self-esteem, learn to treasure their unique value, we pray: ◆ May members of communities filled with fear, work together to ensure safety for all, we pray: ◆ May the curse of war, end, we pray: ◆ May bitterness, prejudice, and persecution cease, we pray: ◆

Our Father . . .

Blessed are you,
Lord our God,
King of the universe.
You bless us with goodness, truth,
and beauty.
Open us, transform us, that we too may
reflect your blessings
for all the world to see.
We ask this through Christ our Lord.
Amen.

✝ Lord, in your great love, answer me.

Tuesday, June 27, 2017
Weekday

✝ **Lord, in your great love, answer me.**

Psalm 69

page 408

Reading

Genesis 13:2, 5–12

Abram was very rich in livestock, silver, and gold.

Lot, who went with Abram, also had flocks and herds and tents, so that the land could not support them if they stayed together; their possessions were so great that they could not dwell together. There were quarrels between the herdsmen of Abram's livestock and those of Lot's. . . .

So Abram said to Lot: "Let there be no strife between you and me, or between your herdsmen and mine, for we are kinsmen. Is not the whole land at your disposal? Please separate from me. If you prefer the left, I will go to the right; if you prefer the right, I will go to the left." Lot looked about and saw how well watered the whole Jordan Plain was as far as Zoar, like the LORD's own garden, or like Egypt. (This was before the LORD had destroyed Sodom and Gomorrah.) Lot, therefore, chose for himself the whole Jordan Plain and set out eastward. Thus they separated from each other; Abram stayed in the land of Canaan, while Lot settled among the cities of the Plain, pitching his tents near Sodom.

Reflection

Even Abram's family sometimes didn't get along. When facing problems directly, families can often find a solution that may at first be hard but ultimately will bring harmony. Abram's family was just like families today with problems that can require difficult solutions. How does your family handle the issues it faces among its members? Do members see value in starting the uncomfortable conversations that are sometimes necessary? Remember to pray for guidance at such times.

Prayers

others may be added

Lord, whose kindness is bountiful,
we pray:

◆ **Gracious Lord, hear our prayer.**

May Church leaders provide a new vision to guide us through churning waters in the world, we pray: ◆ May leaders of nations and communities have the courage to make decisions that empower the poor, we pray: ◆ May our faith give us courage to face adversity and apathy, we pray: ◆ May families be filled with grace, strength, and compassion, we pray: ◆ May we enjoy our time spent with family and friends, and the grace and pleasures God gives us daily, we pray: ◆

Our Father . . .

Father of all,
you have provided us with the gift of family.
Sustain us and bless our family as we seek to nurture each member so that they can bring their gifts to the world.
We ask this through Christ our Lord.
Amen.

✝ **Lord, in your great love, answer me.**

Wednesday, June 28, 2017
Memorial of St. Irenaeus, Bishop and Martyr

✝ Lord, in your great love, answer me.

Psalm 69
page 408

Reading
Genesis 15:2, 4–5, 6–12, 17–18

But Abram said, "O Lord GOD, what good will your gifts be, if I keep on being childless and have as my heir the steward of my house, Eliezer?" Then the word of the LORD came to him: "No, that one shall not be your heir; your own issue shall be your heir." He took him outside and said: "Look up at the sky and count the stars, if you can. Just so," he added, "shall your descendants be."

He then said to him, "I am the LORD who brought you from Ur of the Chaldeans to give you this land as a possession." "O Lord GOD," he asked, "how am I to know that I shall possess it?" He answered him, "Bring me a three-year-old heifer, a three-year-old she-goat, a three-year-old ram, a turtledove, and a young pigeon." Abram brought him all these, split them in two, and placed each half opposite the other; but the birds he did not cut up. Birds of prey swooped down on the carcasses, but Abram stayed with them. As the sun was about to set, a trance fell upon Abram, and a deep, terrifying darkness enveloped him.

When the sun had set and it was dark, there appeared a smoking fire pot and a flaming torch, which passed between those pieces. It was on that occasion that the LORD made a covenant with Abram, saying: "To your descendants I give this land, from the Wadi of Egypt to the Great River the Euphrates."

Reflection
In this version of the making of the covenant, God tells Abram to gather the animals and then puts him in a trance. The cutting of the animals, with parties walking between them signifying their commitment, was how a contract was made. In this case, the flaming torch alone passes through. The covenant is all about God's generosity toward Abram. The blessings are gifts from the Lord. So too is our covenant with the Lord. Grace is a gift.

Prayers
others may be added

To our genersous Lord, we pray:

◆ Gracious Lord, hear our prayer.

May our Church proclaim the generosity of God, we pray: ◆ May nations share their blessings with each other, we pray: ◆ May the gifts of all peoples be treasured as blessings from the Lord, we pray: ◆ May musicians and artists be valued for the blessings of their artistry, we pray: ◆

Our Father . . .

God of our ancestors,
you first made a covenant with Abram,
our father in faith.
In generosity, you made him promises to
which we are heirs.
May this same graciousness overflow in
our world today,
that all might see your bounteous love.
We ask this through Christ our Lord.
Amen.

✝ Lord, in your great love, answer me.

Thursday, June 29, 2017

Solemnity of Sts. Peter and Paul, Apostles

✝ **Lord, in your great love, answer me.**

Psalm 69

page 408

Reading

Acts 12:6–10

On the very night before Herod was to bring him to trial, Peter, secured by double chains, was sleeping between two soldiers, while outside the door guards kept watch on the prison. Suddenly the angel of the Lord stood by him. and a light shone in the cell. He tapped Peter on the side and awakened him, saying, "Get up quickly." The chains fell from his wrists. The angel said to him, "Put on your belt and your sandals." He did so. Then he said to him, "Put on your cloak and follow me." So he followed him out, not realizing that what was happening through the angel was real; he thought he was seeing a vision. They passed the first guard, then the second, and came to the iron gate leading out to the city, which opened for them by itself. They emerged and made their way down an alley, and suddenly the angel left him.

Reflection

This celebration honoring both Peter and Paul is of ancient origin. Both are Apostles, both are martyred in Rome. However, this is where the similarity ends. While contemporaries, they journeyed on different roads. Peter remains a leader in the Jerusalem church while Paul travels the world. They were even in conflict at times over the inclusion of Gentiles into Christianity.

Saints are wonderful heroes for us. However, we each must live our faith in our time. How do you look to a saint to help you as you seek holiness?

Prayers

others may be added

To the Lord, whose kindness is bountiful, we pray:

◆ **Gracious Lord, hear our prayer.**

For N, our pope, N, our bishop, may they follow the example of creativity and compromise exhibited by Sts. Peter and Paul, we pray: ◆ For leaders and all who wield power, may their authority be laden with concern for those with the least influence and the most burdens, we pray: ◆ For the imprisoned and all unjustly accused throughout the world, for freedom and courage, we pray: ◆ For martyrs, may they who still die for the faith be seeds of change and justice, we pray: ◆ For ears to hear God's call, for minds to discern God's will, we pray: ◆

Our Father . . .

Lord God,
you called Sts. Peter and Paul
to guide your fledgling Church.
They responded to the point of offering their lives.
May we too offer our lives for the sake of the Gospel and for the community.
We ask this through Christ our Lord.
Amen.

✝ **Lord, in your great love, answer me.**

Friday, June 30, 2017
Weekday

✝ Lord, in your great love, answer me.

Psalm 69

page 408

Reading

Genesis 17:1, 9–10, 15–16

When Abram was ninety-nine years old, the LORD appeared to him and said: "I am God the Almighty. Walk in my presence and be blameless."

God also said to Abraham: "On your part, you and your descendants after you must keep my covenant throughout the ages. This is my covenant with you and your descendants after you that you must keep: every male among you shall be circumcised."

God further said to Abraham: "As for your wife Sarai, do not call her Sarai; her name shall be Sarah. I will bless her, and I will give you a son by her. Him also will I bless; he shall give rise to nations, and rulers of peoples shall issue from him."

Reflection

Again, we have a story of God making the covenant with Abram. In this story, while the promises are the same, Abram is to do two things. Abram and Sarai are to change their names to Abraham and Sarah. In addition, males are to be circumcised. Scholars tell us these two stories are products of authors from different traditions. An editor put them both in Genesis. While some are frustrated by two accounts, there is wisdom in the editor's choice. Life is more than fact-checking. We rely on perception, influence, memory, and emotions.

Prayers

others may be added

To the Lord, whose kindness is bountiful, we pray

◆ Gracious Lord, hear our prayer.

May the Church help her members embrace diversity, we pray: ◆ May the various perspectives in our world be a source of blessing, we pray: ◆ May business leaders, politicians, judges, and lawmakers open their hearts to justice and the poor, we pray: ◆ May we appreciate and value ourselves, finding joy in becoming all God desires us to be, we pray: ◆ May all who embrace diversity find peace, we pray: ◆

Our Father . . .

Loving God,
your ways are mysterious,
your paths unclear.
You reach out to us in many styles,
fashions, and languages.
Help us to accept and relish the diversity
that speaks of your limitless passion
for us.
We ask this through Christ our Lord.
Amen.

✝ Lord, in your great love, answer me.

Saturday, July 1, 2017
Weekday

✝ Lord, in your great love, answer me.

Psalm 69 *page 408*

Reading *Genesis 18:1–8*

The LORD appeared to Abraham by the Terebinth of Mamre, as Abraham sat in the entrance of his tent, while the day was growing hot. Looking up, he saw three men standing nearby. When he saw them, he ran from the entrance of the tent to greet them; and bowing to the ground, he said: "Sir, if I may ask you this favor, please do not go on past your servant. Let some water be brought, that you may bathe your feet, and then rest yourselves under the tree. Now that you have come this close to your servant, let me bring you a little food, that you may refresh yourselves; and afterward you may go on your way." The men replied, "Very well, do as you have said."

Abraham hastened into the tent and told Sarah, "Quick, three measures of fine flour! Knead it and make rolls." He ran to the herd, picked out a tender, choice steer, and gave it to a servant, who quickly prepared it. Then Abraham got some curds and milk, as well as the steer that had been prepared, and set these before them; and he waited on them under the tree while they ate.

Reflection

Abraham and Sarah are old. Yet, when visitors arrive Abraham jumps up, runs to greet them and puts the whole household on high alert to prepare a meal. The visitors will promise a child to these older adults. Abraham and Sarah don't let age get in the way of serving the Lord. They are ready to change. Are you able to accept any new challenges from God?

Prayers *others may be added*

To the Lord, whose kindness is bountiful, we pray:

◆ Gracious Lord, hear our prayer.

May the Church embrace the vision of youth and the wisdom of age, we pray: ◆ May communities value elders, we pray: ◆ May we respect the dignity of all, despite illness or ailment, we pray: ◆ May those in nursing homes, hospice units, and hospitals, know care and concern, we pray: ◆ May the aged be valued with honor and dignity, we pray: ◆

Our Father . . .

Lord of our years,
you gave Sarah and Abraham a spirit
to still serve in their old age.
Your generosity does not distinguish
between the youthful and elderly.
Keep our spirits lively,
that we may always witness to your love.
We ask this through Christ our Lord.
Amen.

✝ Lord, in your great love, answer me.

Sunday, July 2, 2017
Thirteenth Sunday in Ordinary Time

✝ Forever I will sing the goodness of the Lord.

Psalm 89 *page 412*

Reading *Matthew 10:37–42*

Jesus said to his apostles: "Whoever loves father or mother more than me is not worthy of me, and whoever loves son or daughter more than me is not worthy of me; and whoever does not take up his cross and follow after me is not worthy of me. Whoever finds his life will lose it, and whoever loses his life for my sake will find it.

"Whoever receives you receives me, and whoever receives me receives the one who sent me. Whoever receives a prophet because he is a prophet will receive a prophet's reward, and whoever receives a righteous man because he is a righteous man will receive a righteous man's reward. And whoever gives only a cup of cold water to one of these little ones to drink because the little one is a disciple—amen, I say to you, he will surely not lose his reward."

Reflection

There is something of a descending order in this passage. Jesus begins with the summons of placing our love and commitment to him over and above that of our family and ourself. By the end of the passage the simplest gesture of kindness, giving a cup of cold water, retains our reward. Note that the more difficult challenges lead to receiving Jesus himself, whereas the more general practices yield a reward. Welcoming a prophet, a righteous person, or offering cold water can be done by any conscientious person; being a follower of Jesus demands more than being a good person. It requires total allegiance to Christ.

Prayers *others may be added*

To Christ, who calls us out of darkness into his light, we pray:

◆ Light from Light, hear our prayer.

That the Church remain singular in her allegiance to Christ, we pray: ◆ That nations seek the way of peace together, we pray: ◆ As disciples of Christ, may we seek the Reign of God before all else, we pray: ◆ May we heed the voice of the prophets in our midst, we pray: ◆ For those who minister in soup kitchens and social service agencies, we pray: ◆

Our Father . . .

God of justice and mercy,
you have commanded us
to place no others gods before you.
May we not mix our loyalties
but view all our commitments
through the lens of our covenant with you.
We ask this through our Lord Jesus
Christ, your Son,
who lives and reigns with you in the unity
of the Holy Spirit,
one God, for ever and ever.
Amen.

✝ Forever I will sing the goodness of the Lord.

Monday, July 3, 2017

Feast of St. Thomas, Apostle

✝ Forever I will sing the goodness of the Lord.

Psalm 89

page 412

Reading

John 20:24–29

Thomas, called Didymus, one of the Twelve, was not with them when Jesus came. So the other disciples said to him, "We have seen the Lord." But Thomas said to them, "Unless I see the mark of the nails in his hands and put my finger into the nailmarks and put my hand into his side, I will not believe." Now a week later his disciples were again inside and Thomas was with them. Jesus came, although the doors were locked, and stood in their midst and said, "Peace be with you." Then he said to Thomas, "Put your finger here and see my hands, and bring your hand and put it into my side, and do not be unbelieving, but believe." Thomas answered and said to him, "My Lord and my God!" Jesus said to him, "Have you come to believe because you have seen me? Blessed are those who have not seen and have believed."

Reflection

Though we see at the beginning of this passage that Thomas "doubts," we should not let one event color our image of the Apostle. When Jesus resolved to go to Bethany to raise Lazarus despite the threats on his life, Thomas told his fellow disciples, "Let us also go and die with him" (John 11:16). In Jesus' "farewell discourse," Thomas tells Jesus that "we do not know where you are going; how can we know the way?" (John 14:5). Thomas appears to be a dedicated follower who prefers intellectual clarity and seeks understanding. Do we seek to know more about our faith?

Prayers

others may be added

To Christ, who calls us out of darkness into his light, we pray:

◆ Light from Light, hear our prayer.

May the Church be filled with apostolic zeal, we pray: ◆ For the Church in India, which traces its roots to St. Thomas, we pray: ◆ That we may desire to grow in the knowledge and practice of our faith, we pray: ◆ For seekers and doubters, we pray: ◆ For parishes celebrating their patronal feast today, we pray: ◆

Our Father . . .

Lord Jesus,
you established the Church
on the faith of the Apostles.
May our faith honor their legacy
as we pass it on
to another generation of disciples.
You live and reign with God the Father
in the unity of the Holy Spirit,
one God, for ever and ever.
Amen.

✝ Forever I will sing the goodness of the Lord.

Tuesday, July 4, 2017
Weekday

✝ Forever I will sing the goodness of the Lord.

Psalm 89 *page 412*

Reading *Matthew 8:23–27*

As Jesus got into a boat, his disciples followed him. Suddenly a violent storm came up on the sea, so that the boat was being swamped by waves; but he was asleep. They came and woke him, saying, "Lord, save us! We are perishing!" He said to them, "Why are you terrified, O you of little faith?" Then he got up, rebuked the winds and the sea, and there was great calm. The men were amazed and said, "What sort of man is this, whom even the winds and the sea obey?"

Reflection

Jesus' calming the storm is reminiscent of the Israelites' walking dry shod through the Red Sea. Our ancestors in faith reinterpreted the Exodus to see this as a metaphor for the exodus of Jesus' Death and Resurrection. We share this passage from death to life in Baptism. And so the Exodus functions as an archetype: it was used by those who first came to what would become the United States as a symbol for their journey toward freedom. Likewise, the Exodus figured prominently as a symbol for African-Americans during the civil rights movement. The fullness of freedom is found neither in politics nor economics, but in Christ Jesus.

Prayers *others may be added*

To Christ, who calls us out of darkness into his light, we pray:

◆ Light from Light, hear our prayer.

May the People of God embrace the universality of the Church, we pray: ◆
That the people of the United States work for liberty and justice, we pray: ◆
For Native Americans, we pray: ◆
For prisoners of conscience, we pray: ◆
For all who have given their lives for the freedom of others, we pray: ◆

Our Father . . .

Dear Lord,
you calmed the seas
for the Apostles.
May we look to you
when our lives seem tossed by troubles
and seek refuge in your Word.
Through Christ, our Lord.
Amen.

✝ Forever I will sing the goodness of the Lord.

Wednesday, July 5, 2017
Weekday

✝ Forever I will sing the goodness of the Lord.

Psalm 89 *page 412*

Reading *Genesis 21:9–10, 14–19*

Sarah noticed the son whom Hagar the Egyptian had borne to Abraham playing with her son Isaac; so she demanded of Abraham: "Drive out that slave and her son! No son of that slave is going to share the inheritance with my son Isaac!"

Early the next morning Abraham got some bread and a skin of water and gave them to Hagar. Then, placing the child on her back, he sent her away. As she roamed aimlessly in the wilderness of Beer-sheba, the water in the skin was used up. So she put the child down under a shrub, and then went and sat down opposite him, about a bowshot away; for she said to herself, "Let me not watch to see the child die." As she sat opposite Ishmael, he began to cry. God heard the boy's cry, and God's messenger called to Hagar from heaven: "What is the matter, Hagar? Don't be afraid; God has heard the boy's cry in this plight of his. Arise, lift up the boy and hold him by the hand; for I will make of him a great nation." Then God opened her eyes, and she saw a well of water. She went and filled the skin with water, and then let the boy drink.

Reflection

At the insistence of Sarah, Abraham sends the slave woman who has borne his son, Ishmael, into the wilderness. There, dying of thirst, Ishmael becomes the first person in the Scriptures to cry, and God hears his plight, giving Ishmael the same promise that was made to his father, Abraham, and to his mother, Hagar. That God opens Hagar's eyes is a play on the name Hagar had previously given to God, "The God of Vision" (Genesis 16:13).

Prayers *others may be added*

Called out of darkness into the wonderful light of Christ, we pray:

◆ **Light from Light, hear our prayer.**

May the Church be at the forefront of interreligious dialogue and cooperation, we pray: ◆ For those who observe the Islamic faith, we pray: ◆ For our community leaders, that they will seek to aid abandoned mothers and children, we pray: ◆ For those facing starvation and those who are malnourished, we pray: ◆ That we may see others through the eyes of Christ, we pray: ◆

Our Father . . .

God,
you are compassionate and merciful.
Help all the sons and daughters
of Abraham
to live in peace
and to honor and respect one
another's faith,
for your Son taught us to love others
as ourselves.
We ask this through Christ our Lord.
Amen.

✝ Forever I will sing the goodness of the Lord.

Thursday, July 6, 2017
Weekday

✝ Forever I will sing the goodness of the Lord.

Psalm 89 *page 412*

Reading *Genesis 22:1b–3, 9–12*

God put Abraham to the test. He called to him, "Abraham!" "Here I am," he replied. Then God said: "Take your son Isaac, your only one, whom you love, and go to the land of Moriah. There you shall offer him up as a burnt offering on a height that I will point out to you." Early the next morning Abraham saddled his donkey, took with him his son Isaac, and two of his servants as well, and with the wood that he had cut for the burnt offering, set out for the place of which God had told him.

When they came to the place of which God had told him, Abraham built an altar there and arranged the wood on it. Next he tied up his son Isaac, and put him on top of the wood on the altar. Then he reached out and took the knife to slaughter his son. But the LORD's messenger called to him from heaven, "Abraham, Abraham!" "Here I am," he answered. "Do not lay your hand on the boy," said the messenger. "Do not do the least thing to him. I know now how devoted you are to God, since you did not withhold from me your own beloved son."

Reflection

The parallels between the abandoning of Ishmael and the sacrifice of Isaac are numerous. In both stories a son of Abraham is in mortal danger, God intervenes to save both, the end result is that each will be a father to countless descendants, and both play on the God of Vision. Abraham names the site on which he intended to offer Isaac, "on the mountain the Lord will see." Sadly, the descendants of Abraham, be they Christians, Jews, or Muslims, tend to see mostly their differences, not their commonality.

Prayers *others may be added*

To Christ, our Light, we pray:

◆ **Light from Light, hear our prayer.**

That Christians, Jews, and Muslims honor their unity in Abraham, we pray: ◆ For rabbis and imams, bishops, priests, deacons, and religious, we pray: ◆ That world leaders will urge that religion not be used as a a weapon, we pray: ◆ May religious freedom be honored among all people, we pray: ◆ For children killed in war and in the streets of our cities, we pray: ◆

Our Father . . .

Lover of humankind,
you called your servant Abraham
from whom came three world religions.
May people of faith stop warring and
quarreling among each other
but work together
to alleviate suffering and promote peace.
We ask this through Christ our Lord.
Amen.

✝ Forever I will sing the goodness of the Lord.

Friday, July 7, 2017
Weekday

✝ Be merciful, O Lord, for we have sinned.

Psalm 51

page 406

Reading

Matthew 9:9–13

As Jesus passed by, he saw a man named Matthew sitting at the customs post. He said to him, "Follow me." And he got up and followed him. While he was at table in his house, many tax collectors and sinners came and sat with Jesus and his disciples. The Pharisees saw this and said to his disciples, "Why does your teacher eat with tax collectors and sinners?" He heard this and said, "Those who are well do not need a physician, but the sick do. Go and learn the meaning of the words, / *I desire mercy, not sacrifice.* / I did not come to call the righteous but sinners."

Reflection

"I desire mercy, not sacrifice." These words are a fitting follow-up to the stories of the previous two days in which God disallows the sacrifice of both Ishmael and Isaac. All of us are sinners. None of us can cast the first stone. We are all in need of mercy yet we individually and corporately let racism and ageism influence us and our actions. We often disguise our lack of mercy behind our religiosity. If Pope Francis can identify himself as "a sinner," then we too can drop any façade of self-righteousness and become receivers and givers of mercy.

Prayers

others may be added

To Christ, who calls us out of darkness into his light, we pray:

◆ Light from Light, hear our prayer.

May the Church be willing to eat and drink with sinners, we pray: ◆ May we leave behind our rationalization and admit our sins, we pray: ◆ May our love and charity be a witness to God's mercy, we pray: ◆ May those making end-of-life decisions for another know the compassion of God, we pray: ◆ For all the faithful departed, we pray: ◆

Our Father . . .

God of loving kindness,
your Son, Jesus Christ,
is the embodiment of your mercy in our midst.
May we acknowledge our sins
and learn the meaning of the words,
"I desire mercy, not sacrifice."
We ask this through Christ our Lord.
Amen.

✝ Be merciful, O Lord, for we have sinned.

Saturday, July 8, 2017
Weekday

✝ Forever I will sing the goodness of the Lord.

Psalm 89
page 412

Reading
Matthew 9:14–17

The disciples of John approached Jesus and said, "Why do we and the Pharisees fast much, but your disciples do not fast?" Jesus answered them, "Can the wedding guests mourn as long as the bridegroom is with them? The days will come when the bridegroom is taken away from them, and then they will fast. No one patches an old cloak with a piece of unshrunken cloth, for its fullness pulls away from the cloak and the tear gets worse. People do not put new wine into old wineskins. Otherwise the skins burst, the wine spills out, and the skins are ruined. Rather, they pour new wine into fresh wineskins, and both are preserved."

Reflection
Fasting is a form of penance, an expression of our dependence on God, and is an act of solidarity with the poor and hungry. Only two days of fasting are required during the liturgical year: Ash Wednesday and Good Friday. We also are encouraged to maintain the paschal fast from the time of the Evening Mass of the Lord's Supper on Holy Thursday until the end of the Easter Vigil service. Though the Bridegroom is always with us, consider fasting more often as an act of conversion.

Prayers
others may be added

To Christ, who calls us out of darkness into his light, we pray:

◆ Light from Light, hear our prayer:

Nourished with the Bread of Life and Cup of Salvation, may the Church be in solidarity with the poor and the hungry, we pray: ◆ May we find our security in neither power nor wealth but in God, we pray: ◆ For those who have little or nothing to eat, we pray: ◆ For a simpler lifestyle, we pray: ◆ For the honesty to acknowledge our sins, we pray: ◆

Our Father . . .

God of our longing,
you have provided for all of our needs.
Help us to seek times
to fast from our desires
that we may come to understand
our dependence on you.
We ask this through Christ our Lord.
Amen.

✝ Forever I will sing the goodness of the Lord.

Sunday, July 9, 2017
Fourteenth Sunday in Ordinary Time

✝ I will praise your name forever, my King and my God.

Psalm 145 *page 420*

Reading *Matthew 11:28–30*

[Jesus said to the crowds:] "Come to me, all you who labor and are burdened, and I will give you rest. Take my yoke upon you and learn from me, for I am meek and humble of heart; and you will find rest for yourselves. For my yoke is easy, and my burden light."

Reflection

Nowadays, who is not burdened? In our production-driven world, rest can be considered synonymous with laziness. Rest, though, is part of God's calls to us. We need time away from our work to rejuvenate. Are you able to put work aside to rest in the Lord with family and friends or a hobby? How can you make a place for times of re-creation in your life? Perhaps it will be helpful to ponder Jesus' words, "Come to me . . . find rest . . . my yoke is easy, and my burden light."

Prayers *others may be added*

Seeking the Lord, we pray:

◆ Son of God, hear our prayer.

That the Church persist on proclaiming Sabbath to a weary world, we pray: ◆ For those who labor for minimum wage or less, we pray: ◆ For the gift of humility, we pray: ◆ For those burdened with loved ones yoked to addiction, we pray: ◆ For those weighed down by shame, we pray: ◆

Our Father . . .

God of the earth,
from the beginning of creation,
you rested on the seventh day.
Be with us as we seek to trust in you
so that we will renew ourselves
by resting in your Son,
who lives and reigns with you in the unity of the Holy Spirit,
one God, for ever and ever.
Amen.

✝ I will praise your name forever, my King and my God.

Monday, July 10, 2017
Weekday

✝ I will praise your name forever, my King and my God.

Psalm 145

page 420

Reading

Genesis 28:10–16

Jacob departed from Beer-sheba and proceeded toward Haran. When he came upon a certain shrine, as the sun had already set, he stopped there for the night. Taking one of the stones at the shrine, he put it under his head and lay down to sleep at that spot. Then he had a dream: a stairway rested on the ground, with its top reaching to the heavens; and God's messengers were going up and down on it. And there was the LORD standing beside him and saying: "I, the LORD, am the God of your forefather Abraham and the God of Isaac; the land on which you are lying I will give to you and your descendants. These shall be as plentiful as the dust of the earth, and through them you shall spread out east and west, north and south. In you and your descendants all the nations of the earth shall find blessing. Know that I am with you; I will protect you wherever you go, and bring you back to this land. I will never leave you until I have done what I promised you."

When Jacob awoke from his sleep, he exclaimed, "Truly, the LORD is in this spot, although I did not know it!"

Reflection

What a comforting dream in place of the nightmares that can occupy us either while sleeping or awake. God's messengers ascending and descending the ladder allow for the closeness of the heavenly hosts to ourselves. In this account, the transcendent God is both immanent and accessible. It is the Tower of Babel in reverse, with this being God's initiative. Jacob acknowledges God at his awakening, when he says, "Truly, the Lord is in this spot, although I did not know it." In what situations, times, and places have you been surprised to apprehend the presence of the Holy One?

Prayers

others may be added

Looking to our Savior, who makes our burdens light, we pray:

◆ Son of God, hear our prayer.

May the Church be as Jacob's ladder, we pray: ◆ For greater awareness of God's presence in our lives, we pray: ◆ For priests, religious, lay ecclesial ministers, and parishes that are in transition, we pray: ◆ For those who lie awake at night in fear or anxiety, we pray: ◆ For those who do not believe in God, we pray: ◆

Our Father . . .

God of day and darkness,
though your thoughts are not our thoughts
and your ways are not our ways,
you remain ever close to us.
May we know the comfort of your presence
and be that comfort for others.
We ask this through Christ our Lord.
Amen.

✝ I will praise your name forever, my King and my God.

Tuesday, July 11, 2017
Memorial of St. Benedict, Abbot

✝ I will praise your name forever, my King and my God.

Psalm 145 *page 420*

Reading *Genesis 32:23–29*

In the course of the night, Jacob arose, took his two wives, with the two maidservants and his eleven children, and crossed the ford of the Jabbok. After he had taken them across the stream and had brought over all his possessions, Jacob was left there alone. Then some man wrestled with him until the break of dawn. When the man saw that he could not prevail over him, he struck Jacob's hip at its socket, so that the hip socket was wrenched as they wrestled. The man then said, "Let me go, for it is daybreak." But Jacob said, "I will not let you go until you bless me." The man asked, "What is your name?" He answered, "Jacob." Then the man said, "You shall no longer be spoken of as Jacob, but as Israel, because you have contended with divine and human beings and have prevailed."

Reflection

Jacob seeks the name of the stranger with whom he has wrestled against all night. To know another's name is to have a claim on them. The visitor ignores Jacob's request, which is a hint that he is the Holy One. The stranger then renames Jacob, calling him "Israel," or "one who wrestles with God." Wrestling with God is an apt description of monastic life. St. Benedict (ca. 480–543) is the founder of monastic life. The *Rule of St. Benedict*, his guide on how to live a Christian life and the running of a monastery, continues to be the primary directive for monastic life to this day.

Prayers *others may be added*

Looking to our Savior, who makes our burdens light, we pray:

◆ Son of God, hear our prayer.

That the Church invites her members to live in a more contemplative manner, we pray: ◆ For Benedictine priests, brothers, and sisters throughout the world, we pray: ◆ For those struggling in discernment, we pray: ◆ That we may hear the needs of our youth, we pray: ◆ That we might befriend silence, we pray: ◆

Our Father . . .

God of majesty and awe,
you call to us in silence,
to discern you in community,
to find you in simplicity and service.
Open our minds and hearts
to the wisdom of monastic life
so that we might be contemplatives in a world of action.
We ask this through Christ our Lord.
Amen.

✝ I will praise your name forever, my King and my God.

Wednesday, July 12, 2017
Weekday

✝ I will praise your name forever, my King and my God.

Psalm 145 *page 420*

Reading *Matthew 10:1, 5–7*

Jesus summoned his Twelve disciples and gave them authority over unclean spirits to drive them out and to cure every disease and every illness.

Jesus sent out these Twelve after instructing them thus, "Do not go into pagan territory or enter a Samaritan town. Go rather to the lost sheep of the house of Israel. As you go, make this proclamation: 'The Kingdom of heaven is at hand.'"

Reflection

The names of the Twelve differ in the various Gospel accounts and the Gospel of John admits to no Apostles whatsoever. Paul, Barnabas, Junia, and others also are called "apostles" in the New Testament, so the number twelve is more symbolic than literal. Jesus sends his followers to do what he did: cast out unclean spirits to heal, and proclaim the Kingdom of Heaven. What does this mean for us today? How will I battle the unclean spirits of injustice or judgment? To whom can I bring a healing word? How do I make the Kingdom known?

Prayers *others may be added*

Looking to our Savior, who makes our burdens light, we pray:

◆ Son of God, hear our prayer.

For the Church, that she may encourage all members to proclaim the Good News of God's Reign, we pray: ◆ For the successors to the Apostles, we pray: ◆ That all the baptized embrace their call to ministry and service, we pray: ◆ For medical researchers who seek to find cures and treatments for illness and disease, we pray: ◆ For community leaders, that they will persevere in doing right, we pray: ◆

Our Father . . .

Lord Jesus,
by water and the Holy Spirit,
you claimed us as your own
and gave us the name *Christian.*
Anointed with Sacred Chrism,
we were called to right injustices,
heal those who hurt,
and be your witnesses in word and deed.
Rekindle within us the grace of
our Baptism,
for you live and reign with God the Father
in the unity of the Holy Spirit,
one God, for ever and ever.
Amen.

✝ I will praise your name forever, my King and my God.

Thursday, July 13, 2017
Weekday

✝ I will praise your name forever, my King and my God.

Psalm 145 *page 420*

Reading *Matthew 10:7–13*

Jesus said to his Apostles: "As you go, make this proclamation: 'The Kingdom of heaven is at hand.' Cure the sick, raise the dead, cleanse the lepers, drive out demons. Without cost you have received; without cost you are to give. Do not take gold or silver or copper for your belts; no sack for the journey, or a second tunic, or sandals, or walking stick. The laborer deserves his keep. Whatever town or village you enter, look for a worthy person in it, and stay there until you leave. As you enter a house, wish it peace. If the house is worthy, let your peace come upon it; if not, let your peace return to you."

Reflection

Can you imagine carrying no cash or credit cards, purse or briefcase, no change of clothes? Obviously, Jesus did not live in the twenty-first century where owning a car, computer, and cell phone are necessities. Isn't it interesting that what begins as a luxury soon is regarded as essential? Perhaps the instructions Jesus gives in this Scripture are too impractical for us. But they can help us to reflect on what is necessary and essential; and they remind us that, no matter how much stuff with which we surround ourselves, we remain dependent on God.

Prayers *others may be added*

Looking to our Savior, who makes our burdens light, we pray:

◆ Son of God, hear our prayer.

For N., our pope, and N., our bishop we pray: ◆ That we may not give scandal by living extravagantly or wastefully, we pray: ◆ For those who truly lack the necessities of life, we pray: ◆ For the safety of those who travel on mission trips, we pray: ◆ For the grace of hospitality, we pray: ◆

Our Father . . .

Lord our God,
you accompany us with love as we journey through life.
Help us to travel light both materially and emotionally.
May your love and your grace be enough for us.
We ask this through Christ our Lord.
Amen.

✝ I will praise your name forever, my King and my God.

Friday, July 14, 2017
Memorial of St. Kateri Tekakwitha, Virgin

✝ I will praise your name forever, my King and my God.

Psalm 145
page 420

Reading
Matthew 10:17–22

[Jesus said to his disciples,] "Beware of men, for they will hand you over to the courts and scourge you in their synagogues, and you will be led before governors and kings for my sake as a witness before them and the pagans. When they hand you over, do not worry about how you are to speak or what you are to say. You will be given at that moment what you are to say. For it will not be you who speak but the Spirit of your Father speaking through you. Brother will hand over brother to death, and the father his child; children will rise up against parents and have them put to death. You will be hated by all because of my name, but whoever endures to the end will be saved."

Reflection
"Do not worry about how you are to speak or what you are to say." That is easy for some to do, but others prefer to be prepared. Have you ever had the experience of having the right words come from your mouth, even though you were unprepared? We can trust that it is the Holy Spirit acting within us. It usually is wise to be prepared, but we must allow space for the workings of the Spirit.

Prayers
others may be added

Looking to our Savior, who makes our burdens light, we pray:

◆ Son of God, hear our prayer.

May the Church defend the rights and dignity of indigenous peoples, we pray: ◆ That world leaders may be open to learning from native cultures, we pray: ◆ For Native Americans, we pray: ◆ For a sense of stewardship toward the land, water, and air, we pray: ◆ That we may cultivate respect and reverence for those who have gone before us, we pray: ◆

Our Father . . .

Lord God,
you gave Kateri Tekakwitha
the fortitude to be steadfast in faith
despite the hardships.
May we open our hearts to your love and,
inspired by her example,
accept suffering
for the sake of the Gospel.
We ask this through Christ our Lord.
Amen.

✝ I will praise your name forever, my King and my God.

Saturday, July 15, 2017

Memorial of St. Bonaventure, Bishop and Doctor of the Church

✝ I will praise your name forever, my King and my God.

Psalm 145

page 420

Reading

Matthew 10:24–29

Jesus said to his Apostles: "No disciple is above his teacher, no slave above his master. It is enough for the disciple that he become like his teacher, for the slave that he become like his master. If they have called the master of the house Beelzebul, how much more those of his household!

"Therefore do not be afraid of them. Nothing is concealed that will not be revealed, nor secret that will not be known. What I say to you in the darkness, speak in the light; what you hear whispered, proclaim on the housetops. And do not be afraid of those who kill the body but cannot kill the soul; rather, be afraid of the one who can destroy both soul and body in Gehenna. Are not two sparrows sold for a small coin? Yet not one of them falls to the ground without your Father's knowledge."

Reflection

It is comforting to know that we are worth more than a flock of sparrows! Hyperbole was a common Jewish preaching technique in the first century. The tenderness and assurance in these words, knowing that even a sparrow cannot fall to the ground without God's knowledge, is of unspeakable comfort. In this age of anxiety, fear, and stress, we are reminded of God's love for us.

Prayers

others may be added

Looking to our Savior, who makes our burdens light, we pray:

◆ Son of God, hear our prayer.

That people may know of God's unfathomable love through the ministry of the Church, we pray: ◆ May the baptized seek to grow in knowledge of faith and spirituality, we pray: ◆ For the new evangelization, we pray: ◆ For philosophers and theologians, we pray: ◆ For those who serve the poor and those who seek justice for the oppressed, we pray: ◆

Our Father . . .

God of mystery,
may we seek to know you and your will;
may the gift of your Holy Spirit
inspire us to act in accord with your will.
We ask this through Christ our Lord.
Amen.

✝ I will praise your name forever, my King and my God.

Sunday, July 16, 2017

Fifteenth Sunday in Ordinary Time

✝ The Lord is kind and merciful; slow to anger, and rich in compassion.

Psalm 103 *page 415*

Reading *Matthew 13:1–9*

On that day, Jesus went out of the house and sat down by the sea. Such large crowds gathered around him that he got into a boat and sat down, and the whole crowd stood along the shore. And he spoke to them at length in parables, saying: "A sower went out to sow. And as he sowed, some seed fell on the path, and birds came and ate it up. Some fell on rocky ground, where it had little soil. It sprang up at once because the soil was not deep, and when the sun rose it was scorched, and it withered for lack of roots. Some seed fell among thorns, and the thorns grew up and choked it. But some seed fell on rich soil and produced fruit, a hundred or sixty or thirtyfold. Whoever has ears ought to hear."

Reflection

When it comes to the parable of the sower, we are drawn to the image of the soil and the question, "What kind of soil am I?" The Sower doesn't judge the soil, and perhaps we should not do so either! After all, the same One who made the seed also created the soil. A good harvest would have been about seven percent. To speak of a yield that is a hundred or sixty or thirtyfold suggests an abundance beyond all human imagining, an abundance that more than covers for the seed that fell on the path, rocky soil, or among thorns.

Prayers *others may be added*

To our Lord, who came that we may have life in abundance, we pray:

◆ Hear us, Lord.

May the Church never tire of proclaiming the Good News, we pray: ◆ That our parishes be welcoming communities for all, we pray: ◆ That we strive not to judge ourselves or others but to understand, we pray: ◆ For farmers, migrant workers, and all who work on the land, we pray: ◆ For those who go hungry this day, we pray: ◆

Our Father . . .

Creator of the earth and all
contained therein,
you have declared all you have made to
be good.
Grant that we may recognize, accept,
and cherish
the goodness you have given us,
through our Lord Jesus Christ, your Son,
who lives and reigns with you in the unity
of the Holy Spirit,
one God, for ever and ever.
Amen.

✝ The Lord is kind and merciful; slow to anger, and rich in compassion.

Monday, July 17, 2017
Weekday

✝ The Lord is kind and merciful; slow to anger, and rich in compassion.

Psalm 103

page 415

Reading

Matthew 10:34–36

Jesus said to his Apostles: "Do not think that I have come to bring peace upon the earth. I have come to bring not peace but the sword. For I have come to set a man against his father, a daughter against her mother, and a daughter-in-law against her mother-in-law; and one's enemies will be those of his household."

Reflection

Jesus was a man of peace, but here he says he has not come for peace but for the sword. In context, the "peace" to which Jesus refers is the restoration of the Davidic monarchy, the peace of earthly prosperity. Contrary to those who even today preach "the prosperity Gospel," Jesus denies he brings this peace. The peace of Christ goes deeper than mere material comfort. To this end it will be divisive, hence "the sword." But this is not a sword to be wielded by Christians against others; rather it is the misunderstanding, rejection, and persecution that will result for believing in the *Pax Christi* (peace of Christ) over and against the *pax mundi* (peace of the world).

Prayers

others may be added

To our Lord, who came that we may have life in abundance, we pray:

◆ Hear us, Lord.

That the internal workings of the Church be an example and witness to the peace of Christ, we pray: ◆ That heads of states and governments seek the way of peace together, we pray: ◆ For families that are divided, we pray: ◆ For those we dislike, we pray: ◆ For peacemakers, we pray: ◆

Our Father . . .

Lord Jesus Christ,
you are the Prince of Peace.
Help us to hold fast
to the peace that is beyond all
understanding:
the peace that flows from your life
and ministry,
your Cross and Resurrection.
You live and reign with God the Father in
the unity of the Holy Spirit,
one God, for ever and ever.
Amen.

✝ The Lord is kind and merciful; slow to anger, and rich in compassion.

Tuesday, July 18, 2017
Weekday

☩ The Lord is kind and merciful; slow to anger, and rich in compassion.

Psalm 103
page 415

Reading
Matthew 11:20–24

Jesus began to reproach the towns where most of his mighty deeds had been done, since they had not repented. "Woe to you, Chorazin! Woe to you, Bethsaida! For if the mighty deeds done in your midst had been done in Tyre and Sidon, they would long ago have repented in sackcloth and ashes. But I tell you, it will be more tolerable for Tyre and Sidon on the day of judgment than for you. And as for you, Capernaum:

Will you be exalted to heaven? / You will go down to the netherworld. / For if the mighty deeds done in your midst had been done in Sodom, it would have remained until this day. But I tell you, it will be more tolerable for the land of Sodom on the day of judgment than for you."

Reflection

We tend to overlook the righteous anger of our Lord, but the Gospels do not. Jesus throws the money changers from the Temple and calls Herod a "fox" and Peter "Satan." Jesus curses a fig tree and pronounces a number of woes leveled at the scribes and Pharisees. Anger is not a sin in and of itself. To feel anger is to recognize an injustice. At times, we need to express our anger in a way that can lead to understanding, restoration, and reconciliation.

Prayers
others may be added

To our Lord, who came that we may have life in abundance, we pray:

◆ Lord, hear our prayer.

May the People of God never hesitate in denouncing injustice, we pray: ◆ That the blindness of oppression, discrimination, and prejudice will cease, we pray: ◆ For those whose anger has become rage, we pray: ◆ May we learn cooperation instead of competition, we pray: ◆ For the grace to repent and seek forgiveness, we pray: ◆

Our Father . . .

Lord God,
your gift of anger calls us to seek justice
for ourselves and for others.
In our thirst for fairness,
may we hold ourselves accountable
for using means that are consistent with
the end we seek.
We ask this through Christ our Lord.
Amen.

☩ The Lord is kind and merciful; slow to anger, and rich in compassion.

Wednesday, July 19, 2017
Weekday

✝ **The Lord is kind and merciful; slow to anger, and rich in compassion.**

Psalm 103 *page 415*

page 415

Reading *Exodus 3:1–6, 9–10*

Moses was tending the flock of his father-in-law Jethro, the priest of Midian. Leading the flock across the desert, he came to Horeb, the mountain of God. There an angel of the Lord appeared to him in fire flaming out of a bush. As he looked on, he was surprised to see that the bush, though on fire, was not consumed. So Moses decided, "I must go over to look at this remarkable sight, and see why the bush is not burned."

When the LORD saw him coming over to look at it more closely, God called out to him from the bush, "Moses! Moses!" He answered, "Here I am." God said, "Come no nearer! Remove the sandals from your feet, for the place where you stand is holy ground. I am the God of your father," he continued, "the God of Abraham, the God of Isaac, the God of Jacob. The cry of the children of Israel has reached me, and I have truly noted that the Egyptians are oppressing them. Come now! I will send you to Pharaoh to lead my people, the children of Israel, out of Egypt."

Reflection

All of us need a sanctuary, a place where we can "remove the sandals" so as to be in God's presence, a place of serenity, and renewal. Is there a place in your life that you might identify as holy ground? Where might you find or create such a place in or near your home?

Prayers *others may be added*

To our Lord, who came that we may have life in abundance, we pray:

◆ **Lord, hear our prayer.**

May our Church be holy ground for the world, we pray: ◆ For the inner peace and freedom to become who God calls us to be, we pray: ◆ That we make time for prayer and reflection, we pray: ◆ May parents teach their children to pray, we pray: ◆ For a sense of awe, reverence, and wonder, we pray: ◆

Our Father . . .

O God,
touched by your hand,
our world is holy.
In the midst of our busy lives,
may we pause to remove our sandals
and be attentive to your presence
as it envelops us and holds us.
We ask this through Christ our Lord.
Amen.

✝ **The Lord is kind and merciful; slow to anger, and rich in compassion.**

Thursday, July 20, 2017
Weekday

✝ The Lord is kind and merciful; slow to anger, and rich in compassion.

Psalm 103 *page 415*

Reading *Exodus 3:13–14, 18–20*

Moses, hearing the voice of the Lord from the burning bush, said to him, "When I go to the children of Israel and say to them, 'The God of your fathers has sent me to you,' if they ask me, 'What is his name?' what am I to tell them?" God replied, "I am who am." Then he added, "This is what you shall tell the children of Israel: I AM sent me to you.

"Thus they will heed your message. Then you and the elders of Israel shall go to the king of Egypt and say to him: 'The LORD, the God of the Hebrews, has sent us word. Permit us, then, to go a three-days' journey in the desert, that we may offer sacrifice to the LORD, our God.'

"Yet I know that the king of Egypt will not allow you to go unless he is forced. I will stretch out my hand, therefore, and smite Egypt by doing all kinds of wondrous deeds there. After that he will send you away."

Reflection

When God made his name known to the people of Israel, he was revealing himself to them. By letting them know him, he was opening the relationship to be more intimate. God is made known as the Holy One who is concerned about his people and how they are being treated. God is revealed as one who hears the cry of the poor.

Prayers *others may be added*

To our Lord, who came that we may have life in abundance, we pray:

◆ Teach us your mercy, Lord.

That the cry of the poor be heard by the Church, we pray: ◆ May we be open to simplifying our lifestyle, we pray: ◆ For the grace and courage to reveal our true self, we pray: ◆ For the beggar we see but of whom we never ask their name, we pray: ◆ For those who feel lost, alone, or abandoned, we pray: ◆

Our Father . . .

God of Abraham, Isaac, and Jacob,
in your love you have revealed yourself,
even your very name.
Help us to honor and revere your name
among our families, friends, and in our
workplaces.
We ask this through our Lord Jesus
Christ, your Son,
who lives and reigns with you in the unity
of the Holy Spirit,
one God, for ever and ever.
Amen.

✝ The Lord is kind and merciful; slow to anger, and rich in compassion.

Friday, July 21, 2017
Weekday

✝ The Lord is kind and merciful; slow to anger, and rich in compassion.

Psalm 103

page 415

Reading

Exodus 12:2–4, 11–14

The LORD said to Moses and Aaron in the land of Egypt, "This month shall stand at the head of your calendar; you shall reckon it the first month of the year. Tell the whole community of Israel: On the tenth of this month every one of your families must procure for itself a lamb, one apiece for each household. If a family is too small for a whole lamb, it shall join the nearest household in procuring one and shall share in the lamb in proportion to the number of persons who partake of it.

"This is how you are to eat it: with your loins girt, sandals on your feet and your staff in hand, you shall eat like those who are in flight. It is the Passover of the LORD. For on this same night I will go through Egypt, striking down every first born of the land, both man and beasts, and executing judgment on all the gods of Egypt—I, the LORD! But the blood will mark the houses where you are. Seeing the blood, I will pass over you; thus, when I strike the land of Egypt, no destructive blow will come upon you.

"This day shall be a memorial feast for you, which all your generations shall celebrate with pilgrimage to the LORD, as a perpetual institution."

Reflection

What comes to mind with the phrase, "the Passover of the Lord." Perhaps it is Baptism. Often we think of the Eucharist. But it might be a "death and resurrection" that you have experienced. Where and in what ways do you experience "the Passover of the Lord"?

Prayers

others may be added

To Christ, who gives us life, we pray:

◆ Lord, hear our prayer.

That the joys and hopes, the grief and anguish, of the poor and afflicted, are the joys and hopes, the grief and anguish of the Church, we pray: ◆ May we find in the liturgy of the Church the source and summit of our lives, we pray: ◆ For those held as hostages, we pray: ◆ For those who hold others as hostages, that they may see their victims as persons, we pray: ◆ For our loved ones who have died, we pray: ◆

Our Father . . .

God of salvation,
you make yourself present
to us through the Eucharist.
May we ever be thankful
that you have nurtured us
through the Body and Blood
of your Son
in this sacred mystery.
We ask this through Christ our Lord.
Amen.

✝ The Lord is kind and merciful; slow to anger, and rich in compassion.

Saturday, July 22, 2017
Memorial of St. Mary Magdalene

✝ The Lord is kind and merciful; slow to anger, and rich in compassion.

Psalm 103 *page 415*

Reading *Exodus 12:37–42*

The children of Israel set out from Rameses for Succoth, about six hundred thousand men on foot, not counting the little ones. A crowd of mixed ancestry also went up with them, besides their livestock, very numerous flocks and herds. Since the dough they had brought out of Egypt was not leavened, they baked it into unleavened loaves. They had rushed out of Egypt and had no opportunity even to prepare food for the journey.

The time the children of Israel had stayed in Egypt was four hundred and thirty years. At the end of four hundred and thirty years, all the hosts of the LORD left the land of Egypt on this very date. This was a night of vigil for the LORD, as he led them out of the land of Egypt; so on this same night all the children of Israel must keep a vigil for the LORD throughout their generations.

Reflection

Today's Scripture marks the beginning of Israel's exodus from Egypt. "This was the night of vigil for the Lord." How else to mark the feast of she who is "the apostle to the Apostles"? Mary Magdalene remained present at Jesus' execution. In all four Gospel accounts she is, either alone or with others, the first to be at the empty tomb. In the Gospel accounts of Matthew and John she is the first to see the Risen Christ. Mary of Magdala is the one who carries the shocking word of Jesus' Resurrection to the disciples. In the spirit of Mary of Magdala, each year the Church maintains the solemn vigil of Easter. With Mary of Magdala we proclaim in awe and wonder, "He is risen."

Prayers *others may be added*

To our Lord, who came that we may have life in abundance, we pray:

◆ Teach us your mercy, Lord.

May the Church constantly bear witness to the resurrection, we pray: ◆ For members of the College of Bishops, we pray: ◆ That all disciples may evangelize as did Mary of Magdala, we pray: ◆ For those whose reputation is falsely maligned, we pray: ◆ For those parishes under the patronage of Mary Magdalene, we pray: ◆

Our Father . . .

Lord Jesus,
you gave Mary of Magdala and other women
the faith to nurture the faith of others.
May we too generously give of ourselves
and proclaim to others your Resurrection,
for you live and reign with God the Father
in the unity of the Holy Spirit,
one God, for ever and ever.
Amen.

✝ The Lord is kind and merciful; slow to anger, and rich in compassion.

Sunday, July 23, 2017
Sixteenth Sunday in Ordinary Time

☩ Lord, you are good and forgiving.

Psalm 86
page 412

Reading
Matthew 13:24–30

Jesus proposed another parable to the crowds, saying: "The kingdom of heaven may be likened to a man who sowed good seed in his field. While everyone was asleep his enemy came and sowed weeds all through the wheat, and then went off. When the crop grew and bore fruit, the weeds appeared as well. The slaves of the householder came to him and said, 'Master, did you not sow good seed in your field? Where have the weeds come from?' He answered, 'An enemy has done this.' His slaves said to him, 'Do you want us to go and pull them up?' He replied, 'No, if you pull up the weeds you might uproot the wheat along with them. Let them grow together until harvest."

Reflection
This passage shows how gently Jesus deals with his people. The wheat and the weeds are growing together, and Jesus does not want to uproot one from the other. Sometimes we are eager to judge what is good and what is bad; however, those are not always so identifiable. Perhaps we need to allow ourselves to be tender with all and let the good come to fruition. Openness to mercy while an individual matures can encourage virtue to flourish.

Prayers
others may be added

To the Lord Jesus, who came proclaiming God's Reign, we pray:

◆ Lord, hear our prayer.

For those who serve Christ as missionaries, evangelists, and catechists, we pray: ◆ For farmers and gardeners, we pray: ◆ For patience that is not passivity, we pray: ◆ For people and ideologies that we might judge to be weeds, we pray: ◆ For veterans of war who experience emotional trauma, we pray: ◆

Our Father . . .

God of the earth,
you make the land fruitful.
You send sun and rain to nourish the fruit of the earth.
You sent your Son to nourish us.
May the presence of Christ within us
yield a harvest of justice and mercy.
Through our Lord Jesus Christ, your Son,
who lives and reigns with you in the unity of the Holy Spirit,
one God, for ever and ever.
Amen.

☩ Lord, you are good and forgiving.

Monday, July 24, 2017
Weekday

✝ Lord, you are good and forgiving.

Psalm 86
page 412

Reading
Exodus 14:5–9

When it was reported to the king of Egypt that the people had fled, Pharaoh and his servants changed their minds about them. They exclaimed, "What have we done! Why, we have released Israel from our service!" So Pharaoh made his chariots ready and mustered his soldiers—six hundred first-class chariots and all the other chariots of Egypt, with warriors on them all. So obstinate had the LORD made Pharaoh that he pursued the children of Israel even while they were marching away in triumph. The Egyptians, then, pursued them; Pharaoh's whole army, his horses, chariots and charioteers, caught up with them as they lay encamped by the sea, at Pi-hahiroth, in front of Baal-zephon.

Reflection
Pharaoh is obstinate and now wishes he had not released the Israelites from servitude. A short time ago, all of the houses of Egypt mourned the death of the firstborn. Then, Pharoah told Moses to leave with his people and flocks. Now, Pharaoh changes his mind and sends his warriors to return the Israelites. When have you had a conversion only to discard it in a few days? You may have made a decision to work on your prayer life only to become more lax. What do you need to do to be steadfast with a spiritual resolution?

Prayers
others may be added

To our Lord Jesus, who came proclaiming God's Reign, we pray:

◆ Lord, hear our prayer.

May those holding authority in the Church be beacons of mercy and charity, we pray: ◆ That heads of nations view their leadership through the eyes of the poor and disenfranchised, we pray: ◆ For organized labor and the working poor, we pray: ◆ For those who are abused and those who are discriminated against, we pray: ◆

Our Father . . .

Lord God,
you offer us experiences
to change our hearts.
Help us to be steadfast
in our resolve to grow
in an intimate relationship with you.
We ask this through Christ our Lord.
Amen.

✝ Lord, you are good and forgiving.

Tuesday, July 25, 2017
Feast of St. James, Apostle

✝ Lord, you are good and forgiving.

Psalm 86 *page 412*

Reading *Matthew 20:20–23*

The mother of the sons of Zebedee approached Jesus with her sons and did him homage, wishing to ask him for something. He said to her, "What do you wish?" She answered him, "Command that these two sons of mine sit, one at your right and the other at your left, in your kingdom." Jesus said in reply, "You do not know what you are asking. Can you drink the chalice that I am going to drink?" They said to him, "We can." He replied, "My chalice you will indeed drink, but to sit at my right and at my left, this is not mine to give but is for those for whom it has been prepared by my Father."

Reflection

One wonders if James and John, the sons of Zebedee, were embarrassed by their mother's request. Possibly not. It is comforting to see the flawed humanity of the Apostles. Their weakness affords us some solace as we acknowledge our failings. The Apostle James, not to be confused with the Apostle James the Less, or the author of the Epistle of James, was the first to be martyred (Acts 12:1–3). Despite our flaws, we too are capable of making a great witness for Christ.

Prayers *others may be added*

To our Lord Jesus, who came proclaiming God's Reign, we pray:

◆ Lord, hear our prayer.

Built on the foundation of the Apostles, may the Church not fear opposition but continue to bear witness to God's Reign, we pray: ◆ For Christians and non-Christians who face persecution and torture, we pray: ◆ For mothers and fathers, we pray: ◆ That we may accept our humanity and the humanity of others, we pray: ◆ For parishes celebrating their patronal feast day today, we pray: ◆

Our Father . . .

Lord Jesus,
you called "the sons of thunder," James and John,
to be among your most intimate disciples:
While challenging them to grow you accepted who they were.
May we do the same for ourselves and for each other.
You live and reign with God the Father in the unity of the Holy Spirit,
one God, for ever and ever.
Amen.

✝ Lord, you are good and forgiving.

Wednesday, July 26, 2017

Memorial of Sts. Joachim and Anne,
Parents of the Blessed Virgin Mary

† Lord, you are good and forgiving.

Psalm 86

page 412

Reading

Matthew 13:16–17

Jesus said to his disciples: "Blessed are your eyes, because they see, and your ears, because they hear. Amen, I say to you, many prophets and righteous people longed to see what you see but did not see it, and to hear what you hear but did not hear it."

Reflection

Today we honor Joachim and Anne, the parents of Mary. We know the names of Mary's parents only from tradition. We literally know nothing about them. Why honor such anonymity? Because of Mary herself, whom we can assume was guided by her parents in the way of Judaism, unknowingly preparing her for the great part she would play in the history of salvation. Most of us come from similar anonymity and we will someday be unknown and forgotten. It is a history of the anonymous and the unknowns that have passed on this faith. Many have longed to see what we have seen and to hear what we have heard.

Prayers

others may be added

To our Lord Jesus, who came proclaiming God's Reign, we pray:

◆ Lord, hear our prayer.

That the Church will nurture all its members, we pray: ◆ That we may draw strength from our sharing in the Communion of Saints, we pray: ◆ For those who are unable to conceive, we pray: ◆ For parents, grandparents, godparents, and foster parents, we pray: ◆ For parishes who celebrate their patronal feast today, we pray: ◆

Our Father . . .

God of our forbearers,
we give you thanks
for those who have gone before us
who have,
in ways great and small,
nurtured the gift of faith
planted within us by the Holy Spirit.
May we express our gratitude by kindling
the gift of faith in others.
We ask this through Christ our Lord.
Amen.

† Lord, you are good and forgiving.

Thursday, July 27, 2017
Weekday

✝ Lord, you are good and forgiving.

Psalm 86 *page 412*

Reading *Exodus 19:9–11, 16*

While Israel was encamped here in front of the mountain, the LORD told Moses, "I am coming to you in a dense cloud, so that when the people hear me speaking with you, they may always have faith in you also." When Moses, then, had reported to the LORD the response of the people, the LORD added, "Go to the people and have them sanctify themselves today and tomorrow. Make them wash their garments and be ready for the third day; for on the third day the Lord will come down on Mount Sinai before the eyes of all the people."

On the morning of the third day there were peals of thunder and lightning, and a heavy cloud over the mountain, and a very loud trumpet blast, so that all the people in the camp trembled.

Reflection

"Why don't these kinds of encounters with God happen today?" This is not an uncommon question. It stems from our tendency to overlook poetry and metaphor. Did the encounter with God occur exactly as described in Exodus 19? Possibly. It is also likely that the author uses the language of poetry to convey the experience of the Israelites. Recall a moment in which you felt God's presence. How would you describe it to someone else? Can you identify with the people in the camp who trembled?

Prayers *others may be added*

To our Lord Jesus, who came proclaiming God's Reign, we pray:

◆ Lord, hear our prayer.

May the Church's worship be an experience of encountering the Holy One, we pray: ◆ For an appreciation of myth and metaphor, poetry and symbol, we pray: ◆ For poets, novelists, playwrights, and screenwriters, we pray: ◆ For the willingness to share our faith, we pray: ◆ For those who feel only the absence of God, we pray: ◆

Our Father . . .

Loving God,
you come to us in Word and sacrament,
in work and recreation,
in others and within our being.
Help us to know and to experience
the holiness that envelops our lives.
We ask this through Christ our Lord.
Amen.

✝ Lord, you are good and forgiving.

Friday, July 28, 2017
Weekday

✝ Lord, you are good and forgiving.

Psalm 86

page 412

Reading

Exodus 20:1–6

In those days: God delivered all these commandments:

"I, the LORD, am your God, who brought you out of the land of Egypt, that place of slavery. You shall not have other gods besides me. You shall not carve idols for yourselves in the shape of anything in the sky above or on the earth below or in the waters beneath the earth; you shall not bow down before them or worship them. For I, the LORD, your God, am a jealous God, inflicting punishment for their fathers' wickedness on the children of those who hate me, down to the third and fourth generation; but bestowing mercy down to the thousandth generation on the children of those who love me and keep my commandments."

Reflection

The Ten Commandments are given by God in the context of the covenant, the relational bond of love established between God and Israel. The bond of covenantal love runs deeper than contractual love. In the latter, if one party breaks the agreement, the entire contract is null and void. A covenant is unconditional. Even if one party violates the agreement, the other party remains obligated to it. We live the Commandments not merely as "rules to live by" or "laws to be obeyed"; rather we value the relationship to God and to the community the Commandments uphold.

Prayers

others may be added

To our Lord Jesus, who came proclaiming God's Reign, we pray:

◆ Lord, hear our prayer.

May the Church be again a respected moral voice in the world, we pray: ◆ That we will view law in terms of relationship rather than legalism, we pray: ◆ May people of faith honor the Sabbath even when it requires sacrifice, we pray: ◆ For a lessening of violence in our world, in our streets, and in our hearts, we pray: ◆ For the faithful departed, we pray: ◆

Our Father . . .

Lord Jesus,
you gave us the Great Commandments
of loving God
with the entirety of our being and our
neighbor as ourself.
May we see that these commandments
are so interrelated
that we cannot observe one without
observing the other.
You live and reign with God the Father in
the unity of the Holy Spirit,
one God, for ever and ever.
Amen.

✝ Lord, you are good and forgiving.

Saturday, July 29, 2017
Memorial of St. Martha

☩ Lord, you are good and forgiving.

Psalm 86 *page 412*

Reading *John 11:19–24*

Many of the Jews had come to Martha and Mary to comfort them about their brother [Lazarus, who had died]. When Martha heard that Jesus was coming, she went to meet him; but Mary sat at home. Martha said to Jesus, "Lord, if you had been here, my brother would not have died. But even now I know that whatever you ask of God, God will give you." Jesus said to her, "Your brother will rise." Martha said to him, "I know he will rise, in the resurrection on the last day."

Reflection

Each of the four Gospel accounts presents one person who confesses faith in Jesus. In Mark it is the centurion at the Cross, in Matthew it is Peter, in Luke it is Mary, Jesus' mother, and in John it is Martha. Our first thought of Martha might be that of the burdened homemaker who asks Jesus to make her sister help her. In this passage Martha is a woman who is grieving and angry with Jesus. Still, her wounds do not deplete her faith but inspire her to profess all the more decisively. How do we respond to God when we are hurting?

Prayers *others may be added*

To our Lord Jesus, who came proclaiming God's Reign, we pray:

◆ Lord, hear our prayer.

That the Church gallantly proclaim Jesus as the Resurrection and the life, we pray: ◆ For parents wounded by their children's failure to practice the faith, we pray: ◆ May parishioners champion the virtue of hospitality, we pray: ◆ For homemakers, hosts, servers, and all who work in positions of hospitality, we pray: ◆ For parishes dedicated to St. Martha, we pray: ◆

Our Father . . .

Lord Jesus,
you revealed your humanity
through the bond of love and friendship
you shared
with Martha, Mary, and Lazarus.
Following your example,
may we not run from our humanity but
embrace it;
and may we cherish our friends.
You live and reign with God the Father in
the unity of the Holy Spirit,
one God, for ever and ever.
Amen.

☩ Lord, you are good and forgiving.

Sunday, July 30, 2017
Seventeenth Sunday in Ordinary Time

✝ Lord, I love your commands.

Psalm 119(B) *page 418*

Reading *Matthew 13:44–46*

Jesus said to his disciples: "The kingdom of heaven is like a treasure buried in a field, which a person finds and hides again, and out of joy goes and sells all that he has and buys that field. Again, the kingdom of heaven is like a merchant searching for fine pearls. When he finds a pearl of great price, he goes and sells all that he has and buys it."

Reflection

The Kingdom of Heaven is like a pearl of great price. In the parable the merchant sells everything for the one pearl. Clearly the Lord is talking about our dedication to the Kingdom; it is worth everything we have. There is one more thing about pearls, though. They become more radiant, more full of luster, more beautiful, the more they are worn. It's not enough to recognize the Kingdom and see ourselves in possession of it. No, we must share it. The Reign of God is best when it shines in our lives every day.

Prayers *others may be added*

Looking to our Lord, whose law is more precious than gold, we pray:

◆ Lord, hear our prayer.

For Pope N., for good health, vision, and courage to speak truth to power, we pray: ◆ For a Spirit of wisdom and understanding to guide our community's leaders, we pray: ◆ For an end to war, hunger, and poverty in our world, we pray: ◆ For joy in the Kingdom of Heaven alive in our midst, we pray: ◆ For all who now rest in the peace of Christ, we pray: ◆

Our Father . . .

Gracious One,
your Reign is the center of our lives.
In you we live and move and have
our being.
May our commitment to the Gospel
be a clear and ever-present beacon in
our lives,
drawing others to you.
We ask this through our Lord Jesus
Christ, your Son,
who lives and reigns with you in the unity
of the Holy Spirit,
one God, for ever and ever.
Amen.

✝ Lord, I love your commands.

Monday, July 31, 2017

Memorial of St. Ignatius of Loyola, Priest

† Lord, I love your commands.

Psalm 119(B)

page 418

Reading

Exodus 32:15–20

Moses turned and came down the mountain with the two tablets of the commandments in his hands, tablets that were written on both sides, front and back; tablets that were made by God, having inscriptions on them that were engraved by God himself. Now, when Joshua heard the noise of the people shouting, he said to Moses, "That sounds like a battle in the camp." But Moses answered, "It does not sound like cries of victory, nor does it sound like cries of defeat; the sounds that I hear are cries of revelry." As he drew near the camp, he saw the calf and the dancing. With that, Moses' wrath flared up, so that he threw the tablets down and broke them on the base of the mountain. Taking the calf they had made, he fused it in the fire and then ground it down to powder, which he scattered on the water and made the children of Israel drink.

Reflection

Ignatius of Loyola, the soldier, was bound for glory and fame. Ignatius, the mystic, served others. He put down his military career and placed his will at the service of the Lord and the Church. The Society of Jesus, the Jesuits, founded by Loyola, is known for education and dedication to spreading the faith. Education, however, is not an end. The point for Ignatius is to be willing to surrender ourselves to God. As a soldier he learned to take orders, as a Christian, his orders were from God.

Prayers

others may be added

Looking to our Lord, whose law is more precious than gold, we pray:

◆ Lord, hear our prayer.

For the Church, may we discern the will of the Lord and live it boldly, we pray: ◆ For peacemakers and all who seek justice, we pray: ◆ For an end to bitterness in our world and our lives, we pray: ◆ For teachers, social workers, and all whose lives are given in service to others, we pray: ◆ For members of the Society of Jesus, we pray: ◆

Our Father . . .

Lord God,
you heard the fervent prayer of your servant Ignatius of Loyola.
Hear us as we pray with him,
"Receive, Lord, all my liberty, my memory, my understanding and my whole will.
You have given me all that I have, all that I am,
and I surrender all to your divine will,
that you dispose of me.
Give me only your love and your grace.
With this I am rich enough, and I have no more to ask."
We ask this through Christ our Lord.
Amen.

† Lord, I love your commands.

Tuesday, August 1, 2017

Memorial of St. Alphonsus Ligouri,
Bishop and Doctor of the Church

✝ Lord, I love your commands.

Psalm 119(B) *page 418*

Reading *Exodus 34:5b-9, 28*

Moses stood there with the Lord and proclaimed his name, "LORD." Thus the LORD passed before him and cried out, "The LORD, the LORD, a merciful and gracious God, slow to anger and rich in kindness and fidelity, continuing his kindness for a thousand generations, and forgiving wickedness and crime and sin; yet not declaring the guilty guiltless, but punishing children and grandchildren to the third and fourth generation for their fathers' wickedness!" Moses at once bowed down to the ground in worship. Then he said, "If I find favor with you, O LORD, do come along in our company. This is indeed a stiff-necked people; yet pardon our wickedness and sins, and receive us as your own."

So Moses stayed there with the LORD for forty days and forty nights, without eating any food or drinking any water, and he wrote on the tablets the words of the covenant, the ten commandments.

Reflection

In 1950 Pius XII proclaimed Alphonsus Liguori the patron saint of moral theologians. This founder of the Redemptorists was no rigid rubricist. He left the study of law to become a preacher, confessor, and pastor. He knew the struggles of people's lives, saw their pain, and brought the Gospel to them. He was also known to preach what we would call parish missions. These were aimed at peasants in rural areas. His life was filled with sorrow and pain, physical and emotional. His own Redemptorists even betrayed him. The joy of the Gospel was his solace and friend until his death in 1787.

Prayers *others may be added*

To Christ, who calls us out of darkness into his light, we pray:

◆ Light from Light, hear our prayer.

For our Church, may we be united in the suffering and pain of all people, we pray: ◆ For a world without war or poverty, we pray: ◆ For an end to deceit of every kind, we pray: ◆ For the Redemptorists, we pray: ◆ For spiritual directors, confessors, and moral theologians, we pray: ◆

Our Father . . .

Lord,
your servant Alphonsus Liguori
suffered bravely.
His love for the truth of your Gospel
taught him patience and solidarity
with the struggles of your people.
His physical ailments brought him close
to all who are in pain.
May we too live in unanimity with our
sisters and brothers,
judging not, lest we be judged.
We ask this through Christ our Lord.
Amen.

✝ Lord, I love your commands.

Wednesday, August 2, 2017
Weekday

✝ Lord, I love your commands.

Psalm 119(B)

page 418

Reading

Exodus 34:29–35

As Moses came down from Mount Sinai with the two tablets of the commandments in his hands, he did not know that the skin of his face had become radiant while he conversed with the LORD. When Aaron, then, and the other children of Israel saw Moses and noticed how radiant the skin of his face had become, they were afraid to come near him. Only after Moses called to them did Aaron and all the rulers of the community come back to him. Moses then spoke to them. Later on, all the children of Israel came up to him, and he enjoined on them all that the LORD had told him on Mount Sinai. When he finished speaking with them, he put a veil over his face. Whenever Moses entered the presence of the LORD to converse with him, he removed the veil until he came out again. On coming out, he would tell the children of Israel all that had been commanded. Then the children of Israel would see that the skin of Moses' face was radiant; so he would again put the veil over his face until he went in to converse with the LORD.

Reflection

When Moses speaks with the Lord, his face becomes radiant. The people notice. Are we radiant when we are in the Lord's presence? It seems a bit surreal and overwhelming. Think about people you consider holy. Do they have a glow or peace about them? In Detroit, stories abound about Solanus Casey, a Capuchin friar now on the path to canonization. When people were around him, they felt the presence of God. When he looked at them, people said it seemed God was looking at them. Can we also be like this? Can we so mirror the Lord that our presence reflects the presence of God to others?

Prayers

others may be added

To Christ, who calls us out of darkness into his light, we pray:

◆ Light from Light, hear our prayer.

May our Church radiate the mercy of God to the world, we pray: ◆ May leaders of nations be guided by the light of justice, we pray: ◆ May teachers help their students shine in learning and hope, we pray: ◆ May those who hunger for a peaceful spirit be drawn to the arms of the Lord, we pray: ◆ May we be beacons of the Gospel to all we meet, we pray: ◆

Our Father . . .

Radiant Lord,
your love shines upon the whole world.
In our Baptism,
we promised to keep the flame of
faith burning.
May this light shining within us bring
our light
to places of darkness and hope
for all who struggle with gloom.
We ask this through Christ our Lord.
Amen.

✝ Lord, I love your commands.

Thursday, August 3, 2017
Weekday

✝ Lord, I love your commands.

Psalm 119(B) *page 418*

Reading *Exodus 40:16–21*

Moses did exactly as the LORD had commanded him. On the first day of the first month of the second year the Dwelling was erected. It was Moses who erected the Dwelling. He placed its pedestals, set up its boards, put in its bars, and set up its columns. He spread the tent over the Dwelling and put the covering on top of the tent, as the LORD had commanded him. He took the commandments and put them in the ark; he placed poles alongside the ark and set the propitiatory upon it. He brought the ark into the Dwelling and hung the curtain veil, thus screening off the ark of the commandments, as the LORD had commanded him.

Reflection

Moses builds for his people a physical place where the Lord rests among them. While the Church is the People of God, buildings too have their place. In our tradition, they are where the People of God gather with their Lord. Even when no liturgy is being celebrated, the building itself is a sign of Christ to the community. Our parishes should be beacons of solace and sources of challenge. As we care for our church buildings and grounds, we consider that they herald God to all who see it.

Prayers *others may be added*

To Christ, who calls us out of darkness into his light, we pray:

◆ Light from Light, hear our prayer.

For our Church, a sign of hope and challenge, we pray: ◆ For parish and diocesan leaders, we pray: ◆ For faith communities that struggle with finances, staffing, and participation, we pray: ◆ For our sisters and brothers in need of food and safety, we pray: ◆ For victims of drought, we pray: ◆

Our Father . . .

God of expectations,
you have provided us with faith to share with others.
May our parishes make you known
in our communities by the way
we live your Word.
Send your Spirit to guide us, sustain us, and bring us healing.
We ask this through Christ our Lord.
Amen.

✝ Lord, I love your commands.

Friday, August 4, 2017

Memorial of St. John Vianney, Priest

✝ Lord, I love your commands.

Psalm 119(B)

page 418

Reading

Matthew 13:54–58

Jesus came to his native place and taught the people in their synagogue. They were astonished and said, "Where did this man get such wisdom and mighty deeds? Is he not the carpenter's son? Is not his mother named Mary and his brothers James, Joseph, Simon, and Judas? Are not his sisters all with us? Where did this man get all this?" And they took offense at him. But Jesus said to them, "A prophet is not without honor except in his native place and in his own house." And he did not work many mighty deeds there because of their lack of faith.

Reflection

St. John Vianney knew his share of struggles. His road to priesthood was not an easy one since his education was originally lacking. As a priest, he spent hours as a confessor, listening to people's difficulties, heartbreaks, and sins. When we immerse ourselves in the lives of others, it will bring joy but also sorrow. Solidarity demands a "walking with another." We do not sit in judgment, but stand in mercy. When we understand our shortcomings and problems, we can, like John Vianney, listen to others with an open heart. Be aware today of whom God is placing in your life and may need a friendly ear.

Prayers

others may be added

To Christ, who calls us out of darkness into his light, we pray:

◆ Light from Light, hear our prayer.

For our pope, may he guide the Church in ways of mercy, we pray: ◆ For all bishops and priests, may they hear the pains and sorrows of their people, we pray: ◆ For confessors, may they be instruments of healing and reconciliation, we pray: ◆ For all whose hearts are burdened with sin, we pray: ◆ For victims of our sins and injustice, we pray: ◆

Our Father . . .

Lord of hope and healing,
you blessed John Vianney
with a heart of mercy and a spirit of
reconciliation.
Bless our parish priests with these
same gifts.
May they be pastors of souls
and missionaries of your merciful love.
We ask this through Christ our Lord.
Amen.

✝ Lord, I love your commands.

Saturday, August 5, 2017
Weekday

✝ Lord, I love your commands.

Psalm 119(B) *page 418*

Reading *Leviticus 25:1, 8–14*

The LORD said to Moses on Mount Sinai, "Seven weeks of years shall you count—seven times seven years—so that the seven cycles amount to forty-nine years. Then, on the tenth day of the seventh month, let the trumpet resound; on this, the Day of Atonement, the trumpet blast shall re-echo throughout your land. This fiftieth year you shall make sacred by proclaiming liberty in the land for all its inhabitants. It shall be a jubilee for you, when every one of you shall return to his own property, every one to his own family estate. In this fiftieth year, your year of jubilee, you shall not sow, nor shall you reap the aftergrowth or pick the grapes from the untrimmed vines. Since this is the jubilee, which shall be sacred for you, you may not eat of its produce, except as taken directly from the field.

"In this year of jubilee, then, every one of you shall return to his own property. Therefore, when you sell any land to your neighbor or buy any from him, do not deal unfairly."

Reflection

Today the Lord tells Moses that every fiftieth year is a time of jubilee! Now the land is returned to its original owner. So, as people buy and sell the property, the price should be reckoned with the year of jubilee in mind. The attitude is one of fairness and remembrance. In the end, all belongs to God. Too often our faith is limited to Sunday. Do we live out each day what we profess and pray in the liturgy?

Prayers *others may be added*

To Christ, who calls us out of darkness into his light, we pray:

◆ **Light from Light, hear our prayer.**

May the business of the Church reflect Gospel values, we pray: ◆ May our global economy be governed by justice for all, we pray: ◆ May workers receive fair wages, health care, and safe environments, we pray: ◆ May the Sabbath be respected, we pray: ◆ May greed, avarice, and covetousness cease, we pray: ◆

Our Father . . .

Lord of all,
everything we have is a gift from you.
May our daily labor bring us satisfaction;
our daily bread feed our bodies.
May all people work in honesty, truth,
compassion, and sincerity of heart.
We ask this through Christ our Lord.
Amen.

✝ Lord, I love your commands.

Sunday, August 6, 2017
Feast of the Transfiguration of the Lord

✝ The Lord answers all our needs.

Psalm 145 *page 420*

Reading *Matthew 17:1–5*

Jesus took Peter, James, and John his brother, and led them up a high mountain by themselves. And he was transfigured before them; his face shone like the sun and his clothes became white as light. And behold, Moses and Elijah appeared to them, conversing with him. Then Peter said to Jesus in reply, "Lord, it is good that we are here. If you wish, I will make three tents here, one for you, one for Moses, and one for Elijah." While he was still speaking, behold, a bright cloud cast a shadow over them, then from the cloud came a voice that said, "This is my beloved Son, with whom I am well pleased; listen to him."

Reflection

On the Second Sunday of Lent we read the same Gospel. How different it may appear today. On this date, in 1945, the United States dropped an atomic bomb on Hiroshima. On August 9, another was released on Nagasaki. Our Gospel tells the story of transfiguration, a glimpse of resurrection, and of Jesus' relationship with the Law (Moses) and the prophets (Eilijah). The contrast of stories is striking. We see devastation in the cities that were bombed and hope in Jesus. We see death after the bombing but life with Christ. All of life needs to be viewed in light of the life that Christ brings.

Prayers *others may be added*

Turning to the Lord, who transforms us, we pray:

◆ Lord, hear our prayer.

For the Church, may the Spirit teach us to envision the world as God sees it, we pray: ◆ For an end to nuclear proliferation, we pray: ◆ For the people of Japan, we pray: ◆ For victims of terrorism, we pray: ◆ For all who have died, may they now join the heavenly host in praising God forever, we pray: ◆

Our Father . . .

All powerful and ever-loving God,
you are the giver of life.
Forgive our sins and open our eyes.
May we see the world as you do.
May we love our sisters and brothers as you do.
May we act in justice, charity, and peace.
We ask this through our Lord Jesus Christ, your Son,
who lives and reigns with you in the unity of the Holy Spirit,
one God, for ever and ever.
Amen.

✝ The Lord answers all our needs.

Monday, August 7, 2017
Weekday

✝ The Lord answers all our needs.

Psalm 145 *page 420*

Reading *Numbers 11:4b–6, 10–11*

The children of Israel lamented, "Would that we had meat for food! We remember the fish we used to eat without cost in Egypt, and the cucumbers, the melons, the leeks, the onions, and the garlic. But now we are famished; we see nothing before us but this manna."

When Moses heard the people, family after family, crying at the entrance of their tents, so that the LORD became very angry, he was grieved. "Why do you treat your servant so badly?" Moses asked the LORD. "Why are you so displeased with me that you burden me with all this people?"

Reflection

The people of Israel are beside themselves. They left Egypt for freedom, but they didn't count on hardship. At the beginning, they were grateful for the manna, but day after day of the same food made the people angry. We know the feeling. Sometimes, even when we count our blessings, life feels like drudgery. Discipleship is a commitment, and it is hard to sustain our commitments. Sometimes we prefer an easier path. This is a good time to examine what helps you stay committed to your faith and whether you need to take part in a retreat, Scripture study, or spiritual direction to nourish your commitment.

Prayers *others may be added*

In you O Lord, we place all our trust, we pray:

◆ Lord, hear our prayer.

For our faith community, may we live faithfully to our baptismal promises, we pray: ◆ For married couples, may their daily lives support their wedding promises, we pray: ◆ For nations, may they respect the lives and dignity of other nations, we pray: ◆ For an end to human trafficking, we pray: ◆ For peace, we pray: ◆

Our Father . . .

God of freedom,
you give us every good gift,
yet sometimes we feel burdened by the mundanity of daily life.
Send us a spirit of peace in times of boredom,
a spirit of commitment, when we feel indifferent.
May we always be true to your Gospel.
We ask this through Christ our Lord.
Amen.

✝ The Lord answers all our needs.

Tuesday, August 8, 2017

Memorial of St. Dominic, Priest

✝ The Lord answers all our needs.

Psalm 145

page 420

Reading

Numbers 12:1–10

Miriam and Aaron spoke against Moses on the pretext of the marriage he had contracted with a Cushite woman. They complained, "Is it through Moses alone that the LORD speaks? Does he not speak through us also?" And the LORD heard this. Now, Moses himself was by far the meekest man on the face of the earth. So at once the LORD said to Moses and Aaron and Miriam, "Come out, you three, to the meeting tent." And the three of them went. Then the LORD came down in the column of cloud, and standing at the entrance of the tent, called Aaron and Miriam. When both came forward, he said, "Now listen to the words of the LORD: / Should there be a prophet among you, / in visions will I reveal myself to him, / in dreams will I speak to him; / Not so with my servant Moses! / Throughout my house he bears my trust: / face to face I speak to him; / plainly and not in riddles. / The presence of the LORD he beholds. / Why, then, did you not fear to speak against my servant Moses?"

So angry was the LORD against them that when he departed, and the cloud withdrew from the tent, there was Miriam, a snow-white leper!

Reflection

Dominic was on a journey through France with his bishop when his life was transformed. He encountered the Albigensian heresy, which denied the goodness of the body. He realized his life was to be more than contemplation, that he needed to reach out to others. For Dominic, this meant preaching, which was sorely lacking in the Church. He went on to found the Order of Preachers, also knows as the Dominicans.

Prayers

others may be added

To our Lord, we pray:

◆ Lord, hear our prayer.

For a spirit of evangelization in our Church, we pray: ◆ For preachers, catechists, and all who teach the Gospel, we pray: ◆ For a willingness to share the Good News of Jesus Christ with others, we pray: ◆ For members of the Order of Preachers, the Dominicans, we pray: ◆

Our Father . . .

Heavenly Father,
you gifted Dominic with a well-trained tongue
that he might preach the Gospel
to all who had strayed from the truth.
May we too fearlessly help others
to come to a deeper relationship with you.
We ask this through Christ our Lord.
Amen.

✝ The Lord answers all our needs.

Wednesday, August 9, 2017
Weekday

✝ The Lord answers all our needs.

Psalm 145

page 420

Reading

Numbers 13:1–2, 25–33

The LORD said to Moses [in the desert of Paran,] "Send men to reconnoiter the land of Canaan, which I am giving the children of Israel. You shall send one man from each ancestral tribe, all of them princes."

After reconnoitering the land for forty days they returned . . . . They told Moses: "We went into the land to which you sent us. It does indeed flow with milk and honey, and here is its fruit. However, the people who are living in the land are fierce, and the towns are fortified and very strong. Besides, we saw descendants of the Anakim there. Amalekites live in the region of the Negeb; Hittites, Jebusites, and Amorites dwell in the highlands, and Canaanites along the seacoast and the banks of the Jordan."

Caleb, however, to quiet the people toward Moses, said, "We ought to go up and seize the land, for we can certainly do so." But the men who had gone up with him said, "We cannot attack these people; they are too strong for us." So they spread discouraging reports among the children of Israel about the land they had scouted, saying, "The land that we explored is a country that consumes its inhabitants. And all the people we saw there are huge, veritable giants (the Anakim were a race of giants); we felt like mere grasshoppers, and so we must have seemed to them."

Reflection

The men sent to scout out the Promised Land reported that it was a fruitful and fertile place. However, the people are afraid to take the land and instead turn against Moses and Aaron. Are we afraid of God's blessings? It almost sounds ludicrous but think carefully. How many opportunities and gifts do we turn away from because we are afraid? We like things the way they are, and even if we are in a metaphorical desert, it can seem like a comfortable place. Today, hold out your hands to the favors of the Lord.

Prayers

others may be added

To the Lord, who is worthy of our trust, we pray:

◆ Lord, hear our prayer.

May we revel in the diversity of gifts in our Church, we pray: ◆ May prisoners of conscience be freed, we pray: ◆ May artists, musicians, and writers challenge us to embrace the incredible range of beauty surrounding us, we pray: ◆ May we be open to different ideas, especially from new voices, we pray: ◆

Our Father . . .

You, O Lord,
bless us with every good thing.
Yet, at times, we live in fear of freedom.
Unlock the shackles that bind us.
Remove chains of stagnancy.
Teach us to trust in you.
We ask this through Christ our Lord.
Amen.

✝ The Lord answers all our needs.

Thursday, August 10, 2017

Feast of St. Lawrence, Deacon and Martyr

☩ The Lord answers all our needs.

Psalm 145 *page 420*

Reading *John 12:24–26*

Jesus said to his disciples: "Amen, amen, I say to you, unless a grain of wheat falls to the ground and dies, it remains just a grain of wheat; but if it dies, it produces much fruit. Whoever loves his life loses it, and whoever hates his life in this world will preserve it for eternal life. Whoever serves me must follow me, and where I am, there also will my servant be. The Father will honor whoever serves me."

Reflection

Tradition places St. Lawrence as a deacon in third-century Rome. Entrusted with the Church's finances, the prefect of Rome demanded that Lawrence surrender the Church's treasure to the emperor. Lawrence assembled the poor and disabled, presenting them to the prefect as "the treasure of the church." The prefect had Lawrence executed.

Like the seed that goes into the ground and dies in order to bear good fruit, so the blood of the martyrs and even the small sacrifices we perform deepen faith and can inspire others to good and even heroic deeds. The 2010 rescue of the Chilean miners who were trapped underground for sixty-nine days was named "Operation St. Lawrence" in honor of this deacon.

Prayers *others may be added*

To you, O Lord, in whom we pray:

◆ Strengthen our faith.

That the faithful continue to learn from the legacy of the saints, we pray: ◆ For those who serve as deacons, we pray: ◆ For "the treasury of the Church," we pray: ◆ For those who are abandoned and those who fear abandonment, we pray: ◆ For parishes under the patronage of St. Lawrence, we pray: ◆

Our Father . . .

Lord,
your deacon and martyr Lawrence
served you in prayer, stewardship, and in the poor.
May we find our life's work,
continue to raise up your Kingdom
and may serve and treasure are devalued and dismissed.
We ask this through Christ our Lord.
Amen.

☩ The Lord answers all our needs.

Friday, August 11, 2017
Memorial of St. Clare, Virgin

✝ The Lord answers all our needs.

Psalm 145
page 420

Reading
I Philippians 3:8–14

Brothers and sisters: I consider everything as a loss because of the supreme good of knowing Christ Jesus my Lord. For his sake I have accepted the loss of all things and I consider them so much rubbish, that I may gain Christ and be found in him, not having any righteousness of my own based on the law but that which comes through faith in Christ, the righteousness from God, depending on faith to know him and the power of his resurrection and the sharing of his sufferings by being conformed to his death, if somehow I may attain the resurrection from the dead.

It is not that I have already taken hold of it or have already attained perfect maturity, but I continue my pursuit in hope that I may possess it, since I have indeed been taken possession of by Christ Jesus. Brothers and sisters, I for my part do not consider myself to have taken possession. Just one thing: forgetting what lies behind but straining forward to what lies ahead, I continue my pursuit toward the goal, the prize of God's upward calling, in Christ Jesus.

Reflection

Much is told of the beloved Francis of Assisi, but little is known of his companion in faith, Clare. Like Francis, she left behind a life of wealth and security. She refused to marry at fifteen and at eighteen ran from her father's house. She joined with Francis, gathering a group of women around her. Francis founded this as the "Second Order," the Poor Clares. The women lived in poverty, prayer, and seclusion. Clare was a strong woman, even facing the attacking Saracens with the Blessed Sacrament. Faith was her rock and her peace. Can we say the same thing?

Prayers
others may be added

To the Lord, who is worthy of our trust, we pray:

◆ Lord, hear our prayer.

For a renewal of a spirit of poverty in the Church, we pray: ◆ For the poor, may we serve them in humility, we pray: ◆ For all who suffer from bulimia and anorexia, we pray: ◆ For members of Franciscan communities, we pray: ◆ For faith in times of struggle and pain, we pray: ◆

Our Father . . .

Faithful one,
you embraced Clare as your daughter
and gave her peace in the midst of pain,
courage in the face of attack,
and love in all things.
Bestow these same gifts upon us this day.
Help us to welcome the life you have
chosen for us.
We ask this through Christ our Lord.
Amen.

✝ The Lord answers all our needs.

Saturday, August 12, 2017
Weekday

✝ The Lord answers all our needs.

Psalm 145 *page 420*

Reading *Deuteronomy 6:4–9*

Moses said to the people: "Hear, O Israel! The LORD is our God, the LORD alone! Therefore, you shall love the LORD, your God, with all your heart, and with all your soul, and with all your strength. Take to heart these words which I enjoin on you today. Drill them into your children. Speak of them at home and abroad, whether you are busy or at rest. Bind them at your wrist as a sign and let them be as a pendant on your forehead. Write them on the doorposts of your houses and on your gates."

Reflection

"Hear, O Israel! The Lord is our God, the Lord alone!" This is the prayer Jesus recites in the Gospel, one that Mary and Joseph taught him. It is the foundation of the covenant, the Ten Commandments and the Law. They are words to take to heart and consider each evening as we review our day. Many things compete for out attention during the day, and some of those things may receive our priority over God. Keep these words in your heart to center your life on God.

Prayers *others may be added*

To you, O Lord, in whom we pray:

◆ Strengthen our faith.

For a pervading Spirit of love visible in the actions of Church leaders, we pray: ◆ For a permeating Spirit of love in the choices of legislatures, courts, and councils, we pray: ◆ For parents who teach their children the love of the Lord, we pray: ◆ For an end to bigotry, we pray: ◆ For an abiding love of God in our country, neighborhood, and world, we pray: ◆

Our Father . . .

Lord of love,
you are God alone.
All things are of your making.
All actions obey your will.
Correct us. Nurture us.
Draw us to your arms of mercy
and may our will be one with yours.
We ask this through Christ our Lord.
Amen.

✝ The Lord answers all our needs.

Sunday, August 13, 2017
Nineteenth Sunday in Ordinary Time

☩ Lord, let us see your kindness.

Psalm 85
page 411

Reading
Matthew 14:26–33

When the disciples saw [Jesus] walking on the sea they were terrified. "It is a ghost," they said, and they cried out in fear. At once Jesus spoke to them, "Take courage, it is I; do not be afraid." Peter said to him in reply, "Lord, if it is you, command me to come to you on the water." He said, "Come." Peter got out of the boat and began to walk on the water toward Jesus. But when he saw how strong the wind was he became frightened; and, beginning to sink, he cried out, "Lord, save me!" Immediately Jesus stretched out his hand and caught him, and said to him, "O you of little faith, why did you doubt?" After they got into the boat, the wind died down. Those who were in the boat did him homage, saying, "Truly, you are the Son of God."

Reflection
Jesus is master over the wind and sea. He can walk on water. But what about Peter? Impetuous Peter, he always wants to get in the middle of what he doesn't yet understand. It's almost childlike. Imagine climbing out of the boat and walking toward Jesus. Peter does fine, but when he notices the weather, he sinks. We can make the parallel in our life that we can stay on course as long as we stay focused on God. But when we divert our attention to things of the world, we often have trouble.

Prayers
others may be added

To the Lord, who brings peace with justice, we pray:

◆ Gracious Lord, hear our prayer.

May the Church follow the gentle, yet demanding, voice of God, we pray: ◆ May victims of hatred experience peace, dignity, and respect, we pray: ◆ May we trust Jesus to calm the storms of our lives, we pray: ◆ May people of all nations respect life in all its diversity, from womb to natural death, we pray: ◆ May the dead, now live in the Kingdom of God, we pray: ◆

Our Father . . .

Lord God,
you hold out your hand to us
just as you did with Peter.
Guide us that our trust in you will be our beacon through the rough seas of life.
We ask this through our Lord Jesus Christ, your Son,
who lives and reigns with you in the unity of the Holy Spirit,
one God, for ever and ever.
Amen.

☩ Lord, let us see your kindness.

Monday, August 14, 2017
Memorial of St. Maximilian Kolbe, Priest and Martyr

✝ Lord, let us see your kindness.

Psalm 85 *page 411*

Reading *Deuteronomy 10:12–15*

Moses said to the people: "And now, Israel, what does the LORD, your God, ask of you but to fear the LORD, your God, and follow his ways exactly, to love and serve the LORD, your God, with all your heart and all your soul, to keep the commandments and statutes of the LORD which I enjoin on you today for your own good? Think! The heavens, even the highest heavens, belong to the LORD, your God, as well as the earth and everything on it. Yet in his love for your fathers the LORD was so attached to them as to choose you, their descendants, in preference to all other peoples, as indeed he has now done."

Reflection

Oftentimes saints seem to be so far away. Not Maximilian Kolbe. He was martyred at the Auschwitz concentration camp during World War II. He offered his life in substitution for another man's who had a wife and children. Kolbe was sent with a group of others to starve to death, and in the end was poisoned with a syringe. The similarities to Christ's death are striking, but that wasn't important to Kolbe. He just wanted to do God's will. Each day is an opportunity. In the death camp, his faith was strong and he supported others. Maximillian Kolbe faced evil, and with the grace of God, won. He is the patron saint of people with addictions.

Prayers *others may be added*

To the Lord, who brings peace with justice, we pray:

◆ Graciously hear us, Lord.

For the martyrs of today's Church, we pray: ◆ For a willingness to rely on God's plan and not our own, we pray: ◆ For all who are empty, lost, or searching, may they take refuge in the persistent call of the Spirit, we pray: ◆ For victims of violence, we pray: ◆ For all who suffer with addictions, we pray: ◆

Our Father . . .

Lord of the martyrs,
you offered Maximilian Kolbe the faith
to valiantly follow you
all the way to torture and death.
Give us strength to do your will,
and draw near to all
who live in the shadow of death.
We ask this through Christ our Lord.
Amen.

✝ Lord, let us see your kindness.

Tuesday, August 15, 2017

Solemnity of the Assumption of the Blessed Virgin Mary

✝ Lord, let us see your kindness.

Canticle of Mary

page 422

Reading

Luke 1:39–45

Mary set out in those days and traveled to the hill country in haste to a town of Judah, where she entered the house of Zechariah and greeted Elizabeth. When Elizabeth heard Mary's greeting, the infant leaped in her womb, and Elizabeth, filled with the Holy Spirit, cried out in a loud voice and said, "Most blessed are you among women, and blessed is the fruit of your womb. And how does this happen to me, that the mother of my Lord should come to me? For at the moment the sound of your greeting reached my ears, the infant in my womb leaped for joy. Blessed are you who believed that what was spoken to you by the Lord would be fulfilled."

Reflection

In 1950 the dogma of the Assumption was infallibly declared. The teaching was already present in the Church, so why the necessity of the declaration? Many think that at least some of the reason flows from the conditions of yesterday's feast. World War II was a devastation in many ways, not the least of which was the desecration of human life. The Nazi government deemed some people not worthy of life and executed them. In the face of such sin, the Church upholds the human body. Mary's body was assumed into heaven, and we too look forward to the resurrection of the body. Our bodies are gifts and each person is sacred.

Prayers

others may be added

To the Lord, who brings peace with justice, we pray:

◆ Lord, hear our prayer.

As Church, may we proclaim the inherent goodness of all humanity, we pray: ◆ May we respect our bodies and the bodies of others, we pray: ◆ For food for the hungry and shelter for the homeless, we pray: ◆ For victims of torture, we pray: ◆ May our belief in the resurrection of the dead, bring comfort to all who mourn, and peace to all who struggle, we pray: ◆ As Mary was raised body and soul to heaven, may all who have died also share in the company of the saints, we pray: ◆

Our Father . . .

Lord God,
you assumed the Blessed Virgin Mary,
body and soul, into heaven.
May we honor and respect our bodies on
this earth
even as we look forward to the day of
resurrection with you.
We ask this through Christ our Lord.
Amen.

✝ Lord, let us see your kindness.

Wednesday, August 16, 2017
Weekday

✝ Lord, let us see your kindness.

Psalm 85
page 411

Reading
Deuteronomy 34:1–5

Moses went up from the plains of Moab to Mount Nebo, the headland of Pisgah which faces Jericho, and the LORD showed him all the land—Gilead, and as far as Dan, all Naphtali, the land of Ephraim and Manasseh, all the land of Judah as far as the Western Sea, the Negeb, the circuit of the Jordan with the lowlands at Jericho, city of palms, and as far as Zoar. The LORD then said to him, "This is the land which I swore to Abraham, Isaac, and Jacob that I would give to their descendants. I have let you feast your eyes upon it, but you shall not cross over." So there, in the land of Moab, Moses, the servant of the LORD, died as the LORD had said.

Reflection
Moses dies. He led the people to this place. He, however, did not enter into the land. On the night before he was killed, Dr. Martin Luther King Jr. referenced this passage. "I would like to live—a long life; . . . But I'm not concerned about that now. I just want to do God's will. And He's allowed me to go up to the mountain. And I've looked over. And I've seen the Promised Land. I may not get there with you. But I want you to know tonight, that we, as a people, will get to the Promised Land." Can we live our lives for a cause (the Reign of God) and leave the rest to God?

Prayers
others may be added

To the Lord, who brings peace with justice, we pray:

◆ Lord, hear our prayer.

For a Church, renewed in God's vision, we pray: ◆ For an end to war in the Middle East, may all share in the Promised Land, we pray: ◆ For all who suffer with unequal opportunity, we pray: ◆ For the ability to surrender to the Lord's will, we pray: ◆ For trust in times of conflict, we pray: ◆

Our Father . . .

God of the oppressed,
you offer us a place of promise, a time of justice.
May your vision be our vision, your thoughts, our thoughts.
May we trust in your will.
We ask this through Christ our Lord.
Amen.

✝ Lord, let us see your kindness.

Thursday, August 17, 2017
Weekday

✝ Lord, let us see your kindness.

Psalm 85
page 411

Reading
Joshua 3:7–10a, 11, 13

The LORD said to Joshua, "Today I will begin to exalt you in the sight of all Israel, that they may know I am with you, as I was with Moses. Now command the priests carrying the ark of the covenant to come to a halt in the Jordan when you reach the edge of the waters."

So Joshua said to the children of Israel, "Come here and listen to the words of the LORD, your God. This is how you will know that there is a living God in your midst, who at your approach will dispossess the Canaanites. The ark of the covenant of the LORD of the whole earth will precede you into the Jordan. When the soles of the feet of the priests carrying the ark of the LORD, the Lord of the whole earth, touch the water of the Jordan, it will cease to flow; for the water flowing down from upstream will halt in a solid bank."

Reflection
Our reading today sounds familiar. As the Red Sea split for the Israelites to pass through, so too does the Jordan River. An era has ended and a new one begins. It happens for us too. We move to a new home or job. There is sadness as the keys are turned over and the door, literally, closes. How do you meet transitions in your life with faith?

Prayers
others may be added

To the Lord, who brings peace with justice, we pray:

◆ Lord, hear our prayer.

For members of the Church, that they will seek new opportunities to serve, we pray: ◆ For community leaders, that they will seek to understand new visions, we pray: ◆ For new jobs for the jobless, we pray: ◆ For those facing unwanted transitions, we pray: ◆ For all beginning new eras in their lives, we pray: ◆

Our Father . . .

O Lord,
you bring newness to our lives.
You brought the people of Israel
from slavery to freedom in the
 Promised Land.
Guide our journeys
and help us to embrace
the changes necessary for growth in
 the Spirit.
We ask this through Christ our Lord.
Amen.

✝ Lord, let us see your kindness.

Friday, August 18, 2017
Weekday

✝ Lord, let us see your kindness.

Psalm 85 *page 411*

Reading *Joshua 24:1–4, 5–8a, 10–11, 13*

Joshua gathered together all the tribes of Israel at Shechem, summoning their elders, their leaders, their judges and their officers. When they stood in ranks before God, Joshua addressed all the people: "Thus says the LORD, the God of Israel: . . . I brought your father Abraham from the region beyond the River and led him through the entire land of Canaan. I made his descendants numerous, and gave him Isaac. To Isaac I gave Jacob and Esau. . . .

"Then I sent Moses and Aaron, and smote Egypt with the prodigies which I wrought in her midst. Afterward I led you out of Egypt, and when you reached the sea, the Egyptians pursued your fathers to the Red Sea with chariots and horsemen. Because they cried out to the LORD, he put darkness between your people and the Egyptians, upon whom he brought the sea so that it engulfed them. After you witnessed what I did to Egypt, and dwelt a long time in the desert, I brought you into the land of the Amorites who lived east of the Jordan. Once you crossed the Jordan and came to Jericho, the men of Jericho fought against you, but I delivered them also into your power.

"I gave you a land that you had not tilled and cities that you had not built, to dwell in; you have eaten of vineyards and olive groves which you did not plant."

Reflection

Lest the people forget, Joshua reminds them of their interconnection and roots. Our existence is tied to those who have gone before us. Our ancestors' sins and blessings are part of us. We need to know their stories for guidance, hope, and help. Reflect on your ancestors today. What sins are you still struggling with; what blessings do you revel in? What are you passing on to the next generation?

Prayers *others may be added*

To the Lord, who brings peace with justice, we pray:

◆ Lord, hear our prayer.

For our ancestors in faith, saints and sinners, we pray: ◆ For an end to old rivalries, hatred, and feuds, we pray: ◆ For recognition of the familial ties of all humanity, we pray: ◆ For hearts broken by intolerance, we pray: ◆

Our Father . . .

Creator God,
you made all members of the
human family.
From the beginning,
we are tied together by bonds of love
and history.
Help us to reach out to each other
in tenderness, acceptance,
and recognition
that we are fashioned in your image.
We ask this through Christ our Lord.
Amen.

✝ Lord, let us see your kindness.

Saturday, August 19, 2017
Weekday

✝ Lord, let us see your kindness.

Psalm 85
page 411

Reading
Joshua 24:14–15

Joshua gathered together all the tribes of Israel at Shechem, and addressed them, saying: "Fear the LORD and serve him completely and sincerely. Cast out the gods your fathers served beyond the River and in Egypt, and serve the LORD. If it does not please you to serve the LORD, decide today whom you will serve, the gods your fathers served beyond the River or the gods of the Amorites in whose country you are dwelling. As for me and my household, we will serve the LORD."

Reflection
"As for me and my household, we will serve the Lord." The voice of the elder Joshua reverberates throughout the land. Elders have a responsibility to the community. Having lived a long life, their voice should be respected. However, our society revels in the folly of youth. While youth has it place, so too does wisdom born of years of faithful struggle and joy. Are you an elder? Is there wisdom you can share with your family, godchildren, community? Are you in need of an elder's grace? Who should you search out to aid your journey?

Prayers
others may be added

To the Lord, who brings peace with justice, we pray:

◆ Lord, hear our prayer.

May the wisdom of the Church be a shining example of kindness, compassion, forgiveness, and love, we pray: ◆ May refugees be nourished by daily bread, we pray: ◆ May we have the courage to proclaim God's Word to the powerful and to challenge our society's values, we pray: ◆ May we trust in God's love for us, we pray: ◆ May victims of famine find food and support, we pray: ◆

Our Father . . .

God of our weary years,
Lord of our silent years,
teach us to listen to the elders
you place in our midst.
May their wisdom and courage
guide us ever closer to you.
We ask this through Christ our Lord.
Amen.

✝ Lord, let us see your kindness.

Sunday, August 20, 2017

Twentieth Sunday in Ordinary Time

✝ O God, let all the nations praise you!

Psalm 67 *page 408*

Reading *Matthew 15:21–28*

At that time Jesus withdrew to the region of Tyre and Sidon. And behold, a Canaanite woman of that district came and called out, "Have pity on me, Lord, Son of David! My daughter is tormented by a demon." But he did not say a word in answer to her. His disciples came and asked him, "Send her away, for she keeps calling out after us." He said in reply, "I was sent only to the lost sheep of the house of Israel." But the woman came and did him homage, saying, "Lord, help me." He said in reply, "It is not right to take the food of the children and throw it to the dogs." She said, "Please, Lord, for even the dogs eat the scraps that fall from the table of their masters." Then Jesus said to her in reply, "O woman, great is your faith! Let it be done for you as you wish." And her daughter was healed from that hour.

Reflection

That a non-Jew would seek out Jesus hearkens to one of the basic themes of Matthew: the acceptance of Gentiles into the Christian fold. The woman has great faith and so receives a healing for her daughter. The externals, the fact she is woman and not a Jew, don't matter. Faith is what counts. Do we have an opinion on what "real believers" look like? Let us not be quick to judge but be concerned with the depth of our faith.

Prayers *others may be added*

To the Lord, who nourishes our faith,
we pray:

◆ Hear us, Lord.

That the Church may hear the voice of the outcast and powerless, we pray: ◆ That diversity may be a source of creativity and our various abilities may be valued as gifts from God, we pray: ◆ That power and authority may be used to serve the common good, we pray: ◆ That nations may seek ways of peace together, we pray: ◆ That all who have died may sing forever in the community of the saints, we pray: ◆

Our Father . . .

Father,
your arms embrace all people.
Help us to live freely, welcoming all into
a family of faith.
We ask this through our Lord Jesus
Christ, your Son,
who lives and reigns with you in the unity
of the Holy Spirit,
one God, for ever and ever.
Amen.

✝ O God, let all the nations praise you!

Monday, August 21, 2017
Memorial of St. Pius X, Pope

☩ O God, let all the nations praise you!

Psalm 67 *page 408*

Reading *Judges 2:11–12, 16–19*

The children of Israel offended the LORD by serving the Baals. Abandoning the LORD, the God of their fathers, who led them out of the land of Egypt, they followed the other gods of the various nations around them, and by their worship of these gods provoked the LORD.

Even when the LORD raised up judges to deliver them from the power of their despoilers, they did not listen to their judges, but abandoned themselves to the worship of other gods. They were quick to stray from the way their fathers had taken, and did not follow their example of obedience to the commandments of the LORD. Whenever the LORD raised up judges for them, he would be with the judge and save them from the power of their enemies as long as the judge lived; it was thus the LORD took pity on their distressful cries of affliction under their oppressors. But when the judge died, they would relapse and do worse than their ancestors, following other gods in service and worship, relinquishing none of their evil practices or stubborn conduct.

Reflection

In Judges, the people constantly fall into sin. They start following gods other than the Lord. However, a judge saves the people from suffering and renews their faith. The problem is that without a strong leader, the people will again fall away. Pastoral leaders are important. They have great responsibility. Under a good pastor, faith is nurtured and challenged. Pastors in our parishes need the support of their congregation too. It is a difficult job, for we too can fall into our culture's values, or a faith more mediocre than spirit driven. Today, pray for your pastor. How can you be a support and not a hindrance?

Prayers *others may be added*

To the Lord, who nourishes our faith,
we pray:

◆ Lord, hear our prayer.

For our pope, bishops, and pastors,
that they receive care and guidance,
we pray: ◆ For relief workers and
missionaries, we pray: ◆ For lay ministers
in the Church, we pray: ◆ For our
churches, may we truly be welcoming,
Catholic communities, where the love of
Jesus Christ is learned and lived, sung
and shared, we pray: ◆ For all discerning
a vocation to ministry, we pray: ◆

Our Father . . .

Gentle Shepherd,
you guide us to live in your way.
In the midst of our communities
you gift us with pastors.
Help them to discern your truth.
Support them in times of conflict
and struggle.
Fill them with joyful peace.
We ask this through Christ our Lord.
Amen.

☩ O God, let all the nations praise you!

Tuesday, August 22, 2017

Memorial of the Queenship of the Blessed Virgin Mary

✝ O God, let all the nations praise you!

Psalm 67

page 408

Reading

Judges 6:11–16

The angel of the LORD came and sat under the terebinth in Ophrah that belonged to Joash the Abiezrite. While his son Gideon was beating out wheat in the wine press to save it from the Midianites, the angel of the LORD appeared to him and said, "The LORD is with you, O champion!" Gideon said to him, "My Lord, if the LORD is with us, why has all this happened to us? Where are his wondrous deeds of which our fathers told us when they said, 'Did not the LORD bring us up from Egypt?' For now the LORD has abandoned us and has delivered us into the power of Midian." The LORD turned to him and said, "Go with the strength you have and save Israel from the power of Midian. It is I who send you." But Gideon answered him, "Please, my lord, how can I save Israel? My family is the lowliest in Manasseh, and I am the most insignificant in my father's house." "I shall be with you," the LORD said to him, "and you will cut down Midian to the last man."

Reflection

When called by God, Gideon says he is too insignificant to be a judge. God will make him even more insignificant that the might of the Lord may be revealed. We honor Mary today under the title of queen, but she saw herself as lowly. True humility is found in honestly acknowledging ourselves. How do you see yourself as you stand before our Lord?

Prayers

others may be added

To the Lord, who nourishes our faith, we pray:

◆ **Hear us, Lord.**

For Church leaders, that they will nurture a spirit of humility and meekness, we pray: ◆ For safety for the victimized, we pray: ◆ That disciples seek to love all people as Jesus did, embracing differences in gender, race, language, orientation, and national origin, we pray: ◆ For those who have asked us to pray for them, may they live in the grace of God, we pray: ◆ For those who suffer discrimination, we pray: ◆

Our Father . . .

Almighty God,
you hear the prayer of the meek
and are attentive to the cry of the humble.
Help us to recognize our gifts and
our weaknesses,
calling on you as the Lord of our days
and nights.
We ask this through Christ our Lord.
Amen.

✝ O God, let all the nations praise you!

Wednesday, August 23, 2017
Weekday

✝ O God, let all the nations praise you!

Psalm 67
page 408

Reading
Judges 9:6–15

All the citizens of Shechem and all Beth-millo came together and proceeded to make Abimelech king by the terebinth at the memorial pillar in Shechem.

When this was reported to him, Jotham went to the top of Mount Gerizim and, standing there, cried out to them in a loud voice: "Hear me, citizens of Shechem, that God may then hear you! Once the trees went to anoint a king over themselves. So they said to the olive tree, 'Reign over us.' But the olive tree answered them, 'Must I give up my rich oil, whereby men and gods are honored, and go to wave over the trees?' Then the trees said to the fig tree, 'Come; you reign over us!' But the fig tree answered them, 'Must I give up my sweetness and my good fruit, and go to wave over the trees?' Then the trees said to the vine, 'Come you, and reign over us.' But the vine answered them, 'Must I give up my wine that cheers gods and men, and go to wave over the trees?' Then all the trees said to the buckthorn, 'Come; you reign over us!' But the buckthorn replied to the trees, 'If you wish to anoint me king over you in good faith, come and take refuge in my shadow. Otherwise, let fire come from the buckthorn and devour the cedars of Lebanon.' "

Reflection
Abimelech was the son of Gideon, so he decided that he should be king. Abimelech, however, wanted power for power's sake. Discern the places where you have authority and responsibilities in your family, parish, and community. How have you regarded power? How can you be more faithful to the responsibility you have been given?

Prayers
others may be added

Turning to our Lord, who opens our eyes, we pray:

◆ Hear us, Lord.

For all who govern religious communities, we pray: ◆ For all who seek public office, may they seek the common good, we pray: ◆ For parish pastoral councils and committees, we pray: ◆ For judges and magistrates, we pray: ◆ For dictators and all who rob others of their rights, that they may experience a change of heart, we pray: ◆

Our Father . . .

All powerful God,
you are our leader, king, and guide.
You entrust the world to us, as your stewards.
Free us from undue attachment to power and control.
When we lead, may we do so in a spirit of service to your Reign.
We ask this through Christ our Lord.
Amen.

✝ O God, let all the nations praise you!

Thursday, August 24, 2017

Feast of St. Bartholomew, Apostle

☩ O God, let all the nations praise you!

Psalm 67

page 408

Reading

John 1:45–49

Philip found Nathanael and told him, "We have found the one about whom Moses wrote in the law, and also the prophets, Jesus son of Joseph, from Nazareth." But Nathanael said to him, "Can anything good come from Nazareth?" Philip said to him, "Come and see." Jesus saw Nathanael coming toward him and said of him, "Here is a true child of Israel. There is no duplicity in him." Nathanael said to him, "How do you know me?" Jesus answered and said to him, "Before Philip called you, I saw you under the fig tree." Nathanael answered him, "Rabbi, you are the Son of God; you are the King of Israel."

Reflection

Today we encounter Nathaniel, in whom there is no duplicity. In fact, he sounds naïve to the point of foolishness. But does not our faith invite us to a certain "holy foolishness"? It can appear foolish to believe in the Incarnation, Resurrection, and Real Presence; and foolish to give alms to the poor, shelter the homeless, or welcome the refugee. Therein is the foolishness of holiness.

Prayers

others may be added

Turning to our Lord, who opens our eyes, we pray:

◆ Hear us, Lord.

That a spirit of serenity govern our Church, we pray: ◆ For godparents, sponsors, and all who walk the journey of faith with another disciple, we pray: ◆ For veterans missing in action, we pray: ◆ For the nameless dead who kept the faith, we pray: ◆

Our Father . . .

God of the mystics,
you give us the saints as models of faith.
May we grasp that faith is more than knowledge;
May we know you in your Word,
in the breaking of bread,
in the poor and the stranger,
in patient reflection,
and in the assurance of your grace.
We ask this through Christ our Lord.
Amen.

☩ O God, let all the nations praise you!

Friday, August 25, 2017
Weekday

✝ O God, let all the nations praise you!

Psalm 67 *page 408*

Reading *Ruth 1:1, 3–6, 14b–16*

Once in the time of the judges there was a famine in the land; so a man from Bethlehem of Judah departed with his wife and two sons to reside on the plateau of Moab. Elimelech, the husband of Naomi, died, and she was left with her two sons, who married Moabite women, one named Orpah, the other Ruth. When they had lived there about ten years, both Mahlon and Chilion died also, and the woman was left with neither her two sons nor her husband. She then made ready to go back from the plateau of Moab because word reached her there that the LORD had visited his people and given them food.

Orpah kissed her mother-in-law good-bye, but Ruth stayed with her.

Naomi said, "See now! Your sister-in-law has gone back to her people and her god. Go back after your sister-in-law!" But Ruth said, "Do not ask me to abandon or forsake you! For wherever you go, I will go, wherever you lodge I will lodge, your people shall be my people, and your God my God."

Reflection

People would have understood if Orpah and Ruth had abandoned Naomi. Ruth, however, looks to her mother-in-law with compassion and stays with her. Today when family members are spread across the nation, we need to be creative in showing elders that they are valued.

Prayers *others may be added*

Turning to our Lord, who opens our eyes, we pray:

◆ Teach us, gentle Lord.

May the Church embrace all people, from conception to natural death, we pray: ◆ For nurses, doctors, and aides in our nursing homes and hospitals, we pray: ◆ May lawmakers, budget makers, and unions remember the plight of our senior citizens, we pray: ◆ For families who struggle with medical bills, we pray: ◆ For the lonely, neglected, and abandoned, we pray: ◆

Our Father . . .

Lord,
you are with us always.
Give us strength to love even when it
is difficult,
and to make decisions
that benefit the vulnerable ones in
our care.
We ask this through Christ our Lord.
Amen.

✝ O God, let all the nations praise you!

Saturday, August 26, 2017
Weekday

✝ O God, let all the nations praise you!

Psalm 67 *page 408*

page 408

Reading *Ruth 2:1–3, 8–11*

Naomi had a prominent kinsman named Boaz, of the clan of her husband Elimelech. Ruth the Moabite said to Naomi, "Let me go and glean ears of grain in the field of anyone who will allow me that favor." Naomi said to her, "Go, my daughter," and she went. The field she entered to glean after the harvesters happened to be the section belonging to Boaz of the clan of Elimelech.

Boaz said to Ruth, "Listen, my daughter! Do not go to glean in anyone else's field; you are not to leave here. Stay here with my women servants. Watch to see which field is to be harvested, and follow them; I have commanded the young men to do you no harm. When you are thirsty, you may go and drink from the vessels the young men have filled." Casting herself prostrate upon the ground, Ruth said to him, "Why should I, a foreigner, be favored with your notice?" Boaz answered her: "I have had a complete account of what you have done for your mother-in-law after your husband's death; you have left your father and your mother and the land of your birth, and have come to a people whom you did not know previously."

Reflection

Sometimes we are surprised at the blessings that come from the good that we have done. Naomi's fidelity to Ruth brought others to regard her as a good woman. Impressed with the way Ruth has treated her mother-in-law, Boaz takes care of the young woman and ultimately marries her. Are you known for your loyalty, faithfulness, hard work? What do your actions say about you?

Prayers *others may be added*

Turning to our Lord, who opens our eyes, we pray:

◆ Teach us, gentle Lord.

May the fire of the Spirit fill the mouths of all Church leaders that they may boldly proclaim freedom and justice, we pray: ◆ May government officials throughout the world set aside division and work for the good of all people, we pray: ◆ May we have the courage to speak the truth of Jesus, especially when it is unpopular, we pray: ◆ May we keep our eyes fixed on Jesus, who inspires and perfects our faith, we pray: ◆

Our Father . . .

Lord of all creation,
all goodness comes from you.
As your disciples we seek to show your
image to all we meet.
Help us to radiate your love
and speak your truth.
by our deeds and actions.
We ask this through Christ our Lord.
Amen.

✝ O God, let all the nations praise you!

Sunday, August 27, 2017
Twenty-First Sunday in Ordinary Time

† Glory and praise for ever!

Daniel 3 *page 421*

page 421

Reading *Matthew 16:13–20*

Jesus went into the region of Caesarea Philippi and he asked his disciples, "Who do people say that the Son of Man is?" They replied, "Some say John the Baptist, others Elijah, still others Jeremiah or one of the prophets." He said to them, "But who do you say that I am?" Simon Peter said in reply, "You are the Christ, the Son of the living God." Jesus said to him in reply, "Blessed are you, Simon son of Jonah. For flesh and blood has not revealed this to you, but my heavenly Father. And so I say to you, you are Peter, and upon this rock I will build my church, and the gates of the netherworld shall not prevail against it. I will give you the keys to the kingdom of heaven. Whatever you bind on earth shall be bound in heaven; and whatever you loose on earth shall be loosed in heaven." Then he strictly ordered his disciples to tell no one that he was the Christ.

Reflection

Today we hear Peter's confession of faith in Jesus as "the Christ, the Son of the living God." Often overlooked is the setting: Caesarea Philippi. The city is dedicated to Caesar, who invoked the title, "Son of God" for himself, and Philip, the son of Herod the Great. In this context, the socio-political ramifications of Peter's words are clear: Jesus, not Caesar, is the Son of God. When we confess that "Jesus is Lord," with Peter, we are giving Jesus our complete allegiance. Jesus is Lord of the entirety of our lives.

Prayers *others may be added*

To our Lord, who rules heaven and earth, we pray:

◆ **Son of the living God, hear our prayer.**

For N., our pope, and N., our bishop, we pray: ◆ For Christian unity, we pray: ◆ That all the baptized may be faithful witnesses to the Reign of God, we pray: ◆ May our allegiance to Christ form our political opinions, we pray: ◆ For the willingness to share our faith, we pray: ◆

Our Father . . .

Father for ever,
you revealed to Peter the identity of your Son.
Grant that we who share in Peter's faith
may be steadfast and faithful in living the faith we profess.
We ask this through our Lord Jesus Christ, your Son,
who lives and reigns with you in the unity of the Holy Spirit,
one God, for ever and ever.
Amen.

† Glory and praise for ever!

Monday, August 28, 2017
Memorial of St. Augustine, Bishop and Doctor of the Church

✝ Glory and praise for ever!

Daniel 3 *page 421*

page 421

Reading *1 Thessalonians 1:1–5, 8b–10*

Paul, Silvanus, and Timothy to the Church of the Thessalonians in God the Father and the Lord Jesus Christ: grace to you and peace.

We give thanks to God always for all of you, remembering you in our prayers, unceasingly calling to mind your work of faith and labor of love and endurance in hope of our Lord Jesus Christ, before our God and Father, knowing, brothers and sisters loved by God, how you were chosen. For our Gospel did not come to you in word alone, but also in power and in the Holy Spirit and with much conviction. You know what sort of people we were among you for your sake. In every place your faith in God has gone forth, so that we have no need to say anything. For they themselves openly declare about us what sort of reception we had among you, and how you turned to God from idols to serve the living and true God and to await his Son from heaven, whom he raised from the dead, Jesus, who delivers us from the coming wrath.

Reflection

Seekers in the spiritual life may be able to identify with Augustine. His pilgrimage took him from playboy to Manichean (a dualistic philosophy that viewed creation as essentially flawed) and eventually to Christianity. No wonder he would write, "Our soul cannot rest until it rests in you, O Lord." Augustine came to peace with the imperfections of the world when he came to peace with his sin and imperfections. Augustine's witness is that the more important and difficult search is not one that looks out but the journey inward. This journey continues until we rest in the Lord.

Prayers *others may be added*

To our Lord, who rules heaven and earth, we pray:

◆ **Son of the living God, hear our prayer**

May we, the Body of Christ, be ready to journey with those who are searching, we pray: ◆ For the Church in Africa, we pray: ◆ For theologians, we pray: ◆ For Augustinian priests, brothers, and sisters, we pray: ◆ For parish communities under the patronage of St. Augustine, we pray: ◆

Our Father . . .

God of our journeys,
throughout our restless wanderings,
you hear us.
Help all who search find their way to you.
We ask this through Christ our Lord.
Amen.

✝ Glory and praise for ever!

Tuesday, August 29, 2017
Memorial of the Passion of St. John the Baptist

☩ Glory and praise for ever!

Daniel 3
page 421

Reading
Mark 6:21b–24

Herod, on his birthday, gave a banquet for his courtiers, his military officers, and the leading men of Galilee. His own daughter came in and performed a dance that delighted Herod and his guests. The king said to the girl, "Ask of me whatever you wish and I will grant it to you." He even swore many things to her, "I will grant you whatever you ask of me, even to half of my kingdom." She went out and said to her mother, "What shall I ask for?" Her mother replied, "The head of John the Baptist." The girl hurried back to the king's presence and made her request, "I want you to give me at once on a platter the head of John the Baptist."

Reflection
The execution of John the Baptist has several parallels with the execution of Jesus. Both are arrested, both are condemned reluctantly, both have disciples come and lay their bodies to rest. In Mark's account, Herod and Pilate are similar insofar as neither is strong enough to rule from their convictions. Ignoring their consciences and the stirring of their hearts, they play to their audience. We need to consider whether we act in certain ways to ensure our popularity. Have you agreed to something despite heartfelt misgivings?

Prayers
others may be added

To our Lord, who rules heaven and earth, we pray:

◆ Son of the living God, hear our prayer.

That the Church proclaim the Gospel without compromise and without counting the costs, we pray: ◆ For all who hold public office, we pray: ◆ May we recognize that being unpopular is healthier than betraying our conscience, we pray: ◆ For those who are incarcerated, especially those awaiting execution, we pray: ◆ For those killed while seeking human and civil rights, we pray: ◆

Our Father . . .

Jesus our Lord,
you gave John the Baptist the strength
to herald your Son.
Enkindle within us the Spirit's gifts
of courage and fortitude,
for you live and reign with God the Father
in the unity of the Holy Spirit,
one God, for ever and ever.
Amen.

☩ Glory and praise for ever!

Wednesday, August 30, 2017
Weekday

✝ Glory and praise for ever!

Daniel 3 *page 421*

page 421

Reading *1 Thessalonians 2:9–13*

You recall, brothers and sisters, our toil and drudgery. Working night and day in order not to burden any of you, we proclaimed to you the Gospel of God. You are witnesses, and so is God, how devoutly and justly and blamelessly we behaved toward you believers. As you know, we treated each one of you as a father treats his children, exhorting and encouraging you and insisting that you walk in a manner worthy of the God who calls you into his Kingdom and glory.

And for this reason we too give thanks to God unceasingly, that, in receiving the word of God from hearing us, you received it not as the word of men, but as it truly is, the word of God, which is now at work in you who believe.

Reflection

In this, the oldest part of the New Testament, Paul commends the community at Thessalonica for receiving the Word of God "not as the word of men, but as it truly is, the word of God." This passage can cause us to ponder how we receive God's Word. It is easy for our minds to wander during a reading during Mass. Should that happen just draw your mind back to the reader. Preparation prior to the liturgy aids this process. When we have read the day's readings beforehand, we can listen and receive God's Word more easily.

Prayers *others may be added*

To our Lord, who rules heaven and earth, we pray:

◆ Son of the living God, hear our prayer.

May the community of disciples remain faithful to the Word of God, we pray: ◆ For Scripture scholars and all who are devoted to God's Word, we pray: ◆ That we might demonstrate reverence to the Word of God, we pray: ◆ That we might hear the Word of God and keep it, we pray: ◆ That followers of all faiths accord respect to the sacred books of others, we pray: ◆

Our Father . . .

Lord God,
you send us teachers and preachers of the Word.
May we allow ourselves
to be guided by your Word
by listening to it devotedly and acting on it with joyous resolve.
We ask this through your Word made flesh, Jesus Christ, our Lord,
who lives and reigns with you in the unity of the Holy Spirit,
one God, for ever and ever.
Amen.

✝ Glory and praise for ever!

Thursday, August 31, 2017
Weekday

† Glory and praise for ever!

Daniel 3

page 421

Reading

I Thessalonians 3:7–13

We have been reassured about you, brothers and sisters, in our every distress and affliction, through your faith. For we now live, if you stand firm in the Lord.

What thanksgiving, then, can we render to God for you, for all the joy we feel on your account before our God? Night and day we pray beyond measure to see you in person and to remedy the deficiencies of your faith. Now may God himself, our Father, and our Lord Jesus direct our way to you, and may the Lord make you increase and abound in love for one another and for all, just as we have for you, so as to strengthen your hearts, to be blameless in holiness before our God and Father at the coming of our Lord Jesus with all his holy ones. Amen.

Reflection

Paul praises the church at Thessalonica, saying their faith has been a reassurance. He goes on, however, to write of hoping to "remedy the deficiencies" of their faith and, ultimately, to strengthen their hearts. How open are we to hearing another's evaluation, especially when that means naming our deficiencies? Does the naming of our deficiencies, our weaknesses, and brokenness lead us to guide our growth and strengthen our hearts?

Prayers

others may be added

To our Lord, who rules heaven and earth, we pray:

◆ Son of the living God, hear our prayer.

That when the Church must admonish she does so in love, we pray: ◆ That we may be open to correction and helpful criticism, we pray: ◆ For people with a poor self-image and lacking self-esteem, we pray: ◆ For leaders of our community, that they may exhibit compassion to the many individuals under their care, we pray: ◆ For open minds, strong hearts, and loving spirits, we pray: ◆

Our Father . . .

Lord Jesus,
you send pastors and teachers to guide us.
Help us to hear their direction that we will follow the path
you have set for us.
You live and reign with God the Father in the unity of the Holy Spirit,
one God, for ever and ever.
Amen.

† Glory and praise for ever!

Friday, September 1, 2017
Weekday

✝ Create a clean heart in me, O God.

Psalm 51 *page 406*

Reading *1 Thessalonians 4:1–8*

Brothers and sisters, we earnestly ask and exhort you in the Lord Jesus that, as you received from us how you should conduct yourselves to please God—and as you are conducting yourselves—you do so even more. For you know what instructions we gave you through the Lord Jesus.

This is the will of God, your holiness: that you refrain from immorality, that each of you know how to acquire a wife for himself in holiness and honor, not in lustful passion as do the Gentiles who do not know God; not to take advantage of or exploit a brother or sister in this matter, for the Lord is an avenger in all these things, as we told you before and solemnly affirmed. For God did not call us to impurity but to holiness. Therefore, whoever disregards this, disregards not a human being but God, who also gives his Holy Spirit to you.

Reflection

St. Paul tells the people of Thessalonica that they are conducting themslves as followers of the Lord, but that they can do even more. We also need to consider what to do in addition to following the Commandments. Disciples make the corporal and spiritual works of mercy and the Beatitudes part of their lives. We should never be content that we have done enough. What is "the more" to which God is calling you?

Prayers *others may be added*

To our Lord, who rules heaven and earth, we pray:

◆ Son of the living God, hear our prayer.

May the Church be open to constant reform and conversion, we pray: ◆ May our moral lives be based on more than the avoidance of evil, we pray: ◆ That we commit to the goodness of the body and the dignity of each person, we pray: ◆ For the safety of those who travel this holiday weekend, we pray: ◆ For our beloved dead, we pray: ◆

Our Father . . .

Lord God,
you sent your Son
to show the way to you.
Foster in our hearts a desire to be more
and to do more that is in accord with
your will
so as to be bearers of your Kingdom.
We ask this through Christ our Lord.
Amen.

✝ Create a clean heart in me, O God.

Saturday, September 2, 2017
Weekday

✝ Glory and praise for ever!

Daniel 3
page 421

Reading
I Thessalonians 4:9–11

Brothers and sisters: On the subject of fraternal charity you have no need for anyone to write you, for you yourselves have been taught by God to love one another. Indeed, you do this for all the brothers throughout Macedonia. Nevertheless we urge you, brothers and sisters, to progress even more, and to aspire to live a tranquil life, to mind your own affairs, and to work with your own hands, as we instructed you.

Reflection

Paul notes that the community shows charity and urges them to aspire to a tranquil life. It is not enough to be good, to love one another; one must seek to put complete trust in God. Those who live a tranquil life have taken to heart the Lord's admonition not to worry. Such individuals understand that God provides for them even more than the birds in the air so there is no need to fret. Assured of God's love, they exude an inner calm. When others come upon this tranquility, they are attracted to the peace that it fosters.

Paul's words are for us, too. Perhaps you cannot be faulted for the charity that you show others. Now Paul asks you to "progress even more, and to aspire to live a tranquil life."

Prayers
others may be added

Seeking peace, we turn to the Lord, as we pray:

◆ Son of the living God, hear our prayer.

May the Church be attentive to the prayer life of its members, we pray: ◆ May we make time for prayer and self-reflection, we pray: ◆ For a sense of awe and wonder, we pray: ◆ For those who work this weekend so that we might enjoy a holiday, we pray: ◆ May we be charitable with our possessions, words, and thoughts, we pray: ◆

Our Father . . .

Eternal One,
your Son gave us his farewell gift
of peace.
It is a peace the world cannot give;
a peace that differs greatly from what the
world calls peace.
May we strive to gather this peace
within ourselves
so as to radiate it into our external lives.
We ask this through Christ our Lord.
Amen.

✝ Glory and praise for ever!

Sunday, September 3, 2017

Twenty-Second Sunday in Ordinary Time

✝ My soul is thirsting for you, O Lord my God.

Psalm 63

page 407

Reading

Matthew 16:24–27

Jesus said to his disciples, "Whoever wishes to come after me must deny himself, take up his cross, and follow me. For whoever wishes to save his life will lose it, but whoever loses his life for my sake will find it. What profit would there be for one to gain the whole world and forfeit his life? Or what can one give in exchange for his life? For the Son of Man will come with his angels in his Father's glory, and then he will repay everyone according to his conduct."

Reflection

A few years back one of the luxury car manufactures ran a commercial in which a man in a perfectly tailored suit extolled the benefits of working hard, sixty hours a week or more, to own stuff. A panoramic sweep of the property revealed all the latest technological toys and a built-in swimming pool (which nobody was enjoying). The man then walked outside and stepped into his opulent vehicle that had every bell and whistle available. Nothing was said of the downside of this work ethic: high divorce rates, estranged children, heart disease, alcoholism, and, ultimately, estrangement from one's very self.

Prayers

others may be added

To Jesus Christ, who emptied himself to share in our humanity, we pray:

◆ Lord, hear our prayer.

For a Church of the poor and a Church that is poor, we pray: ◆ That Christians in developed nations learn to simplify their lives, we pray: ◆ For those forced to live in poverty and subhuman conditions, we pray: ◆ That laborers see their efforts as a sharing in the ongoing work of creation, we pray: ◆ For world leaders, that they will continue to work for the conservation of the earth's natural resources, we pray: ◆

Our Father . . .

Loving God,
your Son showed us the way to you.
Guide us as we seek to deny what the world offers and to follow you.
We ask this through our Lord Jesus Christ, your Son,
who lives and reigns with you in the unity of the Holy Spirit,
one God, for ever and ever.
Amen.

✝ My soul is thirsting for you, O Lord my God.

Monday, September 4, 2017
Weekday

✝ My soul is thirsting for you, O Lord my God.

Psalm 63 *page 407*

Reading *1 Thessalonians 4:13–18*

We do not want you to be unaware, brothers and sisters, about those who have fallen asleep, so that you may not grieve like the rest, who have no hope. For if we believe that Jesus died and rose, so too will God, through Jesus, bring with him those who have fallen asleep. Indeed, we tell you this, on the word of the Lord, that we who are alive, who are left until the coming of the Lord, will surely not precede those who have fallen asleep. For the Lord himself, with a word of command, with the voice of an archangel and with the trumpet of God, will come down from heaven, and the dead in Christ will rise first. Then we who are alive, who are left, will be caught up together with them in the clouds to meet the Lord in the air. Thus we shall always be with the Lord. Therefore, console one another with these words.

Reflection

The early Church expected the Second Coming to occur soon. As the first disciples began to die, there was concern as to whether they would be saved. Paul writes to assure the community of the salvation of those who have died. He describes Christ's return as heralded with the voice of command and the blowing of the trumpet. He wants followers to know that, living or dead, they will be with the Lord.

Prayers *others may be added*

To Jesus Christ, who emptied himself to share in our humanity, we pray:

◆ Graciously hear us, Lord.

That the Body of Christ, the Church, stand with those who labor and find life burdensome, we pray: ◆ That the rights of workers, especially the right to unionize and for collective bargaining be recognized and defended, we pray: ◆ For just wages and safe working conditions, we pray: ◆ For people who are unable to work, we pray: ◆ For the unemployed and underemployed, we pray: ◆

Our Father . . .

Lord Jesus, our brother and coworker,
you have promised to be with us always.
In our work and in our rest,
in our struggles and in our
accomplishments,
in our loved ones and in our adversaries,
may we know your presence,
for you live and reign with God the Father
in the unity of the Holy Spirit,
one God, for ever and ever.
Amen.

✝ My soul is thirsting for you, O Lord my God.

Tuesday, September 5, 2017
Weekday

✝ My soul is thirsting for you, O Lord my God.

Psalm 63
page 407

Reading
1 Thessalonians 5:1–5

Concerning the times and seasons, brothers and sisters, you have no need for anything to be written to you. For you yourselves know very well that the day of the Lord will come like a thief at night. When people are saying, "Peace and security," then sudden disaster comes upon them, like labor pains upon a pregnant woman, and they will not escape.

But you, brothers and sisters, are not in darkness, for that day to overtake you like a thief. For all of you are children of the light and children of the day. We are not of the night or of darkness.

Therefore, encourage one another and build one another up, as indeed you do.

Reflection
Every generation tends to think the end of the world is coming in their time. This goes against the clear injunction of Paul that the day of the Lord will overtake you like a thief." Jesus himself says, "you know not the day nor the hour" (Matthew 25:13). Paul counsels that, instead of dwelling on what we cannot know, we should "encourage one another and build one another up." Take time to consider how you can encourage someone in your family, your workplace, or among your friends.

Prayers
others may be added

To Jesus Christ, who emptied himself to share in our humanity, we pray:

◆ Graciously hear us, Lord.

May leaders of the Christian community build up and appreciate the faithful, we pray: ◆ That we may see the Christ that comes to us each day, we pray: ◆ For an end to gossip, we pray: ◆ That we will treat others as we want them to treat us, we pray: ◆ For attentiveness to the present moment, we pray: ◆

Our Father . . .

Lord Jesus,
you provide the way to peace.
Encourage us to look for the light
in our surroundings and in those
we encounter.
May our presence be a beacon that guides
others from darkness to you.
For you live and reign with God the
Father in the unity of the Holy Spirit,
one God, for ever and ever.
Amen.

✝ My soul is thirsting for you, O Lord my God.

Wednesday, September 6, 2017
Weekday

✝ My soul is thirsting for you, O Lord my God.

Psalm 63 *page 407*

Reading *Luke 4:38–44*

After Jesus left the synagogue, he entered the house of Simon. Simon's mother-in-law was afflicted with a severe fever, and they interceded with him about her. He stood over her, rebuked the fever, and it left her. She got up immediately and waited on them.

At sunset, all who had people sick with various diseases brought them to him. He laid his hands on each of them and cured them. And demons also came out from many, shouting, "You are the Son of God." But he rebuked them and did not allow them to speak because they knew that he was the Christ.

At daybreak, Jesus left and went to a deserted place. The crowds went looking for him, and when they came to him, they tried to prevent him from leaving them. But he said to them, "To the other towns also I must proclaim the good news of the Kingdom of God, because for this purpose I have been sent." And he was preaching in the synagogues of Judea.

Reflection

Prayer is both communal and personal. Today's Gospel provides us with Jesus praying in both ways. We are told that Jesus leaves the synagogue, the Jewish place for communal worship. The following morning, he leaves at daybreak to a deserted place to be alone in prayer. We need to practice both forms of prayer. Today reflect on your practice of prayer, considering your expectations and experiences of prayer. As strange as it might sound, we need to pray about and reflect on our prayer as well as the events of our lives.

Prayers *others may be added*

To Jesus Christ, who emptied himself to share in our humanity, we pray:

◆ Graciously hear us, Lord.

For a Church that summons us to prayer and worship, we pray: ◆ For the grace to reflect on our spiritual practices, we pray: ◆ For those who have no one to pray with them, we pray: ◆ For those who struggle with ritual and communal worship, we pray: ◆ That we may be attentive to the holy in this moment of our life, we pray: ◆

Our Father . . .

God of the Covenant,
you command us to keep holy the
Sabbath and to rest.
You speak to us in the silence of
our hearts.
May we, your people,
attune our lives to you
and live in a spirit of constant prayer
and worship.
We ask this through Christ our Lord.
Amen.

✝ My soul is thirsting for you, O Lord my God.

Thursday, September 7, 2017
Weekday

✝ My soul is thirsting for you, O Lord my God.

Psalm 63
page 407

Reading
Luke 5:4–10

[Jesus] said to Simon, "Put out into deep water and lower your nets for a catch." Simon said in reply, "Master, we have worked hard all night and have caught nothing, but at your command I will lower the nets." When they had done this, they caught a great number of fish and their nets were tearing. They signaled to their partners in the other boat to come to help them. They came and filled both boats so that the boats were in danger of sinking. When Simon Peter saw this, he fell at the knees of Jesus and said, "Depart from me, Lord, for I am a sinful man." For astonishment at the catch of fish they had made seized him and all those with him, and likewise James and John, the sons of Zebedee, who were partners of Simon. Jesus said to Simon, "Do not be afraid; from now on you will be catching men."

Reflection
Having fished all night with no results, Peter and his companions, at Jesus' request, make one more attempt and find themselves with so many fish that their nets are tearing. This was the largest catch of their lives and must have represented much income. Amazingly, they leave the fish on the shore to follow Jesus. This reading brings us to consider the value we give to faith and what we need to leave behind to follow Jesus.

Prayers
others may be added

To Jesus Christ, who emptied himself to share in our humanity, we pray:

◆ Graciously hear us, Lord.

For an evangelizing Church, we pray: ◆ May we be moved to share with others what our faith means to us, we pray: ◆ That we will place working for the Reign of God before all else, we pray: ◆ For seekers, we pray: ◆ For those who seek spirituality without a connection to a religion, we pray: ◆

Our Father . . .

Holy God, Lord of all,
you come seeking us.
Help us not to be afraid to leave behind
our desires and dreams
and to be attentive to your voice and
your path.
We ask this through Christ our Lord.
Amen.

✝ My soul is thirsting for you, O Lord my God.

Friday, September 8, 2017
Feast of the Nativity of the Blessed Virgin Mary

✝ My soul is thirsting for you, O Lord my God.

Psalm 63 *page 407*

Reading *Matthew 1:18–21*

Now this is how the birth of Jesus Christ came about. When his mother Mary was betrothed to Joseph, but before they lived together, she was found with child through the Holy Spirit. Joseph her husband, since he was a righteous man, yet unwilling to expose her to shame, decided to divorce her quietly. Such was his intention when, behold, the angel of the Lord appeared to him in a dream and said, "Joseph, son of David, do not be afraid to take Mary your wife into your home. For it is through the Holy Spirit that this child has been conceived in her. She will bear a son and you are to name him Jesus, because he will save his people from their sins."

Reflection

The birth of Mary is not mentioned in the Scriptures. There is no trustworthy historical account of her birth. The names of her parents, Sts. Joachim and Anne, come to us from the apocryphal Gospel of James. That said, the celebration of our Blessed Mother's birth has been a part of the life of the Church since the sixth century. Mary's birth was no less miraculous than the birth of any child. A newborn is a symbol of wonder and hope, promise and potential. In this instance, that wonder and hope, promise and potential made a difference in the lives of all who would follow her Son.

Prayers *others may be added*

To Jesus Christ, who emptied himself to share in our humanity, we pray:

◆ Graciously hear us, Lord.

May the Church, the people of God, bear Christ to the world, we pray: ◆ For expectant parents, we pray: ◆ For the protection of the unborn, we pray: ◆ For children waiting to be adopted, we pray: ◆ For children born with addictions, we pray: ◆

Our Father . . .

God of all,
as we rejoice in the birth of the mother of your Son,
we are mindful of the precariousness of life,
especially the lives of infants and children throughout the world.
Teach us to respect the lives of all.
We ask this through Christ our Lord.
Amen.

✝ My soul is thirsting for you, O Lord my God.

Saturday, September 9, 2017
Memorial of St. Peter Claver, Priest

✝ My soul is thirsting for you, O Lord my God.

Psalm 63 *page 407*

Reading *Luke 6:1–5*

While Jesus was going through a field of grain on a sabbath, his disciples were picking the heads of grain, rubbing them in their hands, and eating them. Some Pharisees said, "Why are you doing what is unlawful on the sabbath?" Jesus said to them in reply, "Have you not read what David did when he and those who were with him were hungry? How he went into the house of God, took the bread of offering, which only the priests could lawfully eat, ate of it, and shared it with his companions?" Then he said to them, "The Son of Man is lord of the sabbath."

Reflection

In 1610, the Jesuit Peter Claver left his native Spain to serve in the New World. He would arrive in what is modern-day Colombia and minister there until his death. Peter Claver's ministry was during the time of the burgeoning slave trade. About ten thousand African slaves were brought to Colombia each year. Peter Claver would meet the ships and present these sons and daughters of God with medicine, food, and drink. With the assistance of an interpreter he proclaimed the Gospel to them. Claver intentionally shunned the hospitality of the plantation owners to live in the slaves' quarters. He is known as "the slave of the slaves."

Prayers *others may be added*

To Jesus Christ, who emptied himself to share in our humanity, we pray:

◆ Graciously hear us, Lord.

May the Church in Africa be at peace with her Muslim neighbors, we pray: ◆ For African-American Catholics, we pray: ◆ That we might be inspired by the humility and justice of St. Peter Claver, we pray: ◆ For the Knights of St. Peter Claver, we pray: ◆ For parishes celebrating their patronal feast today, we pray: ◆

Our Father . . .

God of justice,
you provide for our every need.
Direct us to look to the life of
Peter Claver.
Moved by his holiness,
may we hear the cry of the poor and
the oppressed.
We ask this through Christ our Lord.
Amen.

✝ My soul is thirsting for you, O Lord my God.

Sunday, September 10, 2017
Twenty-Third Sunday in Ordinary Time

☩ If today you hear his voice, harden not your hearts.

Psalm 95 *page 413*

Reading *Matthew 18:15–17*

Jesus said to his disciples: "If your brother sins against you, go and tell him his fault between you and him alone. If he listens to you, you have won over your brother. If he does not listen, take one or two others along with you, so that 'every fact may be established on the testimony of two or three witnesses.' If he refuses to listen to them, tell the Church. If he refuses to listen even to the Church, then treat him as you would a Gentile or a tax collector."

Reflection

Jesus' instructions on handling conflict may be direct, but they are still hard to follow. Go directly to the one you believe has wronged you and talk in private, Jesus tells us. So many hurts would be avoided and misunderstandings cleared up if we followed our Lord's directive. Instead, we display a lack of trust in the other as we tell a third party. Often we tell many third parties, how "so and so" wronged us. Confrontation is never easy. Yet when we confront in love with the goal of understanding and resolution, not revenge and punishment, we affirm and even improve the value of a relationship.

Prayers *others may be added*

To Christ our Light, we pray:

◆ Hear us, Lord.

For transparency in the Church, we pray: ◆ For the work of the United Nations, we pray: ◆ May family members truly listen to one another, we pray: ◆ That leaders of nations seek to settle differences peacefully, we pray: ◆ May we be gentle with ourselves and with one another, we pray: ◆

Our Father . . .

Source of All Truth,
it isn't easy to be honest.
We cover up our faults,
deny our insecurities,
ignore our sins;
we even flee from ourselves.
May we love enough and trust enough
to be honest with others,
with ourselves, and with you, our God.
Through our Lord Jesus Christ, your Son,
who lives and reigns with you in the unity
of the Holy Spirit,
one God, for ever and ever.
Amen.

☩ If today you hear his voice, harden not your hearts.

Monday, September 11, 2017
Weekday

✝ If today you hear his voice, harden not your hearts.

Psalm 95

page 413

Reading

Luke 6:6–11

On a certain sabbath Jesus went into the synagogue and taught, and there was a man there whose right hand was withered. The scribes and the Pharisees watched him closely to see if he would cure on the sabbath so that they might discover a reason to accuse him. But he realized their intentions and said to the man with the withered hand, "Come up and stand before us." Then Jesus said to them, "I ask you, is it lawful to do good on the sabbath rather than to do evil, to save life rather than to destroy it?" Looking around at them all, he then said to him, "Stretch out your hand." He did so and his hand was restored. But they became enraged and discussed what they might do to Jesus.

Reflection

When Jesus cures on a Sabbath the authorities are enraged. The law has been violated. Rules and commands provide us with wisdom, direction, and protection. They are trustworthy guides enabling us to be faithful disciples. However, they are rarely absolute—to be observed in all times, all places, and all circumstances. Jesus shows us the priority of responding in love to human need. When it seems that a rule is in disagreement with human need, the intent and purpose of the tenet should be discerned.

Prayers

others may be added

To Christ our Light, we pray:

◆ Hear us, Lord.

That the Church be a community of healing and acceptance, we pray: ◆ For all who work to heal bodies and spirits, we pray: ◆ For those who plot to harm others, that they may reform and repent, we pray: ◆ For an end to violence in all its forms, we pray: ◆ For those who were killed in attacks sixteen years ago today, we pray: ◆

Our Father . . .

God of mercy and justice,
you provide all that is good.
May we speak, live, serve, and witness
so as to save life and be faithful stewards
of all you, in your goodness, have
entrusted to us.
We ask this through Christ our Lord.
Amen.

✝ If today you hear his voice, harden not your hearts.

Tuesday, September 12, 2017
Weekday

✝ If today you hear his voice, harden not your hearts.

Psalm 95 *page 413*

Reading *Luke 6:12–19*

Jesus departed to the mountain to pray, and he spent the night in prayer to God. When day came, he called his disciples to himself, and from them he chose Twelve, whom he also named Apostles: Simon, whom he named Peter, and his brother Andrew, James, John, Philip, Bartholomew, Matthew, Thomas, James the son of Alphaeus, Simon who was called a Zealot, and Judas the son of James, and Judas Iscariot, who became a traitor.

And he came down with them and stood on a stretch of level ground. A great crowd of his disciples and a large number of the people from all Judea and Jerusalem and the coastal region of Tyre and Sidon came to hear him and to be healed of their diseases; and even those who were tormented by unclean spirits were cured. Everyone in the crowd sought to touch him because power came forth from him and healed them all.

Reflection

"Jesus departed to the mountain to pray." It is said that prayer is conversation with God—speaking and listening. Of course, conversation also includes laughing or crying; asking or thanking. Have you considered prayer as recreating with God; enjoying God's presence; and God enjoying your presence?

Prayers *others may be added*

To Christ, our Light, we pray:

◆ Hear us, Lord.

For bishops and patriarchs, we pray: ◆ May our parishes be attentive to human needs, we pray: ◆ For our parish staff and for the members of our parish council, we pray: ◆ That the faithful will spend time in solitude and prayer, we pray: ◆ For those suffering with a tormented conscience, we pray: ◆

Our Father . . .

Lord Jesus,
throughout your time with your disciples
you showed us how to pray.
Teach us to be faithful to the discipline
of prayer.
May we see prayer as a joy and a delight
for it is time spent with you,
who lives and reigns with God the Father
in the unity of the Holy Spirit,
one God, for ever and ever.
Amen.

✝ If today you hear his voice, harden not your hearts.

Wednesday, September 13, 2017

Memorial of St. John Chrysostom,
Bishop and Doctor of the Church

✝ If today you hear his voice, harden not your hearts.

Psalm 95 *page 413*

page 413

Reading *Luke 6:20–23*

Raising his eyes toward his disciples Jesus said: / "Blessed are you who are poor, / for the Kingdom of God is yours. / Blessed are you who are now hungry, / for you will be satisfied. / Blessed are you who are now weeping, / for you will laugh. / Blessed are you when people hate you, / and when they exclude and insult you, / and denounce your name as evil / on account of the Son of Man.

"Rejoice and leap for joy on that day! Behold, your reward will be great in heaven."

Reflection

John Chrysostom (347–407), was the archbishop of Constantinople. Orthodox Christians and Byzantine Rite Catholics celebrate the Divine Liturgy of St. John Chrysostom as the norm for the Eucharistic liturgy. Nicknamed "golden mouth" for his oratorical skills, Chrysostom rarely minced words. He was a staunch defender of the poor: "Do you wish to honor the Body of the Savior? Do not despise it when it is naked. Do not honor it in church with silk vestments while outside it is naked and numb with cold. Honor him then by sharing your property with the poor. For what God needs is not golden chalices but golden souls" (On the Gospel of St. Matthew, 50, iii).

Prayers *others may be added*

To Christ, our Light, we pray:

◆ Enlighten us, Lord.

May the Church take up the forthrightness of St. John Chrysostom, we pray: ◆ For Eastern Rite Catholics, we pray: ◆ For Orthodox Christians, we pray: ◆ For those who proclaim the Word of God, we pray: ◆ For communities who today celebrate their patronal feast, we pray: ◆

Our Father . . .

Lord God,
East and West share alike
the great legacy of St. John Chrysostom.
Bring unity to your Church
and raise up prophetic leaders
to demand justice for those who are long suffering.
We ask this through Christ our Lord.
Amen.

✝ If today you hear his voice, harden not your hearts.

Thursday, September 14, 2017

Feast of the Exaltation of the Holy Cross

☩ **If today you hear his voice, harden not your hearts.**

Psalm 95

page 413

Reading

John 3:13–17

Jesus said to Nicodemus: "No one has gone up to heaven except the one who has come down from heaven, the Son of Man. And just as Moses lifted up the serpent in the desert, so must the Son of Man be lifted up, so that everyone who believes in him may have eternal life."

For God so loved the world that he gave his only Son, so that everyone who believes in him might not perish but might have eternal life. For God did not send his Son into the world to condemn the world, but that the world might be saved through him.

Reflection

"And just as Moses lifted up the serpent in the desert, so must the Son of Man be lifted up." Today we celebrate that the Cross was transformed from an object of terror and subjugation to the symbol of Christ's victory and the central symbol of our faith. "We should glory in the Cross of our Lord Jesus Christ, / in whom is our salvation, life and resurrection, / through whom we are saved and delivered" (Entrance Antiphon from *The Roman Missal*).

Prayers

others may be added

To Christ, our Light, we pray:

◆ Hear us, Lord.

May Christ crucified be preached by the Church, we pray: ◆ That the cross will remind us of our baptismal identity, we pray: ◆ That the cross will serve as a reminder of God's love and presence, we pray: ◆ May Christians ponder and take to heart the meaning of the Cross, we pray: ◆ For all who share in the sufferings of Christ, we pray: ◆

Our Father . . .

God of wonder and surprises,
you have transformed
a symbol of oppression and shame
into one of love and mercy.
Forgive us for the times and ways
we have crucified one another.
Help us to share the love and life
that flows from the Cross of your Son,
who lives and reigns with you in the unity
of the Holy Spirit,
one God, for ever and ever.
Amen.

☩ **If today you hear his voice, harden not your hearts.**

Friday, September 15, 2017
Memorial of Our Lady of Sorrows

✝ If today you hear his voice, harden not your hearts.

Psalm 95 *page 413*

Reading *John 19:25–27*

Standing by the cross of Jesus were his mother and his mother's sister, Mary the wife of Clopas, and Mary of Magdala. When Jesus saw his mother and the disciple there whom he loved he said to his mother, "Woman, behold, your son." Then he said to the disciple, "Behold, your mother." And from that hour the disciple took her into his home.

Reflection

We can only imagine what Mary endured as she watched helplessly as her son was being condemned, crucified, and finally, breathing his last. The many parents who have watched and suffered through their child's death from disease, accident, or violence can connect to Our Lady of Sorrows. Knowing the loss of a child, she offers herself as a place of refuge for them.

Today, parishes can lift up in prayer parents who grieve the loss of a child. At home, families and individuals can pray for those families who need consolation because of the death of a child.

Prayers *others may be added*

To Christ, our Light, we pray:

◆ Enlighten us, Lord.

May Our Lady of Sorrows move the Church to be in solidarity with the oppressed, we pray: ◆ For parents who have lost a child, we pray: ◆ For parents whose child has been violated by a priest or religious, we pray: ◆ For parents separated from their children due to war, we pray: ◆ For parents who will never see their children again, we pray: ◆

Our Father . . .

Lord Jesus,
yesterday we celebrated the symbol of the Cross
transformed from torture to glory.
Help us to comfort those who mourn so that they know they are not alone.
May we be signs to them of your compassion.
You live and reign with God the Father in the unity of the Holy Spirit,
one God, for ever and ever.
Amen.

✝ If today you hear his voice, harden not your hearts.

Saturday, September 16, 2017

Memorial of Sts. Cornelius, Pope, and Cyprian, Bishop and Martyrs

✝ If today you hear his voice, harden not your hearts.

Psalm 95

page 413

Reading

I Timothy 1:15–17

Beloved: This saying is trustworthy and deserves full acceptance: Christ Jesus came into the world to save sinners. Of these I am the foremost. But for that reason I was mercifully treated, so that in me, as the foremost, Christ Jesus might display all his patience as an example for those who would come to believe in him for everlasting life. To the king of ages, incorruptible, invisible, the only God, honor and glory forever and ever. Amen.

Reflection

In the middle of the third century the Church experienced its first antipope. The bishops affirmed that Cornelius was the rightful successor to Peter. Now there was another concern: could those who had supported the antipope be reconciled to the community? There was also the matter of those who denied the faith under threat of martyrdom. Could these find forgiveness? Or are they to be ostracized forever? It was Cornelius, supported by the theologian Cyprian who maintained both could be reconciled following a period of penance. The theology of Cyprian of Carthage had great influence on the early Church. He is another example of the importance and impact individuals from Africa had on the formation of our faith.

Prayers

others may be added

To Christ, the Light of the World, and so we pray:

◆ Hear us, Lord.

May the People of God be a community of forgiveness and healing, we pray: ◆ For N., our Pope, and N., our bishop we pray: ◆ For all who are persecuted because of their religion, we pray: ◆ For canon lawyers, we pray: ◆ For parishes celebrating their patronal feast today, we pray: ◆

Our Father . . .

Lord Jesus,
as you forgave Peter his denial,
so we see your pardon practiced in the early Church.
Having received your forgiveness
may we forgive one another
and build communities of reconciliation.
You live and reign with God the Father in the unity of the Holy Spirit,
one God, for ever and ever.
Amen.

✝ If today you hear his voice, harden not your hearts.

Sunday, September 17, 2017

Twenty-Fourth Sunday in Ordinary Time

✝ The Lord is kind and merciful, slow to anger, and rich in compassion.

Psalm 103

page 415

Reading

Matthew 18:21–22

Peter approached Jesus and said to him, "Lord, if my brother sins against me, how often must I forgive him? As many as seven times?" Jesus answered, "I say to you, not seven times but seventy-seven times."

Reflection

To forgive one brother seventy-seven times may have seemed to be a lot to Peter. It continues to appear to be a plentiful number to us. We might ask ourselves how one person could need to be forgiven so many times. But then we could consider how many times we have asked God to forgive us. If we are to image God in our encounters with others, we will need to forgive as much as we have been forgiven. The number of times, then, that we will forgive surely will be more than seventy-seven. But that forgiveness will allow us to move on in our relationship with our brother or sister.

Prayers

others may be added

Turning to our Lord, who forgives us, we pray:

◆ Lord, hear our prayer.

May the Christian community be known for its forgiveness, we pray: ◆ That nations find a path to forgive one another, we pray: ◆ For those whom we have hurt or offended, we pray: ◆ For those who have hurt us, we pray: ◆ For those who struggle to forgive others or themselves, we pray: ◆

Our Father . . .

God of mercy and forgiveness,
through your Son you have taught us
that there is no limit to forgiveness.
May we forgive all who have wronged us,
just as you have forgiven us.
We ask this through our Lord Jesus
Christ, your Son,
who lives and reigns with you in the unity
of the Holy Spirit,
one God, for ever and ever
Amen.

✝ The Lord is kind and merciful, slow to anger, and rich in compassion.

Monday, September 18, 2017
Weekday

☩ The Lord is kind and merciful, slow to anger, and rich in compassion.

Psalm 103 *page 415*

page 415

Reading *Luke 7:1–7*

When Jesus had finished all his words to the people, he entered Capernaum. A centurion there had a slave who was ill and about to die, and he was valuable to him. When he heard about Jesus, he sent elders of the Jews to him, asking him to come and save the life of his slave. They approached Jesus and strongly urged him to come, saying, "He deserves to have you do this for him, for he loves our nation and he built the synagogue for us." And Jesus went with them, but when he was only a short distance from the house, the centurion sent friends to tell him, "Lord, do not trouble yourself, for I am not worthy to have you enter under my roof. Therefore, I did not consider myself worthy to come to you; but say the word and let my servant be healed."

Reflection

The centurion's faith so impresses Jesus that he gives high praise to a non-Jew while insulting his own people. "I tell you, not even in Israel have I found such faith." Certainly the remarkable faith of Mahatma Gandhi, Thich Nhat Hanh, Etty Hillesum, or Anne Frank can both teach and chide us for our lack of faith, dedication, and witness to the Reign of God. It is rare for a young movement to acknowledge the fidelity of those beyond its fold. Yet this awareness is part of our faith from its origins. Who are the non-Christians that inspire you? How and why do they touch your life?

Prayers *others may be added*

Turning to our Lord, who forgives us, we pray:

◆ Lord, hear our prayer.

That the People of God never cease to be open to interreligious cooperation and dialogue, we pray: ◆ May we embrace the gifts and witness of those who do not believe in Christ, we pray: ◆ That Jews, Muslims, and Christians come to understanding and peace with one another, we pray: ◆ For people of good will who do not believe in God, we pray: ◆ For the freedom of worship, we pray: ◆

Our Father . . .

God of all,
you have made yourself known to all
and are present in other religions.
May we respect and learn from
one another,
holding fast to our faith in your Son and
the Holy Spirit,
who live and reign with you,
one God, for ever and ever.
Amen.

☩ The Lord is kind and merciful, slow to anger, and rich in compassion.

Tuesday, September 19, 2017
Weekday

✝ The Lord is kind and merciful, slow to anger, and rich in compassion.

Psalm 103 *page 415*

Reading *Luke 7:11–17*

Jesus journeyed to a city called Nain, and his disciples and a large crowd accompanied him. As he drew near to the gate of the city, a man who had died was being carried out, the only son of his mother, and she was a widow. A large crowd from the city was with her. When the Lord saw her, he was moved with pity for her and said to her, "Do not weep." He stepped forward and touched the coffin; at this the bearers halted, and he said, "Young man, I tell you, arise!" The dead man sat up and began to speak, and Jesus gave him to his mother. Fear seized them all, and they glorified God, exclaiming, "A great prophet has arisen in our midst," and "God has visited his people." This report about him spread through the whole of Judea and in all the surrounding region.

Reflection

This passage illustrates both that Jesus is Lord of Life and his concern for the poor. In the first century, it was expected that children would provide for their elderly parents. With the death of her son, this widow faced certain poverty. In returning life to her son, Jesus insured the widow's ability to live out her days in dignity. Ponder the implications of this account in light of Jesus and his mother, who also was a widow.

Prayers *others may be added*

Turning to Christ, who forgives our sins, we pray:

◆ Lord, hear our prayer.

May we never forget that those who have died remain united with the Church, we pray: ◆ For grieving parents, we pray: ◆ For those who minister to the bereaved, we pray: ◆ For older adults, we pray: ◆ For widows and orphans, we pray: ◆

Our Father . . .

Author of Life,
in your Son, Jesus Christ,
you have indeed visited your people.
Strengthen our awareness
of the many ways your Son
remains present to us,
for he lives and reigns with you in the unity of the Holy Spirit,
one God, for ever and ever.
Amen.

✝ The Lord is kind and merciful, slow to anger, and rich in compassion.

Wednesday, September 20, 2017

Memorial of Sts. Andrew Kim Tae-gŏn, Priest, and Paul Chŏng Ha-sang, and Companions, Martyrs

† The Lord is kind and merciful, slow to anger, and rich in compassion.

Psalm 103

page 415

Reading

Luke 9:23–26

Jesus said to all, "If anyone wishes to come after me, he must deny himself and take up his cross daily and follow me. For whoever wishes to save his life will lose it, but whoever loses his life for my sake will save it. What profit is there for one to gain the whole world yet lose or forfeit himself? Whoever is ashamed of me and of my words, the Son of Man will be ashamed of when he comes in his glory and in the glory of the Father and of the holy angels."

Reflection

It is unclear how Christianity was introduced to Korea. A leading theory posits that Japanese soldiers introduced the faith when they invaded Korea in 1592. When the first missionaries arrived in the 1800s they were astounded to discover several thousand Catholics. The faith had been established and survived without the Eucharist and without clergy. Families and catechists had passed on the faith through the Scriptures. Andrew Kim was the first native priest of Korea. He, together with Paul Chŏng and 102 others were martyred in 1846. Without diminishing the centrality of the Eucharist, the history of the Korean Church is a testimony to the power and sublimity of the Word of God.

Prayers

others may be added

Turning to Christ, who forgives our sins, we pray:

◆ Lord, hear our prayer.

For a Church that evangelizes through her words and actions, we pray: ◆ That parents be faithful to their promise to raise their children in the practice of the faith, we pray: ◆ For missionaries, we pray: ◆ For the Church in Korea, we pray: ◆ For parishes celebrating their patronal feast today, we pray: ◆

Our Father . . .

God of all,
your grace and mercy extend
beyond the boundaries of race and nation.
May we learn from the Church in Korea
so that your Word will ever be on
our minds,
upon our lips, and in our hearts.
We ask this through Christ our Lord.
Amen.

† The Lord is kind and merciful, slow to anger, and rich in compassion.

Thursday, September 21, 2017
Feast of St. Matthew, Apostle and Evangelist

✝ The Lord is kind and merciful, slow to anger, and rich in compassion.

Psalm 103
page 415

Reading
Matthew 9:9–13

As Jesus passed by, he saw a man named Matthew sitting at the customs post. He said to him, "Follow me." And he got up and followed him. While he was at table in his house, many tax collectors and sinners came and sat with Jesus and his disciples. The Pharisees saw this and said to his disciples, "Why does your teacher eat with tax collectors and sinners?" He heard this and said, "Those who are well do not need a physician, but the sick do. Go and learn the meaning of the words, / *I desire mercy, not sacrifice.* / I did not come to call the righteous but sinners."

Reflection
In the Gospel bearing his name, Matthew is identified as a tax collector. As a Jew collecting taxes for Rome he would have been viewed as a traitor to his people. Tax collectors made their living by overcharging the people and keeping the extra money for themselves. This helps us to understand the consternation of the Pharisees. It also helps us to understand one of the tensions played out in Matthew's Gospel: judgment or mercy? Read cover to cover, a great deal of judgment can be found in Matthew, yet this Gospel consistently emphasizes mercy over and against judgment. Are we perceived as people of judgment or as people of mercy?

Prayers
others may be added

Turning to Christ, who forgives our sins, we pray:

◆ Lord, hear our prayer.

That mercy may pervade every action of the Church, we pray: ◆ That we will learn the meaning of the words, "I desire mercy, not sacrifice," we pray: ◆ For accountants, bankers, bookkeepers, and tax collectors, we pray: ◆ For those living with an overwhelming sense of guilt, we pray: ◆ For parishes that hold St. Matthew as their patron, we pray: ◆

Our Father . . .

Lord Jesus,
in choosing Matthew to be an Apostle,
you looked to those we would have
ignored, rejected, and even despised.
Make us aware of how we judge
and remind us to be merciful to others
and ourselves.
You live and reign with God the Father in
the unity of the Holy Spirit,
one God, for ever and ever.
Amen.

✝ The Lord is kind and merciful, slow to anger, and rich in compassion.

Friday, September 22, 2017
Weekday

✝ The Lord is kind and merciful, slow to anger, and rich in compassion.

Psalm 103 *page 415*

Reading *1 Timothy 6:6–10*

[Beloved,] indeed, religion with contentment is a great gain. For we brought nothing into the world, just as we shall not be able to take anything out of it. If we have food and clothing, we shall be content with that. Those who want to be rich are falling into temptation and into a trap and into many foolish and harmful desires, which plunge them into ruin and destruction. For the love of money is the root of all evils, and some people in their desire for it have strayed from the faith and have pierced themselves with many pains.

Reflection

Is "rich Christian" an oxymoron? Paul warns against those who abuse religion for personal profit. He also urges us to be content with having food and clothing. Beyond that, "love of money is the root of all evils." Wealth can distort our view so we can no longer see the world from the perspective of the poor and oppressed.

Some mistakenly equate wealth for security, but true security comes from God. Some confuse wealth with power, but true power is "the ability of love to bring about justice" (Paul Tillich). Wealth is a blessing when it is used to bless others, especially the poor.

Prayers *others may be added*

Turning to the Lord, who forgives our sins, we pray:

◆ Lord, hear our prayer.

For a Church of the poor and a Church that is poor, we pray: ◆ For the gift of contentment with what we have, we pray: ◆ That we view wealth as a stewardship rather than a personal possession, we pray: ◆ For those who lead lives of voluntary poverty, we pray: ◆ For those who have died from hunger, we pray: ◆

Our Father . . .

God of all creation,
the earth and everything it contains
is yours.
May we not treat what is yours
as our personal claim or property
but understand that we are responsible
before you and to one another.
We ask this through Christ our Lord.
Amen.

✝ The Lord is kind and merciful, slow to anger, and rich in compassion.

Saturday, September 23, 2017
Memorial of St. Pius of Pietrelcina, Priest

† The Lord is kind and merciful, slow to anger, and rich in compassion.

Psalm 103

page 415

Reading

1 Timothy 6:13–16

Beloved: I charge you before God, who gives life to all things, and before Christ Jesus, who gave testimony under Pontius Pilate for the noble confession, to keep the commandment without stain or reproach until the appearance of our Lord Jesus Christ that the blessed and only ruler will make manifest at the proper time, the King of kings and Lord of lords, who alone has immortality, who dwells in unapproachable light, and whom no human being has seen or can see. To him be honor and eternal power. Amen.

Reflection

Having entered eternal life in 1968 and canonized in 2002, Padre Pio, as St. Pius of Pietrelcina is more commonly called, is a recent saint. Known for bearing the wounds of Christ in his body, the stigmata, Padre Pio was sought after as a confessor, spiritual counselor, and intercessor. He was subject to numerous investigations and his spiritual gifts were discounted even by some popes.

Prayers

others may be added

Turning to the Lord, who forgives our sins, we pray:

◆ Lord, hear our prayer.

That the Holy Spirit will continue to raise up men and women of holiness to inspire the People of God, we pray: ◆ For the ability to join our sufferings with Christ and all humanity, we pray: ◆ For those who are questioned, silenced, or dismissed by the Church, we pray: ◆ For Capuchins and all in religious life, we pray: ◆ That the chronically ill find a companion and friend in St. Padre Pio, we pray: ◆

Our Father . . .

God of life,
you allowed St. Pius of Pietrelcina
to witness to you through
miraculous ways.
May the memory of this saint
remind us to disagree with gentleness
and respect.
We ask this through Christ our Lord.
Amen.

† The Lord is kind and merciful, slow to anger, and rich in compassion.

Sunday, September 24, 2017
Twenty-Fifth Sunday in Ordinary Time

✝ The Lord is near to all who call upon him.

Psalm 145

page 420

Reading

Matthew 20:8–13, 15

"When it was evening the owner of the vineyard said to his foreman, 'Summon the laborers and give them their pay, beginning with the last and ending with the first.' When those who had started about five o'clock came, each received the usual daily wage. So when the first came, they thought that they would receive more, but each of them also got the usual wage. And on receiving it they grumbled against the landowner, saying, 'These last ones worked only one hour, and you have made them equal to us, who bore the day's burden and the heat.' He said to one of them in reply, 'My friend, I am not cheating you. Are you envious because I am generous?' "

Reflection

It is easy to be troubled by the parable and wonder why the owner is not paying the men for the time spent in labor. Rather than being troubled by this parable we should consider our response to it. Why are we so quick to side with those who labored all day? Reading the parable from the perspective of those who worked just one hour might provide another insight. Do not the families of these workers have the same need for food, clothing, and shelter as those who worked longer? Would we deprive them of these necessities just so some can have more?

Prayers

others may be added

To our compassionate God, we pray:

◆ Lord, hear our prayer.

May the Church engage in action on behalf of justice, we pray: ◆ For our nation's leaders, that they consider the needs of the working poor, we pray: ◆ For migrant workers and those subsisting on minimum wage or less, we pray: ◆ For those whom no one has hired, we pray: ◆ That our resentment be transformed into joy, we pray: ◆

Our Father . . .

God of the vineyard,
you see to all of our needs.
May we not be envious because you
are generous
but rejoice with all
as undeserving recipients
of your boundless mercy and forgiveness.
Through our Lord Jesus Christ, your Son,
who lives and reigns with you in the unity
of the Holy Spirit,
one God, for ever and ever.
Amen.

✝ The Lord is near to all who call upon him.

Monday, September 25, 2017
Weekday

☩ The Lord is near to all who call upon him.

Psalm 145

page 420

Reading

Ezra 1:1–4

In the first year of Cyrus, king of Persia, in order to fulfill the word of the LORD spoken by Jeremiah, the LORD inspired King Cyrus of Persia to issue this proclamation throughout his kingdom, both by word of mouth and in writing: "Thus says Cyrus, king of Persia: 'All the kingdoms of the earth the LORD, the God of heaven, has given to me, and he has also charged me to build him a house in Jerusalem, which is in Judah. Therefore, whoever among you belongs to any part of his people, let him go up, and may his God be with him! Let everyone who has survived, in whatever place he may have dwelt, be assisted by the people of that place with silver, gold, goods, and cattle, together with free-will offerings for the house of God in Jerusalem.'"

Reflection

This Scripture tells of "the second Exodus," when Jews were allowed to return to their homeland after being exiled to Babylon. Not all Jews returned. Many had intermarried, had jobs, and created new lives in Babylon. These would be part of the "Diaspora" (Jews living outside of Israel). By the time of Jesus more Jews lived abroad than in the Holy Land. Not all had been taken into exile. Those left behind also married with non-Jews and their religion and culture developed differently from those returning from Babylon. Some of these are the Samaritans whom we meet in the Gospel accounts: hence the enmity between Jews and Samaritans.

Prayers

others may be added

To our compassionate God, we pray:

◆ Lord, hear our prayer.

For the Church, that her members may serve as peacemakers, we pray: ◆ For religious dialogue among Christians, Muslims, and Jews, we pray: ◆ For peace for all in the Middle East, we pray: ◆ For those living in exile, may they be able to return home, we pray: ◆ For refugees and immigrants, that nations look after their needs, we pray: ◆

Our Father . . .

Prince of Peace,
you have shown us the way to harmony.
May we return our swords to their sheaths
and proclaim,
"No more war, war never again,"
(Pope Paul VI),
for you live and reign with God the Father
in the unity of the Holy Spirit,
one God, for ever and ever.
Amen.

☩ The Lord is near to all who call upon him.

Tuesday, September 26, 2017
Weekday

✝ The Lord is near to all who call upon him.

Psalm 145
page 420

Reading
Ezra 6:7–8, 12

King Darius issued an order to the officials of West-of-Euphrates: "Let the governor and the elders of the Jews continue the work on that house of God; they are to rebuild it on its former site. I also issue this decree concerning your dealing with these elders of the Jews in the rebuilding of that house of God: From the royal revenue, the taxes of West-of-Euphrates, let these men be repaid for their expenses, in full and without delay. I, Darius, have issued this decree; let it be carefully executed."

Reflection
Having returned from exile the Jews are now to rebuild the house of God. This is a powerful image. We can think of the literal building of our parish church. We might think of the charge given to St. Francis of Assisi to "rebuild my Church," referring not to a building but to reforming the spirituality and mission of the Church. We can ponder Jesus as the New Temple, or the People of God as the Temple of the Holy Spirit. As Church we are always under reform, we are always being built and rebuilt. How is this happening in your community?

Prayers
others may be added

To our compassionate God, we pray:

◆ Lord, hear our prayer.

That the Church be open to the gift of continual conversion, we pray: ◆ That our parishes be perceived as spiritual centers within their local community, we pray: ◆ For our parish staff, we pray: ◆ For lay leaders who freely serve in positions of parish leadership, we pray: ◆ For our nation's leaders, that they will listen to the Church, we pray: ◆

Our Father . . .

God of the covenant,
you continually call to yourself
a people to be the visible sign of
your presence.
Guide us and our Church to be holy
as you are holy so that our worship, work,
and witness
point to you.
We ask this through Christ our Lord.
Amen.

✝ The Lord is near to all who call upon him.

Wednesday, September 27, 2017

Memorial of St. Vincent de Paul, Priest

✝ The Lord is near to all who call upon him.

Psalm 145

page 420

Reading

Luke 9:1–6

Jesus summoned the Twelve and gave them power and authority over all demons and to cure diseases, and he sent them to proclaim the Kingdom of God and to heal the sick. He said to them, "Take nothing for the journey, neither walking stick, nor sack, nor food, nor money, and let no one take a second tunic. Whatever house you enter, stay there and leave from there. And as for those who do not welcome you, when you leave town, shake the dust from your feet in testimony against them." Then they set out and went from village to village proclaiming the good news and curing diseases everywhere.

Reflection

The simplicity to which Jesus calls his disciples was not lost on St. Vincent de Paul. He is known as the "Great Apostle of Charity" because of his devotion to the poor. His legacy includes being founder of the Congregation of the Mission (Vincentians) and the inspiration behind the St. Vincent de Paul Society. St. Vincent was instrumental in supporting the reform called for by the Council of Trent, especially the education of priests and formation of seminaries. While it is difficult for us to fathom today, for the first fifteen-hundred years of Christianity, there was no formal program to prepare men for the priesthood.

Prayers

others may be added

To our compassionate God, we pray:

◆ Lord, hear our prayer.

May the Church remain in solidarity with the poor and marginalized, we pray: ◆ For legislators, that they advocate on behalf of the poor, we pray: ◆ For those who serve as Vincentian priests and brothers, we pray: ◆ For the members of the St. Vincent de Paul Society, we pray: ◆ For seminary faculty and staff, we pray: ◆

Our Father . . .

Lord God,
you always defend the poor.
May the zeal of St. Vincent de Paul
challenge us to simplify our lives,
give generously to the needy,
and summon us to see life from the
perspective of the poor.
We ask this through Christ our Lord.
Amen.

✝ The Lord is near to all who call upon him.

Thursday, September 28, 2017
Weekday

✝ The Lord is near to all who call upon him.

Psalm 145 *page 420*

Reading *Haggai 1:1–8*

On the first day of the sixth month in the second year of King Darius, The word of the LORD came through the prophet Haggai to the governor of Judah, Zerubbabel, son of Shealtiel, and to the high priest Joshua, son of Jehozadak:

Thus says the LORD of hosts: This people says: "The time has not yet come to rebuild the house of the LORD." (Then this word of the LORD came through Haggai, the prophet:) Is it time for you to dwell in your own paneled houses, while this house lies in ruins? / Now thus says the LORD of hosts: / Consider your ways! / You have sown much, but have brought in little; / you have eaten, but have not been satisfied; / You have drunk, but have not been exhilarated; / have clothed yourselves, but not been warmed; / And whoever earned wages / earned them for a bag with holes in it. / Thus says the LORD of hosts: / Consider your ways! / Go up into the hill country; / bring timber, and build the house / That I may take pleasure in it / and receive my glory, says the LORD. /

Reflection

The prophet Haggai informs us that, in returning from exile in Babylon and given the order to rebuild the Temple, all did not go well. Sounding as angry as Amos, Haggai criticizes his people for focusing on "what's in it for me," and neglecting the house of the Lord. They have fashioned homes for themselves, clothed themselves, made money, and planted food, while the house of the Lord "lies in ruins." Where is God in our day-to-day priorities? Do God, the poor, justice, and the Church receive our leftovers or our firstfruits?

Prayers *others may be added*

To our compassionate God, we pray:

◆ Lord, hear our prayer.

May God's will guide the Church, we pray: ◆ That disciples will make the Reign of God the first priority in their lives, we pray: ◆ That our community leaders will listen to the prophets in our midst, we pray: ◆ For attentiveness and awareness of our liturgical space, we pray: ◆ For architects, builders, and construction workers, we pray: ◆

Our Father . . .

Lord God,
you give us what satisfies.
May we consider our ways and set our hearts firmly upon glorifying you.
We ask this through Christ our Lord.
Amen.

✝ The Lord is near to all who call upon him.

Friday, September 29, 2017

Feast of Sts. Michael, Gabriel, and Raphael, Archangels

✝ The Lord is near to all who call upon him.

Psalm 145 *page 420*

Reading *Revelation 12:7–9*

War broke out in heaven; Michael and his angels battled against the dragon. The dragon and its angels fought back, but they did not prevail and there was no longer any place for them in heaven. The huge dragon, the ancient serpent, who is called the Devil and Satan, who deceived the whole world, was thrown down to earth, and its angels were thrown down with it.

Reflection

We understand angels to be celestial beings without bodies. The word *angel* simply means *messenger*. Gabriel announces the birth of both John the Baptist and Jesus; Michael is the protector and guardian against evil; Raphael appears in the Book of Tobit and journeys with the young Tobias.

We can all think of "angels" who have touched our lives. They might have helped us in distress, told us things we needed to hear, or walked with us through a difficult time. Though they had bodies, they were "angelic" insofar as God sent them into our lives at the right time and place.

Prayers *others may be added*

To our compassionate God, we pray:

◆ Lord, hear our prayer.

That the Church may be as angels and proclaim tidings of great joy, we pray: ◆ That the baptized earnestly engage in evangelization and announce the Good News, we pray: ◆ For all who work to protect the vulnerable, we pray: ◆ For parishes celebrating their patronal feast today, we pray: ◆ For all the faithful departed, we pray: ◆

Our Father . . .

Providential God,
you are with us always and watch over your people.
Open our eyes and hearts
so that we will be signs of your compassion and care
to those who are lonely, discouraged, or in need.
We ask this through Christ our Lord.
Amen.

✝ The Lord is near to all who call upon him.

Saturday, September 30, 2017

Memorial of St. Jerome, Priest and Doctor of the Church

☩ The Lord is near to all who call upon him.

Psalm 145

page 420

Reading

2 Timothy 3:14–17

Beloved: Remain faithful to what you have learned and believed, because you know from whom you learned it, and that from infancy you have known the sacred Scriptures, which are capable of giving you wisdom for salvation through faith in Christ Jesus. All Scripture is inspired by God and is useful for teaching, for refutation, for correction, and for training in righteousness, so that one who belongs to God may be competent, equipped for every good work.

Reflection

St. Jerome stated that "Ignorance of Scripture is ignorance of Christ." To be a follower of Jesus we must listen not only to his teaching but come to know Jesus himself; to do that we must enter into the Word of God, especially the Gospel. To that end, Jerome translated the Bible into Latin, what became known as "the Vulgate" because it was the "vulgar" language of the people.

Jerome was, in fact a prolific writer. He was also known for his acerbic personality. He preferred the quiet, reflective life associated with monasticism and displayed little tolerance for those enamored with society.

Prayers

others may be added

To our compassionate God, we pray:

◆ Lord, hear our prayer.

For Scripture scholars, we pray: ◆ For parish Bible study and reflection groups, we pray: ◆ For those who struggle with issues of anger, we pray: ◆ For parishes under the patronage of St. Jerome, we pray: ◆ For our nation's leaders, that they may put their trust in God, we pray: ◆

Our Father . . .

Lord Jesus,
you are the Word made flesh.
Inspire us to open the Word
to be drawn into a deeper relationship
with you,
who lives and reigns with God the Father
in the unity of the Holy Spirit,
one God, for ever and ever.
Amen.

☩ The Lord is near to all who call upon him.

Sunday, October 1, 2017
Twenty-Sixth Sunday in Ordinary Time

† Remember your mercies, O Lord.

Psalm 25 *page 404*

Reading *Matthew 21:28–31*

Jesus said to the chief priests and elders of the people: "What is your opinion? A man had two sons. He came to the first and said, 'Son, go out and work in the vineyard today.' He said in reply, 'I will not,' but afterwards changed his mind and went. The man came to the other son and gave the same order. He said in reply, 'Yes, sir,' but did not go. Which of the two did his father's will?" They answered, "The first." Jesus said to them, "Amen, I say to you, tax collectors and prostitutes are entering the kingdom of God before you."

Reflection

Who are we and how do we act as baptized disciples of Jesus? Today's Gospel asks us to reflect on our discipleship. In examining of the way we live, we can consider the extent we act on Christ's teachings. It is possible to attend Mass and to pray daily and still ignore the will of God in our lives. Being a Christian is not nearly as much about words as actions.

Prayers *others may be added*

To our Lord, who guides us in truth, we pray:

◆ Lord, hear our prayer.

For our Church, that she grow in wisdom, we pray: ◆ For our community's leaders, that they have the courage to do God's will, no matter the cost, we pray: ◆ For the humility to admit our sins and sinfulness and the strength and grace to change our lives, we pray: ◆ For a heart open to the joys and struggles of families, we pray: ◆ For all who have died, especially those for whom no one prays, we pray: ◆

Our Father . . .

Gracious Lord,
you offer us the way to the Kingdom.
Open us to your guidance
that others may see in us
a reflection of your truth and goodness.
We ask this through our Lord Jesus
Christ, your Son,
who lives and reigns with you in the unity
of the Holy Spirit,
one God, for ever and ever.
Amen.

† Remember your mercies, O Lord.

Monday, October 2, 2017
Memorial of the Holy Guardian Angels

✝ Remember your mercies, O Lord.

Psalm 25
page 404

Reading
Exodus 23:20–23

Thus says the LORD: "See, I am sending an angel before you, to guard you on the way and bring you to the place I have prepared. Be attentive to him and heed his voice. Do not rebel against him, for he will not forgive your sin. My authority resides in him. If you heed his voice and carry out all I tell you, I will be an enemy to your enemies and a foe to your foes.

"My angel will go before you and bring you to the Amorites, Hittites, Perizzites, Canaanites, Hivites, and Jebusites; and I will wipe them out."

Reflection
When I was little, my parents hung a picture in my room of two children walking along with an angel hovering over them, protecting them. We are comforted by images like these. Angels are messengers from God and their forms vary. They symbolize for us a link to heaven. In them, we remember that God is not far away.

The spiritual world is intimately tied to our daily life. There is no division. Today, let us seek to view all of God's creation as a unity of life.

Prayers
others may be added

To our Lord, who guides us in truth, we pray:

◆ Lord, hear our prayer.

For encouragement in Christ, solace in love, and participation in the Spirit alive in our parish communities, we pray: ◆ For all victims of famine, we pray: ◆ For those who are selfish, that they open their eyes to others, we pray: ◆ For an openness to the common good, we pray: ◆ For all who struggle for safety and freedom, we pray: ◆

Our Father . . .

Lord of heaven and earth,
in you all things have their origin
and being.
Protect us on our journey in this world
and bring us safely home to you.
We ask this through Christ our Lord.
Amen.

✝ Remember your mercies, O Lord.

Tuesday, October 3, 2017
Weekday

✝ Remember your mercies, O Lord.

Psalm 25

page 404

Reading

Zechariah 8:20–23

Thus says the LORD of hosts: There shall yet come peoples, the inhabitants of many cities; and the inhabitants of one city shall approach those of another, and say, "Come! let us go to implore the favor of the LORD"; and, "I too will go to seek the LORD." Many peoples and strong nations shall come to seek the LORD of hosts in Jerusalem and to implore the favor of the LORD. Thus says the LORD of hosts: In those days ten men of every nationality, speaking different tongues, shall take hold, yes, take hold of every Jew by the edge of his garment and say,

"Let us go with you, for we have heard that God is with you."

Reflection

Evangelization is essential to the mission of the Gospel. Our responsibility is to proclaim the Gospel to all people, because the world is in need of its truth.

But how are we to announce the Good News? Most of us are not comfortable talking to strangers in a parking lot. Zechariah provides an inspiring image. If we truly live as disciples, if we don't cut corners in our faith, or give in to social pressure, then others will come to us. They will be "taking hold" of us and begging us to tell them about the Lord. Are our actions today this stimulating?

Prayers

others may be added

To our Lord, who guides us in truth, we pray:

◆ Lord, hear our prayer.

For the growth of evangelization in the Church, we pray: ◆ For an end to divisiveness in our world, we pray: ◆ For those who seek God, we pray: ◆ For our catechumens and candidates, we pray: ◆ For runaways, we pray: ◆

Our Father . . .

Holy One,
you provide justice for all peoples.
May our witness to the Gospel
be a beacon to the parts of our world
that still live in darkness.
Guide us to share your light of peace.
We ask this through Christ our Lord.
Amen.

✝ Remember your mercies, O Lord.

Wednesday, October 4, 2017
Memorial of St. Francis of Assisi

☩ Remember your mercies, O Lord.

Psalm 25 *page 404*

Reading *Galatians 6:14–18*

Brothers and sisters: May I never boast except in the cross of our Lord Jesus Christ, through which the world has been crucified to me, and I to the world. For neither does circumcision mean anything, nor does uncircumcision, but only a new creation. Peace and mercy be to all who follow this rule and to the Israel of God.

From now on, let no one make troubles for me; for I bear the marks of Jesus on my body.

The grace of our Lord Jesus Christ be with your spirit, brothers and sisters. Amen.

Reflection

Francis of Assisi is quite the popular saint, though he seems to have more admirers than followers. The simple man from Assisi did not have an easy life. He rejected wealth and embraced poverty. He rejected comfort, preferring a life filled with hunger and even disgrace. Francis was a humble man, accepting the Gospel at face value. He didn't try to make adjustments to Christ's words. His life preached the following: Love your enemies. Do good to those who hate you. Pray for those who persecute you. Reject riches. Live simply. Yes, we admire Francis, but can we accept the radicalism of the Gospel and follow the Lord?

Prayers *others may be added*

Guide us in truth, O Lord, we pray:

◆ Teach your people.

For a Church, embracing simplicity and peace, we pray: ◆ For a world that lives in harmony, we pray: ◆ For all who find it difficult to abandon an attachment to violence, we pray: ◆ For members of Franciscan communities, we pray: ◆ For our nation's leaders, that they will promote a concern for the environment, we pray: ◆

Our Father . . .

Loving God,
you gave your servant Francis the
humility to live an unassuming life.
May we too embrace your Gospel
with fullness of heart and action.
We ask this through Christ our Lord.
Amen.

☩ Remember your mercies, O Lord.

Thursday, October 5, 2017
Weekday

✝ Remember your mercies, O Lord.

Psalm 25

page 404

Reading

Nehemiah 8:1–3, 6

The whole people gathered as one in the open space before the Water Gate, and they called upon Ezra the scribe to bring forth the book of the law of Moses which the LORD prescribed for Israel. On the first day of the seventh month, therefore, Ezra the priest brought the law before the assembly, which consisted of men, women, and those children old enough to understand. Standing at one end of the open place that was before the Water Gate, he read out of the book from daybreak until midday, in the presence of the men, the women, and those children old enough to understand; and all the people listened attentively to the book of the law. Ezra blessed the LORD, the great God, and all the people, their hands raised high, answered, "Amen, amen!"

Reflection

This passage reflects the reverence the people had for the Word of God. At Mass, the Book of the Gospels is honored as it is carried in the Entrance Procession. During the Liturgy of the Word, we seek to be attentive in listening to the Word. The time you spend daily with the readings in this book shows your interest in Scripture. To further your understanding of the Word of God, purchase a Bible with commentaries or invest in a biblical commentary.

Prayers

others may be added

To our Lord, who guides us in truth, we pray:

◆ Lord, hear our prayer.

May our Church communities grow in knowledge of the Scriptures, we pray: ◆ For theologians and Scripture scholars, we pray: ◆ For deeper insight into God's revelation in the biblical message, we pray: ◆ For students, and all who seek wisdom, we pray: ◆ For those who are denied an education, we pray: ◆

Our Father . . .

God of our ancestors,
your holy scribes wrote for us stories of revelation and love.
Help us to see your truths, Spirit, guidance, and mercy found in Scripture.
We ask this through Christ our Lord.
Amen.

✝ Remember your mercies, O Lord.

Friday, October 6, 2017
Weekday

✝ Remember your mercies, O Lord.

Psalm 25
page 404

Reading
Baruch 19–22

During the Babylonian captivity, the exiles prayed: "From the time the Lord led our ancestors out of the land of Egypt until the present day, we have been disobedient to the Lord, our God, and only too ready to disregard his voice. And the evils and the curse that the Lord enjoined upon Moses, his servant, at the time he led our ancestors forth from the land of Egypt to give us the land flowing with milk and honey, cling to us even today. For we did not heed the voice of the Lord, our God, in all the words of the prophets whom he sent us, but each one of us went off after the devices of his own wicked heart, served other gods, and did evil in the sight of the Lord, our God."

Reflection
Where is prophecy in our lives? Culturally, we relegate prophets to ancient men whose words can no longer rouse us. But in Baptism we are anointed as prophets. We are a people who are to see our world in light of the Gospel. We are to affirm, critique, and challenge. Can we embrace this role? It is easier to act like sheep, following the popular trends of the day. Though it is difficult to speak out with family and friends, we are anointed to acknowledge what needs to be said about justice and peace.

Prayers
others may be added

To our Lord, who guides us in truth, we pray:

◆ Lord, hear our prayer.

For an increase of prophecy in the Church, we pray: ◆ For an ability to honor the voices that challenge us, we pray: ◆ For a world overflowing with just actions, we pray: ◆ For those who are marginalized, we pray: ◆ For community leaders who work against human trafficking, we pray: ◆

Our Father . . .

Voice of the prophets,
throughout the ages you call forth men and women
to proclaim your truths of justice.
May we too join their call
and in our time seek transformation for our world.
We ask this through Christ our Lord.
Amen.

✝ Remember your mercies, O Lord.

Saturday, October 7, 2017
Memorial of Our Lady of the Rosary

✝ Remember your mercies, O Lord.

Psalm 25 *page 404*

Reading *Baruch 4:5–8*

Fear not, my people! / Remember, Israel, / You were sold to the nations / not for your destruction; / It was because you angered God / that you were handed over to your foes. / For you provoked your Maker / with sacrifices to demons, to no-gods; / You forsook the Eternal God who nourished you, / and you grieved Jerusalem who fostered you.

Reflection

Actions have consequences. Baruch reminds the people that their exile was the outcome of their deeds. We teach this lesson to children, but we too need to heed it. Sometimes we are tempted to blame God for the calamities that occur in the world. It would be better to look inward to see when we have disregarded God and sacrificed our time and resources selfishly to the gods that our culture holds up. We may not be able to cure the world of its ills but putting God first can make a difference in our lives.

Prayers *others may be added*

To our Lord, who guides us in truth, we pray:

◆ Lord, hear our prayer.

For a Church that acts in justice, we pray: ◆ For all who work in sweatshops, we pray: ◆ For our community leaders, that they will seek to act justly, we pray: ◆ For devotion to the Rosary as a prayer for peace, we pray: ◆ For a spirit of tranquility, we pray: ◆

Our Father . . .

Merciful Lord,
you always offer yourself to us.
Open our eyes so that we forsake the gods of our culture.
May we choose to follow you and act out of goodness, humility, and love,
We ask this through Christ our Lord.
Amen.

✝ Remember your mercies, O Lord.

Sunday, October 8, 2017
Twenty-Seventh Sunday in Ordinary Time

✝ My soul trusts in the Lord.

Psalm 130 *page 419*

Reading *Matthew 21:33–39a, 43*

"There was a landowner who planted a vineyard, put a hedge around it, dug a wine press in it, and built a tower. Then he leased it to tenants and went on a journey. When vintage time drew near, he sent his servants to the tenants to obtain his produce. But the tenants seized the servants and one they beat, another they killed, and a third they stoned. Again he sent other servants, more numerous than the first ones, but they treated them in the same way. Finally, he sent his son to them, thinking, 'They will respect my son.' But when the tenants saw the son, they said to one another, 'This is the heir. Come, let us kill him and acquire his inheritance.' They seized him, threw him out of the vineyard and killed him. . . . Therefore, I say to you, the kingdom of God will be taken away from you and given to a people that will produce its fruit."

Reflection

For the Matthean community, this parable is about the Jewish people's rejection of prophets, priests, and finally Jesus. Hence, the early Church reached beyond Judaism, proclaiming the Gospel to Gentiles. Try to put yourself in the story and determine who you would be. It can be difficult to hear the prophets of the day and the challenge of the Gospel.

Prayers *others may be added*

Calling on the Lord, we pray:

◆ Lord, hear our prayer.

For the Church, may we respond to the Lord's nurturing and grow in ways God intends, we pray: ◆ For world leaders, may their hearts be guided by all that is true, honorable, and just, we pray: ◆ For a respect for all life, from conception to natural death, we pray: ◆ For an end to bitterness, we pray: ◆ For those who now sleep in the peace of death, we pray: ◆

Our Father . . .

Lord,
you have provided a vineyard for us
to cultivate.
Help us to till your soil and plant
your seeds.
May your harvest be one of peace, justice,
and truth.
We ask this through our Lord Jesus
Christ, your Son,
who lives and reigns with you in the unity
of the Holy Spirit,
one God, for ever and ever.
Amen.

✝ My soul trusts in the Lord.

Monday, October 9, 2017
Weekday

✝ My soul trusts in the Lord.

Psalm 130 *page 419*

Reading *Jonah 1:1:–5a, 12, 15—2:2, 11*

This is the word of the LORD that came to Jonah, son of Amittai:

"Set out for the great city of Nineveh, and preach against it; their wickedness has come up before me." But Jonah made ready to flee to Tarshish away from the LORD. He went down to Joppa, found a ship going to Tarshish, paid the fare, and went aboard to journey with them to Tarshish, away from the LORD.

The LORD, however, hurled a violent wind upon the sea, and in the furious tempest that arose the ship was on the point of breaking up. Then the mariners became frightened and each one cried to his god.

Jonah said to them, "Pick me up and throw me into the sea, that it may quiet down for you; since I know it is because of me that this violent storm has come upon you."

Then they took Jonah and threw him into the sea, and the sea's raging abated. Struck with great fear of the LORD, the men offered sacrifice and made vows to him.

But the LORD sent a large fish, that swallowed Jonah; and Jonah remained in the belly of the fish three days and three nights. From the belly of the fish Jonah prayed to the LORD, his God. Then the LORD commanded the fish to spew Jonah upon the shore.

Reflection

Jonah didn't just refuse God, he tried to run away. His running put the lives of others in danger. Unable to deter the Lord, Jonah is swallowed by a fish. We too try to run from God. As fugitives from the Lord, we cause damage to ourselves and to others. The route back is arduous. Fear is the enemy, but we join with it because we lack courage. What is God asking you to do? Do you fear doing it? Why?

Prayers *others may be added*

Calling on the Lord, we pray:

◆ Lord, hear our prayer.

May our Church be willing to follow wherever the Lord leads, we pray: ◆ May victims of fear find courage, we pray: ◆ May fishers know safety and prosperity, we pray: ◆ May teens who are discerning God's call have the audacity to live in faith, we pray: ◆ May those we hurt by our sin forgive us and find healing, we pray: ◆

Our Father . . .

Lord of the lost,
you call us to follow you,
but we are afraid of so many things.
Send upon us your Spirit of courage
and insight.
Make us willing and faithful servants.
We ask this through Christ our Lord.
Amen.

✝ My soul trusts in the Lord.

Tuesday, October 10, 2017
Weekday

✝ My soul trusts in the Lord.

Psalm 130 *page 419*

Reading *Jonah 3:1–5*

The word of the LORD came to Jonah a second time: "Set out for the great city of Nineveh, and announce to it the message that I will tell you." So Jonah made ready and went to Nineveh, according to the LORD's bidding. Now Nineveh was an enormously large city; it took three days to go through it. Jonah began his journey through the city, and had gone but a single day's walk announcing, "Forty days more and Nineveh shall be destroyed," when the people of Nineveh believed God; they proclaimed a fast and all of them, great and small, put on sackcloth.

Reflection

God's will for Jonah is to preach to Nineveh. So, what's the problem? These are not Israelites, as Jonah is. Jonah is asked to evangelize. He is to go to people he doesn't know who have different ideas. Yet, they heard the truth and were converted.

Consider how we live our faith. Do we feel free to talk about family Confirmations and Baptisms with coworkers or friends, or are we reticent to mention attendance at liturgies? Evangelization is about living the faith in such an organic way that its truths shine. When we pray for others, and our faith and its symbols are a part of our daily lives, others will take notice of the Gospel.

Prayers *others may be added*

Calling on the Lord, we pray:

◆ Lord, hear our prayer.

For a spirit of evangelization to be lived out in the Church, we pray: ◆ For peace among nations, we pray: ◆ For a greater love of the Sacred Scriptures, we pray: ◆ For married people who are persevering through difficult times, we pray: ◆ For our community leaders, may they nurture their faith, we pray: ◆

Our Father . . .

Dear Lord,
you have made yourself known to us.
Renew in us joy so profound
that it cannot be hidden.
By our lives may we share your Good
News with all we meet.
We ask this through Christ our Lord.
Amen.

✝ My soul trusts in the Lord.

Wednesday, October 11, 2017
Weekday

☩ My soul trusts in the Lord.

Psalm 130 *page 419*

Reading *Jonah 4:1–4*

Jonah was greatly displeased and became angry that God did not carry out the evil he threatened against Nineveh. He prayed, "I beseech you, LORD, is not this what I said while I was still in my own country? This is why I fled at first to Tarshish. I knew that you are a gracious and merciful God, slow to anger, rich in clemency, loathe to punish. And now, LORD, please take my life from me; for it is better for me to die than to live." But the LORD asked, "Have you reason to be angry?"

Reflection

What a contrary character is Jonah. He is fuming because his preaching was heard. He is irritated that the people repented. He is angry because God is merciful! Jonah wanted to see the people of Nineveh destroyed. But God is merciful, even to Jonah. Are we more like God or Jonah today? Do we seek retribution and prefer vengeance? Do we hide behind laws and create walls with Scripture to keep others away from God's grace? Do we feel we have a privileged place with God, or are we open enough to see the Lord's love flowing upon all people?

Prayers *others may be added*

Calling on the Lord, we pray:

◆ Lord, hear our prayer.

For a Spirit of welcome and forgiveness in the Church, we pray: ◆ For an end to vengeance among family members, we pray: ◆ For dignity, love, and respect for all people, despite differences of age, gender, race, national origin, orientation, or economic status, we pray: ◆ For world leaders, that they will foster a bond of solidarity with refugees, we pray: ◆ For an end to bullying, we pray: ◆

Our Father . . .

Merciful One,
your love is boundless and reaches beyond human comprehension.
Fill us with peace and confidence in your love.
We ask this through Christ our Lord.
Amen.

☩ My souls trusts in the Lord.

Thursday, October 12, 2017
Weekday

✝ My soul trusts in the Lord.

Psalm 130 *page 419*

Reading *Malachi 3:13–15*

You have defied me in word, says the LORD, / yet you ask, "What have we spoken against you?" / You have said, "It is vain to serve God, / and what do we profit by keeping his command, / And going about in penitential dress / in awe of the LORD of hosts? / Rather must we call the proud blessed; / for indeed evildoers prosper, / and even tempt God with impunity."

Reflection

Clearer vision is the work of the prophets. Their gift is to cut through the fog that fills our minds, clouding our sense of right and wrong. Malachi tells the people that they are embracing the mist. They prefer the wickedness of their actions. Yet, they claim that they are not sinning. Can we see clearly what is right and what is wrong? Just a quick perusal of the television guide demonstrates this lack of clarity. People yell, attack, and abuse others, and we not only call it entertainment, but we justify their actions. Can you easily see what is good and what is evil?

Prayers *others may be added*

Calling on the Lord, we pray:

◆ Lord, hear our prayer.

For prophets in the Church and an acceptance of their vision, we pray: ◆ For the courage to name what is wicked and discern what is good, we pray: ◆ For victims of slanderous tongues and vindictive actions, we pray: ◆ For anger to be replaced with compassion, we pray: ◆ For all who struggle with depression, we pray: ◆

Our Father . . .

Source of Goodness,
you send us prophets to point out
your path.
Remove the scales from our eyes
and hearts.
Train us to do good and live in ways
that are pleasing to you.
We ask this through Christ our Lord.
Amen.

✝ My soul trusts in the Lord.

Friday, October 13, 2017
Weekday

✝ My soul trusts in the Lord.

Psalm 130 *page 419*

Reading *Joel 1:15, 2:1–2*

Alas, the day! / for near is the day of the LORD, / and it comes as ruin from the Almighty.

Blow the trumpet in Zion, / sound the alarm on my holy mountain! / Let all who dwell in the land tremble, / for the day of the LORD is coming; / Yes, it is near, a day of darkness and of gloom, / a day of clouds and somberness! / Like dawn spreading over the mountains, / a people numerous and mighty! / Their like has not been from of old, / nor will it be after them, / even to the years of distant generations.

Reflection

The original understanding of the day of the Lord was a time of salvation for Israel from their enemies and judgment on those who had dared to go against the Lord. But the tables have been turned. Israel is the one who has defied God. Joel sounds the alarm, attempting to awaken a spirit of repentance.

Have we too become complacent? Do we think God is on our side, so we can do no wrong? Are we so sure of our sanctity and other people's sins? Take some time for a careful examination of conscience.

Prayers *others may be added*

Calling on the Lord, we pray:

◆ Lord, hear our prayer.

For the Church, may she renew herself and continue to seek sanctity, we pray: ◆ For peace to fill the world, we pray: ◆ For a willingness to accept goodness wherever it is found, we pray: ◆ For all who wallow in guilt, that they may accept forgiveness, we pray: ◆ For community leaders, may they look to the holy for guidance, we pray: ◆

Our Father . . .

Gracious Lord,
you are the God of all nations
and peoples.
Be present to us as we seek to make your
Good News known to all we meet.
Support us as we help others know you by
the way we live.
We ask this through Christ our Lord.
Amen.

✝ My soul trusts in the Lord.

Saturday, October 14, 2017
Weekday

✝ My soul trusts in the Lord.

Psalm 130 *page 419*

Reading *Joel 4:12–16*

Thus says the LORD: / Let the nations bestir themselves and come up / to the Valley of Jehoshaphat; / For there will I sit in judgment / upon all the neighboring nations.

Apply the sickle, / for the harvest is ripe; / Come and tread, / for the wine press is full; / the vats overflow, / for great is their malice. / Crowd upon crowd / in the valley of decision; / For near is the day of the LORD / in the valley of decision. / Sun and moon are darkened, / and the stars withhold their brightness. / The LORD roars from Zion, / and from Jerusalem raises his voice; / The heavens and the earth quake, / but the LORD is a refuge to his people, / a stronghold to the children of Israel.

Reflection

The day of the Lord has arrived in Joel's vision. God sits in judgment over the nations and avenges the people of Judah. Evil is punished and Jerusalem is again called holy. Sometimes we forget that this world will end. What we do matters, but it is not the last word. God has that. When we have given all, loved all, it is still not about us. Our discipleship finds its roots in faith. We trust and hope in the Lord, not in our actions. We must lay down our weapons of self-importance, even when it comes to doing good, and rest in the knowledge that God is in charge.

Prayers *others may be added*

Calling on the Lord, we pray:

◆ Lord, hear our prayer.

For the Church, that divisions within her will be healed, we pray: ◆ For our faith, that it will increase, we pray: ◆ For sinners, that they will seek forgiveness, we pray: ◆ For world leaders, that they will seek peace, we pray: ◆ For the sick, that they will feel your presence, we pray: ◆

Our Father . . .

Almighty God,
you are the One God, living and true.
In you is found justice; in you is
found peace.
May we live encircled by your grace.
We ask this through Christ our Lord.
Amen.

✝ My soul trusts in the Lord.

Sunday, October 15, 2017

Twenty-Eighth Sunday in Ordinary Time

✝ You guide us in right paths for your name's sake.

Psalm 23

page 403

Reading

Matthew 22:1b–9

[Jesus said:] "The kingdom of heaven may be likened to a king who gave a wedding feast for his son. He dispatched his servants to summon the invited guests to the feast, but they refused to come. A second time he sent other servants, saying, 'Tell those invited: "Behold, I have prepared my banquet, my calves and fattened cattle are killed and everything is ready; come to the feast."' Some ignored the invitation and went away, one to his farm, another to his business. The rest laid hold of his servants, mistreated them, and killed them. The king was enraged and sent his troops, destroyed those murderers, and burned their city. Then the king said to his servants, 'The feast is ready, but those who were invited were not worthy to come. Go out, therefore, into the main roads and invite to the feast whomever you find.' "

Reflection

Those who were first invited to the wedding feast refused, giving their work priority. We have been invited to the Eucharistic banquet. Our prayer lives prepare us for this feast. As we pray, we grow closer to God and our need for Christ's presence in the Eucharist is nurtured. Prayer and sacrament ready us to feast in the Kingdom.

Prayers

others may be added

Turning to our God, who awaits us at the heavenly banquet, we pray:

◆ Graciously hear us, Lord.

For the Church, may we extravagantly invite all people to share in the feast of our Lord, we pray: ◆ For hearts open to the banquet of the Lord, for a yearning for the food that satisfies, we pray: ◆ For our nation's leaders, that they protect those who risk their lives for freedom, we pray: ◆ For a sense of calm, we pray: ◆ For all who have gone before us marked with the sign of faith, may they now rejoice at the heavenly table, we pray: ◆

Our Father . . .

Dear Lord,
you offer us your Word and your Body
and Blood.
Through these we are renewed in faith.
May we welcome your nurturing
presence so that we can enjoy the feast
at the heavenly banquet.
We ask this through our Lord Jesus
Christ, your Son,
who lives and reigns with you in the unity
of the Holy Spirit,
one God, for ever and ever.
Amen.

✝ You guide us in right paths for your name's sake.

Monday, October 16, 2017
Weekday

✝ You guide us in right paths for your name's sake.

Psalm 23
page 403

Reading
Romans 1:1–7

Paul, a slave of Christ Jesus, called to be an Apostle and set apart for the Gospel of God, which he promised previously through his prophets in the holy Scriptures, the Gospel about his Son, descended from David according to the flesh, but established as Son of God in power according to the Spirit of holiness through resurrection from the dead, Jesus Christ our Lord. Through him we have received the grace of apostleship, to bring about the obedience of faith, for the sake of his name, among all the Gentiles, among whom are you also, who are called to belong to Jesus Christ; to all the beloved of God in Rome, called to be holy. Grace to you and peace from God our Father and the Lord Jesus Christ.

Reflection
With this letter, Paul writes to a community he did not found and has not met. In essence today we hear his introduction to them. Paul not only tells of the importance of his faith but acknowledges the honor of the community. He tells them that they have received the grace of apostleship and are called to be holy. Our hospitality to another acknowledges that they are a child of God. Our faith is shared through our words and actions.

Prayers
others may be added

To our merciful God, we pray:

◆ Lord, hear our prayer.

For a Church filled with peace, serenity, and hope, we pray: ◆ For those who live in fear of violence, we pray: ◆ For a willingness to let God guide our daily lives, we pray: ◆ For peace in our work, we pray: ◆ For all who live with chronic health problems, we pray: ◆

Our Father . . .

Father of hope,
you bless us with the gift of faith.
May we have insight as we reach out
to others.
Let us hear their stories and offer them
truth and peace.
We ask this through Christ our Lord.
Amen.

✝ You guide us in right paths for your name's sake.

Tuesday, October 17, 2017
Memorial of St. Ignatius of Antioch, Bishop and Martyr

☩ You guide us in right paths for your name's sake.

Psalm 23

page 403

Reading

Romans 1:16–17

Brothers and sisters: I am not ashamed of the Gospel. It is the power of God for the salvation of everyone who believes: for Jew first, and then Greek. For in it is revealed the righteousness of God from faith to faith; as it is written, "The one who is righteous by faith will live."

Reflection

Ignatius of Antioch was born in Syria and made a bishop in the first decades of Christianity. In 107 AD, the Roman Emperor Trajan began persecution of the Christians in Antioch. They were given a choice to renounce the Lord or be killed. Ignatius chose martyrdom. He was taken to Rome to be executed. Ignatius too was unashamed of the Gospel. On the journey to his death, he wrote seven letters encouraging the early churches to be faithful during this time of persecution. He met his death bravely, seeing it as a sign of his faith.

Prayers

others may be added

To our merciful God, we pray:

◆ Lord, hear our prayer.

For our Church, may we be courageous in time of persecution, we pray: ◆ For martyrs and all who witness the Gospel, we pray: ◆ For bishops, that a spirit of mercy to guide them, we pray: ◆ For our legislators, that laws they enact will protect all who work the land, we pray: ◆ For a love that includes all people unconditionally, we pray: ◆

Our Father . . .

Almighty Lord,
you gave your servant Ignatius
the gifts of knowledge, faith, and courage.
Shower these upon us too,
that in times of trial
we may boldly confess your name
and bear witness to your love.
We ask this through Christ our Lord.
Amen.

☩ You guide us in right paths for your name's sake.

Wednesday, October 18, 2017

Feast of St. Luke, Evangelist

✝ *You guide us in right paths for your name's sake.*

Psalm 23

page 403

Reading

2 Timothy 4:10–17b

Beloved: Demas, enamored of the present world, deserted me and went to Thessalonica, Crescens to Galatia, and Titus to Dalmatia. Luke is the only one with me. Get Mark and bring him with you, for he is helpful to me in the ministry. I have sent Tychicus to Ephesus. When you come, bring the cloak I left with Carpus in Troas, the papyrus rolls, and especially the parchments.

Alexander the coppersmith did me a great deal of harm; the Lord will repay him according to his deeds. You too be on guard against him, for he has strongly resisted our preaching.

At my first defense no one appeared on my behalf, but everyone deserted me. May it not be held against them! But the Lord stood by me and gave me strength, so that through me the proclamation might be completed and all the Gentiles might hear it.

Reflection

Scholars are pretty certain that the Luke noted in this reading was a Gentile Christian who wrote for other Gentile Christians. We honor him for writing the Gospel that bears his name and the Acts of the Apostles. Without his Gospel account and Acts, a perspective of the Gospel and the history of the early Church would be lost. We give thanks for his testimony.

Prayers

others may be added

To our merciful God, we pray:

◆ Lord, hear our prayer.

For theologians, we pray: ◆ For teachers and catechists, we pray: ◆ For those unable to receive an education, we pray: ◆ For all who grapple with illiteracy and its effects, we pray: ◆ For children who struggle with learning disabilities, we pray: ◆ For all considered different, we pray: ◆

Our Father . . .

Father,
you gave Luke the ability
to put into words the struggles and joys of the early Church.
Increase our love for your Sacred Scriptures
and may our knowledge of the Bible foster and nurture our love for you.
We ask this through Christ our Lord.
Amen.

✝ *You guide us in right paths for your name's sake.*

Thursday, October 19, 2017

Memorial of Sts. John de Brébeuf and Isaac Jogues, Priests, and Companions, Martyrs

✝ You guide us in right paths for your name's sake.

Psalm 23

page 403

Reading

2 Corinthians 4:7–15

Brothers and sisters: We hold this treasure in earthen vessels, that the surpassing power may be of God and not from us. We are afflicted in every way, but not constrained; perplexed, but not driven to despair; persecuted, but not abandoned; struck down, but not destroyed; always carrying about in the body the dying of Jesus, so that the life of Jesus may also be manifested in our body. For we who live are constantly being given up to death for the sake of Jesus, so that the life of Jesus may be manifested in our mortal flesh.

So death is at work in us, but life in you. Since, then, we have the same spirit of faith, according to what is written, I believed, therefore I spoke, we too believe and therefore speak, knowing that the one who raised the Lord Jesus will raise us also with Jesus and place us with you in his presence. Everything indeed is for you, so that the grace bestowed in abundance on more and more people may cause the thanksgiving to overflow for the glory of God.

Reflection

In the 1600s, Europeans conquered, settled, and explored the Americas. The Jesuits were part of the explorers, seeking to bring the Gospel to Native Americans. This European immigration is a complex history, as is the missionary activity that accompanied it. The North American Martyrs were a mixture of priests and lay ministers, all working toward the common goal of evangelization. The saints we honor today labored with various Native American tribes. They taught and translated and in the end were tortured and killed. Yet, it was through their efforts that Christianity took hold in North America.

Prayers

others may be added

To our merciful God, we pray:

◆ Lord, hear our prayer.

For missionaries in the Church, we pray: ◆ For priests, lay ministers and all all who tirelessly work in our parishes, we pray: ◆ For our nation's leaders, that they do not give in to bigotry, we pray: ◆ For a willingness to be receptive to new ideas and different ways of life, we pray: ◆ For a spirit of inculturation and inclusivity, we pray: ◆

Our Father . . .

Lord of all nations,
you sent the Jesuit missionaries
to a new world to proclaim your Gospel.
Make us willing to reach out to others
of differing races, places, and histories.
Let us see your goodness and generosity
active in their lives.
We ask this through Christ our Lord.
Amen.

✝ You guide us in right paths for your name's sake.

Friday, October 20, 2017
Weekday

☩ You guide us in right paths for your name's sake.

Psalm 23
page 403

Reading
Romans 4:1–8

Brothers and sisters: What can we say that Abraham found, our ancestor according to the flesh? Indeed, if Abraham was justified on the basis of his works, he has reason to boast; but this was not so in the sight of God. For what does the Scripture say? *Abraham believed God, and it was credited to him as righteousness.* A worker's wage is credited not as a gift, but as something due. But when one does not work, yet believes in the one who justifies the ungodly, his faith is credited as righteousness. So also David declares the blessedness of the person to whom God credits righteousness apart from works: *Blessed are they whose iniquities are forgiven / and whose sins are covered. / Blessed is the man whose sin the Lord does not record.*

Reflection
Why is Abraham remembered four millennia later? Is it because of all he did? Is it because of his accomplishments? No, it is for he who is a man of faith. Works are often rooted in self-importance. We accomplish something, and we have pride in that. However, this is not why Abraham is accounted as righteous. It is because he trusted God enough to choose him. God, in turn, blessed him.

Prayers
others may be added

To our merciful God, we pray:

◆ Lord, hear our prayer.

For the gift of wisdom to guide, protect, discipline, and teach our Church, we pray: ◆ For the gift of faith and a simple trust in the Lord, we pray: ◆ For contemplatives, and all who pray for us and our world, we pray: ◆ For our Jewish and Islamic sisters and brothers, the other children of Abraham, we pray: ◆ For our lawmakers, that they will work to end capital punishment, we pray: ◆ For a willingness to let go and rely on God, we pray: ◆

Our Father . . .

O God,
you provided our father in faith Abraham
with a deep trust in you,
and so he was counted among
the righteous.
Be with us as we seek to remove barriers
to faith
and all that binds us to self-importance
and self-indulgence.
We ask this through Christ our Lord.
Amen.

☩ You guide us in right paths for your name's sake.

Saturday, October 21, 2017
Weekday

✝ You guide us in right paths for your name's sake.

Psalm 23

page 403

Reading

Romans 4:13, 16–18

Brothers and sisters: It was not through the law that the promise was made to Abraham and his descendants that he would inherit the world, but through the righteousness that comes from faith. For this reason, it depends on faith, so that it may be a gift, and the promise may be guaranteed to all his descendants, not to those who only adhere to the law but to those who follow the faith of Abraham, who is the father of all of us, as it is written, *I have made you father of many nations*. He is our father in the sight of God, in whom he believed, who gives life to the dead and calls into being what does not exist. He believed, hoping against hope, that he would become the father of many nations, according to what was said, *Thus shall your descendants be*.

Reflection

Paul returns to his common themes of the law and faith. The law does not provide salvation, righteousness, or justification. All of these come through faith. Law has its place but so does mercy. In *The Joy of the Gospel*, Pope Francis quotes Thomas Aquinas regarding mercy. "The foundation of the New Law is in the grace of the Holy Spirit, who is manifested in the faith which works through love" (37).

Prayers

others may be added

To our merciful God, we pray:

◆ Lord, hear our prayer.

For teachers in the Church, may their words challenge and guide, we pray: ◆ For a greater love of the Scriptures, we pray: ◆ For an openness to hear God challenging us to deeper discipleship, we pray: ◆ For an end to the idolatry of wealth, fame, or power, we pray: ◆ For a heart that seeks forgiveness, from God and those we have wounded, we pray: ◆

Our Father . . .

Lord of the covenant,
you seek a deep relationship with us.
May we, like our father in faith Abraham,
put our trust in you
and nurture our faith
as a gift from you.
We ask this through Christ our Lord.
Amen.

✝ You guide us in right paths for your name's sake.

Sunday, October 22, 2017
Twenty-Ninth Sunday in Ordinary Time

☩ Great is the Lord and highly to be praised.

Psalm 96
page 413

Reading
Matthew 22:15, 17–21

The Pharisees . . . plotted how they might entrap Jesus in speech, . . . saying, . . . "Tell us, then, what is your opinion: Is it lawful to pay the census tax to Caesar or not?" Knowing their malice, Jesus said, "Why are you testing me, you hypocrites? Show me the coin that pays the census tax." Then they handed him the Roman coin. He said to them, "Whose image is this and whose inscription?" They replied, "Caesar's." At that he said to them, "Then repay to Caesar what belongs to Caesar and to God what belongs to God."

Reflection
The Pharisees and Herodians try to trap Jesus. In essence, they are attempting to set the stage for Jesus' conviction of treason. They want to twist his words to use against him. As on other occasions, Jesus does not fall into the trap. Instead, he tells his questioners to give to give the emperor what is due and to return to God what is his. We might reflect on what we recognize as God's and how we treat those gifts. In the encyclical *Laudato Si'*, Pope Francis reminds us of the reverence that St. Francis regarded creation. "He felt called to care for all that exists" (11). We too need to care for what belongs to our Creator.

Prayers
others may be added

Turning to our Lord, who shows us the way, we pray:

◆ Hear our prayer, O Lord.

For the Church, may the Gospel continue to transform us, we pray: ◆ For leaders of nations, for integrity in governance, transparency in intent, we pray: ◆ For an end to hatred, we pray: ◆ For conviction to scrutinize laws and policies with the vision of the Gospel, we pray: ◆ For all who have died, may they live forever in the heavenly Jerusalem, we pray: ◆

Our Father . . .

Gentle Shepherd,
you are the Lord of all truthfulness.
May we honestly review our intentions and actions
in light of your Gospel of love.
We ask this through our Lord Jesus Christ, your Son,
who lives and reigns with you in the unity of the Holy Spirit,
one God, for ever and ever.
Amen.

☩ Great is the Lord and highly to be praised.

Monday, October 23, 2017
Weekday

✝ Great is the Lord and highly to be praised.

Psalm 96 *page 413*

Reading *Romans 4:20–25*

Brothers and sisters: Abraham did not doubt God's promise in unbelief; father, he was empowered by faith and gave glory to God and was fully convinced that what God had promised he was able to do. That is why *it was credited to him as righteousness.* But it was not for him alone that it was written that *it was credited to him*; it was also for us, to whom it will be credited, who believe in the one who raised Jesus our Lord from the dead, who was handed over for our transgressions and was raised for our justification.

Reflection

Abraham's trust in the Lord is expressed in giving glory to God. St. Paul tells the Romans that their lives are to follow Abraham's. They who believe in Christ Jesus as Lord are righteous and are to live in faith. Their lives too are to be given to glorifying God. As believers, our words and actions are to praise God. We can take comfort that, as we begin our day in thanksgiving and prayer, we are following in the steps of our ancestors in faith. Their work of praising God is our work too.

Prayers *others may be added*

Turning to our Lord, who shows us the way, we pray:

◆ Hear our prayer, O Lord.

For the Church, that she may be joyful in her love of the Lord, we pray: ◆ For honesty in speech and charity in action, we pray: ◆ For a deepening of our baptismal commitment to the Lord, we pray: ◆ For a respect for all life, from conception to natural death, we pray: ◆ For an end to hunger, we pray: ◆

Our Father . . .

Most wonderful God,
you shower us with blessings each day.
May we see the grace
with which you surround us
and offer you an unguarded sacrifice
of praise.
We ask this through Christ our Lord.
Amen.

✝ Great is the Lord and highly to be praised.

Tuesday, October 24, 2017
Weekday

✝ Great is the Lord and highly to be praised.

Psalm 96 *page 413*

Reading *Romans 5:12, 15b, 17*

Brothers and sisters: Through one man sin entered the world, and through sin, death, and thus death came to all men, inasmuch as all sinned.

If by that person's transgression the many died, how much more did the grace of God and the gracious gift of the one man Jesus Christ overflow for the many. For if, by the transgression of the one, death came to reign through that one, how much more will those who receive the abundance of grace and the gift of justification come to reign in life through the one Jesus Christ.

Reflection

We turn to another common image for Paul: Christ as the new Adam. In essence, sin and death came through Adam, but life, grace, and righteousness came through Jesus Christ. Paul's parallels are striking, with much theological nuance. Where do we fit into the picture? As disciples of Christ, we seek to be accepting and show love and forgiveness. When we falter in acts of charity, we know to ask God's forgivness and try again. Ours is a life of hope, for death no longer reigns.

Prayers *others may be added*

Turning to our Lord, who shows us the way, we pray:

◆ Hear our prayer, O Lord.

As Church, may we model the goodness and graciousness of the Gospel, we pray: ◆ For peace, we pray: ◆ For missionaries throughout the world, we pray: ◆ For godparents and sponsors, and for all who promise to mentor others in the ways of discipleship, we pray: ◆ For those struggling on their journey to God, we pray: ◆

Our Father . . .

Holy One,
your Son Jesus Christ
brought us life and righteousness.
As his disciples,
may we too bless the world
with your wisdom, grace, example,
and hope.
We ask this through Christ our Lord.
Amen.

✝ Great is the Lord and highly to be praised.

Wednesday, October 25, 2017
Weekday

✝ Great is the Lord and highly to be praised.

Psalm 96 *page 413*

Reading *Romans 6:12–14*

Brothers and sisters: Sin must not reign over your mortal bodies so that you obey their desires. And do not present the parts of your bodies to sin as weapons for wickedness, but present yourselves to God as raised from the dead to life and the parts of your bodies to God as weapons for righteousness. For sin is not to have any power over you, since you are not under the law but under grace.

Reflection

We are to be weapons not for wickedness but for righteousness. Not sin, but grace shall live in us. The real struggle is the discernment between sin and grace. It sounds easy, but our daily decisions are complex. Remember too that discipleship is not about following the law for Paul. This is why the *Catechism of the Catholic Church* speaks of following a well-formed conscience. The key is in the formation. We need to reflect on the Gospel, listen to the guidance of the Church and, of course, pray. All is found in that deep, abiding relationship with the Lord. Struggle is inevitable, but let grace prevail.

Prayers *others may be added*

Turning to our Lord, who shows us the way, we pray:

◆ Hear our prayer, O Lord.

For the wisdom of the Church, bringing to bear on our joys and sorrows, we pray: ◆ For a life of prayer and trust in grace, we pray: ◆ For those forgotten by the powerful and wealthy, we pray: ◆ For the poor in spirit, we pray: ◆ For those in nursing homes, we pray: ◆

Our Father . . .

Lord,
you hold the truth for us.
In humility we come seeking your guidance so that sin does not have power over us.
Fill us with your gift of wisdom
and may we live days of prayer and grace.
We ask this through Christ our Lord.
Amen.

✝ Great is the Lord and highly to be praised.

Thursday, October 26, 2017
Weekday

☩ Great is the Lord and highly to be praised.

Psalm 96
page 413

Reading
Romans 6:21–23

[Brothers and sisters:] But what profit did you get from the things of which you are now ashamed? For the end of those things is death. But now that you have been freed from sin and have become slaves from God, the benefit that you have leads to sanctification, and its end is eternal life. For the wages of sin is death, but the gift of God is eternal life in Christ Jesus our Lord.

Reflection
Reflecting on our lives can be painful, but it is necessary for spiritual growth. We must acknowledge both our sins and the grace of God. Seeing our failings, how we have hurt others and ourselves, requires courage. Since such sight is a gift of the Spirit, our contemplating, even of sin, is guided by God.

Questioning how we thought we would profit from sin allows us to dig into the roots of our iniquities. When we find the reasons for our choices, then, perhaps we can heal and grow. Pray for courage to find time to make this walk with the Lord.

Prayers
others may be added

Turning to our Lord, who shows us the way, we pray:

◆ Hear our prayer, O Lord.

May our Church exercise compassion, we pray: ◆ May world leaders see the wickedness of war, we pray: ◆ May we find forgiveness from those we have wronged, we pray: ◆ May bitterness be removed from our homes, we pray: ◆ May the balm of healing fill hurting hearts, we pray: ◆

Our Father . . .

Gracious One,
you forgive us when we fail you.
May our sins be ever before our eyes.
May your grace fill us, heal us, and
help us
to repair the damage we have
caused ourselves,
others, and our world.
We ask this through Christ our Lord.
Amen.

☩ Great is the Lord and highly to be praised.

Friday, October 27, 2017
Weekday

✝ Great is the Lord and highly to be praised.

Psalm 96 *page 413*

Reading *Romans 7:18–23*

Brothers and sisters: I know that good does not dwell in me, that is, in my flesh. The willing is ready at hand, but doing the good is not. For I do not do the good I want, but I do the evil I do not want. Now if I do what I do not want, it is no longer I who do it, but sin that dwells in me. So, then, I discover the principle that when I want to do right, evil is at hand. For I take delight in the law of God, in my inner self, but I see in my members another principle at war with the law of my mind, taking me captive to the law of sin that dwells in my members.

Reflection

Paul has great insight into the shortcomings of disciples. We want to do good; we want to follow Jesus. But, then the day begins and soon we find that we have spoken harshly.

We need to root the Gospel deeply within us. To do so, we need to nurture the discipline of daily prayer and spiritual practices that wise teachers pass on to us. Such discipline helps us grow in faith. And no matter how well-disciplined our practices, we need to periodically step back and review our prayer life. Consider whether your prayer life needs some renewal.

Prayers *others may be added*

Turning to our Lord, who shows us the way, we pray:

◆ Hear our prayer, O Lord.

May we be guided by the spiritual wisdom of our Church community, we pray: ◆ May those who seek violence hear the voice of peace calling them to be transformed, we pray: ◆ May the Holy Spirit rest on spiritual directors, we pray: ◆ May those who suffer from natural disaster find support and peace, we pray: ◆ May our farms yield a fruitful harvest, we pray: ◆

Our Father . . .

All powerful God,
you call us to live as your daughters and sons.
We hear your voice alive in our hearts.
Send your Spirit upon us this day
and help us to continue our journey,
trusting in your forgiveness and love.
We ask this through Christ our Lord.
Amen.

✝ Great is the Lord and highly to be praised.

Saturday, October 28, 2017

Feast of Sts. Simon and Jude, Apostles

† Great is the Lord and highly to be praised.

Psalm 96 *page 413*

Reading *Ephesians 2:19–22*

Brothers and sisters: You are no longer strangers and sojourners, but you are fellow citizens with the holy ones and members of the household of God, built upon the foundation of the Apostles and prophets, with Christ Jesus himself as the capstone. Through him the whole structure is held together and grows into a temple sacred in the Lord; in him you also are being built together into a dwelling place of God in the Spirit.

Reflection

We often see ourselves as individuals sharing a common space. Yes, we are unique creations of God. However, we are also members of the household of God. We are a family whose bonds make us stronger than each is separately. The beauty of diversity joins with the strength of unity. Simon and Jude are honored today as Apostles, but little is known about them. Jude is also known as Thaddeus. Simon is also called a Zealot, a member of the political party that worked for Jewish freedom from the Romans. The Apostles too were a mixed group. Let's pray today for those with whom we have differences but are one with us in the family of God.

Prayers *others may be added*

Turning to our Lord, who shows us the way, we pray:

◆ Hear our prayer, O Lord.

For the beauty of diversity in the Church, we pray: ◆ For a willingness to hear the voices of those with whom we do not agree, we pray: ◆ For a respect of all cultures, languages, and ways of life, we pray: ◆ For an end to vindictive self-righteousness, we pray: ◆ For those whom this world does not value, we pray: ◆

Our Father . . .

Father of all,
you created this world in amazing diversity.
Help us to accept the differences among us and to live
as sisters and brothers in you.
We ask this through Christ our Lord.
Amen.

† Great is the Lord and highly to be praised.

Sunday, October 29, 2017
Thirtieth Sunday in Ordinary Time

✝ *Your words, Lord, are Spirit and life.*

Psalm 19 *page 402*

Reading *Matthew 22:34–40*

When the Pharisees heard that Jesus had silenced the Sadducees, they gathered together, and one of them a scholar of the law, tested him by asking, "Teacher, which commandment in the law is the greatest?" Jesus said to him, "You shall love the Lord, your God, with all your heart, with all your soul, and with all your mind. This is the greatest and the first commandment. The second is like it: You shall love your neighbor as yourself. The whole law and the prophets depend on these two commandments."

Reflection

Again the Pharisees question Jesus. His answer is rooted in his upbringing. When asked about the greatest Commandment, he replies not with one of the Ten Commandments. Rather, Jesus repeats the *Shema*. He would have learned this prayer as a small child and recited it often. The second command also comes from the Book of Leviticus in the Torah.

We too need to immerse ourselves in the faith. When tested by life's struggles, we will then be able to rely on our faith. If children are in our care, their faith will grow as we teach them prayers and read stories from the Bible to them.

Prayers *others may be added*

Turning to our Lord, who shows us the way, we pray:

◆ Lord, hear our prayer.

For the Church, may we model the love of the Gospel to all we meet, we pray: ◆ For immigrants, may they be welcomed and find a home among us, we pray: ◆ For the trust to love God with all our hearts, we pray: ◆ For the openness to love our neighbor, we pray: ◆ For our nation's leaders, that they will seek to protect refugees, we pray: ◆ For all who have died, may they now rejoice in the new and eternal Jerusalem, we pray: ◆

Our Father . . .

God of our ancestors,
your truth is eternal
and your goodness is from age to age.
May our elders impart all they know of
your love
and may our children's children
sing your praises in every generation.
We ask this through our Lord Jesus
Christ, your Son,
who lives and reigns with you in the unity
of the Holy Spirit,
one God, for ever and ever.
Amen.

✝ *Your words, Lord, are Spirit and life.*

Monday, October 30, 2017
Weekday

✝ Your words, Lord, are Spirit and life.

Psalm 19
page 402

Reading
Romans 8:12–17

Brothers and sisters: We are not debtors to the flesh, to live according to the flesh. For if you live according to the flesh, you will die, but if by the spirit you put to death the deeds of the body, you will live.

For those who are led by the Spirit of God are sons of God. For you did not receive a spirit of slavery to fall back into fear, but you received a spirit of adoption, through which we cry, "*Abba*, Father!" The spirit himself bears witness with our spirit that we are children of God, and if children, then heirs, heirs of God and joint heirs with Christ, if only we suffer with him so that we may also be glorified with him.

Reflection

What language do you use when you pray? How do you perceive your relationship with the Lord? Words matter. In the Lord's Prayer, Jesus refers to the Father as *Abba*, a child's word more like Daddy. Paul echoes this understanding. We are not slaves, but children of God. We are beloved. Our relationship is not one of fear; rather we live in the Spirit already. Do we act as if we are afraid of the Lord? Are we living as those awaiting condemnation or punishment? Or do we live freely, joyously? Does seeing yourself as a beloved daughter or son change how you live?

Prayers
others may be added

To our Lord, who holds out the truth, we pray:

◆ Hear us, Lord.

For cloistered contemplatives, for the work of prayer in the Church, we pray: ◆ For the freedom to live as children of God, we pray: ◆ For lawmakers, that they will defend the rights of the oppressed, we pray: ◆ For an end to the death penalty, throughout the world, we pray: ◆ For those struggling with debt, we pray: ◆

Our Father . . .

Our Father,
you are a God of love.
You call us your beloved daughters
and sons.
Today, may we live in the freedom of the
children of God,
loving others as you first loved us.
We ask this through Christ our Lord.
Amen.

✝ Your words, Lord, are Spirit and life.

Tuesday, October 31, 2017
Weekday

✝ *Your words, Lord, are Spirit and life.*

Psalm 19 *page 402*

Reading *Romans 8:18–21*

Brothers and sisters: I consider that the sufferings of this present time are as nothing compared with the glory to be revealed for us. For creation awaits with eager expectation the revelation of the children of God; for creation was made subject to futility, not of its own accord but because of the one who subjected it, in hope that creation itself would be set free from slavery to corruption and share in the glorious freedom of the children of God.

Reflection

Suffering is an inevitable part of life. This is a truth we know well. Today commemorates the five hundredth anniversary of the Reformation. Great strides have been made toward healing, including a joint document on justification between Catholics and Lutherans. Yet division and pain remain. We look forward to a day when our mutual wounds strengthen our bond of unity with one another. The time of mutual respect has come, with even some shared ministry. But we still struggle toward a new bond, a new way of living as true sisters and brothers in Christ. We look forward to the glory to be revealed for us.

Prayers *others may be added*

To our Lord, who holds out the truth, we pray:

◆ Hear us, Lord.

As Church, may we live in solidarity with the suffering and oppressed, we pray: ◆ For the Lutheran-Catholic dialogue, we pray: ◆ For our Protestant sisters and brothers, we pray: ◆ As children of God, may we live in hope and abide in love, we pray: ◆ As community, may we reach out to victims of abuse, we pray: ◆

Our Father . . .

God of our silent tears,
you are with us in our suffering.
Hear us when we cry out to you.
Bring us solace and give us courage to wipe the tears
of our sisters and brothers.
We ask this through Christ our Lord.
Amen.

✝ *Your words, Lord, are Spirit and life.*

Wednesday, November 1, 2017
Solemnity of All Saints

✝ O God, you are my God.

Psalm 63 *page 407*

Reading *1 John 3:1–3*

Beloved: See what love the Father has bestowed on us that we may be called the children of God. Yet so we are. The reason the world does not know us is that it did not know him. Beloved, we are God's children now; what we shall be has not yet been revealed. We do know that when it is revealed we shall be like him, for we shall see him as he is. Everyone who has this hope based on him makes himself pure, as he is pure.

Reflection

Many days of the liturgical year are set aside to honor holy heroes who have gone before us. Today we recall the righteous throng, a sacred assembly. We remember sanctity is not the prize of the few. It is not a brass ring that only a select number can grasp.

Each of us receives the call to holiness. Saints in this life are imperfect but seeeking perfection. Saints are sinners who never stop in their journey. Saints are us, stumbling, flawed, but working to build up God's reign. We celebrate today and join in the parade. "O how I want to be that number, when the saints go marching in."

Prayers *others may be added*

To our Lord, who holds out the truth, we pray:

◆ Hear us, Lord.

May we look to Sts. Ephrem and Cecilia to help us joyfully sing God's praises, we pray: ◆ May Church leaders shepherd us courageously, we pray: ◆ May leaders of nations look to Sts. Elizabeth of Portugal, Wenceslaus, and Louis of France as they seek justice, we pray to the Lord: ◆ May we seek to serve the poor as did Sts. Martin de Porres, Francis of Assisi, and Damien of Molokai, we pray: ◆ May we look to Sts. Charles Lwanga, Lawrence Ruiz, and Kateri Tekakwitha for examples of lives dedicated to service to the Gospel, despite persecution, we pray: ◆

Our Father . . .

Lord of all the saints,
today we honor our sisters and brothers
who have gone before us in faith.
May their dedication to you be an
example for us.
May their courage inspire us.
When we lie in death,
raise us up to sing their song of praise.
We ask this through Christ our Lord.
Amen.

✝ O God, you are my God.

Thursday, November 2, 2017

Commemoration of All the Faithful Departed (All Souls' Day)

✝ O God, you are my God.

Psalm 27 *page 404*

Reading *Wisdom 3:1–9*

The souls of the just are in the hand of God, / and no torment shall touch them. / They seemed, in the view of the foolish, to be dead; / and their passing away was thought an affliction / and their going forth from us, utter destruction. / But they are in peace. / For if before men, indeed they be punished, / yet is their hope full of immortality; / chastised a little, they shall be greatly blessed, / because God tried them and found them worthy of himself. / As gold in the furnace, he proved them, / and as sacrificial offerings he took them to himself. / In the time of their visitation they shall shine, / and shall dart about as sparks through stubble; / they shall judge nations and rule over peoples, / and the LORD shall be their King forever. / Those who trust in him shall understand truth, / and the faithful shall abide with him in love: / Because grace and mercy are with his holy ones, / and his care is with his elect.

Reflection

Today we remember all the deceased. In many cultures families visit cemeteries on this day, clean the graves, light candles, and tell stories. Profound truths that lie deep in our hearts rise to the surface. What we believe about love, forgiveness, faith, and resurrection fills our thoughts. Whom do you still need to forgive? Do so today. Is there anger or pain still wrapped around your heart? Release it today. Does love cause you to weep? Go ahead, and tell your children and your children's children stories they need to know about relatives and friends.

Today we also pray for those who most need our prayers: those forgotten.

Prayers *others may be added*

To our Lord, who holds out the truth, we pray:

◆ Hear us, Lord.

When suffering and pain overwhelm us, may the gentle care of the Church be our balm, solace, and strength, we pray: ◆ When world leaders make decisions, may God's Word inspire them to bring about peace, we pray: ◆ When we feel lost, or confused, may we find shelter in the loving arms of God, we pray: ◆ When family and friends die, may our belief in the resurrection sustain us, we pray: ◆ When people struggle to persevere in this life, may the Giver of all life be their hope, we pray: ◆

Our Father . . .

Lord of Life,
you provide us hope in the resurrection.
When our loved ones are called from
this life
may their souls, and the souls of all the
faithful departed
through your mercy, rest in peace.
We ask this through Christ our Lord.
Amen.

✝ O God, you are my God.

Friday, November 3, 2017
Weekday

✝ Your words, Lord, are Spirit and life.

Psalm 19 *page 402*

Reading *Romans 9:1–5*

Brothers and sisters: I speak the truth in Christ, I do not lie; my conscience joins with the Holy Spirit in bearing me witness that I have great sorrow and constant anguish in my heart. For I could wish that I myself were accursed and cut off from Christ for the sake of my own people, my kindred according to the flesh. They are children of Israel; theirs the adoption, the glory, the covenants, the giving of the law, the worship, and the promises; theirs the patriarchs, and from them, according to the flesh, is the Christ, who is over all, God blessed forever. Amen.

Reflection

Can you hear the anguish in Paul's voice? He was schooled in the Law, raised as a devout Jew, by some accounts even studied in Jerusalem, and he persecuted this renegade movement called Christianity. However, he experienced a deep conversion. Now he is an evangelist of the Gospel but cannot ignore his roots.

Transition is painful and the pain should not be ignored. God calls us to move along a journey, and that entails choosing to leave behind part of our past. What is God asking you to leave so that you can embrace more fully the Lord's plan for you?

Prayers *others may be added*

To our Lord, who holds out the truth, we pray:

◆ Hear us, Lord.

May our Church hold on to truth and embrace what is new and good as we continue to proclaim the Gospel, we pray: ◆ May the sins of the past be forgiven, we pray: ◆ May we welcome the new challenges the Lord places before us, we pray: ◆ May those who struggle with change, find confidence in their relationship with Jesus, we pray: ◆

Our Father . . .

God of all ages,
you walk with us on our journeys
through life.
Each age brings new challenges and
new sorrows,
new struggles, and new joys.
Teach us to retain what is worthy,
adopt what is true, and
adapt to the changes that we face.
We ask this through Christ our Lord.
Amen.

✝ Your words, Lord, are Spirit and life.

Saturday, November 4, 2017

Memorial of St. Charles Borromeo, Bishop

✝ *Your words, Lord, are Spirit and life.*

Psalm 19

page 402

Reading

Romans 11:1–2a, 11–12,

Brothers and sisters: I ask, then, has God rejected his people? Of course not! God has not rejected his people whom he foreknew. Do you not know what the Scripture says about Elijah, how he pleads with God against Israel?

Hence, I ask, did they stumble so as to fall? Of course not! But through their transgression salvation has come to the Gentiles, so as to make them jealous. Now if their transgression is enrichment for the worlds, and if their diminished number is enrichment for the Gentiles, how much more their full number.

Reflection

Charles Borromeo lived during the great upheaval of the Reformation. He left behind power and riches to embrace poverty and the administration of the reform of the Church. It is through his strength of character and hard work that the Council of Trent issued changes, reorganized administration, and affirmed teachings. He was made the bishop of Milan (present-day Italy) and there continued his work in renewing the faith. When the plague hit the city, Charles stayed and ministered to the sick. Administration is a difficult and thankless job. In addition, it is easy to get caught up in the paperwork and forget the people. Charles took care of both, seeing his ministry as caring for the Church he loved.

Prayers

others may be added

To our Lord, who holds out the truth,
we pray:

◆ Hear us, Lord.

For administrators in our Church, may they minister as servants to the Gospel, we pray: ◆ For leaders of nations, may they serve the needs of their people, we pray: ◆ For managers, that they may bring joy and integrity to their work, we pray: ◆ For all who seem lost in rules and regulations, may a spirit of justice and clarity guide them to resolutions, we pray: ◆ For the voiceless, we pray: ◆

Our Father . . .

Father of our Church,
you provided your servant Charles with
skills that helped the Church reform.
Draw near to our leadership.
May they too renew your people,
and make decisions that serve the Gospel.
We ask this through Christ our Lord.
Amen.

✝ *Your words, Lord, are Spirit and life.*

Sunday, November 5, 2017
Thirty-First Sunday in Ordinary Time

☩ In you, Lord, I have found my peace.

Psalm 131 *page 419*

Reading *Matthew 23:1–12*

Jesus spoke to the crowds and to his disciples, saying, "The scribes and the Pharisees have taken their seat on the chair of Moses. Therefore, do and observe all things whatsoever they tell you, but do not follow their example. For they preach but they do not practice. They tie up heavy burdens hard to carry and lay them on people's shoulders, but they will not lift a finger to move them. All their works are performed to be seen. They widen their phylacteries and lengthen their tassels. They love places of honor at banquets, seats of honor in synagogues, greetings in marketplaces, and the salutation 'Rabbi.' As for you, do not be called 'Rabbi.' You have but one teacher, and you are all brothers. Call no one on earth your father; you have but one Father in heaven. Do not be called 'Master'; you have but one master, the Christ. The greatest among you must be your servant. Whoever exalts himself will be humbled; but whoever humbles himself will be exalted."

Reflection

Listening to Jesus rail against the Pharisees can lead us into self-righteousness. After all, it is easy to use the failings of others as an excuse to ignore or reject what they represent, especially if that teaching is a challenge to us. The Pharisees were holy men. They erred by considering faith a body of prohibitions, warnings, and threats. Pope Francis has reminded us that we must show that the Good News really is cause for joy.

Prayers *others may be added*

To the Lord, who teaches us to serve, we pray:

◆ **Lord, hear our prayer.**

That the Church be an instrument of liberation from heavy burdens, we pray: ◆ May the baptized practice what they preach, we pray: ◆ For those in positions of leadership and authority, we pray: ◆ For the grace of humility and a spirit of servanthood, we pray: ◆ For those ignored or forgotten in the halls of power, we pray: ◆

Our Father . . .

Hope of the poor,
you are our refuge.
Teach us to be faithful servants,
who hear the cry of the poor
and recognize the need of the one in our midst.
We ask this through our Lord Jesus Christ, your Son,
who lives and reigns with you in the unity of the Holy Spirit,
one God, for ever and ever.
Amen.

☩ In you, Lord, I have found my peace.

Monday, November 6, 2017
Weekday

✝ In you, Lord, I have found my peace.

Psalm 131 *page 419*

Reading *Romans 11:29–32*

Brothers and sisters: The gifts and the call of God are irrevocable.

Just as you once disobeyed God but have now received mercy because of their disobedience, so they have now disobeyed in order that, by virtue of the mercy shown to you, they too may now receive mercy. For God delivered all to disobedience, that he might have mercy upon all.

Reflection

Paul finishes his explanation of why his own people, the Jews, will be saved. Paul reasons that, just as the Gentiles were once delivered from disobedience, so now his own people are so delivered, so that God "might have mercy on all." Here salvation is not about our faith or good works. Salvation concerns God's unfathomable and undeserved mercy. God cannot renege on his word or promise: "The gifts and the call of God are irrevocable." Repeat those words, pray them, meditate on them, trust them, and take them into your being.

Prayers *others may be added*

To the Lord, who teaches us to serve, we pray:

◆ Lord, hear our prayer.

For the Body of Christ, that members bear witness to the irrevocable love of God, we pray: ◆ That we will have greater trust in God's mercy and acceptance, we pray: ◆ For those who preach the Gospel, we pray: ◆ For Catholic Relief Services, we pray: ◆ For our beloved dead, we pray: ◆

Our Father . . .

Lord Jesus,
you are Light from Light, true God from true God,
in you we come to know God's grace and mercy.
Strengthen us to be confident
in the salvation you have won for us,
for you live and reign with God the Father, in the unity of the Holy Spirit,
one God, for ever and ever.
Amen.

✝ In you, Lord, I have found my peace.

Tuesday, November 7, 2017
Weekday

✝ In you, Lord, I have found my peace.

Psalm 131 *page 419*

Reading *Romans 12:5–10*

Brothers and sisters: We, though many, are one Body in Christ and individually parts of one another. Since we have gifts that differ according to the grace given to us, let us exercise them: if prophecy, in proportion to the faith; if ministry, in ministering; if one is a teacher, in teaching; if one exhorts, in exhortation; if one contributes, in generosity; if one is over others, with diligence; if one does acts of mercy, with cheerfulness.

Let love be sincere; hate what is evil, hold on to what is good; love one another with mutual affection; anticipate one another in showing honor.

Reflection

Paul returns to a topic he wrote about in his First Letter to the Corinthians, that we are, all of us, part of the Body of Christ. Here he says we are "parts of one another." In November we can especially experience this unity, this sense of being bound up in and to one another. On our minds and in our hearts are those who have gone before us. Their presence continues to impact and shape us.

November is also a time of charity and we connect with those who struggle financially and emotionally. Reflect on our interconnectedness and name some ways we are "parts of one another."

Prayers *others may be added*

To the Lord, who teaches us to serve, we pray:

◆ Lord, hear our prayer.

For N., our Pope, N., our bishop, and N., our pastor, we pray: ◆ May we grow in awareness of our unity with all that is, we pray: ◆ For those in public office and those seeking public office, we pray: ◆ For those who are sick, we pray: ◆ For those who are imprisoned, we pray: ◆

Our Father . . .

Lover of humanity,
you charge us with being our brother's
and sister's keeper.
Your Son taught us to love our neighbor
and that what we do to the least we do
to him.
Help us to live and act
as consciously being part of one another.
We ask this through Christ our Lord.
Amen.

✝ In you, Lord, I have found my peace.

Wednesday, November 8, 2017
Weekday

✝ In you, Lord, I have found my peace.

Psalm 131 *page 419*

Reading *Romans 13:8–10*

Brothers and sisters: Owe nothing to anyone, except to love one another; for the one who loves another has fulfilled the law. The commandments, *You shall not commit adultery; you shall not kill; you shall not steal; you shall not covet,* and whatever other commandment there may be, are summed up in this saying, namely, *You shall love your neighbor as yourself.* Love does no evil to the neighbor; hence, love is the fulfillment of the law.

Reflection

Can you imagine living in a society in which no one owed anyone anything but love? The credit cards in our wallets and purses, in their very existence, let alone their use, undermine Paul's words! Then there are the emotional debts, the debts of time and of having asked for a favor. Yet if we turn this around, would those to whom we are indebted lord it over us? Would they want us to avoid them, feel guilty, or less powerful in their presence? That would hardly be "love." If we live out debt to love one another, the issues of who has the power, who owes whom, who feels inferior or superior, begin to fade as we own and claim our common humanity.

Prayers *others may be added*

To the Lord who teaches us to serve, we pray:

◆ Lord, hear our prayer.

That the Church may serve as a catalyst for love, we pray: ◆ May world leaders be committed to peace, we pray: ◆ For those who share in the Sacrament of Matrimony, we pray: ◆ For those living with feelings of guilt or indebtedness, we pray: ◆ For those who feel unloved and those who are afraid to give themselves in love, we pray: ◆

Our Father . . .

God of loving kindness,
your sent your only Son to us in a love
that is unsurpassed.
Help us to see each person as neighbor
and to embrace them for who they are.
We ask this through Christ our Lord.
Amen.

✝ In you, Lord, I have found my peace.

Thursday, November 9, 2017

Feast of the Dedication of the Lateran Basilica

✝ In you, Lord, I have found my peace.

Psalm 131 *page 419*

Reading *Ezekiel 47:1–2, 8–9, 12*

The angel brought me back to the entrance of the temple, and I saw water flowing out from beneath the threshold of the temple toward the east, for the façade of the temple was toward the east; the water flowed down from the southern side of the temple, south of the altar. He led me outside by the north gate, and around to the outer gate facing the east, where I saw water trickling from the southern side. He said to me, "This water flows into the eastern district down upon the Arabah, and empties into the sea, the salt waters, which it makes fresh. Wherever the river flows, every sort of living creature that can multiply shall live, and there shall be abundant fish, for wherever this water comes the sea shall be made fresh. Along both banks of the river, fruit trees of every kind shall grow; their leaves shall not fade, nor their fruit fail. Every month they shall bear fresh fruit, for they shall be watered by the flow from the sanctuary. Their fruit shall serve for food, and their leaves for medicine."

Reflection

Ezekiel sees water flowing from the side of the Temple. When Jesus hung on the Cross, his side was pierced and blood and water flowed out. Jesus is the Temple and on the Cross becomes the font of sacramental life for the Church.

Today we honor the Basilica of St. John Lateran, the cathedral church of Rome. Because St. John Lateran is the cathedral of Rome and the oldest basilica (ca. 313) it ranks ahead of all churches in Catholicism. An inscription in the basilica proclaims it to be "the mother and head of all churches in the city and the world."

Prayers *others may be added*

To the Lord, who teaches us to serve, we pray:

◆ Lord, hear our prayer.

For the Church universal, we pray: ◆ For bishops and patriarchs, we pray: ◆ For all the baptized, we pray: ◆ For the work of ecumenism, we pray: ◆

Our Father . . .

God of endless ages,
by our sharing in the Paschal Mystery
we become one with the holy People
of God,
the Body of Christ, the Church.
Rejoicing in this unity may our worship,
faith, and service
bear witness to the Reign of God
that is now and that is to come,
through our Lord Jesus Christ, your Son,
who lives and reigns with you in the unity
of the Holy Spirit,
one God, for ever and ever.
Amen.

✝ In you, Lord, I have found my peace.

Friday, November 10, 2017

Memorial of St. Leo the Great, Pope and Doctor of the Church

☩ In you, Lord, I have found my peace.

Psalm 131 *page 419*

Reading *Romans 15:14–16*

I myself am convinced about you, my brothers and sisters, that you yourselves are full of goodness, filled with all knowledge, and able to admonish one another. But I have written to you rather boldly in some respects to remind you, because of the grace given me by God to be a minister of Christ Jesus to the Gentiles in performing the priestly service of the Gospel of God, so that the offering up of the Gentiles may be acceptable, sanctified by the Holy Spirit.

Reflection

As Paul wrote to Rome so Pope Leo I wrote from Rome to the Council of Chalcedon (451), which was wrestling with how Christ's identity was to be understood. Reportedly, when "Leo's Tome" was read at the council, those gathered exclaimed, "Peter has spoken thus through Leo." Chalcedon and Leo became synonymous that day, as both proclaimed Christ to be a divine person with both a human and a divine nature. Leo extended the concept of papal primacy. He is also credited for convincing Attila the Hun to turn back and not attack Rome. Though often involved with high-level diplomacy, Leo never tired of asserting the fundamental dignity that is proper to all the baptized.

Prayers *others may be added*

To the Lord, who teaches us to serve, we pray:

◆ Lord, hear our prayer.

In the spirit of St. Leo, may Church leaders respect the dignity of the baptized, we pray: ◆ For those who seek alternatives to war and violence, we pray: ◆ That we may embrace the stewardship entrusted to us, we pray: ◆ For families, we pray: ◆ For parishes celebrating their patronal feast this day, we pray: ◆

Our Father . . .

Wisdom of the Father,
as you enlightened St. Leo the Great
so enlighten us on our journey to you.
May we learn ways of nonviolent resolution
to conflicts and insist on the dignity of all.
You live and reign with God the Father in the unity of the Holy Spirit,
one God, for ever and ever.
Amen.

☩ In you, Lord, I have found my peace.

Saturday, November 11, 2017
Memorial of St. Martin of Tours, Bishop

† In you, Lord, I have found my peace.

Psalm 131 *page 419*

Reading *Isaiah 61:1–3abcd*

The Spirit of the Lord GOD is upon me, / because the LORD has anointed me; / He has sent me to bring glad tidings to the lowly, / to heal the brokenhearted, / To proclaim liberty to the captives and release to the prisoners, / To announce a year of favor from the LORD and a day of vindication by our God, / to comfort all who mourn; / To place on those who mourn in Zion / a diadem instead of ashes, / To give them oil of gladness in place of mourning, / a glorious mantle instead of a listless spirit.

Reflection

Martin became a catechumen at a young age and against the wishes of his parents. As expected, he followed in his father's footsteps and entered the Roman military. According to legend, one day he came across a cold, hungry beggar. Martin cut his cloak in half and wrapped the man in it. That night he had a dream in which the beggar wrapped in his cloak was Christ. He then was baptized and came to the realization that being a disciple of Jesus was incompatible with military service. "I am a soldier of Christ and it is not lawful for me to fight."

Prayers *others may be added*

To the Lord, who teaches us to serve, we pray:

◆ Lord, hear our prayer.

May we be a Church of peace, we pray ◆ For those who conscientiously object to military service, we pray: ◆ That those in public office be attentive to the cry of the poor, we pray: ◆ That we see Christ in one another, we pray: ◆ For parishes whose patronal feast is today, we pray: ◆

Our Father . . .

Lord God,
send forth your Spirit of courage
that we may live in accord
with our conscience and our faith
as did your servant Martin of Tours.
We ask this through Christ our Lord.
Amen.

† In you, Lord, I have found my peace.

Sunday, November 12, 2017
Thirty-Second Sunday in Ordinary Time

✝ My soul is thirsting for you, O Lord my God.

Psalm 63 *page 407*

Reading *Matthew 25:1–13*

Jesus told his disciples this parable: "The kingdom of heaven will be like ten virgins who took their lamps and went out to meet the bridegroom. Five of them were foolish and five were wise. The foolish ones, when taking their lamps, brought no oil with them, but the wise brought flasks of oil with their lamps. Since the bridegroom was long delayed, they all became drowsy and fell asleep. At midnight, there was a cry, 'Behold, the bridegroom! Come out to meet him!' Then all those virgins got up and trimmed their lamps. The foolish ones said to the wise, 'Give us some of your oil, for our lamps are going out.' But the wise ones replied, 'No, for there may not be enough for us and you. Go instead to the merchants and buy some for yourselves.' While they went off to buy it, the bridegroom came and those who were ready went into the wedding feast with him. Then the door was locked. Afterwards the other virgins came and said, 'Lord, Lord, open the door for us!' But he said in reply, 'Amen, I say to you, I do not know you.' Therefore, stay awake, for you know neither the day nor the hour."

Reflection

The point of this parable is not sharing, but rather preparedness. We participate in Sunday Mass, pray, act rightly, make sacrifices, and even study our faith, often seemingly with little "result." Sometimes we think that, for all of our effort, we don't feel closer to God. Yet, in all this, we are storing oil for our lamp (our baptismal candle). These spiritual practices are preparing us to see and recognize the Bridegroom and the Reign of God that unexpectedly comes upon us both in this life and the next.

Prayers *others may be added*

To our God, who always looks for us, we pray

◆ Lord, hear our prayer.

May the Church always be at the service of the Reign of God, we pray: ◆ May the baptized be prepared to welcome the Christ who comes, we pray: ◆ For inquirers, we pray: ◆ For the homebound, we pray: ◆

Our Father . . .

Good and Gracious God,
you provide your teachings to guide us.
May we be confident in your presence
even when we fail to notice
you are with us.
Through our Lord Jesus Christ, your Son,
who lives and reigns with you in the unity
of the Holy Spirit,
one God, for ever and ever.
Amen.

✝ My soul is thirsting for you, O Lord my God.

Monday, November 13, 2017
Memorial of St. Frances Xavier Cabrini, Virgin

✝ My soul is thirsting for you, O Lord my God.

Psalm 63

page 407

Reading

Luke 17:1–6

Jesus said to his disciples, "Things that cause sin will inevitably occur, but woe to the one through whom they occur. It would be better for him if a millstone were put around his neck and he be thrown into the sea than for him to cause one of these little ones to sin. Be on your guard! If your brother sins, rebuke him; and if he repents, forgive him. And if he wrongs you seven times in one day and returns to you seven times saying, 'I am sorry,' you should forgive him."

And the Apostles said to the Lord, "Increase our faith." The Lord replied, "If you have faith the size of a mustard seed, you would say to this mulberry tree, 'Be uprooted and planted in the sea,' and it would obey you."

Reflection

Frances Cabrini came to the United States with six members of the Missionary Sisters of the Sacred Heart, the religious institute she founded. Her community was instrumental in assisting Italian immigrants arriving in the Americas. She founded numerous schools, hospitals, and orphanages. Her legacy should cause us to reflect on the welcome that we show to those who come to the United States today. Honoring her, what might our parish do to assist immigrants?

Prayers

others may be added

Searching for the living God,
we pray:

◆ Lord, hear our prayer.

For the Body of Christ, may she be one with immigrants, we pray: ◆ For the grace of hospitality, we pray: ◆ For orphans and those in foster care, we pray: ◆ For Catholic schools and religious-education programs, we pray: ◆ For parishes and institutions celebrating their patronal feast today, we pray: ◆

Our Father . . .

God of all nations,
you looked after the Chosen People
enslaved in Egypt;
and the Holy Family who fled their
homeland as refugees,
so fill our hearts with compassion
toward immigrants
seeking respite and freedom.
May they find in our parishes welcome
and warmth.
We ask this through Christ our Lord.
Amen.

✝ My soul is thirsting for you, O Lord my God.

Tuesday, November 14, 2017
Weekday

✝ My soul is thirsting for you, O Lord my God.

Psalm 63 *page 407*

Reading *Luke 17:7–10*

Jesus said to the Apostles: "Who among you would say to your servant who has just come in from plowing or tending sheep in the field, 'Come here immediately and take your place at table'? Would he not rather say to him, 'Prepare something for me to eat. Put on your apron and wait on me while I eat and drink. You may eat and drink when I am finished'? Is he grateful to that servant because he did what was commanded? So should it be with you. When you have done all you have been commanded, say, 'We are unprofitable servants; we have done what we were obliged to do.'"

Reflection

"We are unprofitable servants; we have done what we were obliged to do." That phrase may seem surprising to some. When we have done a task well, we expect at least words of appreciation. This passage makes it clear that our prayer, volunteering, and ministry are never about us. As disciples, we are servants, and as servants, we do as Jesus did. That means we wash feet and do not look to be rewarded for our service. We rest in the knowledge that God showed love for us by doing the same.

Prayers *others may be added*

Searching for the living God,
we pray:

◆ **Lord, hear our prayer.**

May we be a servant Church, we pray: ◆ For the grace to center our lives on God, we pray: ◆ For maids and other domestic workers, we pray: ◆ For those living on minimum wage, we pray: ◆ For victims of human trafficking, we pray: ◆

Our Father . . .

Lord God,
"you have no need of our praise
and even our desire to thank you is itself your gift" (Weekday Preface IV, Sacramentary).
Help us to know and remember
that all we have
and all we are comes from you.
We ask this through Christ our Lord.
Amen.

✝ My soul is thirsting for you, O Lord my God.

Wednesday, November 15, 2017
Weekday

✝ My soul is thirsting for you, O Lord my God.

Psalm 63
page 407

Reading
Luke 17:11–19

As Jesus continued his journey to Jerusalem, he traveled through Samaria and Galilee. As he was entering a village, ten lepers met him. They stood at a distance from him and raised their voice, saying, "Jesus, Master! Have pity on us!" And when he saw them, he said, "Go show yourselves to the priests." As they were going they were cleansed. And one of them, realizing he had been healed, returned, glorifying God in a loud voice; and he fell at the feet of Jesus and thanked him. He was a Samaritan. Jesus said in reply, "Ten were cleansed, were they not? Where are the other nine? Has none but this foreigner returned to give thanks to God?" Then he said to him, "Stand up and go; your faith has saved you."

Reflection
A theme other than gratitude may be within this passage. Jesus often stresses the observance of mercy, justice, and charity over and above the Law. Did the other nine not return because they had been told to show themselves to the priests? Did they fear that by not doing so their illness would return? Only one recognized that giving thanks is more important than literal observance. Because of his example, giving thanks acquires the same importance as mercy, justice, and charity.

Prayers
others may be added

Searching for the living God,
we pray:

◆ Lord, hear our prayer.

May the Eucharist truly be the source and summit of our lives as the Church, we pray: ◆ That we grow in becoming a thankful people, we pray: ◆ For those who are ostracized, we pray: ◆
For those unable to see beyond the literal, we pray: ◆ For people living with Hansen's disease, we pray: ◆

Our Father . . .

God of abundance,
you have provided all that we have.
Trusting in you, may we possess
the assurance
that we are and have all we truly need.
We ask this through Christ our Lord.
Amen.

✝ My soul is thirsting for you, O Lord my God.

Thursday, November 16, 2017
Weekday

✝ My soul is thirsting for you, O Lord my God.

Psalm 63 *page 407*

Reading *Luke 17:20–25*

Asked by the Pharisees when the Kingdom of God would come, Jesus said in reply, "The coming of the Kingdom of God cannot be observed, and no one will announce, 'Look, here it is,' or, 'There it is.' For behold, the Kingdom of God is among you."

Then he said to his disciples, "The days will come when you will long to see one of the days of the Son of Man, but you will not see it. There will be those who will say to you, 'Look, there he is,' or 'Look, here he is.' Do not go off, do not run in pursuit. For just as lightning flashes and lights up the sky from one side to the other, so will the Son of Man be in his day. But first he must suffer greatly and be rejected by this generation."

Reflection

Jesus seems to be saying three essential things about the coming of the Kingdom: First, the Kingdom of God is already in our midst. We do not merely wait for it but witness to it and reveal it by living our faith. Second, he explains that we should not chase after those who have the answer as to when and how the end times are to come. Third, we need to keep in mind that the Kingdom is already triumphant in the Son of Man's Passion, Death, and Resurrection.

Prayers *others may be added*

Searching for the living God,
we pray:

◆ Lord, hear our prayer.

May the Church be an effective symbol of the Reign of God in our midst, we pray: ◆ May the baptized be transparent witnesses and builders of the Kingdom, we pray: ◆ For those who manipulate the good faith of others for their personal profit, we pray: ◆ For those who prey upon the elderly, may they reform and repent, we pray: ◆ That those who have gone before us rejoice in the heavenly banquet, we pray: ◆

Our Father . . .

God of endless ages,
there is no time in your presence;
all is now, all is eternal.
May we, your servants,
be less concerned with hours and days
and more resolute in being faithful to you
and to the Gospel of your Son,
Jesus Christ,
who lives and reigns with you in the unity of the Holy Spirit,
one God, for ever and ever.
Amen.

✝ My soul is thirsting for you, O Lord my God.

Friday, November 17, 2017
Memorial of St. Elizabeth of Hungary, Religious

✝ My soul is thirsting for you, O Lord my God.

Psalm 63
page 407

Reading
Luke 6:36–38

[Jesus said to his disciples:] "Be merciful, just as your Father is merciful.

"Stop judging and you will not be condemned. Forgive and you will be forgiven. Give and gifts will be given to you; a good measure, packed together, shaken down, and overflowing, will be poured into your lap. For the measure with which you measure will in return be measured out to you."

Reflection
The daughter of the king of Hungary, Elizabeth embraced a life of voluntary poverty. At age fourteen, she married Louis of Thuringia (a German principality). Unlike many of the noblewomen saints, her marriage was a happy one and Louis, also known for his faith and charity, supported Elizabeth in her concern for the poor. Tragically, he was killed during the Crusades. A widow at 20, Elizabeth continued to spin clothes for the poor and assist those stricken from plague and famine. It is reported that near the end of her short life she became a Third Order Franciscan and received a personal message of blessing from St. Francis of Assisi.

Prayers
others may be added

Searching for the living God,
we pray:

◆ Lord, hear our prayer.

That the Body of Christ be the Defender of the Poor in word and in deed, we pray: ◆ May leaders of nations be inspired by the example of Elizabeth of Hungary, we pray: ◆ For the grace to simplify our lifestyles, we pray: ◆ For those who have made the decision to live in voluntary poverty, we pray: ◆ For those who are forced to live in poverty, we pray: ◆

Our Father . . .

Lord God,
you gave Elizabeth of Hungary the
humility to not allow wealth or status
to prevent her from seeing Christ in the
poor and the sick.
Grant that we will use the gifts
you entrust to us
to serve not our self-interests but the
common good.
We ask this through Christ our Lord.
Amen.

✝ My soul is thirsting for you, O Lord my God.

Saturday, November 18, 2017
Weekday

✝ My soul is thirsting for you, O Lord my God.

Psalm 63 *page 407*

Reading *Luke 18:1–8*

Jesus told his disciples a parable about the necessity for them to pray always without becoming weary. He said, "There was a judge in a certain town who neither feared God nor respected any human being. And a widow in that town used to come to him and say, 'Render a just decision for me against my adversary.' For a long time the judge was unwilling, but eventually he thought, 'While it is true that I neither fear God nor respect any human being, because this widow keeps bothering me I shall deliver a just decision for her lest she finally come and strike me.'" The Lord said, "Pay attention to what the dishonest judge says. Will not God then secure the rights of his chosen ones who call out to him day and night? Will he be slow to answer them? I tell you, he will see to it that justice is done speedily. But when the Son of Man comes, will he find faith on earth?"

Reflection

Some of the world's great cathedrals took centuries to build. Prayer, faith, the liturgy, symbols, and the spiritual life are akin to a slow process as building a cathedral or parenting. Growth is slow and almost imperceptible. We don't pray to get God's attention; we give our attention to God in prayer. We don't pray to get what we want; we pray to know God's will. Over and over again, it is good to remind ourselves that our lives are about God.

Prayers *others may be added*

Searching for the living God,
we pray:

◆ Lord, hear our prayer.

May the spiritual heritage of the Church be explored by the faithful, we pray: ◆ For monks and mystics, pilgrims and people of prayer, we pray: ◆ For parents worrying over their children's lack of faith, we pray: ◆ That the right to life from conception to natural death be respected, we pray: ◆ For the grace to persist and to persevere, we pray: ◆

Our Father . . .

Holy One, Ancient Light,
you invite us to the path that is long
and slow.
May we be unhurried in your presence
and persist in fidelity to the Baptism
we have received through Jesus Christ
our Lord.
Amen.

✝ My soul is thirsting for you, O Lord my God.

Sunday, November 19, 2017
Thirty-Third Sunday in Ordinary Time

☩ Blessed are they who follow the law of the Lord.

Psalm 119 *page 417*

Reading *Matthew 25:14–15, 19–21*

Jesus told his disciples this parable: "A man going on a journey called in his servants and entrusted his possessions to them. To one he gave five talents; to another, two; to a third, one—to each according to his ability. Then he went away.

"After a long time the master of those servants came back and settled accounts with them. The one who had received five talents came forward bringing the additional five. He said, 'Master, you gave me five talents. See, I have made five more.' His master said to him, 'Well done, my good and faithful servant. Since you were faithful in small matters, I will give you great responsibilities. Come, share your master's joy.'"

Reflection

Barbara Reid, OP, in her book, *Abiding Word.* makes a convincing case for the third servant. One talent equals fifteen years' wages, so this master is unimaginably rich. In contrast, a worker in those days hoped to earn the daily bread for the family. The third servant refuses to cooperate with a system whereby his master amasses wealth while others lack basic necessities. He is cast into the darkness—so too was Jesus, on the Cross. From this perspective, the parable is a warning about being co-opted by an unjust system.

Prayers *others may be added*

To the Lord, who hears the cry of the poor, we pray:

◆ Lord, hear us.

For the Church, may we live as well as preach the preferential option for the poor, we pray: ◆ That those who possess many gifts use them to relieve the suffering of others, we pray: ◆ For those who struggle with a conflicted conscience, we pray: ◆ For an end to discrimination based on religion, race, age, gender, orientation, and disability, we pray: ◆ May those who sleep in Christ find light, happiness, and peace, we pray: ◆

Our Father . . .

The earth is yours, O Lord,
and all it contains comes from your bountiful hand.
May we not claim your work as our possession
but share your blessings abundantly with others,
especially the poor and the marginalized.
We ask this through our Lord Jesus Christ, your Son,
who lives and reigns with you in the unity of the Holy Spirit,
one God, for ever and ever.
Amen.

☩ Blessed are they who follow the law of the Lord.

Monday, November 20, 2017
Weekday

✝ Blessed are they who follow the law of the Lord.

Psalm 119 *page 417*

Reading *1 Maccabees 1:11–15, 62–63*

In those days there appeared in Israel men who were breakers of the law, and they seduced many people, saying: "Let us go and make an alliance with the Gentiles all around us; since we separated from the, many evils have come upon us." The proposal was agreeable; some from among the people promptly went to the king, and he authorized them to introduce the way of living of the Gentiles. Thereupon they built a gymnasium in Jerusalem according to the Gentile custom. They covered over the mark of their circumcision and abandoned the holy covenant; they allied themselves with the Gentiles and sold themselves to wrongdoing.

Whoever was found with a scroll of the covenant, and whoever observed the law, was condemned to death by royal decree. But many in Israel were determined and resolved in their hearts not to eat anything unclean; they preferred to die rather than to be defiled with unclean food.

Reflection

The Jewish people had been under foreign rule for centuries: first the Assyrians had power over them, then the Perisians, and next the Greeks. From around 164 to 63 BC, a successful revolt allowed a period of relative independence. The text of 1 Maccabees describes this turbulent period. King Antiochus desired to impose a completely Greek way of life upon the Jews. He forbade the keeping of the Sabbath, banned circumcision, the mark of the covenant, built a gymnasium that would include public nudity, and installed a statue of Zeus on the altar in the Temple. Some Jews went along with these sacrileges, others engaged in organized protest and resistance.

Prayers *others may be added*

To the Lord, who hears the cry of the poor, we pray:

◆ Lord, hear us.

For the Church persecuted, we pray: ◆ That all nations will recognize freedom of religion, we pray: ◆ That greater efforts be made to embrace nonviolent conflict resolution, we pray: ◆ For those denied religious liberty, we pray: ◆ That the faith of others is respected, we pray: ◆

Our Father . . .

Lord Jesus,
you have revealed the Father to us.
Guide us toward appreciating faiths
that differ from ours
so that we may live in concord and
harmony together.
You live and reign with God the Father in
the unity of the Holy Spirit,
one God, for ever and ever.
Amen.

✝ Blessed are they who follow the law of the Lord.

Tuesday, November 21, 2017
Memorial of the Presentation of the Blessed Virgin Mary

† Blessed are they who follow the law of the Lord.

Psalm 119 *page 417*

Reading *2 Maccabees 6:18–20*

Eleazar, one of the foremost scribes, a man of advanced age and noble appearance, was being forced to open his mouth to eat pork. But preferring a glorious death to a life of defilement, he spat out the meat, and went forward of his own accord to the instrument of torture, as people ought to do who have the courage to reject the food which it is unlawful to taste even for the love of life.

Reflection

Today's celebration is not found in the Bible nor based on historical fact. It comes from the realm of spiritual truth. Mary, from the beginning of her life, was dedicated to God. She who is presented in the Temple will give birth to the new Temple, one not made by human hands but begotten of God's love. It is fitting that we read today of Eleazar's refusal to even pretend to eat pork. Eleazar, like Mary, is a model of fidelity to the covenant. As Our Lady of Sorrows will grieve for her Son, Eleazar dies as a model and mentor to the young rather than dishonor God.

Prayers *others may be added*

To the Lord, who hears the cry of the poor, we pray:

◆ Lord, hear us.

May the Living Temple, the Church, be wholly dedicated to God, we pray: ◆ That Catholics and Orthodox, who both celebrate this day, find a path to unity, we pray: ◆ For peace in the world through the intercession of Mary, we pray: ◆ May we embrace the vocation to which God calls us, we pray: ◆ May we be open to making sacrifices and enduring hardships for the Gospel, we pray: ◆

Our Father . . .

Lord our God,
as Mary was presented in the Temple and dedicated to you,
inspire us to give ourselves completely
to the Reign of your Son,
who lives and reigns with you in the unity of the Holy Spirit,
one God, for ever and ever.
Amen.

† Blessed are they who follow the law of the Lord.

Wednesday, November 22, 2017

Memorial of St. Cecilia, Virgin and Martyr

☩ Blessed are they who follow the law of the Lord.

Psalm 119

page 417

Reading

Hosea 2:16bc, 17cd, 21–22

Thus says the LORD: I will lead her into the desert and speak to her heart. / She shall respond there as in the days of her youth, / when she came up from the land of Egypt. /

I will espouse you to me forever: / I will espouse you in right and in justice, / in love and in mercy; / I will espouse you in fidelity, / and you shall know the LORD.

Reflection

We know nothing for certain about Cecilia, the patron of musicians. According to legend, she heard heavenly music in her head the day she wedded Valerian. Their marriage was never consummated as both were martyred very shortly thereafter. Faith, love, and music are intimately related to one another. St. Augustine said, "In the song of the lover (there is) love." Today we give thanks for the gift of music and how it stirs our souls and reflects our many moods. Music and song are ways of praying and this need not be limited in understanding or practice to psalms and hymns. Other music too can inspire prayer and guide us to the holy.

Prayers

others may be added

To the Lord, who hears the cry of the poor, we pray:

◆ Lord, hear us.

May the song of faith be sung in the lives of the People of God, we pray: ◆ For musicians who share their gifts with the Church, we pray: ◆ For singers, instrumentalists, composers, and all who help to make music, we pray: ◆ For those deprived of hearing music and song, we pray: ◆ May parishes celebrating their feast this day make a joyful noise, we pray: ◆

Our Father . . .

Lover of humankind,
you have gifted us with music.
Encourage us to embrace this gift and
allow music to flow through
our bodies
and move our souls in prayer.
We ask this through Christ our Lord.
Amen.

☩ Blessed are they who follow the law of the Lord.

Thursday, November 23, 2017
Thanksgiving Day

✝ Blessed are they who follow the law of the Lord.

Psalm 119 *page 417*

Reading *Luke 19:41–44*

As Jesus drew near Jerusalem, he saw the city and wept over it, saying, "If this day you only knew what makes for peace—but now it is hidden from your eyes. For the days are coming upon you when your enemies will raise a palisade against you; they will encircle you and hem you in on all sides. They will smash you to the ground and your children within you, and they will not leave one stone upon another within you because you did not recognize the time of your visitation."

Reflection

Thanksgiving Day is not, strictly speaking, a feast of the Church. However, the word Eucharist is Greek for *thanksgiving*. Each time we gather for Mass we celebrate thanksgiving; and every time we give thanks we are tacitly acknowledging our unity and interdependence with one another and creation. Today's Gospel states, "If this day you only knew what makes for peace." Clearly giving thanks and having a heart filled with genuine gratitude and appreciation brings peace. A truly thankful heart is content to be with loved ones and for what is given by God.

Prayers *others may be added*

To the Lord, who hears the cry of the poor, we pray:

◆ Lord, hear us.

May the Body of Christ, the Church, exude thankfulness, we pray: ◆ For Native Americans and all indigenous peoples, we pray: ◆ For farmers, migrant workers, transportation workers, bakers, cooks, and all who provide us with our daily bread, we pray: ◆ For those who must work today, we pray: ◆ May those who cannot be with loved ones today find ways to spiritually connect with one another, we pray: ◆

Our Father . . .

God of the Harvest,
you have provided for us in abundance.
We give you thanks for what you have
provided in Christ and through
the Church.
May we cherish these gifts
and all the gifts that fill our lives.
We ask this through Christ, our Lord.
Amen.

✝ Blessed are they who follow the law of the Lord.

Friday, November 24, 2017
Memorial of St. Andrew Dũng-Lạc, Priest, and Companions, Martyrs

✝ **Blessed are they who follow the law of the Lord.**

Psalm 119 *page 417*

Reading *1 Maccabees 4:36–37, 56–58*

Judas and his brothers said, "Now that our enemies have been crushed, let us go up to purify the sanctuary and rededicate it."

For eight days they celebrated the dedication of the altar and joyfully offered burnt offerings and sacrifices of deliverance and praise. They ornamented the façade of the temple with gold crowns and shields; they repaired the gates and the priests' chambers and furnished them with doors. There was great joy among the people now that the disgrace of the Gentiles was removed.

Reflection

This reading forms the basis for the feast of Hanukkah, the rededication of the Temple. It is a fitting complement to today's memorial of the Vietnamese martyrs. Portuguese missionaries introduced Christianity to Vietnam in the seventeenth century. In the nineteenth century, a violent persecution broke out. Andrew Dũng-Lạc and his 116 companions were martyred between 1820 and 1862. They are representative of the estimated one hundred thousand to three hundred thousand Catholics in Vietnam killed for their faith. As the blood of Jewish martyrs led to the rededication of the Temple, so the Vietnamese martyrs continue to deepen the faith and fervor of Vietnamese Catholics and of all the Church.

Prayers *others may be added*

To the Lord, who hears the cry of the poor, we pray:

◆ **Lord, hear us.**

May the witness of the martyrs continue to inspire the Body of Christ, we pray: ◆ For the Church in Vietnam, we pray: ◆ That we may be willing to share our faith, we pray: ◆ For the ability to listen to the faith stories of others, we pray: ◆ For parishes celebrating their patronal feast today, we pray: ◆

Our Father . . .

God of all nations,
you have provided people of stalwart faith
to guide us.
May we allow the witness of martyrs
to enrich our faith
and deepen our appreciation
for knowing Jesus Christ,
who lives and reigns with you in the unity
of the Holy Spirit,
one God, for ever and ever.
Amen.

✝ **Blessed are they who follow the law of the Lord.**

Saturday, November 25, 2017
Weekday

✝ Blessed are they who follow the law of the Lord.

Psalm 119 *page 417*

Reading *1 Maccabees 6:1–2, 5–9*

While King Antiochus was traversing the inland provinces, he heard that in Persia there was a city called Elymais, famous for its wealth in silver and gold, and that its temple was very rich, containing gold helmets, breastplates, and weapons left there by Alexander, son of Philip, king of Macdon, the first king of the Greeks.

While he was in Persia, a messenger brought him news that the armies sent into the land of Judah had been put to flight; that Lysias had gone at first with a strong arm and been driven back by the children of Israel; that they had grown strong by reason of the arms, men, and abundant possessions taken from the armies they had destroyed; they had pulled down the Abomination which he had built upon the altar in Jerusalem; and that they had surrounded with high walls both the sanctuary as it had been before, and his city of Beth-zur.

When the king heard this news, he was struck with fear and very much shaken. Sick with grief because his design had failed, he took to his bed. There he remained many days, overwhelmed with sorrow, for he knew he was going to die.

Reflection

King Antiochus, approaching the end of his days, comes to understand the evil he committed in his treatment of the Jewish people and their faith. One of the spiritual exercises of St. Ignatius Loyola is to imagine our death. What are our regrets? How and for what will our loved ones remember us?

Prayers *others may be added*

To the Lord, who hears the cry of the poor, we pray:

◆ Lord, hear us.

For N., our pope, and N., our bishop, we pray: ◆ For leaders of nations and heads of state, we pray: ◆ That we may grasp the brevity of our lives, we pray: ◆ For those who have gone before us marked with the sign of faith, we pray: ◆

Our Father . . .

Infinite God,
you have given us each day.
May we dedicate our time
to actions that speak of mercy, justice,
gratitude, and compassion.
We ask this through Christ, our Lord.
Amen.

✝ Blessed are they who follow the law of the Lord.

Sunday, November 26, 2017

Solemnity of Our Lord Jesus Christ, King of the Universe

✝ The Lord is my shepherd; there is nothing I shall want.

Psalm 23

page 403

Reading

Matthew 25:31–36

Jesus said to his disciples: "When the Son of Man comes in his glory, and all the angels with him, he will sit upon his glorious throne, and all the nations will be assembled before him. And he will separate them one from another, as a shepherd separates the sheep from the goats. He will place the sheep on his right and the goats on his left. Then the king will say to those on his right, 'Come, you who are blessed by my Father. . . . For I was hungry and you gave me food, I was thirsty and you gave me drink, a stranger and you welcomed me, naked and you clothed me, ill and you cared for me, in prison and you visited me.'"

Reflection

On this last Sunday of the liturgical year we read of the Last Judgment and the spiritual practices known to us as the corporal works of mercy. Further in this reading it is clear that those who feed the hungry, welcome the stranger, and visit the sick and imprisoned are unaware they are serving Christ. Recall Matthew's warning about performing religious acts to gain recognition (Matthew 6:1–18). This group has followed the way of Christ but not so that they would be rewarded. Disciples respond to human need simply because of the need.

Prayers

others may be added

To the Son of God, the Lord of Life, and the King of the Universe, we pray:

◆ Prince of Peace, hear us.

That the Church will hear the cry of the poor, we pray: ◆ That governments be attentive to the poor in their midst, we pray: ◆ For seekers of justice and makers of peace, we pray: ◆ For the ongoing work of the Catholic Campaign for Human Development, we pray: ◆ For those in paupers' graves, we pray: ◆

Our Father . . .

Christ our Lord,
you have shown us the way to you
through service to one another.
May we see you in broken lives as well as
in the breaking of bread.
Shepherd us in the path of justice, mercy,
and peace,
for you live and reign with God the Father
in the unity of the Holy Spirit,
one God, for ever and ever.
Amen.

✝ The Lord is my shepherd; there is nothing I shall want.

Monday, November 27, 2017
Weekday

✝ The Lord is my shepherd; there is nothing I shall want.

Psalm 23

page 403

Reading

Daniel 1:8, 12–17

Daniel was resolved not to defile himself with the king's food or wine; so he begged the chief chamberlain to spare him this defilement. "Please test your servants for ten days. Give us vegetables to eat and water to drink. Then see how we look in comparison with the other young men who eat from the royal table, and treat your servants according to what you see." He acceded to this request, and tested them for ten days; after ten days they looked healthier and better fed than any of the young men who ate from the royal table. So the steward continued to take away the food and wine they were to receive, and gave them vegetables.

To these four young men God gave knowledge and proficiency in all literature and science, and to Daniel the understanding of all visions and dreams.

Reflection

The Book of Daniel was written during the persecution of Antiochus IV, which led to the Jewish revolt related in 1 Maccabees. The book is named not for its author but for the book's hero, Daniel. The story, set during the time of the Babylonian exile, tells the story of this hero of former days under a previous time of captivity and persecution. In telling this story, the author intends to inspire his contemporaries to endure great sacrifice to remain faithful to God and the covenant. Who are heroes of the past who inspire you? How do their lives and witness speak to your situation?

Prayers

others may be added

To the Son of God, the Lord of Life, and the King of the Universe, we pray:

◆ Prince of Peace, hear us.

May the People of God draw wisdom and fortitude from those who have gone before us, we pray: ◆ For our local civic leaders, we pray: ◆ For those experiencing marital difficulties, we pray: ◆ That young adults may find models and mentors for living the faith, we pray: ◆ For the coldhearted, we pray: ◆

Our Father . . .

God of our ancestors,
from one generation to the next
you are our refuge and our strength.
Teach us to learn from our past and the history of our faith.
May this collective wisdom steer us through confusing and uncertain times.
We ask this through Christ our Lord.
Amen.

✝ The Lord is my shepherd; there is nothing I shall want.

Tuesday, November 28, 2017
Weekday

✝ The Lord is my shepherd; there is nothing I shall want.

Psalm 23

page 403

Reading

Daniel 2:31, 37–40a, 44

Daniel said to Nebuchadnezzar: "In your vision, O king, you saw a statue, very large and exceedingly bright, terrifying in appearance as it stood before you.

"You, O king, are the king of kings; to you the God of heaven has given dominion and strength, power and glory; men, wild beasts, and birds of the air, wherever they may dwell, he has handed over to you, making you ruler over them all; you are the head of gold. Another kingdom shall take your place, inferior to yours, then a third kingdom of bronze, which shall rule over the whole earth. Then there shall be a fourth kingdom as strong as iron. In the lifetime of those kings the God of heaven will set up a kingdom that shall never be destroyed or delivered up to another people; rather, it shall break in pieces all these kingdoms and put an end to them, and it shall stand forever."

Reflection

Although Daniel is often grouped with the Old Testament prophets, the Book of Daniel is properly considered an apocalyptic text, like the Book of Revelation. *Apocalyptic* means *revelation.* This writing style was popular from about 200 BC through the time of Jesus. It arises as a response to persecution and is characterized by symbols, cosmic battles between good and evil, and divine intervention.

The materials comprising the great statue are understood to represent the past kingdoms that have conquered and suppressed the Jewish people for centuries. Daniel concludes with the promise that God will establish a kingdom that will stand forever.

Prayers

others may be added

To the Son of God, the Lord of Life, and the King of the Universe, we pray:

◆ Prince of Peace, hear us.

May the Church and all people of good will advance together toward the Reign of God, we pray: ◆ May we remain faithful to our Baptism, we pray: ◆ For peace in our world, in our homes, and in our hearts, we pray: ◆ May people be lifted up through their faith, we pray: ◆ That those facing the end of their days be thankful for what has been and be confident in God's love, we pray: ◆

Our Father . . .

Source of Life and Goodness,
for all eternity you live in
unapproachable light.
Stir our hearts
to know your presence in the activities
and events of our lives.
We ask this through Christ our Lord.
Amen.

✝ The Lord is my shepherd; there is nothing I shall want.

Wednesday, November 29, 2017
Weekday

✝ The Lord is my shepherd; there is nothing I shall want.

Psalm 23 *page 403*

Reading *Daniel 5:17, 23–24*

Daniel answered the king: "You may keep your gifts or give your presents to someone else; but the writing I will read for you, O king, and tell you what it means. You have rebelled against the Lord of heaven. You had the vessels of his temple brought before you, so that you and your nobles, your wives and your entertainers, might drink wine from them; and you praised the gods of silver and gold, bronze and iron, wood and stone, that neither see nor hear nor have intelligence. But the God in whose hand is your life breath and the whole course of your life, you did not glorify. By him were the wrist and hand sent, and the writing sent down."

Reflection

Daniel is empowered to read what nobody else can. He chastises the king for rebelling against the Lord and for worshipping idols. Soon, this kingdom will be history. Similar to Daniel, the Servant of God Dorothy Day, who died on this day in 1980, heard God's summons to conversion. Together with Peter Maurin she founded the Catholic Worker. Her memory continues to challenge the idols of our era as her legacy calls us to embrace voluntary poverty, shelter the homeless, resist violence, and practice the corporal works of mercy (Matthew 25).

Prayers *others may be added*

To the Son of God, the Lord of Life, and the King of the Universe, we pray:

◆ Prince of Peace, hear us.

Through the practice of mercy may the Church evangelize and change hearts, we pray: ◆ That we, the baptized, may examine the idols in our lives, we pray: ◆ For those who minister at Catholic Worker houses of hospitality, we pray: ◆ For catechumens, we pray: ◆ For pacifists, we pray: ◆

Our Father . . .

Lord Jesus,
you lived in solidarity with the poor and the outcasts.
As Advent draws near,
may we know you both in the breaking of bread
and in the person who is looking for our care and concern.
You live and reign with God the Father in the unity of the Holy Spirit,
one God, for ever and ever.
Amen.

✝ The Lord is my shepherd; there is nothing I shall want.

Thursday, November 30, 2017

Feast of St. Andrew, Apostle

✝ The Lord is my shepherd; there is nothing I shall want.

Psalm 23

page 403

Reading

Matthew 4:18–22

As Jesus was walking by the Sea of Galilee, he saw two brothers, Simon who is called Peter, and his brother Andrew, casting a net into the sea; they were fishermen. He said to them, "Come after me, and I will make you fishers of men." At once they left their nets and followed him. He walked along from there and saw two other brothers, James, the son of Zebedee, and his brother John. They were in a boat, with their father Zebedee, mending their nets. He called them, and immediately they left their boat and their father and followed him.

Reflection

St. Andrew is highly esteemed in the Orthodox Church. In Matthew, Simon Peter and Andrew are called together; but in John, Andrew follows Jesus and then invites his brother, Simon Peter, to discipleship. Thus, in Eastern Orthodoxy, Andrew is known as "the first called." Legend has Andrew founding the See of Byzantium (Constantinople.) Feeding this tradition is the oddity that the name *Andrew* is Greek in origin and has no Aramaic or Hebrew equivalent. Also, in John 12, Andrew acts as a bridge to the Gentiles when some Greeks ask to see Jesus. Andrew is clearly a "fisher of men" and one who summons us to the ministry of evangelization.

Prayers

others may be added

To Christ, the King of the Universe, we pray:

◆ Prince of Peace, hear us.

May the Church preach the Gospel to all nations, we pray: ◆ For the Eastern Orthodox Church, we pray: ◆ For those who fish commercially, we pray: ◆ For parishes celebrating their patronal feast today, we pray: ◆

Our Father . . .

Lamb of God,
you gave Andrew the insight to want to follow you.
Fill us with confidence in sharing our faith
so that we too will guide others to believe in you,
who live and reign with God the Father in the unity of the Holy Spirit,
one God, for ever and ever.
Amen.

✝ The Lord is my shepherd; there is nothing I shall want.

Friday, December 1, 2017
Weekday

✝ The Lord is my shepherd; there is nothing I shall want.

Psalm 23
page 403

Reading
Luke 21:29–33

Jesus told his disciples a parable. "Consider the fig tree and all the other trees. When their buds burst open, you see for yourselves and know that summer is now near; in the same way, when you see these things happening, know that the Kingdom of God is near. Amen, I say to you, this generation will not pass away until all these things have taken place. Heaven and earth will pass away, but my words will not pass away."

Reflection
"Know that the Kingdom of God is near." Jesus says this generation will not pass away until these things take place. Yet clearly that generation has passed away. In Luke's Gospel, we are now on the threshhold of Jesus' Passion, Death, and Resurrection. In these life-giving events, the Kingdom of God is realized, thus "this generation" did not pass away before these things took place. As Advent draws near, we too must read the signs of the times.

Prayers
others may be added

To the Son of God, the Lord of Life, and the King of the Universe, we pray:

◆ Prince of Peace, hear us.

For the Church universal, we pray: ◆ For the cessation of violence in our streets, we pray: ◆ That we will make time to prepare ourselves for a new liturgical year, we pray: ◆ For writers, we pray: ◆ For those who have died, we pray: ◆

Our Father . . .

God of all times and seasons,
you have given us your Word that will never pass away.
Be with us as we move forward into a new liturgical year.
Keep us attentive to the grace given us
and help us to read the signs of the times and the presence of your Son,
who lives and reigns with you in the unity of the Holy Spirit,
one God, for ever and ever.
Amen.

✝ The Lord is my shepherd; there is nothing I shall want.

Saturday, December 2, 2017
Weekday

✝ The Lord is my shepherd; there is nothing I shall want.

Psalm 23
page 403

Reading
Luke 21:34–36

Jesus said to his disciples: "Beware that your hearts do not become drowsy from carousing and drunkenness and the anxieties of daily life, and that day catch you by surprise like a trap. For that day will assault everyone who lives on the face of the earth. Be vigilant at all times and pray that you have the strength to escape the tribulations that are imminent and to stand before the Son of Man."

Reflection
The cry to be vigilant informs us that Advent is knocking on our door. How hard it is to be vigilant and attentive, especially with the busyness already buzzing around us. Then again, perhaps the coming mayhem would be less stressful if we practiced being attentive. Vigilance and prayer might help us to escape the imminent tribulations. Those spiritual practices can also, however, direct us into the eye of the storm. Some today will pause to remember Ursuline Sister Dorothy Kazel, Maryknoll Sisters Ita Ford and Maura Clarke, and lay missionary Jean Donovan, who were raped and murdered in El Salvador on December 2, 1980.

Prayers
others may be added

To the Son of God, the Lord of Life, and the King of the Universe, we pray:

◆ Prince of Peace, hear us.

May the blood of the martyrs and the witness of holy men and women strengthen the faith of the Church, we pray: ◆ For those serving the Church as missionaries, we pray: ◆ For those who seek justice for the poor, we pray: ◆ That we practice attentiveness, we pray: ◆ May the joy that is ours from following Christ be apparent in our lives, we pray: ◆

Our Father . . .

God of tenderness,
you offer us your loving embrace.
In being attentive to your Word,
may we be gentle to those we meet.
We ask this through Christ our Lord.
Amen.

✝ The Lord is my shepherd; there is nothing I shall want.

Sunday, December 3, 2017
First Sunday of Advent

✝ Come to us, O Emmanuel.

Psalm 80 *page 411*

Reading *Mark 13:33–37*

Jesus said to his disciples: "Be watchful! Be alert! You do not know when the time will come. It is like a man traveling abroad. He leaves home and places his servants in charge, each with his own work, and orders the gatekeeper to be on the watch. Watch, therefore; you do not know when the Lord of the house is coming, whether in the evening, or at midnight, or at cockcrow, or in the morning. May he not come suddenly and find you sleeping. What I say to you, I say to all: 'Watch!'"

Reflection

Watching or waiting? Which are we engaged in this Advent? Waiting implies passivity, a tacit acceptance of one's fate. This is not the Gospel of Mark, the Gospel account that begins today that we will read throughout the year. The sacred author propels his Gospel forward. From his language, to the images he uses, to his style, Mark encourages us to press forward to the Cross. Watching is an active word. We are to be attentive. All our senses are alert and ready for Jesus to come into our lives and our world. So, which are we? Are our lives about a passive acceptance of events, or are we helping with the building of the Reign of God?

Prayers *others may be added*

To Emmanuel, we pray:

◆ Hear us, O Lord.

That the Church will be a beacon of compassion and a voice of justice, we pray: ◆ That when the Lord comes, he will meet us doing right, we pray: ◆ That hearts hardened by bitterness will be softened, we pray: ◆ That the Lord will protect those who face violence at home, we pray: ◆ That God will remember all who sleep in the peace of death, we pray: ◆

Our Father . . .

Come, Emmanuel,
Holy One of God.
Empower us to continue to build up
your Reign.
When you come in glory,
may you find your disciples alive in
the Spirit
and watchful for your return.
We ask this through our Lord Jesus
Christ, your Son,
who lives and reigns with you in the unity
of the Holy Spirit,
one God, for ever and ever.
Amen.

✝ Come to us, O Emmanuel.

Monday, December 4, 2017
Advent Weekday

✝ Come to us, O Emmanuel.

Psalm 80

page 411

Reading

Matthew 8:5–11

When Jesus entered Capernaum, a centurion approached him and appealed to him, saying, "Lord, my servant is lying at home paralyzed, suffering dreadfully." He said to him, "I will come and cure him." The centurion said in reply, "Lord, I am not worthy to have you enter under my roof; only say the word and my servant will be healed. For I too am a man subject to authority, with soldiers subject to me. And I say to one, 'Go,' and he goes; and to another, 'Come here,' and he comes; and to my slave, 'Do this,' and he does it." When Jesus heard this, he was amazed and said to those following him, "Amen, I say to you, in no one in Israel have I found such faith. I say to you, many will come from the east and the west, and will recline with Abraham, Isaac, and Jacob at the banquet in the Kingdom of heaven."

Reflection

Today's image of the centurion is a familiar one, as his response to Jesus is our response just prior to Communion. "Lord, I am not worthy . . . ." This statement is not one of shame, but of humility. The truly humble person acknowledges his/her rightful place. Jesus Christ is Lord. He has the authority. The type of authority Jesus wields is one of compassion. How do we lead? When we exercise authority at home or work, do we seek to follow Jesus?

Prayers

others may be added

To Emmanuel, we pray:

◆ Hear us, O Lord.

May our Church lead with compassion and mercy, we pray: ◆ May we hear the voice of the powerless, we pray: ◆ May nations be powerful in ways of peace, we pray: ◆ May those who speak with anger, be converted to love and tenderness, we pray: ◆ May victims of violence find healing, we pray: ◆

Our Father . . .

All powerful God,
in you is found supreme authority,
yet you wield your command in love
and mercy.
Teach us to be like you.
May understanding and kindness be our
only weapons.
We ask this through Christ our Lord.
Amen.

✝ Come to us, O Emmanuel.

Tuesday, December 5, 2017
Advent Weekday

✝ Come to us, O Emmanuel.

Psalm 80
page 411

Reading
Luke 10:21–24

Jesus rejoiced in the Holy Spirit and said, "I give you praise, Father, Lord of heaven and earth, for although you have hidden these things from the wise and the learned you have revealed them to the childlike. Yes, Father, such has been your gracious will. All things have been handed over to me by my Father. No one knows who the Son is except the Father, and who the Father is except the Son and anyone to whom the Son wishes to reveal him."

Turning to the disciples in private he said, "Blessed are the eyes that see what you see. For I say to you, many prophets and kings desired to see what you see, but did not see it, and to hear what you hear, but did not hear it."

Reflection

"Jesus rejoiced in the Holy Spirit." This theme of the Holy Spirit regarding prayer is constant in the Gospel of Luke. When we pray we place ourselves consciously in the presence of God. We always live in God, but prayer adds the dimension of recognition. We acknowledge God's movement, love, and wisdom. Too often we want to "feel something" when we pray. Or we want an answer to our request. The more important facet of praying is remembering the presence of God and seeking communion with the Lord.

Prayers
others may be added

To Emmanuel, we pray:

◆ Hear us, O Lord.

May our Church be a constant witness to God's presence in the world, we pray: ◆ May the Spirit transform places of war to lands of abundant peace, we pray: ◆ May we seek to deepen our prayer life, we pray: ◆ For all whose prayer feels arid, we pray: ◆ For communities of contemplative women and men, we pray: ◆

Our Father . . .

In you, O Lord,
we live and move and have our being.
Each day is filled with your
abundant blessings.
May we be ever mindful of your presence
and embrace your Spirit blowing through
our world.
We ask this through Christ our Lord.
Amen.

✝ Come to us, O Emmanuel.

Wednesday, December 6, 2017
Optional Memorial of St. Nicholas, Bishop

✝ Come to us, O Emmanuel.

Psalm 80 *page 411*

Reading *Isaiah 6:1–8*

In the year King Uzziah died, I saw the Lord seated on a high and lofty throne, with the train of his garment filling the temple. Seraphim were stationed above; each of them had six wings: with two they veiled their faces, with two they veiled their feet, and with two they hovered aloft.

"Holy, holy, holy is the LORD of hosts!" they cried, one to the other. All the earth is filled with his glory!" At the sound of that cry, the frame of the door shook and the house was filled with smoke.

Then I said, "Woe is me, I am doomed! For I am a man of unclean lips, living among a people of unclean lips; yet my eyes have seen the King, the LORD of hosts!" Then one of the seraphim flew to me, holding an ember which he had taken with tongs from the altar.

He touched my mouth with it and said, "See, now that this has touched your lips, your wickedness is removed, your sin purged."

Then I heard the voice of the LORD saying, "Whom shall I send? Who will go for us?" "Here I am," I said; "send me!"

Reflection

This section of Isaiah exemplifies the biblical motif of a call story. A mission is always attached to a call. Nicholas, bishop of Myra, heard such a call. The most famous story of his good work tells about how, in the dead of night, he threw a bag of gold into a poor man's home as a dowry for his daughter. He did this two more times, ensuring the marriage and care for three young women. Thus is the origin of the Santa Claus myth. However, Nicholas was much more than a nocturnal present giver. He guided his church community though a turbulent time of heresy by his active prayer life and care for them.

Prayers *others may be added*

To Emmanuel, we pray:

◆ Hear us, O Lord.

For the Church, that in her benevolence, she hears the cry of the poor, we pray: ◆ For hearts freely giving to all in need, we pray: ◆ For world leaders, that they will encourage their citizens to share their bounty, that all might be fed, we pray: ◆ For a spirit of courage in the face of hostility, we pray: ◆ For hostages and all who live in terror today, we pray: ◆

Our Father . . .

Gracious God,
you inspired St. Nicholas to creatively
care for the poor.
Open our minds as well.
May we think beyond standard ways of
doing things
and seek to be imaginative in our love.
We ask this through Christ our Lord.
Amen.

✝ Come to us, O Emmanuel.

Thursday, December 7, 2017
Memorial of St. Ambrose, Bishop and Doctor of the Church

✝ Come to us, O Emmanuel.

Psalm 80

page 411

Reading

Matthew 7:21, 24–27

Jesus said to his disciples: "Not everyone who says to me, 'Lord, Lord,' will enter the Kingdom of heaven, but only the one who does the will of my Father in heaven.

"Everyone who listens to these words of mine and acts on them will be like a wise man who built his house on rock. The rain fell, the floods came, and the winds blew and buffeted the house. But it did not collapse; it had been set solidly on rock. And everyone who listens to these words of mine but does not act on them will be like a fool who built his house on sand. The rain fell, the floods came, and the winds blew and buffeted the house. And it collapsed and was completely ruined."

Reflection

St. Ambrose of Milan is one of the most influential theologians, liturgists, and ecclesiastical administrators of the early Church. He led the Church in Milan, though he was chosen to be bishop by popular acclamation against his wishes. During a turbulent time in the fourth-century Church in which Arianism was debated, he led with wisdom, insight, and understanding. While he upheld the divinity of Jesus, he was merciful to the followers of Arianism.

Prayers

others may be added

To Emmanuel, we pray:

◆ Hear us, O Lord.

For bishops, may they lead by first listening to all their people, we pray: ◆ For the lost, lonely, and all who struggle with depression, we pray: ◆ For insight in times of moral chaos, we pray: ◆ For liturgists and theologians, we pray: ◆ For a willingness to live in mercy and peace with those who disagree with us, we pray: ◆

Our Father . . .

Lord of all,
you guided your servant Ambrose to lead
his people
with your love and wisdom.
Guide all who lead our Church today.
May they recognize the unity that is
found in diversity,
and embrace all who are entrusted
to their care.
We ask this through Christ our Lord.
Amen.

✝ Come to us, O Emmanuel.

Friday, December 8, 2017

Solemnity of the Immaculate Conception of the Blessed Virgin Mary

✝ Hail Mary full of grace! The Lord is with you.

Canticle of Mary

page 422

Reading

Luke 1:26–33

The angel Gabriel was sent from God to a town of Galilee called Nazareth, to a virgin betrothed to a man named Joseph, of the house of David, and the virgin's name was Mary. And coming to her, he said, "Hail, full of grace! The Lord is with you." But she was greatly troubled at what was said and pondered what sort of greeting this might be. Then the angel said to her, "Do not be afraid, Mary, for you have found favor with God. Behold, you will conceive in your womb and bear a son, and you shall name him Jesus. He will be great and will be called Son of the Most High, and the Lord God will give him the throne of David his father, and he will rule over the house of Jacob forever, and of his Kingdom there will be no end."

Reflection

Today's solemnity celebrates that Mary was conceived without Original Sin. Her willingness to do the will of God shows how she is a person who is "full of grace," as the Hail Mary states. As a person free from Original Sin, she embraces the place God has for her in the mystery of salvation.

Mary is an example of faith and trust in God. We know her by many names, and can look to her as a disciple. When we feel that God expects much of us, we can look to how she lived her faith.

Prayers

others may be added

To Emmanuel, we pray:

◆ Hear us, O Lord.

May your Church trust in your mysterious ways, we pray: ◆ May all peoples of the earth respect life from conception to natural death, we pray: ◆ May those who live in fear and oppression we pray: ◆ May pregnant woman have safety and health care, we pray: ◆ May we bring to birth the dreams God plans within us, we pray: ◆

Our Father . . .

Creator God,
you chose the Blessed Virgin Mary
to birth Jesus into our world.
Guide us as we seek to be your obedient servants too.
Show us the vision you have designed
and make us willing to take our place in your plan.
We ask this through Christ our Lord.
Amen.

✝ Hail Mary full of grace! The Lord is with you.

Saturday, December 9, 2017
Advent Weekday

✝ Come to us, O Emmanuel.

Psalm 80
page 411

Reading
Matthew 9:35–36, 10:1, 5a, 7

Jesus went around to all the towns and villages, teaching in their synagogues, proclaiming the Gospel of the Kingdom, and curing every disease and illness. At the sight of the crowds, his heart was moved with pity for them because they were troubled and abandoned, like sheep without a shepherd.

Then he summoned his Twelve disciples and gave them authority over unclean spirits to drive them out and to cure every disease and every illness.

Jesus sent out these Twelve after instructing them, "As you go, make this proclamation: 'The Kingdom of heaven is at hand.'"

Reflection
Jesus moves around a lot. He teaches; he heals. What does the Lord see in the crowds that are drawn to him? These individuals comprise lost sheep, individuals who are troubled and abandoned. They had leaders, both religious and civil, who did not serve them.

Jesus sends out the Twelve to care for other sheep. All of the baptized have been anointed to care for others. When you look around, do you see people who are troubled, who could be helped by a kind word, by a comforting look?

Prayers
others may be added

To Emmanuel, we pray:

◆ Hear us, O Lord.

May pastors see the pain of their parishioners, we pray: ◆ May minds tainted by racism and prejudice be healed, we pray: ◆ May those who hide domestic violence and abuse find healing and comfort, we pray: ◆ For victims of human trafficking, we pray: ◆ For all who struggle, we pray: ◆

Our Father . . .

God of all hopefulness,
open our eyes to the lost, lonely, and sorrowful in our community.
Support us as we seek to remove barriers between ourselves and others.
May we see as you see and act as you would act.
We ask this through Christ our Lord.
Amen.

✝ Come to us, O Emmanuel.

Sunday, December 10, 2017
Second Sunday of Advent

✝ Lord, let us see your kindness

Psalm 85

page 411

Reading

Mark 1:1–5, 7–8

The beginning of the gospel of Jesus Christ the Son of God.

As it is written in Isaiah the prophet: / *Behold, I am sending my messenger ahead of you; / he will prepare your way. / A voice of one crying out in the desert: / "Prepare the way of the Lord, / make straight his paths."* / John the Baptist appeared in the desert proclaiming a baptism of repentance for the forgiveness of sins. People of the whole Judean countryside and all the inhabitants of Jerusalem were going out to him and were being baptized by him in the Jordan River as they acknowledged their sins. . . . And this is what he proclaimed: "One mightier than I is coming after me. I am not worthy to stoop and loosen the thongs of his sandals. I have baptized you with water; he will baptize you with the Holy Spirit."

Reflection

The Gospel of Mark begins with John the Baptist in the desert. Dressed in camel's hair and eating locusts, he is not a pretty sight. The people, however, are drawn to John. What is there about John that captures your interest?

Advent is not a season to cover up our hunger, loneliness, or loss. Now is the time to hope and remember the power of the Gospel and Jesus' presence in the Gospel.

Prayers

others may be added

Turning to you, Lord, who offers salvation, we pray:

◆ Lord, give us hope.

May the Church proclaim comfort to the oppressed, and blessed assurance to all who walk in your way, we pray: ◆ May hardened hearts be softened, we pray: ◆ May our nation's leaders be filled with courage to speak the truth, we pray: ◆ May hope and trust in the Lord be restored, we pray: ◆ May the dying hear tender words at the end of life, we pray: ◆

Our Father . . .

Lord of hope,
you sent John the Baptist
to prepare the way to you.
Be with us as we ready our hearts
for your coming.
May your Gospel renew the face of
the earth.
We ask this through our Lord Jesus
Christ, your Son,
who lives and reigns with you in the unity
of the Holy Spirit,
one God, for ever and ever.
Amen.

✝ Lord, let us see your kindness.

Monday, December 11, 2017
Advent Weekday

✝ Lord, let us see your kindness.

Psalm 85
page 411

Reading
Luke 5:18–24

And some men brought on a stretcher a man who was paralyzed; they were trying to bring him in and set him in his presence. But not finding a way to bring him in because of the crowd, they went up on the roof and lowered him on the stretcher through the tiles into the middle in front of Jesus. When Jesus saw their faith, he said, "As for you, your sins are forgiven."

Then the scribes and Pharisees began to ask themselves, "Who is this who speaks blasphemies? Who but God alone can forgive sins?" Jesus knew their thoughts and said to them in reply, "What are you thinking in your hearts? Which is easier, to say, 'Your sins are forgiven,' or to say, 'Rise and walk'? But that you may know that the Son of Man has authority on earth to forgive sins"—he said to the man who was paralyzed, "I say to you, rise, pick up your stretcher, and go home."

Reflection
As you read today's Scripture, try to remove any negative images of the Pharisees. They are sitting at Jesus' feet while he heals. Yes, they ask themselves about his authority, but there is no anger in the story, just wonder and awe. Advent asks us to remember who is king and ruler in the world, ultimately. Let us seek to see God's work in the world with new eyes.

Prayers
others may be added

Turning to you, Lord, who offers salvation, we pray:

◆ Lord, hear us.

For a Church renewed in joy, delighting in the goodness of God, we pray: ◆ For a world without hatred, prejudice, or duplicitousness, we pray: ◆ For lives filled with bliss and wonder in the goodness of creation, we pray: ◆ For a greater effort to preserve our world from pollution, and all that destroys the earth, we pray: ◆ For those who today are in sorrow and who awaken in pain, we pray: ◆

Our Father . . .

God with us,
you teach us through your works.
We sit at your feet eager to learn.
As we contemplate your mystery, help us
to become people of hope and joy,
able to see the blessings you bestow on us
each day
and ready to share the Good News
with others.
We ask this through Christ our Lord.
Amen.

✝ Lord, let us see your kindness.

Tuesday, December 12, 2017

Feast of Our Lady of Guadalupe

☩ Lord, let us see your kindness.

Psalm 85

page 411

Reading

Luke 1:39–45

Mary set out in those days and traveled to the hill country in haste to a town of Judah, where she entered the house of Zechariah and greeted Elizabeth. When Elizabeth heard Mary's greeting, the infant leaped in her womb, and Elizabeth, filled with the Holy Spirit, cried out in a loud voice and said, "Most blessed are you among women, and blessed is the fruit of your womb. And how does this happen to me, that the mother of my Lord should come to me? For at the moment the sound of your greeting reached my ears, the infant in my womb leaped for joy. Blessed are you who believed that what was spoken to you by the Lord would be fulfilled."

Reflection

"And how does it happen that the mother of my Lord should come to me?" While these words are placed on the lips of Elizabeth in the Gospel, they could easily have been uttered by St. Juan Diego. In his humility he meets Our Lady and is given a message and a miracle of roses. Are we open to messages and miracles? Remember, a miracle in the Scriptures is a marvel or sign of God's power. So, are we able to hear the Word of God? Do we have eyes to see the work of God? Yes, sometimes it's hard to miss a spectacle, but more often miracles are simple and subtle. What will we witness today?

Prayers

others may be added

Turning to you, Lord, who offers salvation, we pray:

◆ **Lord, give us hope.**

May your Church give witness to the Gospel in humility, we pray: ◆ May the poor today receive food; may the homeless find shelter, we pray: ◆ May those deprived of dignity be given respect, we pray: ◆ May those who live in oppression find freedom, we pray: ◆ May pregnant women have just health care, we pray: ◆

Our Father . . .

Come to us, Gracious One.
Be with us in our need and in our longing.
In this Advent Time,
help us to live in humility before you
and in peace with each sister and brother
we meet.
We ask this through Christ our Lord.
Amen.

☩ Lord, let us see your kindness.

Wednesday, December 13, 2017

Memorial of St. Lucy, Virgin and Martyr

☩ Lord, let us see your kindness.

Psalm 85

page 411

Reading

Matthew 11:28–30

Jesus said to the crowds: "Come to me, all you who labor and are burdened, and I will give you rest. Take my yoke upon you and learn from me, for I am meek and humble of heart; and you will find rest for yourselves. For my yoke is easy, and my burden light."

Reflection

In these short days of December we celebrate St. Lucy, patron saint of those who are blind. Little is known for sure about Lucy, other than that she suffered and died during the persecution of Diocletian. However, many legends abound concerning her. The most common legend is that Lucy preferred to dedicate her life to Christ, rather than get married. The jilted suitor, in his anger, turned her over to the Roman authorities. They put out her eyes, so statues may be seen with Lucy holding them on a plate. The root of her name means "light" and so other images portray Lucy with an Advent wreath crowning her head.

We remember today a courageous young woman who could not be bullied into denying her Lord.

Prayers

others may be added

Turning to you, Lord, who offers salvation, we pray:

◆ Lord, hear our prayer.

For our Church, may we be a beacon to all who struggle to see the truth, we pray: ◆ For all who are blind in body or spirit, we pray: ◆ For community leaders, that they will seek an end to bullying in our schools, we pray: ◆ For victims of violence and intimidation, we pray: ◆ For a willingness to embrace our baptismal commitment to be light to our world, we pray: ◆

Our Father . . .

Wondrous Light,
St. Lucy willingly offered her life rather than deny you.
May we too be brave in times of trouble and may our faith shine brightly in the midst of conflict and hatred.
We ask this through Christ our Lord.
Amen.

☩ Lord, let us see your kindness.

Thursday, December 14, 2017

Memorial of St. John of the Cross,
Priest and Doctor of the Church

✝ Lord, let us see your kindness.

Psalm 85 *page 411*

Reading *Matthew 11:11–15*

Jesus said to the crowds: "Amen, I say to you, among those born of women there has been none greater than John the Baptist; yet the least in the Kingdom of heaven is greater than he. From the days of John the Baptist until now, the Kingdom of heaven suffers violence, and the violent are taking it by force. All the prophets and the law prophesied up to the time of John. And if you are willing to accept it, he is Elijah, the one who is to come. Whoever has ears ought to hear."

Reflection

John of the Cross was born in Spain in the mid-1500s, a child of poverty and hunger. As a teenager, he worked in a hospital amid the poor and ill. In all this he realized that true happiness is found only in God.

After John joined the Carmelites, St. Teresa of Avila asked him to help reform the Order. This work proved unpopular, and John was imprisoned. It was in prison that this great mystic wrote poetry about the love of God. He escaped and lived his life proclaiming the happiness found in the immensity of God's love.

Prayers *others may be added*

Turning to you, Lord, who offers salvation, we pray:

◆ Lord, hear our prayer.

For a Church overflowing with joy that comes from God, we pray: ◆ For the poor, we pray: ◆ For those in hospice units, we pray: ◆ For those experiencing the dark night of the soul, we pray: ◆ For members of the Carmelites, we pray: ◆

Our Father . . .

Lord of love,
you gave John of the Cross
the tenacity to endure great suffering
and still proclaim the immensity
of your love.
Give us a glimmer of the vision
you gave to him.
May we rejoice and find solace in you.
We ask this through Christ our Lord.
Amen.

✝ Lord, let us see your kindness.

Friday, December 15, 2017
Advent Weekday

✝ Lord, let us see your kindness.

Psalm 85
page 411

Reading
Matthew 11:16–19

Jesus said to the crowds: "To what shall I compare this generation? It is like children who sit in marketplaces and call to one another, 'We played the flute for you, but you did not dance, we sang a dirge but you did not mourn.' For John came neither eating nor drinking, and they said, 'He is possessed by a demon.' The Son of Man came eating and drinking and they said, 'Look, he is a glutton and a drunkard, a friend of tax collectors and sinners.' But wisdom is vindicated by her works."

Reflection
Have you ever felt trapped? No matter what you say, you're wrong? Jesus acknowledges this conundrum. The people say John the Baptist, who fasted, was possessed. They say that Jesus, who eats and drinks, is a drunkard. There is no pleasing them. What it comes down to is that these individuals are not interested in a spiritual life.

Where are you in your spiritual life today? What disciplines make up your spiritual practices? Consider which spiritual disciplines to add to your life during this new year. A new year's resolution may be to begin a new spiritual discipline.

Prayers
others may be added

Turning to you, Lord, who offers salvation, we pray:

◆ Lord, hear our prayer.

For mystics in the Church, we pray: ◆ For all who have lost faith and wander without direction, we pray: ◆ For all who struggle to find time to pray, we pray: ◆ For those with whom we have differences, we pray: ◆ For young adults and all who search for meaning in life, we pray: ◆

Our Father . . .

Lord of the Universe,
you are the source of all being and
all life.
You have gifted us with many paths
by which we may draw nearer to you.
Increase our faith;
guide our steps
so that we will be pulled into your
radiant peace.
We ask this through Christ our Lord.
Amen.

✝ Lord, let us see your kindness.

Saturday, December 16, 2017
Advent Weekday

✝ Lord, let us see your kindness.

Psalm 85 *page 411*

Reading *Matthew 17:9a, 10–13*

As they were coming down from the mountain, the disciples asked Jesus, "Why do the scribes say that Elijah must come first?" He said in reply, "Elijah will indeed come and restore all things; but I tell you that Elijah has already come, and they did not recognize him but did to him whatever they pleased. So also will the Son of Man suffer at their hands." Then the disciples understood that he was speaking to them of John the Baptist.

Reflection

The story of John the Baptist is told in snippets in the Gospel. Little is truly known about the man, but it is clear that he was a prophet in the image of Elijah. The prophet Elijah was carried away in a fiery chariot, and he was to return at the end time. Today's story links the two men, reminding us that with the Incarnation, Death, and Resurrection of Christ, the Reign of God has begun.

With Advent, we revel in the thought of God entering into human history. We are blessed to live in this glorious age.

Prayers *others may be added*

Turning to you, Lord, who offers salvation, we pray:

◆ Lord, hear our prayer.

For prophets in the Church, we pray: ◆ For blessed assurance in the power and Reign of God, we pray: ◆ For our nation's leaders, that they will speak out against injustice, we pray: ◆ For all who live on death row, we pray: ◆ For courage to speak truth to power, we pray: ◆

Our Father . . .

All powerful God,
the world is yours and all that dwells within it.
Your prophets proclaim truth to the powerful,
compassion to the sinful, and hope to all who despair.
As your disciples,
may we be counted worthy to lift our voices
in announcing your time of justice and peace to all the world.
We ask this through Christ our Lord.
Amen.

✝ Lord, let us see your kindness.

Sunday, December 17, 2017
Third Sunday of Advent

✝ Maranatha! Come, Emmanuel!

Psalm 85

page 411

Reading

John 1:6–8

A man named John was sent from God. He came for testimony, to testify to the light, so that all might believe through him. He was not the light, but came to testify to the light.

Reflection

From the onset of adolescence, to the end of our days we struggle with our identity. John the Baptist's certainty as to who he is not, and who he is, might make us envious. In considering who you are, you might want to reflect on the question, "Am I already in Christmas, or am I still in Advent?"

Much of the world around us is already in Christmas. To a certain extent, that is fine. Christ comes for all and therefore Christmas is for everyone. But Advent is a time just for believers, for those who are already aware of Christ's presence and with joy and patience await the fullness of his glory.

Prayers

others may be added

To the One who is coming soon,
we pray:

◆ O Wisdom, come.

May those who teach, preach, and proclaim the joy of the Gospel, we pray: ◆ For catechumens and candidates, we pray: ◆ For those who do not recognize the presence of Christ, we pray: ◆ For those who are filled with stress and anxiety, we pray: ◆ For those in prison, we pray: ◆

Our Father . . .

Lord God,
you are the ground of our being.
Confident in your love and providence,
may we go forward in hope and joy
this Advent
and trust in the promise of Christ's return
in glory.
We ask this through our Lord Jesus
Christ, your Son,
who lives and reigns with you in the unity
of the Holy Spirit,
one God, for ever and ever.
Amen.

✝ Maranatha! Come, Emmanuel!

Monday, December 18, 2017
Advent Weekday

✝ Maranatha! Come, Emmanuel!

Psalm 85 *page 411*

Reading *Matthew 1:18–21*

This is how the birth of Jesus Christ came about. When his mother Mary was betrothed to Joseph, but before they lived together, she was found with child through the Holy Spirit. Joseph her husband, since he was a righteous man, yet unwilling to expose her to shame, decided to divorce her quietly. Such was his intention when, behold, the angel of the Lord appeared to him in a dream and said, "Joseph, son of David, do not be afraid to take Mary your wife into your home. For it is through the Holy Spirit that this child has been conceived in her. She will bear a son and you are to name him Jesus, because he will save his people from their sins."

Reflection

The time of Advent is sadly abbreviated this year. Even though it is the Third Week of Advent, we are within a week from Christmas Day. Our attention turns to the first coming of Christ. Matthew focuses on Joseph, who, like his namesake in Genesis, receives God's Word in his dreams. More than one link to Judaism is at work here, however. In refusing to bring the weight of the Law upon Mary and by his willingness to take her into his home, Matthew establishes one of the central themes of his Gospel: fidelity to God demands not only observing the Law, but the understanding to go beyond it.

Prayers *others may be added*

To the One who is coming soon, we pray:

◆ O Adonai, hear our prayer.

May the Church be guided to compassion, we pray: ◆ May followers of Christ live not merely by the letter of the law, we pray: ◆ For husbands and wives dealing with the pain of infidelity, we pray: ◆ For those struggling with unwanted pregnancies, we pray: ◆ May our young see visions and our aged dream dreams, we pray: ◆

Our Father . . .

God of the covenant,
we are often limited by our perceptions.
Free us from the limitations we impose on ourselves
and guide us to be agents of your mercy.
We ask this through Christ our Lord.
Amen.

✝ Maranatha! Come, Emmanuel!

Tuesday, December 19, 2017
Advent Weekday

✝ Maranatha! Come, Emmanuel!

Psalm 85

page 411

Reading

Luke 1:13–16, 18–20, 25

But the angel said to him, "Do not be afraid, Zechariah, because your prayer has been heard. Your wife Elizabeth will bear you a son, and you shall name him John. And you will have joy and gladness, and many will rejoice at his birth, for he will be great in the sight of the Lord. He will drink neither wine nor strong drink. He will be filled with the Holy Spirit even from his mother's womb, and he will turn many of the children of Israel to the Lord their God."

Then Zechariah said to the angel, "How shall I know this? For I am an old man, and my wife is advanced in years." And the angel said to him in reply, "I am Gabriel, who stand before God. I was sent to speak to you and to announce to you this good news. But now you will be speechless and unable to talk until the day these things take place, because you did not believe my words, which will be fulfilled at their proper time."

After this time his wife Elizabeth conceived, and she went into seclusion for five months, saying, "So has the Lord done for me at a time when he has seen fit to take away my disgrace before others."

Reflection

Having a sense of purpose and a plan for our lives, managing our time, organization, communication these are all vital, especially in these stress-filled days. Still, we need to know that we are not in control. Elizabeth's words are filled with wisdom. "The Lord has done for me at a time when he has seen fit." Our Baptism charges us with growing in faith, being charitable, seeking justice, practicing the works of mercy. Through it all we remember that grace will come in God's time.

Prayers

others may be added

To the One who is coming soon,
we pray:

◆ O Stump of Jesse, come to our aid.

May your Church be the voice of the voiceless, we pray: ◆ May the earth learn justice and mercy, we pray: ◆ For all liturgical ministers, we pray: ◆ That our community leaders will encourage all to respect older adults, we pray: ◆ For those who are deaf or mute, we pray: ◆

Our Father . . .

Lord of the Universe,
your Word informs us
that there is a time to be silent and a time
to speak
May we learn from the silence of Sts.
Joseph and Zechariah
and those in monastic life.
Help us to quiet our lives and our minds
so as to simply be in your presence.
We ask this through Christ our Lord.
Amen.

✝ Maranatha! Come, Emmanuel!

Wednesday, December 20, 2017
Advent Weekday

✝ Maranatha! Come, Emmanuel!

Psalm 85 *page 411*

Reading *Luke 1:26–33*

The angel Gabriel was sent from God to a town of Galilee called Nazareth, to a virgin betrothed to a man named Joseph, of the house of David, and the virgin's name was Mary. And coming to her, he said, "Hail, favored one! The Lord is with you." But she was greatly troubled at what was said and pondered what sort of greeting this might be. Then the angel said to her, "Do not be afraid, Mary, for you have found favor with God. Behold, you will conceive in your womb and bear a son, and you shall name him Jesus. He will be great and will be called Son of the Most High, and the Lord God will give him the throne of David his father, and he will rule over the house of Jacob forever, and of his Kingdom there will be no end."

Reflection

The first lines of the Annunciation, which we hear today, seize our hearts with a hope beyond all hope. We can scarcely breathe, for something awesome is about to occur. The passage concludes with Mary's "fiat," spoken with the enthusiasm of one who places her trust in God. May we look to her as we profess the Creed, renew our baptismal promises, or declare our "Amen" to the Body and Blood of Christ. With Mary, we trust unconditionally in the One who has given the promise.

Prayers *others may be added*

To the One who is coming soon,
we pray:

◆ O Key of David, hear our prayer.

That the Church puts her trust in the promise of God, we pray: ◆ For our legislators that they exhibit an openness to life, we pray: ◆ For a spirit of awe and wonder, we pray: ◆ For the overlooked, we pray: ◆ For those who have gone before us, we pray: ◆

Our Father . . .

God of Life,
with the aid of your Holy Spirit,
help us to join with Mary in saying "yes"
to your will.
May we place our trust in you and in
your Wisdom.
We ask this through Christ our Lord.
Amen.

✝ Maranatha! Come, Emmanuel!

Thursday, December 21, 2017
Advent Weekday

✝ Maranatha! Come, Emmanuel!

Psalm 85
page 411

Reading
Luke 1:39–45

Mary set out in those days and traveled to the hill country in haste to a town of Judah, where she entered the house of Zechariah and greeted Elizabeth. When Elizabeth heard Mary's greeting, the infant leaped in her womb, and Elizabeth, filled with the Holy Spirit, cried out in a loud voice and said, "Most blessed are you among women, and blessed is the fruit of your womb. And how does this happen to me, that the mother of my Lord should come to me? For at the moment the sound of your greeting reached my ears, the infant in my womb leaped for joy. Blessed are you who believed that what was spoken to you by the Lord would be fulfilled."

Reflection
The Visitation, like the Annunciation, is a favorite scene for artists. The encounter of Mary and Elizabeth is a meeting of the generations. The elder, Elizabeth, filled with wisdom learned from life experience welcomes her young, frightened, and tentative kinswoman, Mary. Yet by her words, Elizabeth defers to Mary, calling her and the child in her womb blessed. She wonders how it is that Mary came to her, implying she should have gone to Mary who is carrying her Lord. It is a great irony that we should go before the Lord with our praise and thanksgiving, but instead, in Christ, God comes to us.

Prayers
others may be added

To the One who is coming soon,
we pray:

◆ O Radiant Dawn, hear our prayer.

That the Christian community be a sign of God's presence, we pray: ◆ For the ministry of evangelization, we pray: ◆ For the many women who so faithfully serve Christ and the Church, we pray: ◆ For expectant mothers, we pray: ◆ For those who will be setting out in haste to visit family and friends, we pray: ◆

Our Father . . .

Lord God,
as your Son humbled himself to share
in our humanity,
so too your servant Elizabeth
humbled herself
to defer to the mother of our Lord.
In doing the work of evangelization,
may we be willing to listen with openness
to another's story
and defer to them out of reverence
for Christ,
who lives and reigns with you in the unity
of the Holy Spirit,
one God, for ever and ever.
Amen.

✝ Maranatha! Come, Emmanuel!

Friday, December 22, 2017
Advent Weekday

✝ Maranatha! Come, Emmanuel!

Psalm 85 *page 411*

Reading *Luke 1:46–56*

"My soul proclaims the greatness of the Lord; / my spirit rejoices in God my savior, / for he has looked upon his lowly servant. / From this day all generations will call me blessed: / the Almighty has done great things for me, / and holy is his Name. / He has mercy on those who fear him / in every generation. / He has shown the strength of his arm, / and has scattered the proud in their conceit. / He has cast down the mighty from their thrones / and has lifted up the lowly. / He has filled the hungry with good things, / and the rich he has sent away empty. / He has come to the help of his servant Israel / for he remembered his promise of mercy, / the promise he made to our fathers, / to Abraham and his children for ever." /

Mary remained with Elizabeth about three months and then returned to her home.

Reflection

Mary's song has many similarities with the lesser known Song of Hannah in 1 Samuel 2:1–10. Luke may have used the verses from Samuel as the basis for Mary's proclamation. The woman behind the *Magnificat* is filled with the fire of faith and social change. Here Luke brings together his key themes: the dignity of women, the liberation of the poor, God's protection of the lowly, and prayer.

Prayers *others may be added*

To the One who is coming soon,
we pray:

◆ O King of all nations, hear us.

For the bishop of Rome and all bishops, we pray: ◆ May the hungry be fed with good things, we pray: ◆ May we too remember the promise of mercy, we pray: ◆ For community organizers and all who advocate on behalf of the poor, we pray: ◆ May we respond to the call of peace in a world of violence, we pray: ◆

Our Father . . .

God of holiness,
as we make ready to celebrate the
mystery of the Incarnation,
may we come to those in need
as you came to us in your Son:
lifting up the lowly, feeding the hungry,
and remembering your mercy.
We ask this through Christ our Lord.
Amen.

✝ Maranatha! Come, Emmanuel!

Saturday, December 23, 2017
Advent Weekday

☩ Maranatha! Come, Emmanuel!

Psalm 85 *page 411*

Reading *Luke 1:57–63*

When the time arrived for Elizabeth to have her child she gave birth to a son. Her neighbors and relatives heard that the Lord had shown his great mercy toward her, and they rejoiced with her. When they came on the eighth day to circumcise the child, they were going to call him Zechariah after his father, but his mother said in reply, "No. He will be called John." But they answered her, "There is no one among your relatives who has this name." So they made signs, asking his father what he wished him to be called. He asked for a tablet and wrote, "John is his name," and all were amazed.

Reflection

Both the birth of John the Baptist and the birth of Christ are gifts from God. Both Mary and Elizabeth accepted with love their sons as unexpected gifts. Through these births, we see how God surprises and leads people to new ways and paths. It is up to the recipient of the marvels that God works to trust in the ways of the Lord. Once Zechariah showed that he trusted in God, the gift of speech was returned to him.

Prayers *others may be added*

To the One who is coming soon,
we pray:

◆ O Emmanuel, hear our prayer.

For the universal Church, we pray: ◆ That we may seek to live in a way that is worthy of the call we have received, we pray: ◆ That we may be grateful for gifts given and received, we pray: ◆ That our community leaders encourage cooperation, we pray: ◆ For those working in retail stores, we pray: ◆

Our Father . . .

Lover of humanity,
we give thanks for all the gifts you pour forth upon us.
May we be less concerned with ranking their value
but see all as important signs of your love and mercy.
We ask this through Christ our Lord.
Amen.

☩ Maranatha! Come, Emmanuel!

Sunday, December 24, 2017

Fourth Sunday of Advent

✝ Forever I will sing the goodness of the Lord.

Psalm 89

page 412

Reading

Luke 1:26–30a, 35b–38b

The angel Gabriel was sent from God to a town of Galilee called Nazareth, to a virgin betrothed to a man named Joseph, of the house of David, and the virgin's name was Mary. And coming to her, he said, "Hail, full of grace! The Lord is with you." But she was greatly troubled at what was said and pondered what sort of greeting this might be. Then the angel said to her, "Do not be afraid, Mary . . . the Holy Spirit will come upon you, and the power of the Most High will overshadow you. Therefore the child to be born will be called holy, the Son of God. And behold, Elizabeth, your relative, has also conceived a son in her old age, and this is the sixth month for her who was called barren; for nothing will be impossible for God." Mary said, "Behold, I am the handmaid of the Lord. May it be done to me according to your word."

Reflection

Scripture scholar Raymond E. Brown, ss, maintained that Matthew's genealogy contains the essential theology of the Old and New Testaments. He also stated that we need to read it at least once a year (*A Coming Christ in Advent*. Collegeville: The Liturgical Press, 1988). Jesus comes from the Jewish patriarchs; from noble kings and scoundrel kings that were unfaithful to God; from Jews and non-Jews; from holy women and women with checkered pasts; and from those who are only names to us. Reflect on who called you to faith and the people you have called to faith.

Prayers

others may be added

To the Word made flesh, we pray:

◆ Lord Jesus, hear our prayer:

May all the Church rejoice this night, we pray: ◆ Prince of Peace, move our hearts to choose forgiveness, we pray: ◆ Splendor of the Father, allow us to experience awe and wonder of your Incarnation, we pray: ◆ Word made flesh, may your becoming human help us to know the dignity of our body and the bodies of others, we pray: ◆

Our Father . . .

God of endless ages,
generations have kept vigil
to see what we see but did not see it
and to hear what we hear but did not
hear it.
May our joy in the mystery of
the Incarnation
resound in words and acts of
loving kindness.
Through our Lord Jesus Christ, your Son,
who lives and reigns with you in the unity
of the Holy Spirit,
one God, for ever and ever.
Amen.

✝ Forever I will sing the goodness of the Lord.

Monday, December 25, 2017
Solemnity of the Nativity of the Lord

☩ Let the heavens be glad and the earth rejoice!

Psalm 96 *page 413*

Reading *Luke 2:8–14*

Now there were shepherds in that region living in the fields and keeping the night watch over their flock. The angel of the Lord appeared to them and the glory of the Lord shone around them, and they were struck with great fear. The angel said to them, "Do not be afraid; for behold, I proclaim to you good news of great joy that will be for all the people. For today in the city of David a savior has been born for you who is Christ and Lord. And this will be a sign for you: you will find an infant wrapped in swaddling clothes and lying in a manger." And suddenly there was a multitude of the heavenly host with the angel, praising God and saying: / "Glory to God in the highest / and on earth peace to those on whom his favor rests." /

Reflection

Consider your favorite Christmas story. Christmas stories vary in terms of setting, character, and context; yet the great stories of Christmas are stories of redemption. They mimic and summon us to do what God does in the Incarnation: embrace humanity. As stories of redemption, they call us to live the reclamation that we confess by being people of mercy, generosity, peace, and forgiveness.

Prayers *others may be added*

To the Word made flesh, we pray:

◆ Lord Jesus, hear our prayer.

May our celebration of the coming of Emmanuel, enkindle the flame of faith given to us in Baptism, we pray: ◆ May leaders of nations pursue true and lasting peace, we pray: ◆ May divided families feel solace, we pray: ◆ May those who are homeless be protected, we pray: ◆ May those who have gone be received with mercy, we pray: ◆

Our Father . . .

Lover of humankind,
by the Incarnation of your Son,
you invite us to love and to ponder
more deeply
the mystery of our wondrous humanity.
May we be confident in your gift
of redemption.
Through our Lord Jesus Christ, your Son,
who lives and reigns with you
in the unity of the Holy Spirit,
one God, for ever and ever.
Amen.

☩ Let the heavens be glad and the earth rejoice!

Tuesday, December 26, 2017
Feast of St. Stephen, the First Martyr

✝ Let the heavens be glad and the earth rejoice!

Psalm 96
page 413

Reading
Acts 6:8–10; 7:54–59

Stephen, filled with grace and power, was working great wonders and signs among the people. Certain members of the so-called Synagogue of Freedmen, Cyrenians, and Alexandrians, and people from Cilicia and Asia, came forward and debated with Stephen, but they could not withstand the wisdom and the spirit with which he spoke.

When they heard this, they were infuriated, and they ground their teeth at him. But he, filled with the Holy Spirit, looked up intently to heaven and saw the glory of God and Jesus standing at the right hand of God, and he said, "Behold, I see the heavens opened and the Son of Man standing at the right hand of God." But they cried out in a loud voice, covered their ears, and rushed upon him together. They threw him out of the city, and began to stone him. . . . As they were stoning Stephen, he called out "Lord Jesus, receive my spirit."

Reflection
On the day after Christmas, the Church commemorates the first martyr, the deacon, Stephen. All we know of Stephen is found in the Acts of the Apostles. He was among those chosen to ensure that food was distributed fairly to the Greek-speaking widows. His death highlights the tragedy of religious persecution that continues to be all too real in the twenty-first century.

Prayers
others may be added

To the Word made flesh, we pray:

◆ **Lord Jesus, hear our prayer.**

For those who serve the Church as deacons, we pray: ◆ That religious leaders will engage in interreligious dialogue leading to mutual understanding and acceptance, we pray: ◆ That governments refrain from using the faith of people for political opportunism or an excuse for aggressive violence, we pray: ◆ For those persecuted for obeying the dictates of their conscience, we pray: ◆

Our Father . . .

God of creation,
you give us all that is good.
Guide us to act as Stephen and care for
the bodily needs of the poor.
By the words and example of your Son
and the witness of the martyrs,
may we be inspired to share our
abundance with those dwelling in want.
We ask this through Christ our Lord.
Amen.

✝ Let the heavens be glad and the earth rejoice!

Wednesday, December 27, 2017

Feast of St. John, Apostle and Evangelist

✝ Let the heavens be glad and the earth rejoice!

Psalm 96

page 413

Reading

I John 1:1–4

Beloved: What was from the beginning, / what we have heard, / what we have seen with our eyes, / what we looked upon / and touched with our hands / concerns the Word of life— / for the life was made visible; / we have seen it and testify to it / and proclaim to you the eternal life / that was with the Father and was made visible to us— / what we have seen and heard / we proclaim now to you, / so that you too may have fellowship with us; / for our fellowship is with the Father / and with his Son, Jesus Christ. / We are writing this so that our joy may be complete.

Reflection

So much of what of what comprises our Christmas celebrations and gatherings has been handed on to us. We make the foods we do, for example, because that is what our mother did (and probably our grandmother and beyond). We hang ornaments that have been on our tree for generations, and we tell their story.

Today's Epistle honors St. John by capturing the theme from the Johannine writings of disciples calling other disciples. We share with our children, family members, friends, and coworkers what we have seen and heard, our stories of faith. This is the work of evangelization. This is how we pass on our story and the story of Jesus Christ.

Prayers

others may be added

To the Word made flesh, we pray:

◆ Lord Jesus, hear us.

That the ministry of evangelization take hold in the hearts of all God's people, we pray: ◆ For continued ecumenical dialogue, we pray: ◆ That parents act as the first teachers for their children in the life of faith, we pray: ◆ That we make room to prayerfully reflect on what we have seen and heard, we pray: ◆ For parishes celebrating their patronal feast today, we pray: ◆

Our Father . . .

God of enlightenment,
as we observe the feast of St. John,
may we contemplate the mystery of your
Son's Incarnation.
Help us to see that this is not only
a central belief
but one that gives meaning
to who we are and to what we do.
We ask this through Christ our Lord.
Amen.

✝ Let the heavens be glad and the earth rejoice!

Thursday, December 28, 2017

Feast of the Holy Innocents, Martyrs

✝ Let the heavens be glad and the earth rejoice!

Psalm 96

page 413

Reading

Matthew 2:13–15

When the magi had departed, behold, the angel of the Lord appeared to Joseph in a dream and said, "Rise, take the child and his mother, flee to Egypt, and stay there until I tell you. Herod is going to search for the child to destroy him." Joseph rose and took the child and his mother by night and departed for Egypt. He stayed there until the death of Herod, that what the Lord had said through the prophet might be fulfilled, / *Out of Egypt I called my son.*

Reflection

As we commemorate the Holy Innocents we think of all whose lives have ended prematurely due to illness, war, abuse, neglect, accident, or poverty. We might also recall those who were never afforded the chance to become who they are or share their skills. Convinced of their worthlessness, afflicted with mental illness, having no one to believe in or encourage them, they perish and remain forever unopened presents and gifts not given.

Prayers

others may be added

To the Word made flesh, we pray:

◆ Lord Jesus, hear our prayer.

For the Church, may she call forth the gifts of all her people, we pray: ◆ For all young lives taken prematurely, we pray: ◆ For women dealing with guilt and remorse in the aftermath of an abortion, we pray: ◆ For all victims of war, oppression, and violence, we pray: ◆ For those prevented from becoming who God intends them to be, we pray: ◆

Our Father . . .

Author of life,
your Son came that we might have life
and have it in abundance.
May we be a salve for those
who find it difficult
to discover the joy in this season,
so that they too will rejoice
in the Good News.
We ask this through Christ our Lord.
Amen.

✝ Let the heavens be glad and the earth rejoice!

Friday, December 29, 2017

Fifth Day within the Octave of Christmas

☩ Let the heavens be glad and the earth rejoice!

Psalm 96

page 413

Reading

1 John 2:3–6

Beloved: The way we may be sure that we know Jesus is to keep his commandments. Whoever says, "I know him," but does not keep his commandments is a liar, and the truth is not in him. But whoever keeps his word, the love of God is truly perfected in him. This is the way we may know that we are in union with him: whoever claims to abide in him ought to walk just as he walked.

Reflection

To know Christ means much more than to know of Christ or to believe in certain doctrines about Christ. Knowing Christ refers to a personal relationship that results in union with Christ. How many of us, when young, thought we were clever in discovering that biblically "to know" someone meant physically. How little did we grasp what is entailed in getting to know another, to know them so well that you can finish their sentences, discern their moods, and reverence their heart. This is the profoundly intimate union to which we are called and invited to live with Christ.

Prayers

others may be added

To the Word made flesh, we pray:

◆ Lord Jesus, hear us.

May we, the Church, love one another as Christ has loved us, we pray: ◆ May we love God with all our heart, all our soul, and all our mind, we pray: ◆ May we love our neighbor as ourself, we pray: ◆ May we love our enemies and pray for those who would harm us, we pray: ◆ May we do to others as we would want done to us we pray: ◆

Our Father . . .

God of the Covenant,
your Beloved Son became one with us in our humanity.
Through Word, sacrament, and ministry may we become one with Christ,
who lives and reigns with you in the unity of the Holy Spirit,
one God, for ever and ever.
Amen.

☩ Let the heavens be glad and the earth rejoice!

Saturday, December 30, 2017

Sixth Day within the Octave of Christmas

✝ Let the heavens be glad and the earth rejoice!

Psalm 96

page 413

Reading

Luke 2:36–38

There was a prophetess, Anna, the daughter of Phanuel, of the tribe of Asher. She was advanced in years, having lived seven years with her husband after her marriage, and then as a widow until she was eighty-four. She never left the temple, but worshiped night and day with fasting and prayer. And coming forward at that very time, she gave thanks to God and spoke about the child to all who were awaiting the redemption of Jerusalem.

Reflection

Luke tells us that Anna "never left the temple." Obviously she must return to her home, but Luke is speaking metaphorically.

Anna is a model of prayer for us, as she worships night and day. This Scripture suggests we think about our place in the worshipping assembly. Do we reflect on the interplay between Sunday worship and our daily life? Do we experience the liturgy of our life and our life in the liturgy? How aware are we that the Spirit of God dwells within us?

Prayers

others may be added

To the Word made flesh, we pray:

◆ Lord Jesus, hear our prayer.

For the bishop of Rome and all bishops, we pray: ◆ For all who serve the Church in lay ecclesial ministry, we pray: ◆ For catechumens and candidates, we pray: ◆ For older adults who are infirm, especially those in long-term care facilities, we pray: ◆ For the people of our parish, we pray: ◆

Our Father . . .

God ever faithful,
you call us to be your people,
to be builders of communities that praise you
in worship, service, education, and the nurturing of faith.
May we be worthy of the calling we have received.
We ask this through Christ our Lord.
Amen.

✝ Let the heavens be glad and the earth rejoice!

Sunday, December 31, 2017

The Feast of the Holy Family of Jesus, Mary, and Joseph

✝ The Lord has come to his people
and set them free.

Canticle of Zechariah *page 423*

Reading *Luke 2:25–32*

Now there was a man in Jerusalem whose name was Simeon. This man was righteous and devout, awaiting the consolation of Israel, and the Holy Spirit was upon him. It had been revealed to him by the Holy Spirit that he should not see death before he had seen the Christ of the Lord. He came in the Spirit into the temple; and when the parents brought in the child Jesus to perform the custom of the law in regard to him, he took him into his arms and blessed God, saying: / Now, Master, you may let your servant go / in peace, according to your word, / for my eyes have seen your salvation, / which you prepared in sight of all the peoples, / a light for revelation to the Gentiles, / and glory for your people Israel."

Reflection

As we honor the Holy Family, we also honor the family of the Church, the family of humankind, and our own family. Our feast coincides with the end of the calendar year. Shall we resist the celebrations of the secular new year? There is plenty worthy of resistance this night. Yet our faith is born of dying and rising, of endings and new beginnings; we are in this together. There is no "them." We are one family of God. "All belong to you, and you to Christ, and Christ to God" (1 Corinthians 3:23).

Prayers *others may be added*

To the Lord, who offers salvation,
we pray:

◆ Lord Jesus, hear our prayer.

For the family of the Church, we pray: ◆ That the human family will find the way to peace and understanding, we pray: ◆ May our nuclear family and extended family be a wellspring of safety, acceptance, and unconditional love, we pray: ◆ May our young look forward in hope and our elders look back in thanksgiving, we pray: ◆ For those who have died this year, may they know the fullness of life in the Kingdom of God, we pray: ◆

Our Father . . .

Holy One,
you dwell in eternity, where there are no years, months, or hours.
But we, your people, mark the shortness of time.
Help us to remain one in you and in peace with one another
as we claim the bond of humanity that unites us.
Through our Lord Jesus Christ, your Son,
who lives and reigns with you in the unity of the Holy Spirit,
one God, for ever and ever.
Amen.

✝ The Lord has come to his people
and set them free.

Psalter

Psalm 8:2ab and 5, 6–7, 8–9

O LORD, our Lord,
How glorious is your name over all the earth!
What is man that you should be mindful of him,
or the son of man that you should care for him?

You have made him little less than the angels,
and crowned him with glory and honor.
You have given him rule over the work of your hands,
putting all things under his feet.

All sheep and oxen,
yes, and the beasts of the field,
The birds of the air, the fishes of the sea,
and whatever swims the paths of the seas.

Psalm 16:1–2, 5, 7–8, 9–10, 11

Keep me, O God, for in you I take refuge;
I say to the LORD, "My Lord are you."
O LORD, my allotted portion and my cup,
you it is who hold fast my lot.

I bless the LORD who counsels me;
even in the night my heart exhorts me.
I set the LORD ever before me;
with him at my right hand I shall not be disturbed.

Therefore my heart is glad and my soul rejoices,
my body, too, abides in confidence;
because you will not abandon my soul to the netherworld,
nor will you suffer your faithful one to undergo corruption.

You will show me the path to life,
fullness of joys in your presence,
the delights at your right hand forever.

Psalm 19:8, 9, 10, 11

The law of the LORD is perfect,
refreshing the soul,
The decree of the LORD is trustworthy,
giving wisdom to the simple.

The precepts of the LORD are right,
rejoicing the heart.
The command of the LORD is clear,
enlightening the eye.

The fear of the LORD is pure,
enduring forever.
The ordinances of the LORD are true,
all of them just.

Psalm 22

All who see me scoff at me;
they mock me with parted lips, they wag their heads:
"He relied on the LORD; let him deliver him,
let him rescue him, if he loves him."

Indeed, many dogs surround me,
a pack of evildoers closes in upon me;
They have pierced my hands and my feet;
I can count all my bones.

They divide my garments among them,
and for my vesture they cast lots.
But you, O LORD, be not far from me;
O my help, hasten to aid me.

I will proclaim your name to my brethren;
in the midst of the assembly I will praise you:
"You who fear the LORD, praise him;
all you descendants of Jacob, give glory to him;
revere him, all you descendants of Israel!"

Psalm 23:1–3a, 3b–4, 5, 6

The LORD is my shepherd; I shall not want.
In verdant pastures he gives me repose;
Beside restful waters he leads me;
he refreshes my soul.
He guides me in right paths
for his name's sake.
Even though I walk in the dark valley
I fear no evil; for you are at my side
With your rod and your staff
that give me courage.

You spread the table before me
In the sight of my foes;
You anoint my head with oil;
my cup overflows.
Only goodness and kindness follow me
all the days of my life;
And I shall dwell in the house of the LORD
for years to come.

Psalm 24:1–2, 3–4, 5–6

The LORD's are the earth and its fullness;
the world and those who dwell in it.
For he founded it upon the seas
and established it upon the rivers.

Who can ascend the mountain of the LORD?
or who may stand in his holy place?
One whose hands are sinless, whose heart is clean,
who desires not what is vain.

He shall receive a blessing from the LORD,
a reward from God his savior.
Such is the race that seeks for him,
that seeks the face of the God of Jacob.

Psalm 25:4–5, 6–7, 8–9

Your ways, O LORD, make known to me;
teach me your paths,
Guide me in your truth and teach me,
for you are God my savior.

Remember that your compassion, O LORD,
and your love are from of old.
The sins of my youth and my frailties remember not;
in your kindness remember me,
because of your goodness, O LORD.

Good and upright is the LORD;
thus he shows sinners the way.
He guides the humble to justice,
and teaches the humble his way.

Psalm 27:1, 4, 13–14

The LORD is my light and my salvation;
whom should I fear?
The LORD is my life's refuge;
of whom should I be afraid?

One thing I ask of the LORD
all the days of my life,
That I may gaze on the loveliness of the LORD
and contemplate his temple.

I believe that I shall see the bounty of the LORD
in the land of the living.
Wait for the LORD with courage;
be stouthearted, and wait for the LORD.

Psalm 33:4–5, 18–19, 20, 22

Upright is the word of the LORD,
  and all his works are trustworthy.
He loves justice and right;
  of the kindness of the LORD the earth is full.

See, the eyes of the LORD are upon those who fear him,
  upon those who hope for his kindness,
To deliver them from death
  and preserve them in spite of famine.

Our soul waits for the LORD,
  who is our help and our shield.
May your kindness, O LORD, be upon us
  who have put our hope in you.

Psalm 40:2, 4, 7–8, 8–9, 10

I have waited, waited for the LORD
  and he stooped toward me and heard my cry.
And he put a new song into my mouth,
  a hymn to our God.

Sacrifice or oblation you wished not,
  but ears open to obedience you gave me.
Holocausts or sin-offerings you sought not;
  then said I, "Behold, I come."

"In the written scroll it is prescribed for me,
  to do your will, O my God, is my delight,
  and your law is within my heart!"

I announced your justice in the vast assembly;
  I did not restrain my lips, as you, O LORD, know.

Psalm 47:2–3, 6–7, 8–9

All you peoples, clap your hands,
shout to God with cries of gladness.
For the LORD, the Most High, the awesome,
is the great king over all the earth.

God mounts his throne amid shouts of joy;
the LORD, amid trumpet blasts.
Sing praise to God, sing praise;
sing praise to our king, sing praise.

For king of all the earth is God;
sing hymns of praise.
God reigns over the nations,
God sits upon his holy throne.

Psalm 51:3–4, 5–6a, 6b–7

Have mercy on me, O God, in your goodness;
in the greatness of your compassion wipe out my offense.
Thoroughly wash me from my guilt
and of my sin cleanse me.

For I acknowledge my offense,
and my sin is before me always:
"Against you only have I sinned,
and done what is evil in your sight"—

That you may be justified in your sentence,
vindicated when you condemn.
Indeed, in guilt was I born,
and in sin my mother conceived me.

Psalm 62:2–3, 6–7, 8–9

Only in God is my soul at rest,
from him comes my salvation.
He only is my rock and my salvation,
my stronghold; I shall not be disturbed at all.

Only in God be at rest, my soul,
for from him comes my hope.
He only is my rock and my salvation,
my stronghold; I shall not be disturbed.

With God is my safety and my glory,
he is the rock of my strength; my refuge is in God.
Trust in him at all times, O my people!
Pour out your hearts before him.

Psalm 63:2, 3–4, 5–6, 8–9

O God, you are my God, whom I seek;
for you my flesh pines and my soul thirsts.

Thus have I gazed toward you in the sanctuary
to see your power and your glory,
For your kindness is a greater good than life;
my lips shall glorify you.

Thus I will bless you as I live;
lifting up my hands, I will call upon your name.
As with the riches of the banquet shall my soul be satisfied,
and with exultant lips my mouth shall praise you.

You are my help,
and in the shadow of your wings I shout for joy.
My soul clings fast to you;
your right hand upholds me.

Psalm 67:2–3, 5, 6, 8

May God have pity on us and bless us;
may he let his face shine upon us.
So may your way be known upon the earth;
among all nations, your salvation.

May the nations be glad and exult
because you rule the people in equity;
the nations on the earth you guide.

May the people praise you, O God;
may all the peoples praise you!
May God bless us,
and may all the ends of the earth fear him!

Psalm 69:8–10, 14, 17, 33–35

For your sake I bear insult,
and shame covers my face.
I have become an outcast to my brothers,
a stranger to my mother's sons,
Because zeal for your house consumes me,
and the insults of those who blaspheme you fall upon me.

I pray to you, O LORD,
for the time of your favor, O God!
In your great kindness answer me
with your constant help.
Answer me, O LORD, for bounteous is your kindness;
in your great mercy turn toward me.

"See, you lowly ones, and be glad;
you who seek God, may your hearts revive!
For the LORD hears the poor,
and his own who are in bonds he spurns not.
Let the heavens and the earth praise him,
the seas and whatever moves in them!"

Psalm 71:1–2, 3–4a, 5–6, 15, 17

In you, O LORD, I take refuge;
let me never be put to shame.
In your justice rescue me, and deliver me;
incline your ear to me, and save me.

Be my rock of refuge,
a stronghold to give me safety,
for you are my rock and my fortress.
O my God, rescue me from the hand of the wicked.

For you are my hope, O Lord;
my trust, O God, from my youth.
On you I depend from birth;
from my mother's womb you are my strength.

My mouth shall declare your justice,
day by day your salvation.
O God, you have taught me from my youth,
and till the present I proclaim your wondrous deeds.

Psalm 72:1–2, 7–8, 12–13, 17

O God, with your judgment endow the king,
and with your justice, the king's son;
He shall govern your people with justice
and your afflicted ones with judgment.

Justice shall flower in his days,
and profound peace, till the moon be no more.
May he rule from sea to sea,
and from the River to the ends of the earth.

For he shall rescue the poor man when he cries out,
and the afflicted when he has no one to help him.
He shall have pity for the lowly and the poor;
the lives of the poor he shall save.

May his name be blessed forever;
as long as the sun his name shall remain.
In him shall all the tribes of the earth be blessed;
all the nations shall proclaim his happiness.

Psalm 79: 8, 9, 11, 13

Remember not against us the iniquities of the past;
may your compassion quickly come to us,
for we are brought very low.

Help us, O God our savior,
because of the glory of your name;
Deliver us and pardon our sins
for your name's sake.

Let the prisoners' sighing come before you;
with your great power free those doomed to death.
Then we, your people and the sheep of your pasture,
will give thanks to you forever;
through all generations we will declare your praise.

Psalm 80:2– 3, 15–16, 18–19

O shepherd of Israel, hearken,
From your throne upon the cherubim, shine forth.
Rouse your power.
  and come to save us.

Once again, O LORD of hosts,
  look down from heaven, and see;
Take care of this vine,
  and protect what your right hand has planted
  [the son of man whom you yourself made strong].

May your help be with the man of your right hand,
  with the son of man whom you yourself made strong.
Then we will no more withdraw from you;
  give us new life, and we will call upon your name.

Psalm 85:9ab, and 10, 11–12, 13–14

I will hear what God proclaims;
  the LORD—for he proclaims peace to his people.
Near indeed is his salvation to those who fear him,
  glory dwelling in our land.

Kindness and truth shall meet;
  justice and peace shall kiss.
Truth shall spring out of the earth,
  and justice shall look down from heaven.

The LORD himself will give his benefits;
  our land shall yield its increase.
Justice shall walk before him,
  and salvation, along the way of his steps.

Psalm 86:5–6, 9–10, 15–16

You, O Lord, are good and forgiving,
  abounding in kindness to all who call upon you.
Hearken, O LORD, to my prayer
  and attend to the sound of my pleading.

All the nations you have made shall come
  and worship you, O Lord,
  and glorify your name.
For you are great, and you do wondrous deeds;
  you alone are God.

You, O Lord, are a God merciful and gracious,
  slow to anger, abounding in kindness and fidelity.
Turn toward me, and have pity on me;
  give your strength to your servant.

Psalm 89:2–3, 4–5, 27 and 29

The favors of the LORD I will sing forever;
  through all generations my mouth shall proclaim your
    faithfulness.
For you have said, "My kindness is established forever";
  in heaven you have confirmed your faithfulness.

"I have made a covenant with my chosen one,
  I have sworn to David my servant:
Forever will I confirm your posterity
  and establish your throne for all generations."

"He shall say of me, 'You are my father,
  my God, the Rock, my savior.'
Forever I will maintain my kindness toward him,
  and my covenant with him stands firm."

Psalm 95:1–2, 6–7, 8–9

Come, let us sing joyfully to the LORD;
let us acclaim the Rock of our salvation.
Let us come into his presence with thanksgiving;
let us joyfully sing psalms to him.

Come, let us bow down in worship;
let us kneel before the LORD who made us.
For he is our God,
and we are the people he shepherds, the flock he guides.

Oh, that today you would hear his voice:
"Harden not your hearts as at Meribah,
as in the day of Massah in the desert.
Where your fathers tempted me;
they tested me though they had seen my works."

Psalm 96:1–2, 2–3, 11–12, 13

Sing to the LORD a new song;
sing to the LORD, all you lands.
Sing to the LORD; bless his name.

Announce his salvation, day after day.
Tell his glory among the nations;
among all peoples, his wondrous deeds.

Let the heavens be glad and the earth rejoice;
let the sea and what fills it resound;
let the plains be joyful and all that is in them!
Then shall all the trees of the forest exult.

They shall exult before the LORD, for he comes;
for he comes to rule the earth.
He shall rule the world with justice
and the peoples with his constancy.

Psalm 97:1, 6, 11–12

The LORD is king; let earth rejoice;
let the many isles be glad.
The heavens proclaim his justice,
and all peoples see his glory.

Light dawns for the just;
and gladness, for the upright of heart.
Be glad in the LORD, you just,
and give thanks to his holy name.

Psalm 98:1, 2–3, 3–4, 5–6

Sing to the LORD a new song,
for he has done wondrous deeds;
His right hand has won victory for him,
his holy arm.

The LORD has made his salvation known:
in the sight of the nations he has revealed his justice.
He has remembered his kindness and his faithfulness
toward the house of Israel.

All the ends of the earth have seen
the salvation by our God.
Sing joyfully to the LORD, all you lands:
break into song; sing praise.

Sing praise to the LORD with the harp,
with the harp and melodious song.
With trumpets and the sound of the horn
sing joyfully before the King, the LORD.

Psalm 103:1–2, 3–4, 9–10, 11–12

Bless the LORD, O my soul;
   and all my being, bless his holy name.
Bless the LORD, O my soul,
   and forget not all his benefits.

He pardons all your iniquities,
   he heals all your ills.
He redeems your life from destruction,
   he crowns you with kindness and compassion.

He will not always chide,
   nor does he keep his wrath forever.
Not according to our sins does he deal with us,
   nor does he requite us according to our crimes.

For as the heavens are high above the earth,
   so surpassing is his kindness toward those who fear him.
As far as the east is from the west,
   so far has he put our transgressions from us.

Psalm 104:1–2a, 5–6, 10, 12, 24 and 35

Bless the LORD, O my soul!
O LORD, my God, you are great indeed!
You are clothed with majesty and glory,
robed in light as with a cloak.

You fixed the earth upon its foundation,
not to be moved forever;
With the ocean, as with a garment, you covered it;
above the mountain the waters stood.

You send forth springs into the watercourses
that wind among the mountains.
Beside them the birds of heaven dwell;
from among the branches they send forth their song.

How manifold are your works, O LORD!
In wisdom you have wrought them all—
the earth is full of your creatures;
Bless the LORD, O my soul! Alleluia.

Psalm 116:12–13, 15–16bc, 17–18

How shall I make a return to the LORD
for all the good he has done for me?
The cup of salvation I will take up,
and I will call upon the name of the LORD.

Precious in the eyes of the LORD
is the death of his faithful ones,
I am your servant, the son of your handmaid;
you have loosed my bonds.

To you will I offer sacrifice of thanksgiving,
and I will call upon the name of the LORD.
My vows to the LORD I will pay
in the presence of all his people.

Psalm 118:1–2, 16–17, 22–23

Give thanks to the LORD, for he is good,
for his mercy endures forever.
Let the house of Israel say,
"His mercy endures forever."

The right hand of the LORD has struck with power;
the right hand of the LORD is exalted.
I shall not die, but live,
and declare the works of the LORD.

The stone which the builders rejected
has become the cornerstone.
By the LORD has this been done;
it is wonderful in our eyes.

Psalm 119:1–2, 4–5, 17–18, 33–34

Blessed are they whose way is blameless,
who walk in the law of the LORD
Blessed are they who observe his decrees,
who seek him with all their heart.

You have commanded that your precepts
be diligently kept.
Oh, that I might be firm in the ways
of keeping your statutes!

Be good to your servant, that I may live
and keep your words.
Open my eyes, that I may consider
the wonders of your law.

Instruct me, O LORD, in the way of your statutes,
that I may exactly observe them.
Give me discernment, that I may observe your law
and keep it with all my heart.

Psalm 119(B):57, 72, 76–77, 127–128, 129–130

I have said, O Lord, that my part
  is to keep your words.
The law of your mouth is to me more precious
  than thousands of gold and silver pieces.

Let your kindness comfort me
  according to your promise to your servants.
Let your compassion come to me that I may live,
  for your law is my delight.

For I love your commands
  more than gold, however fine.
For in all your precepts I go forward;
  every false way I hate.

Wonderful are your decrees;
  therefore I observe them.
The revelation of your words sheds light,
  giving understanding to the simple.

Psalm 130:1–2, 3–4, 5b and 7a, 7bc

Out of the depths I cry to you, O LORD;
LORD, hear my voice!
Let your ears be attentive
to my voice in supplication.

If you, O LORD, mark our iniquities,
LORD, who can stand?
But with you is forgiveness,
that you may be revered.

I trust in the LORD;
my soul trusts in his word.
My soul waits for the LORD
More than sentinels wait for the dawn.
let Israel wait for the LORD.

For with the LORD is kindness,
and with him is plenteous redemption.

Psalm 131:1, 2, 3

O LORD, my heart is not proud,
nor are my eyes haughty;
I busy not myself with great things,
nor with things too sublime for me.

Nay rather, I have stilled and quieted
my soul like a weaned child.
Like a weaned child on its mother's lap,
so is my soul within me.

O Israel, hope in the LORD,
both now and forever.

Psalm 145:1–2, 8–9, 10–11, 13b–14

I will extol you, O my God and King,
and I will bless your name for ever and ever.
Every day will I bless you,
and I will praise your name for ever and ever.

The LORD is gracious and merciful,
slow to anger and of great kindness.
The LORD is good to all
and compassionate toward all his works.

Let all your works give you thanks, O LORD,
and let your faithful ones bless you.
Let them discourse of the glory of your kingdom
and speak of your might.

The LORD is faithful in all his words
and holy in all his works.
The LORD lifts up all who are falling
and raises up all who are bowed down.

Psalm 146:6c–7, 8–9a, 9bc–10

The LORD keeps faith forever,
secures justice for the oppressed,
gives food to the hungry.
The LORD sets captives free.

The LORD gives sight to the blind.
The LORD raises up those who are bowed down;
the LORD loves the just.
The LORD protects strangers.

The fatherless and the widow he sustains,
but the way of the wicked he thwarts
The LORD shall reign forever,
your God, O Zion, through all generations! Alleluia.

Daniel 3:52, 53, 54, 55, 56

Blessed are you, O Lord, the God of our fathers,
 praiseworthy and exalted above all forever;
and blessed is your holy and glorious name,
 praiseworthy and exalted above all for all ages.

Blessed are you in the temple of your holy glory,
 praiseworthy and glorious above all forever.

Blessed are you on the throne of your kingdom,
 praiseworthy and exalted above all forever.

Blessed are you who look into the depths
 from your throne upon the cherubim,
 praiseworthy and exalted above all forever.

Blessed are you in the firmament of heaven,
 praiseworthy and glorious forever.

The Canticle of Mary

My soul proclaims the greatness of the Lord,
my spirit rejoices in God my savior
for he has looked with favor on his lowly servant.

From this day all generations will call me blessed:
the Almighty has done great things for me,
and holy is his Name.

He has mercy on those who fear him
in every generation.

He has shown the strength of his arm,
he has scattered the proud in their conceit.

He has cast down the mighty from their thrones,
and has lifted up the lowly.

He has filled the hungry with good things,
and the rich he has sent away empty.

He has come to the help of his servant Israel
for he has remembered his promise of mercy,
the promise he made to our fathers,
to Abraham and his children forever.

Canticle of Zechariah

Blessed be the Lord, the God of Israel;
for he has come to his people and set them free.

He has raised up for us a mighty savior,
born of the house of his servant David.

Through his prophets he promised of old
  that he would save us from our enemies,
  from the hands of all who hate us.

He promised to show mercy to our fathers
and to remember his holy covenant.

This was the oath he swore to our father Abraham:
To set us free from the hand of our enemies,
free to worship him without fear,
holy and righteous in his sight
  all the days of our life.

You, my child, shall be called the prophet of the Most High,
for you will go before the Lord to prepare his way,
to give his people knowledge of salvation
by the forgiveness of their sins.

In the tender compassion of our God
the dawn from on high shall break upon us,
to shine on those who dwell in the darkness and the shadow of
    death,
and to guide our feet into the way of peace.